HOOFED MAMMALS
of Alberta

HOOFED MAMMALS
of Alberta

Edited by

J. Brad Stelfox

Written by

Jan Adamczewski
Wiktor L. Adamowicz
Peter C. Boxall
Ludwig N. Carbyn
Denis Chabot
John R. Gunson
Robert J. Hudson
Martin Jalkotzy
Heather C.H. McIntyre

George Mitchell
Lyle A. Renecker
Laurence D. Roy
William M. Samuel
J. Brad Stelfox
John G. Stelfox
Edmund S. Telfer
Shawn Wasel
William D. Wishart

Foreword by
Valerius Geist

LONE PINE

The publisher:

Lone Pine Publishing
206, 10426-81 Avenue
Edmonton, Alberta, Canada
T6E 1X5

Lone Pine Publishing
202A - 1110 Seymour Street
Vancouver, British Columbia, Canada
V6B 3N3

Canadian Cataloguing in Publication Data
Hoofed mammals of Alberta

     includes bibliographical references and
index.
     ISBN 1-55105-035-8 (bound)— ISBN
1-55105-037-4 (pbk.)
     1. Ungulate—Alberta. 2. Wildlife management—
Alberta. I. Stelfox, (John Brad), 1958-
QL737.U4H65 1993   599.73'5'097123   C93-091801-0

In-house editorial: Debby Shoctor, Glenn Rollans
Cover & book design: B. Timothy Keith
Layout: B. Timothy Keith, David Baker
Colour illustrations: Robert Neaves
Additional illustrations: Linda Dunn
Front-cover photograph: Dan and Sue Foley
Back-cover photographs: Dan and Sue Foley, R.J. Hudson (wapiti), B. Smith (goats), W.M. Samuel (fawn)
Printing: Quality Colour Press, Edmonton, Alberta, Canada

The publisher gratefully acknowledges the assistance of Heritage Canada and Alberta Community Development, and the financial support provided by the Alberta Foundation for the Arts in the production of this book.

Financial assistance for this publication was provided by the Alberta Environmental Research Trust; Alberta Recreation, Parks & Wildlife Foundation; Alberta Fish and Wildlife Services; Alberta Environmental Centre; and Alberta-Pacific Forest Industries Inc.

Recreation, Parks & Wildlife Foundation

ENVIRONMENTAL PROTECTION
Fish and Wildlife

ALBERTA
PACIFIC
FOREST INDUSTRIES INC.

CREATED BY LEGISLATIVE ENACTMENT APRIL 16, 1971

ENVIRONMENTAL CENTRE

Contents

List of Figures

List of Tables and Keys

Foreword

Valerius Geist

Faculty of Environmental Design
University of Calgary
Calgary, Alberta
March 1993

Hoofed Mammals of Alberta is an interesting and useful compilation of facts and views about some important animals. The list of contributors reads a little like a biological Who's Who, for many names are known well beyond Alberta's borders. While much has been contributed by Albertans to current wildlife science and conservation, as shown in this book, it is but a continuation of an honourable tradition. Alberta was, after all, central to the national effort to conserve wildlife, in particular elk, pronghorn, and bison. The national parks established to protect bison and in 1914 to protect the last of the northern pronghorn are now history, and pronghorn, long recovered, have paid many thousandfold for the concern that once saved them from extinction. So have other species.

Canada's bison conservation, with all its great achievements and blunders, is centred in Alberta. In the now defunct Buffalo National Park (BNP) near Wainwright, 631 of 716 of Michel Don Pablo's bison, shipped from Montana between 1907–1912, found their new home; the rest went to Elk Island Park, where their descendants still reside. Between 1925–1928, 6,673 BNP bison, many infected with bovine tuberculosis and brucellosis by cattle they met during domestication experiments, were sent on their infamous trek north to Wood Buffalo National Park. Tuberculosis and brucellosis are still in the continent's only natural herd in that park, and they are a source of controversy and friction with agriculture. Alas, the old lesson, "never allow a disease bridge between livestock and wild populations via captive wildlife," was forgotten in the current rush into elk ranching. So was the transfer of swine brucellosis from domestic reindeer to native people and our northern caribou, grizzly bear, wolves, foxes and domestic dogs. Will captive elk, in time, insure a repeat of what happened to bison, or recently to deer in New Zealand? In a decade we will know.

After the turn of the century, when wildlife had been reduced to mere remnants by commerce, military policy, and subsistence hunting, a decade of hearings by commissions on conservation formed the basis for continental wildlife management and its recovery. The wildlife we enjoy today is here not by the grace of nature, but by the grace of far-sighted management. Elk, virtually exterminated in Alberta by 1910 with possibly the last four killed in 1914 near the Brazeau River, were reintroduced in Banff Park from Jackson Hole by 1916. With elk expanding out of British Columbia's Kootenay population, they were in full recovery by 1930. So were moose, which had been absent from the east slopes and Dominion parks in 1915. Mule deer, which quickly colonized the many burns and profited from the virtual absence of wolves, were also in recovery by that time. The recovery happened none too soon to save many rural Albertans from losing it all in the "dirty thirties". A glimpse of this is provided by George Mitchell's contribution. Yet, when have we acknowledged the "welfare role" of wildlife? How many prospectors, trappers, and rural families, let alone native people, have been nurtured by wildlife? Occasionally it intrudes into our consciousness, such as when the Lubicons, began making headlines — after their annual moose harvest had dropped from a comfortable 350 to a desperate 35.

There is still too little recognition that public wildlife creates wealth and jobs. When abundant, accessible, and managed for deliberate inefficiency in harvest, it attracts users by the hundreds of thousands, creating big, diverse economic demands. Thousands of dollars are then expended per living head of big game per year! The demand for affordable wildlife on this continent is insatiable. Unfortunately, Alberta is no leader here and urgently needs to learn from others.

Wildlife, historically, has always been "in trouble". It is always dependent on foresight, good will, and sympathy, and on bold public and private initiatives for its survival. It will continue to be so. Vigilance is called for. Alberta was a vibrant part of the great American success story in wildlife conservation. Economic depression has taken its toll on Alberta's ability to do as well today as it did in the past. May it again rise to the occasion, and may this splendid, useful book help and inspire those towards greater effort who cannot live without wildlife.

Preface

J. Brad Stelfox

As a student attending the University of Alberta in the 1970s, I frequently found myself searching for a book that provided an in-depth look at Alberta's hoofed mammals. Now, in the early 1990s, recreationalists, sport hunters, research scientists, conservationists, game farmers and wildlife managers urgently require a comprehensive review of Alberta's hoofed mammals in light of intensifying human land use practices. This book was written to help fill that void.

Hoofed mammals are perceived differently by various sectors of society. The questions we ask about the animals vary considerably, depending on whether we view them through the eyes of sport hunters, game farmers, conservationists, game managers, tourists, research scientists, or resource developers. I hope this book offers each reader some special and useful insight.

Chapter 1, Introduction to Alberta's Hoofed Mammals, introduces the reader to the diversity of hoofed mammals found in Alberta and the substantial benefits they provide. A brief review of their classification and evolution is included.

Chapter 2, Identification, familiarizes the reader with identification of hoofed mammals using scat, hair, antlers and horns, body conformation, skulls, and tracks. Useful distinguishing features separating mule deer from white-tailed deer and plains bison from wood bison are presented.

Chapter 3, Communication, describes the ways hoofed mammals convey messages and the information these signals contain. A full description of visual, acoustic, olfactory, and tactile signals is provided.

Chapter 4, Distribution, details the habitat requirements and distributional patterns of each species. Distribution maps illustrate the range of each species in Alberta and indicate relative densities. Good viewing locations for each species are recommended and a list of ungulate translocations has been assembled.

Chapter 5, Population Dynamics and Reproduction, chronicles changes in provincial population numbers of Alberta's hoofed mammals and explores their causes. An array of reproductive parameters is presented for each species.

Chapter 6, Predation, describes the interactions between Alberta's hoofed mammals and their predators (wolf, coyote, bear, cougar), and discusses the relative impact of predators on their ungulate prey. Management options for predator/prey systems in Alberta are explored. Mortality sources of hoofed mammals other than predation are identified.

Chapter 7, Parasites and Disease, introduces the reader to various viral, bacterial, helminth, and tick infections and their consequences. A complete listing of ecto- and endo-parasites and diseases documented for Alberta's hoofed mammal community is provided.

Chapter 8, Hunting and Harvest, discusses the history and importance of hunting and outfitting in Alberta. Detailed tables document hunting tag sales and estimates of annual offtake. Figures illustrate the age-class structure of Alberta's hunters. Decline in hunting as a recreational activity in Alberta is discussed and the level of participation in Alberta relative to other regions of Canada is illustrated. The locations from which Alberta's top trophy heads have been taken are mapped and a table comparing the contribution of trophy heads from Alberta and the rest of Canada and the United States has been assembled.

Chapter 9, Management, chronicles the arrival and nature of modern wildlife management in Alberta. The strengths and weaknesses of various census techniques and harvest strategies are discussed. Such topical issues as habitat management, poaching, aboriginal hunting, depredation and wolf management are explored.

Chapter 10, Economic Aspects, examines hoofed mammals from the perspective of monetary value and attempts to ascertain their economic and aesthetic worth to Albertans. The importance of both consumptive and non-consumptive use of ungulates is discussed relative to management practices in Alberta.

Chapter 11, Commercialization, addresses the ongoing debate concerning game farming and ranching in Alberta. The potential strengths and weaknesses of commercial consumptive use of hoofed mammals are explored, and the development and growth of Alberta's game farming community are presented.

Chapter 12, Morphology, Bioenergetics and Resource Use, combines a diverse array of principles and theories into an integrated explanation of form and function of Alberta's hoofed mammals. This chapter, intended primarily for an academic audience, describes the physical attributes of Alberta's hoofed mammals and discusses the patterns and processes that link body form to energy requirements, growth, reproduction, foraging strategies, resource use, and population dynamics. Tables documenting morphometrics, forages, and physiological indicators are provided.

Appendix 1, Glossary, defines terms that may be unfamiliar to the reader.

Appendix 2, Capture and Restraint, details various drugs and practices involved in the capture and restraint of hoofed mammals.

Appendix 3, Indices of Body Condition and Nutritional Status, describes and evaluates various techniques for measuring body condition and nutritional status on both living and dead animals.

Appendix 4, Age Determination Techniques, describes techniques that can be used to estimate the age of individuals.

Appendix 5, Field Dressing, Handling and Aging Big Game Meat, provides the hunter with information about processing big game animals. Particular attention is paid to proper evisceration, skinning, caping and aging of meat.

Appendix 6, A Seasoned Hunter's Perspective, chronicles the experiences and attitudes of a long-time sportsman in a previous hunting era in Alberta.

Appendix 7, Boone and Crockett Club Scoring Forms, offers scoring sheets on which hunters can "rough score" their trophies.

References lists those articles, arranged by chapters, that are cited in the book.

Acknowledgments

J. Brad Stelfox

Wildlife Ecology Branch

Alberta Environmental Centre

Vegreville, Alberta

August 1993

After I began writing this book, it became apparent that I did not have sufficient expertise to do justice to each of the various topics that needed to be addressed. Approaching selected biologists to write chapters on their specialty fields, I received both encouragement and a shared urgency for the need for such a book. I am very thankful to these people who found time in their busy schedules to complete their chapters. I also appreciate their patience, for this book did not evolve along predicted schedules.

Numerous people were instrumental in getting this project off the drawing board and on its way. My father, John Stelfox, and Bob Hudson and Bill Wishart provided continual encouragement and advice on structuring the book and getting project funding. Each provided valuable editorial comments on several chapters. Not surprisingly, these three scientists were largely responsible for shaping my interest in Alberta's hoofed mammals and their management.

I am thankful for the financial support provided by the Alberta Environmental Research Trust, Alberta Recreation, Parks and Wildlife Foundation, Alberta Fish and Wildlife Division, Alberta Environmental Centre, and Alberta-Pacific Forest Industries. Without their financial assistance, the development and publication of the book would not have been possible. When funding seemed far away, Brent Markham (Alberta Fish and Wildlife Division), Brian Hammond (Alberta Environment), Malcolm Wilson (Alberta Environmental Centre), and Daryll Hebert (Alberta-Pacific Forest Industries Inc.) offered undaunted encouragement and helped sell the project to prospective funders.

Through countless phone calls, correspondence, and interviews, many people generously provided important information. In addition to those authors that contributed chapters in this book, these people included Morley Barrett, Barbara Bertch, Sylvia Birkholz, Chuck Blyth, Wes Bradford, Mabel Brick, Judd Bunnage, James Burns, Susan Crites, Ken Crutchfield, Betty Dlugosz, Frank Dunn, Jan Edmonds, Albert England, Lyle Fullerton, Val Geist, Bill Glasgow, Jack Graham, Norma Gutteridge, Jim Halfpenny, Bill Hall, Daryll Hebert, Bud Hughes, Rick Kunelius, Gerry Lynch, Andrew MacPherson, Bob McClymont, Janet Mercer, Luigi Morgantini, John Nishi, Chris Olsen, Wes Olson, Jack Ondrack, Don Pattie, Dave Poll, Margo Pybus, Dennis Quintilio, Rob Ramey, Jack Reneau, Hal Reynolds, Blair Rippin, Wayne Roberts, Hugh Smith, Kirby Smith, Dave Spalding, Harry Stelfox, Bob Stevenson, Curtis Strobeck, Michael Sullivan, Bruce Treichel, Robb Watt, Dwight Welch and Jerry Wilde. Thanks to Susan Crites, Marco Festa-Bianchet, Mark Drew, Val Geist, Jon Jorgenson, Frank Miller, Marie Nietfeld, Jack Nolan, Glen Rowan, William Samuel, Charles Schwartz, Bruce Smith and Harry Stelfox for providing photographic plates. The beautiful colour illustrations of ungulates provided by Robert Neaves add much to the appearance of the book. My sincere apologies to those I have forgotten to acknowledge.

Important to the completion of this book were the university students who attended the hoofed mammal ecology courses I taught in Jasper National Park during the summers of 1988 and 1989. These students served as a constant reminder of the need for this book. Their refreshing inquisitiveness about hoofed mammals and questions about ecological patterns and processes helped shape the contents of the book.

I am thankful for the many forms of assistance provided by the Alberta Environmental Centre, including the administrative support of Malcolm Wilson, Fayyaz Qureshi, Richard Johnson and Stan Selinger, technical reviews provided by Larry Roy, Jack Nolan, Kelly Sturgess and Len Peleshok of the Wildlife Ecology Branch, and graphic productions by Phil Henry and Marion Herbut. Gloria Horon, Valerie Golka and Arhlene Hrynyk kindly assisted with the many episodes of manuscript preparation and photocopying.

Permission from the Boone and Crockett Club to use their scoring forms is greatly appreciated.

During my two years at the Teton Science School in Jackson Hole, Wyoming, Director Jack Shea provided me with an opportunity to work on the book and to use the laser printer. Billy Helprin and Lynne Lawrence offered helpful comments on several chapters and shared many enjoyable days with me watching wapiti, bison, pronghorn and mule deer in Jackson Hole.

Thorough editorial and technical reviews of the entire manuscript were completed by Bob Holmes and Marie Nietfeld. Their attention to detail and recommendations improved the book significantly. I acknowledge their efforts warmly but personally accept responsibility for all errors and omissions.

My fascination with ungulates started early when my parents encouraged an appreciation for wilderness and provided countless opportunities to view wildlife. For this and much more, I thank them.

Lastly, I am indebted to my wife, Sarah, for the understanding, tolerance and assistance required to complete such a project. Her illustrations and editorial efforts have added greatly to the book.

1

Introduction to Alberta's Hoofed Mammals

J. Brad Stelfox

Alberta hosts a diverse and spectacular array of natural resources. Indeed, our government spends considerable time and money promoting our wildlands to prospective out-of-province tourists and encouraging Albertans to experience their natural heritage. To many Albertans, the most conspicuous of our wildlife are those animals referred to as hoofed mammals or ungulates. These mammals differ from all others by their unique foot structure, for they support their weight on hooves (or unguis) which are anatomically equivalent to the human fingernail or toenail. Of the twelve ungulate species native to North America, nine are presently found in Alberta: a greater representation than any other province, territory, or state on the continent can lay claim to. These are the white-tailed deer, mule deer, caribou, wapiti, moose, pronghorn, mountain goat, bighorn sheep and bison.

INTRODUCTION

From the points of view of ecological and societal importance, aesthetics and economics, one could hardly find a more important group of wildlife in Alberta. Attributes of hoofed mammals that contribute to our fascination include their large size and hence conspicuous presence, their role as symbols of pristine wildlands (the majestic bighorn sheep of the Rockies), their speed (the pronghorn is the fastest land mammal in North America), their historical value in providing meat and hides to aboriginal people and early settlers, their value as quarry for sport hunters and as prey to large and newsworthy predators, and, more recently, their controversial potential as commercial meat producers in emerging game farms.

Not all land uses have treated Alberta's native hoofed mammals favourably, and there are some people who consider wild ungulates to be an impediment to progress. Today, human activities affect wild populations in complex and manifold ways. Evidence of a tumultuous human/ungulate relationship can be seen in the decline in numbers and distribution of several species in historic times as a result of agriculture, commercial hunting, forestry, mining and the petro-chemical industry.

The societal and economic importance of our native ungulates, their population numbers (~320,000 in 1992), and province-wide distribution all point toward the critical need for serious and far-sighted management. Their future prosperity depends on it. Unfortunately, the situation in Alberta is far from ideal. Caught in the wake of budgetary constraints, the number of government personnel and dollars committed to ungulate research, management, and extension education has been reduced significantly. This undesirable situation has been exacerbated by past decades of inadequate environmental protection measures from agriculture, forestry, mining, and the petrochemical industries.

Those whose interests are guided more by monetary considerations than environmental conscience should note that approximately 125,000 hunters contribute in excess of $100 million dollars to our provincial economy each fall. This revenue depends on the sustained use of a healthy ungulate community. The intangible value of hoofed mammals to such non-consumptive users as recreationalists, conservationists, and the tourism industry, although more difficult to calculate, cannot be over-stated. By informing more Albertans about our renewable ungulate resource, and the uncertain status of some species, it is hoped that people will press their elected officials to ensure proper conservation and management of ungulates.

Finally, a word about the format of this book. After the literature searches and interviews were completed, it was apparent that far too much information existed to permit a fully narrative approach to writing this book. Alternatively, it was decided to present as much information as possible in comparative tables, illustrations and keys. Thousands of published and unpublished reports, articles, and dissertations deal with Alberta's ungulates. A thorough listing of these references, arranged topically, can be found in A Selected Bibliography of Research, Management, and Biology of Alberta's Native Ungulates (Stelfox et al., 1991).

EVOLUTION AND TAXONOMY

Alberta's ungulate fauna today differs considerably from the one that grazed and browsed here during the late Pliocene (3.0–1.8 million years ago) and much of the Pleistocene epochs (1.8 million years to 10,000 years before present). For example, the 12 ungulate species found in North America today (peccary, white-tailed deer, mule deer, caribou, wapiti, moose, pronghorn, mountain goat, Dall's sheep, bighorn sheep, muskoxen and bison) offer a meager diversity in comparison to the 47 species present during the Wisconsinan glacial period less than 90,000 years ago. This exceptionally diverse fauna included 10 horselike species in the Family Equidae, 3 tapirs (Tapiridae), 2 peccaries (Tayassuidae), 4 camels (Camelidae), 9 deer (Cervidae), 6 pronghorns (Antilocapridae), and 13 members of Bovidae (true horned ungulates) (Kurten and Anderson, 1980). With the exception of pronghorn, all of today's North American hoofed mammals, or their ancestors, can be traced back to Eurasia. Since crossing the Bering land bridge connecting Eurasia and North America during the ice-dominated Pleistocene periods, hoofed mammals have colonized most of the continent. The reasons for the loss of many species, and all representatives of the camel, tapir, and horse families, are uncertain, but probably relate to such events as glaciation (and associated climate change), intense competition among species within the grazing community, the arrival of man in North America, and evolutionary developments among predators.

Alberta's cervid species (white-tailed deer, mule deer, caribou, wapiti and moose) owe their evolutionary development to ancestors that moved across the Bering land bridge from Asia. It is believed that these immigrants were responsible for the disappearance, presumably by acute competition, of several unusual looking deer-like species that had evolved in North America. The earliest deer of the genus Odocoileus appeared approximately 3.5 million years ago and subsequently evolved into forms leading to white-tailed deer, and later, mule deer about 2 million years ago. Numerous bones of white-tailed deer have been excavated from early Paleo-Indian archeological sites, indicating their importance as an aboriginal food source. The ancestry of caribou is unclear, but their early evolutionary history (1.5–2.0 million y.b.p.) probably occurred in Beringia or northern Asia (Kurten and Anderson, 1980). Most of their evolutionary development is thought to have been along the southern edges of the expanding and receding Pleistocene glaciers. The world's largest living cervid, the moose, is thought to have evolved from a much larger predecessor found in Europe, likely Alces latifrons. North America's moose are recognized as conspecific (same species) with those now found in Eurasia.

The family Antilocapridae to which pronghorn belong is the only living family of ungulates that is endemic to North America. Remains of members of this family have been excavated from sites dating back to the Hemingfordian Land Mammal Age of the Miocene (16–20 million years ago). Of the 12 genera of Antilocaprids roaming North America in the late Cenozoic, only one species, the pronghorn, remains today. Modern pronghorn probably existed by 100,000 years ago.

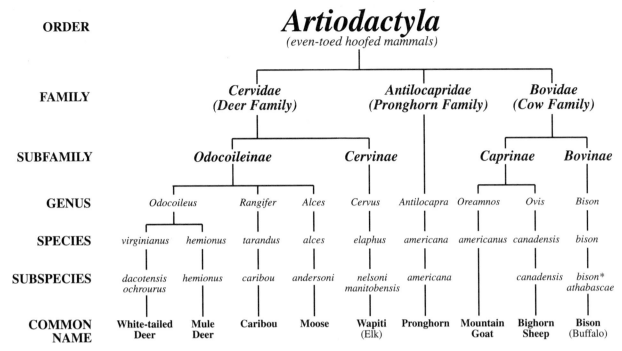

ORDER	**_Artiodactyla_** (even-toed hoofed mammals)							
FAMILY	_Cervidae_ (Deer Family)			_Antilocapridae_ (Pronghorn Family)	_Bovidae_ (Cow Family)			
SUBFAMILY	_Odocoileinae_			_Cervinae_		_Caprinae_		_Bovinae_
GENUS	_Odocoileus_		_Rangifer_ _Alces_	_Cervus_	_Antilocapra_	_Oreamnos_	_Ovis_	_Bison_
SPECIES	_virginianus_	_hemionus_	_tarandus_ _alces_	_elaphus_	_americana_	_americanus_	_canadensis_	_bison_
SUBSPECIES	_dacotensis_ _ochrourus_	_hemionus_	_caribou_ _andersoni_	_nelsoni_ _manitobensis_	_americana_		_canadensis_	_bison*_ _athabascae_
COMMON NAME	**White-tailed Deer**	**Mule Deer**	**Caribou** **Moose**	**Wapiti** (Elk)	**Pronghorn**	**Mountain Goat**	**Bighorn Sheep**	**Bison** (Buffalo)

*The validity of distinct bison subspecies is presently in doubt.

Figure 1.1
Taxonomic classification of Alberta's ungulates.

The family Bovidae, the true horned ungulates, has an impressive history that dates back to the Miocene in the Old World and Africa. Most ancestors of present-day bovids came across the Bering land bridge to North America during the Rancholabrean Land Mammal Age (beginning 700,000 years ago). The mountain goat, more closely related to the European chamois than to true goats, is poorly represented by fossils. Its earliest fossil records date back to approximately 120,000 years ago. The true sheep of the genus _Ovis_ first arose in Europe and Asia before spreading to North America. According to Kurten and Anderson (1980), bighorn sheep may have evolved from earlier forms while occupying glacial refugia in Siberia (possibly Alaska-Yukon) approximately 500,000 y.b.p. It is believed that bighorn and Dall's sheep to the north share a common ancestry with the Siberian snow sheep (_Ovis nivicola_) of Eurasia.

The largest of Alberta's hoofed mammals, the bison, may be conspecific with the European wisent (_Bison bonasus_). During the evolutionary development of the North American _Bison bison_, advancing and receding glacial sheets may have allowed it to interbreed periodically with Eurasian populations of _Bison priscus_, the species from which it most likely evolved. Another species, _Bison latifrons_, existed in North America since the late Illinoian, or about 200,000 years ago, and sported horns with a span greater than 2 meters.

Many biologists treat the plains and wood bison of North America as distinct subspecies, yet taxonomists are uncertain about their genetic status. Although plains and wood bison appear to differ in body measurements (van Zyll de Jong, 1986), genetic studies have failed to reveal significant differences (Neuman, 1971; Peden and Kraay, 1979; Bork et al., 1991).

Currently, an attempt to document possible external phenotypic differences between bison subspecies is being conducted by the Taxonomy Subcommittee of the Wood Bison Recovery Team. This approach is based on an examination of seven external characteristics (hump shape, cape demarcation, chap hair, front display hair, ventral neck mane, beard and cape variegation) of both male and female bison. Bison from herds of known genetic composition in both Canada and the United States will be examined and photographed prior to ranking their phenotypes (Anonymous, 1992).

The taxonomic status of bison goes beyond academic interest and has some significant management implications. For example, the listing of wood bison as a "threatened" subspecies by CITES (Convention on International Trade in Endangered Species) is one justification for the proposed extermination of diseased wood/plains hybrid bison in Wood Buffalo National Park. The control measure is being proposed to prevent the infection of a nearby disease-free herd of pure wood bison in the Mackenzie Delta sanctuary.

Table 1.1 summarizes the evolutionary history of Alberta's ungulates, Table 1.2 explains the meaning or derivation of scientific names, and Figure 1.1 illustrates the taxonomic relationships of Alberta's ungulates.

ACKNOWLEDGEMENTS

Paleontology revisions and comments provided by Dr. James Burns, Curator, Quaternary Paleontology, Provincial Museum of Alberta, are greatly appreciated.

TABLE 1.1

EVOLUTIONARY ORIGIN OF ALBERTA'S UNGULATES
(based on Kurten and Anderson, 1980) and J.A. Burns (personal communication).

Species	Evolutionary Origin	Earliest Fossil Record in North America
White-tailed deer	North America	~2.5 million years before present; later Blancan period
Mule Deer	North America	~1.5 million years before present; later Blancan period approximately
Caribou	Eurasia, Beringia	~1.5–2.0 million years before present; *Rangifer* genus appeared
Wapiti (Elk)	Eurasia	~100,000–250,000 years before present
Moose	Eurasia	~30,000–150,000 years before present; late Wisconsinan period
Pronghorn	North America	~100,000 years before present; late Wisconsinan period of Pleistocene
Bighorn Sheep	Asia	~250,000–500,000 years before present
Mountain Goat	Asia	~250,000–500,000 years before present
Bison (Buffalo)	Eurasia	~250,000–300,000 years before present; late Pleistocene

TABLE 1.2

DERIVATIONS OF SCIENTIFIC NAMES

Common Name	Scientific Name	Derivation of Scientific Name
White-tailed Deer	*Odocoileus virginianus*	*Odocoileus* (well-hollowed tooth); *virginianus* (of Virginia)
Mule Deer	*Odocoileus hemionus*	*Odocoileus* (well-hollowed tooth); *hemionus* (a half-ass, mule)
Caribou	*Rangifer tarandus*	*Rangifer* (derived from French word *rangifere* [reindeer] *tarandus* (animal of the north) "caribou" is a Micmac Indian name
Wapiti (Elk)[1]	*Cervus elaphus*	*Cervus* (Latin for deer or stag); *elaphus* (a deer); "wapiti" is a Shawnee Indian name meaning "white rump"; "elk" is derived from the Germanic "elch", which refers to the European moose
Moose	*Alces alces*	*Alces* (Elk)[1]; "Musee" is an Algonkian Indian word for "eater of twigs"
Pronghorn	*Antilocapra americana*	*Antilocapra* (horned animal); *americana* (of America)
Mountain Goat	*Oreamnos americanus*	*Oreamnos* (mountain lamb); *americanus* (of America)
Bighorn Sheep	*Ovis canadensis*	*Ovis* (sheep); *canadensis* (of Canada)
Bison (Buffalo)	*Bison*[2] *bison*	*Bison* (wild ox or buffalo)

[1] To avoid confusion between the moose, referred to as "elk" in Europe, and the wapiti, referred to as "elk" in North America, it is recommended that the term "wapiti" be used for *Cervus elaphus.*

[2] Recently, some taxonomists (see Jones et al., 1992) have suggested that the genus *Bison* be changed to *Bos.*

2
Identification

J. Brad Stelfox

This chapter introduces the reader to some helpful clues and keys for identifying Alberta's hoofed mammals. After reviewing appropriate names for different genders and ages of ungulates, some clues to help separate males from females are offered. The strengths and weaknesses of scat as an identification tool are discussed, as is the value of hair structure to predator ecologists or forensic officers for determining the identity of hoofed mammals. Following an identification key based on antler and horn shape, a series of drawings of ungulates is provided. For those naturalists lucky enough to come across a skull while hiking, a series of detailed skull illustrations should help you identify your find. Hoofed mammal tracks can generally be found if you look in the right places, such as along the muddy edges of lakes and creeks, or in the winter snowpack. After defining a few basic measurements, illustrated track imprints of each species are provided. Some hoofed mammals can be confusing to identify, so some special attention is given to our two deer species and two bison subspecies. Should you be fortunate enough to catch a glimpse of a youngster, a brief description and photos should be of considerable help.

INTRODUCTION

Although sightings of native ungulates are common in Alberta, many recreationalists cannot readily identify the animals they see. Those who can recognize hoofed mammals generally rely on conspicuous body features such as the curving horns of the bighorn sheep, the massive size of the bison, or the contrasting tail flag of the alarmed white-tailed deer. As useful as these diagnostic body features are, they are only a few of the many identification tools available to the outdoor enthusiast. Other valuable, though seldom used, clues to the presence of ungulate species are shed antlers, "pick-up" skulls, hoof prints, scats, vocalizations, beds and browsed vegetation. For wary species or those that inhabit forest habitats, these "signs" can provide important information on distribution and abundance.

The rest of this book uses the following common terms to refer to the age and sex of ungulates:

Buck	An adult male deer or pronghorn
Doe	An adult female deer or pronghorn
Fawn	A deer or pronghorn less than a year old
Bull[*]	An adult male caribou, wapiti, moose, or bison
Cow[*]	An adult female caribou, wapiti, moose, or bison
Calf	A caribou, wapiti, moose, bison less than one year of age
Billy	An adult male mountain goat
Nanny	An adult female mountain goat
Kid	A mountain goat less than one year of age
Ram	An adult male bighorn sheep
Ewe	An adult female bighorn sheep
Lamb	A bighorn sheep less than one year of age
Yearling	An individual between one and two years of age.

[*] *With the advent of game-farmed wapiti (elk) in Alberta, both game farmers and biologists are beginning to use the European terms of "stag" and "hind" as common names for male and female wapiti, respectively.*

Billy (male)

Nanny (female)

Figure 2.1
Differences in the horn shape of male and female mountain goats.

- *Horns of adult males exhibit a greater and more gradual curvature.*
- *Nannies' horns are generally straighter, and often display a pronounced hook toward the tip.*
- *Billy horns are larger and have a greater basal circumference than do nanny horns.*

The dichotomous keys, tables, and illustrations of this chapter help the recreationalist, hunter and wildlife biologist identify Alberta's hoofed mammals. Particular attention is paid to the two deer species and the two bison subspecies, which can be difficult to tell apart.

SEXING ADULT INDIVIDUALS

Accurate identification of males and females is valuable for many reasons. When wildlife biologists survey the composition of ungulate herds, it becomes essential to differentiate animal gender. Hunters must be skilled with field identification of sexes to abide by hunting regulations that specify which sex they can legally kill. A naturalist who can readily identify an animal's sex will observe some fascinating behavioural differences between males and females.

Several useful field clues help distinguish between the sexes, except in young-of-the-year animals. Look for the following characteristics:

Appearance:
- For all species, a visible scrotum or penile button indicates a male.
- For all species, adult males are larger than adult females. **Caution:** To see this difference, it is often necessary to compare an adult male to a nearby female.
- For deer, wapiti and moose, visible antlers indicate a male. (Remember that female caribou often have antlers!)
- A long fold of skin, or bell, hanging from the throat of a moose generally indicates a bull. Females also have bells, but they are usually smaller. It is not uncommon for the bell to freeze off during a particularly cold winter.
- A white vulva patch is often visible around the genitalia of female moose.
- For bighorn sheep, both sexes possess horns, but the horns of adult rams are much longer and more curved. It is often difficult to distinguish the horns of an adult ewe from the horns of yearling and two-year-old rams.
- Horns of mountain goat billies are larger and longer than those of nannies. The difference, however, is often difficult to see in the field. A better feature seems to be the tips of the horns, which are usually bent back at a sharper angle in nannies (Figure 2.1). For mountain goats seen at a distance, look carefully at social groupings, for billies are usually solitary, whereas nannies and kids usually congregate.
- A black vulva patch is visible in nanny mountain goats when the tail is raised.
- The horns of female pronghorn, when present, are usually not visible, except when viewed at very close range. In contrast, the horns of adult males are conspicuous.
- A black cheek patch is usually visible in adult male pronghorn and is absent in females.

Behaviour:
- Male and female ungulates often differ in the sounds they make. Complete descriptions of these are presented in Chapter 3.
- Wallowing (rolling in a wet muddy depression) is generally a behaviour of rutting males.
- Males generally stretch to urinate, while females usually squat.
- Track marks of hooves being dragged through shallow snow often indicates a buck deer in the rut. Foot-dragging enables the buck to transfer his scent to the ground as a signal to other deer.
- When individuals of the same species fight they are generally males. Females may chase and strike other females, but intense body contact or prolonged chasing generally involves males.
- Adults in prolonged, close contact with newborn or young individuals are usually females. Individuals that are nursing offspring are females.
- Single individuals defending offspring from predators are generally females.

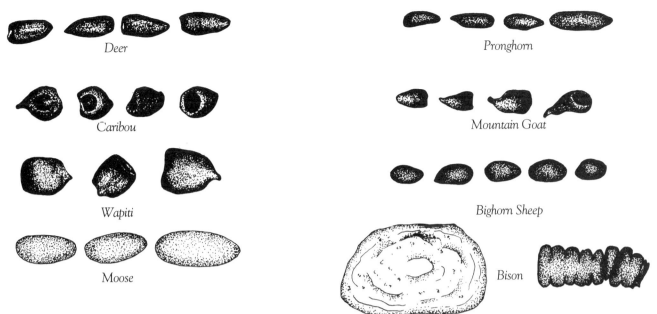

Figure 2.2
Winter fecal pellets
from adult ungulates
(not drawn to scale)
Drawings by Sarah Stelfox.

IDENTIFICATION USING SCATS

Many outdoor enthusiasts can identify scats (fecal pellets), yet it is difficult to construct a dichotomous scat key that works reliably. The main obstacle to this task is the variation in scat dimensions, texture, and shape caused by the scat's age and differences in the quality and moisture content of the animal's diet. For example, droppings are generally moister, more clumped and darker in late spring and summer. Drier and more distinct pellets are common during the fall and winter, and a softer, amorphous clump appears shortly after the vegetation flush of late spring. With these problems in mind, a description of fecal pellets is cautiously offered in Table 2.1 and a few examples are illustrated in Figure 2.2. When using scats for identification purposes, also consider their surroundings (e.g., habitat, slope, elevation, possible tracks) to guide your selection of possible ungulate candidates. For example, bighorn sheep and pronghorn often produce similar pellets, yet their distinctive habitat preferences enable us to eliminate the bighorn sheep as the producer of scats found in short-grass prairie or the pronghorn of pellets found in a subalpine meadow.

TABLE 2.1

CHARACTERISTICS OF FECAL PELLETS FROM ADULT INDIVIDUALS

Species	Description	Pellet length (mm)	Can be confused with:
Deer	Generally more heart-shaped than bighorn sheep or pronghorn	10–22	mountain goat bighorn sheep pronghorn
Caribou	Distinctive crater often present on each pellet similar to deer, but larger	20–25	deer
Wapiti (Elk)	Distinctive nipple/dimple appearance	18–25	moose
Moose	Pellets rounded at both ends, texture of pellets is coarse, reflecting woody diet, generally brown in colour	22–30	scats of young moose may look like wapiti
Pronghorn	Teardrop shaped, one end blunt and one pointed; relatively small, pellet sides irregular	15–20	bighorn sheep
Mountain Goat	Colour brown to black; pellets similar to bighorn sheep or deer in shape, but smaller	12–16	bighorn sheep, deer
Bighorn Sheep	Dry pellets generally have rounded ends, moist pellets often display a depression; moist pellets tend to clump, colour varies from brown to black	13–16	pronghorn
Bison (Buffalo)	Distinct pellets absent, moist diet causes large (~30 cm) brown semi-soft patty	pellets absent	domestic cow

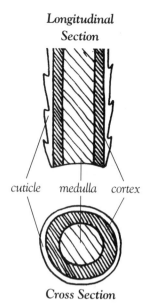

Longitudinal
Section

cuticle   medulla   cortex

Cross Section

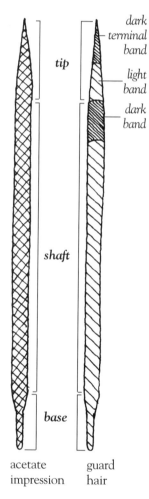

tip

dark
terminal
band

light
band

dark
band

shaft

base

acetate   guard
impression   hair

Figure 2.3
*Ungulate hair morphology;
generalized drawing of a
deer guard hair.*

IDENTIFICATION USING HAIR

Ungulate hair is seldom thought of as an identification clue except by wildlife forensic officers involved in criminal investigations and ecologists who study predator/prey relationships. Since hair is indigestible and passage through the gastro-intestinal tract does not alter its cuticular scale pattern, examination of hair found in predator scats offers ecologists a valuable tool to determine diet composition. The structural basis for hair identification is the relatively unique scale pattern which can be found on the cuticle (outer layer) of guard hairs. Before these patterns can be examined, selected hairs must first be cleaned and heat-pressed between a slide and acetate film. After the hair is carefully removed from the acetate strip, the resulting impression and the hair can be examined microscopically. A detailed description of this procedure, and a dichotomous key for identification, have been written by Kennedy and Carbyn (1981). Considerable knowledge of hair morphology and practice with the key is required to master this technique. Those components of guard hairs used for identification purposes are shown in Figure 2.3. It remains for someone to conduct a "blind test" of known-identity hairs before the accuracy and precision of this technique can be determined.

IDENTIFICATION USING ANTLERS AND HORNS

The presence and shape of antlers or horns provide a quick and accurate way to identify species. Before proceeding, it is necessary to understand that cervids (deer, caribou, wapiti, moose) have antlers, while bovids (mountain goat, bighorn sheep, bison) and antilocaprids (pronghorn) possess horns (although it is common to hear hunters talk about deer horns, this usage is incorrect). The difference between antlers and horns lies in their appearance, tissue origin and permanence. Antlers are grown and shed annually, are made of bone (extensions of the frontal bones), and have multiple tines. With the exception of caribou, they are found only on males. A small proportion (about 1 percent; Wishart, 1984) of female deer grow antlers because of excessive testosterone. Bear in mind that the antlers of immature males are small and may not show all the characteristics of the species. Unlike antlers, horns are permanent structures composed of a bony core and an outer sheath of keratin, the same material found in fingernails and hooves. The horns of bovids never branch, whereas antilocaprid (pronghorn) horns have a forward-projecting prong. For Alberta's bovids, horns are found on both sexes, though they are invariably smaller on females. Some pronghorn females (~25%) do not have horns.

The colour illustrations on pages 13–20 illustrate typical horns and antlers for each species. Maximum antler weights and months in which antlers are commonly shed are listed in Table 12.1.

For hunters who wish to measure the horns or antlers of their trophies using the Boone and Crockett scoring system, refer to the scoring sheets and instructions provided in Appendix 7.

IDENTIFICATION USING BODY CONFORMATION AND COLOUR

Knowledge of body conformation and hair colour is a useful identification tool that all naturalists and hunters should master. For members of the deer family, it is not uncommon to have only a quick and obscured glimpse of an animal in dense vegetation. Problems identifying members of the deer family are compounded by the absence of antlers on females (except caribou) and on males during the late winter and early spring. If no snow is present for tracking, body shape and colour may be your only clues.

Detailed drawings of each species (see the figures on pages 13–20) illustrate conformational differences. Various body measurements including height and weight are provided in Table 12.1. Don't forget that newborn or juvenile individuals may appear decidedly different than adult individuals (the reddish coat of the bison calf is a good example).

IDENTIFICATION USING "PICK-UP" SKULLS

Anyone who has spent much time in the bush has found either intact ungulate skulls or remnants of them. For Alberta's native ungulates, the following skull features apply and will help you distinguish ungulate skulls from those of other wildlife:

- 0 upper incisors and 3 lower incisors on each side
- upper canines present only in wapiti and caribou
- lower canines incisor-like and adjoin lower incisors
- wide gap between lower canines and cheekteeth
- cheekteeth selenodont (ridged)
- post-orbital bar (zygomatic arch) complete

Skulls represent a fascinating piece of natural history and provide a good opportunity to test identification skills. Intact skulls generally represent recent deaths, since many cranial bones are thin and easily broken. Gnawings by rodents seeking minerals also quicken the rate of skull decay. If the skull is relatively intact, one can often tell the gender of the animal. Pedicels, or projections from the frontal bone from which antlers arise, are present only in males of deer, wapiti and moose. Bony horn cores from pronghorn, bighorn sheep and bison are generally larger in adult males than females. An examination of teeth can also reveal the age of the ungulate at time of death (see Appendix 4). Identification of skulls at kill sites assists biologists in determining the predator's diet. The following diagram (Figure 2.4) indicates the name and location of several key skull bones used in identification. Detailed skull illustrations of each species are presented in Figures 2.5–2.13.

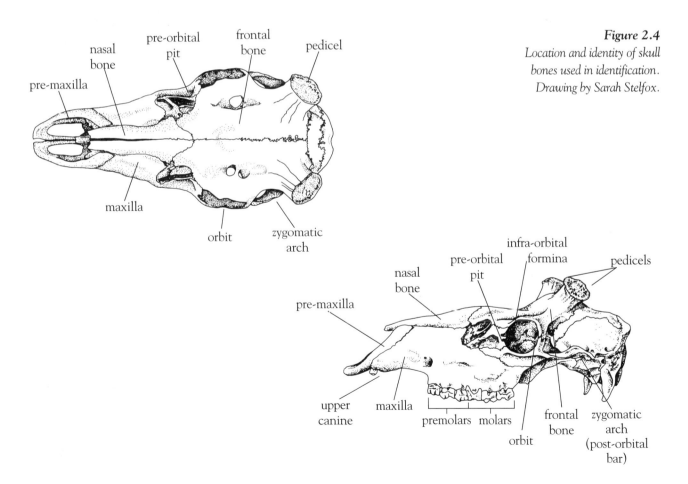

Figure 2.4
Location and identity of skull bones used in identification. Drawing by Sarah Stelfox.

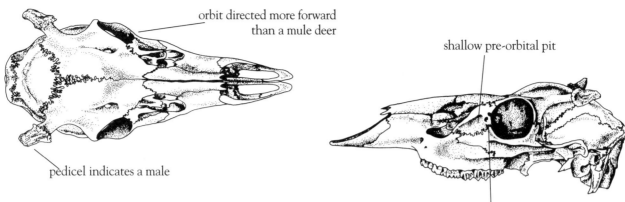

orbit directed more forward than a mule deer

pedicel indicates a male

shallow pre-orbital pit

two formina (holes) at the leading edge of the orbit indicate a member of the deer or pronghorn family

Figure 2.5
Male white-tailed deer skull
(redrawn by Sarah Stelfox from Gilbert, 1990;
average skull length 27 cm, males; 26 cm, females).

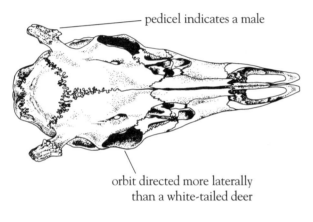

pedicel indicates a male

orbit directed more laterally than a white-tailed deer

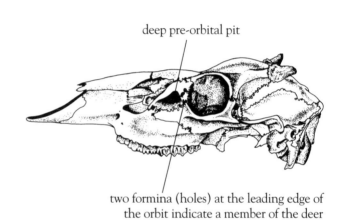

deep pre-orbital pit

two formina (holes) at the leading edge of the orbit indicate a member of the deer family

Figure 2.6
Male mule deer skull
(redrawn by Sarah Stelfox from Gilbert, 1990;
average skull length 24 cm, males; 23 cm, females).

premaxilla does not contact the nasal bone

antler pedicels on both male and females

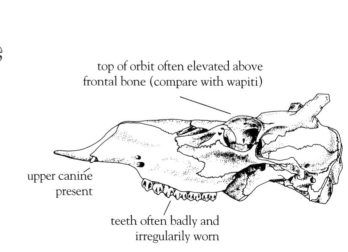

top of orbit often elevated above frontal bone (compare with wapiti)

upper canine present

teeth often badly and irregularily worn

Figure 2.7
Male caribou skull
(redrawn by Sarah Stelfox from Gilbert, 1990;
average skull length 40 cm, males; 34 cm, females).

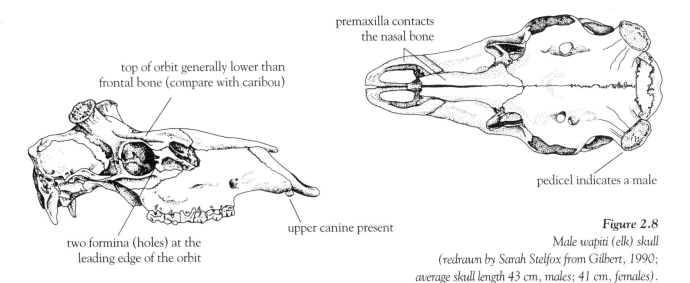

top of orbit generally lower than
frontal bone (compare with caribou)

premaxilla contacts
the nasal bone

upper canine present

two formina (holes) at the
leading edge of the orbit

pedicel indicates a male

Figure 2.8
Male wapiti (elk) skull
(redrawn by Sarah Stelfox from Gilbert, 1990;
average skull length 43 cm, males; 41 cm, females).

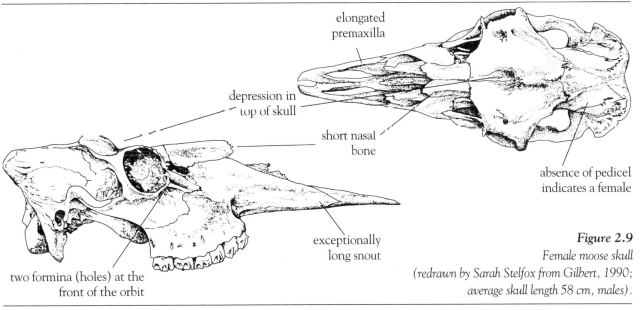

elongated
premaxilla

depression in
top of skull

short nasal
bone

absence of pedicel
indicates a female

two formina (holes) at the
front of the orbit

exceptionally
long snout

Figure 2.9
Female moose skull
(redrawn by Sarah Stelfox from Gilbert, 1990;
average skull length 58 cm, males).

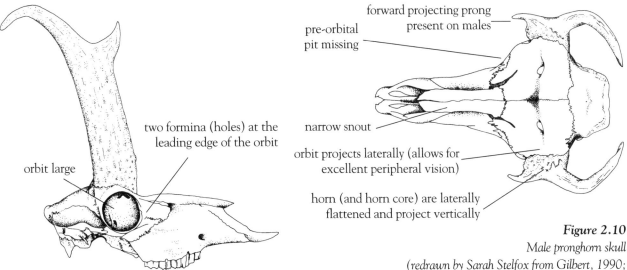

forward projecting prong
present on males

pre-orbital
pit missing

two formina (holes) at the
leading edge of the orbit

narrow snout

orbit large

orbit projects laterally (allows for
excellent peripheral vision)

horn (and horn core) are laterally
flattened and project vertically

Figure 2.10
Male pronghorn skull
(redrawn by Sarah Stelfox from Gilbert, 1990;
average skull length 24 cm, males).

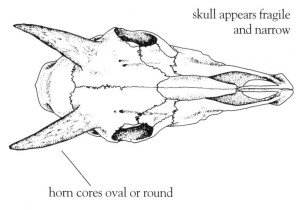

skull appears fragile
and narrow

horn cores oval or round

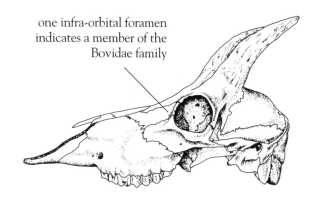

one infra-orbital foramen
indicates a member of the
Bovidae family

Figure 2.11
*Male mountain goat skull
(redrawn by Sarah Stelfox from Gilbert, 1990;
average skull length 29 cm, males; 28 cm, females).*

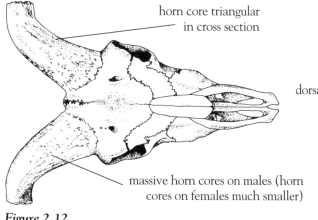

horn core triangular
in cross section

massive horn cores on males (horn
cores on females much smaller)

dorsal skull profile
is triangular

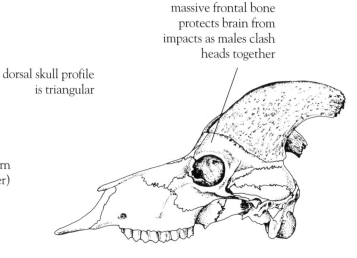

massive frontal bone
protects brain from
impacts as males clash
heads together

Figure 2.12
*Male bighorn sheep skull
(redrawn by Sarah Stelfox from Gilbert, 1990;
average skull length 28 cm, males; 25 cm, females).*

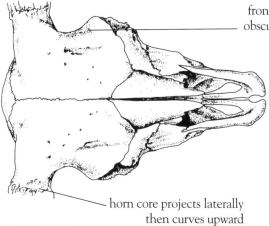

horn core projects laterally
then curves upward

frontal expanded laterally behind orbit,
obscuring view of zygomatic arch below;
arch visible in domestic cattle

massive skull

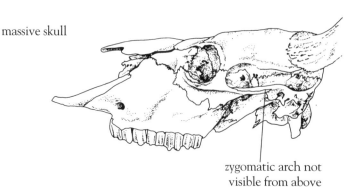

zygomatic arch not
visible from above

Figure 2.13
*Male bison (buffalo) skull
(redrawn by Sarah Stelfox from Gilbert, 1990;
skull length 50–60 cm).*

Figure 2.14 White-tailed Deer: buck (left); doe (right). *White tailed deer are usually brownish-grey to brownish-red in colour. Their name is derived from the white underside of their tail, which is elevated and exposed when the animal is alarmed. The rump and top of the tail are brownish, and the belly is whitish. The antlers of the buck have one central beam from which all tines branch upwards. Females lack antlers. Illustration by Robert Neaves.*

Figure 2.15 Mule Deer: buck (left); doe (right). *Mule deer are usually brownish-grey in colour. In late fall and winter their colour tends to be more grey than brown. Their name is derived from their large mule-like ears. The forehead is dark and the chin and throat are white. The tail is narrow and primarily white except for a solid black tip, and the belly is darkish. The antlers have Y-shaped forks. Females lack antlers. Illustration by Robert Neaves.*

Figure 2.16 (left) *White-tailed deer fawn in hiding position. Photo by M.T. Nietfeld.*

Figure 2.17 (above) *Mule deer fawn in hiding position. Photo by W.M. Samuel.*

Figure 2.18 Caribou: bull. *Caribou have brown coats, often with distinctive white patches on the rump, belly, backs of legs, and tip of nose. In addition, white bands may be found just above the hooves. A mane of long white hair on the neck is especially pronounced in winter. Males and most females have distinctive antlers, although those of the female are considerably smaller.*
Illustration by Robert Neaves.

Figure 2.19
Caribou calf.
Photo by F.L. Miller.

Figure 2.20
Wapiti calf in hiding position.
Photo by M.T. Nietfeld.

Figure 2.21 Wapiti (elk): **bull (left); cow (right)**.
Wapiti are generally a reddish-brown colour with a distinctive light, cream-coloured rump patch. The head, neck and legs are darker than the rest of the body. Cows are more evenly coloured than bulls. Antlers are large, and sweep back and upward. A mature bull will have 5–7 tines, or points, projecting from each main beam. Cows lack antlers. Illustration by Robert Neaves.

Figure 2.22 Moose: bull (left); cow (right). *Gangly in appearance and having extremely long legs, moose are the largest member of the deer family. Body colour generally appears black, but varies from dark brown to reddish or greyish brown with grey or white leg stockings. The nose is long and ends in a large, flexible upper lip. The ears are similar to those of a mule, although not quite as long. From the upper neck of most moose hangs a long pendant of fur covered skin called a "bell." Male moose have large palmate antlers while females lack antlers.*
Illustration by Robert Neaves.

Figure 2.23
Moose calf bedded.
Photo by C. Schwartz.

Figure 2.24 Mountain Goat: billy (right); nanny (left). *The mountain goat is white except for black horns and hooves. Unlike many animals which change colour seasonally, mountain goats remain white during all seasons, though it shed its long, shaggy coat in late spring. Both sexes have long white chin hairs that form distinctive beards. The short, sharp horns are cone-shaped, and slightly curved back from the head. Horns of a mature adult are 20–30 cm in length.*
Illustration by Robert Neaves.

Figure 2.25
Mountain goat kids.
Photo by J. Jorgenson.

Figure 2.26
Bighorn sheep lambs with ewes.
Photo by M. Festa-Bianchet.

Figure 2.27 Bighorn Sheep: ram (left); ewe (right). *The colour of bighorn sheep varies from dark to light tan or cream, with a yellowish-white belly. Seen from the rear, the creamy white rump patch around a small brown tail is very distinctive. Both sexes have horns, but those of the ewe are seldom longer than 20 cm. The spiralled horns of an old ram are massive, may measure up to 115 cm, and weigh as much as 15 kg. Bighorn sheep horns, which are never shed, grow longer each year and are marked by annual growth rings. The age of a bighorn sheep can be determined by counting these horn growth sections.*

Figure 2.28 **Pronghorn** *(Antelope)*: **buck (left); doe (right)**. *Pronghorn are rusty brown with white stripes across their necks. They have white bellies and large white rumps. The hair on their rump flares out when they are frightened, serving as a visual flag for the herd. They have black and dark brown markings on their heads; males also have dark markings on their necks. The horns are black, with a fork or prong projecting forward in males. Females also have horns although the horns generally do not have forks and are much smaller than those of the males (rarely rising above the ears). Pronghorn lack dewclaws.*
Illustration by Robert Neaves.

Figure 2.29
Pronghorn fawn in hiding position.
Photo by W.M. Samuel.

Figure 2.30 Bison (Buffalo): **bull (left); cow (right).** The largest of North America's mammals can be readily identified by its massive size, pronounced shoulder development and shaggy hair hanging from the front legs of adult individuals. Bison have a large head and are dark brown in colour. Young calves are reddish brown. The horns, which are larger on bulls, curve outwards laterally then upwards.
Illustration by Robert Neaves.

Figure 2.31
Bison calves.
Photo by L. Carbyn.

IDENTIFICATION USING FRESH TRACKS OF ADULT INDIVIDUALS

Of the various forms of ungulate sign (scats, tracks, pick-up skulls, hair on vegetation), tracks are probably the most frequently found if ground conditions are favourable (either snow or moist soil). Not only are tracks useful for identification, they also reveal considerable adaptation to the terrain over which different species travel (see Chapter 12). Tracks can also be a source of considerable frustration, since hoof sizes vary, and once an impression is made, it undergoes shape and size changes as it ages. For species with hooves of different size but similar shape, one can easily confuse young individuals of larger species with the mature ones of smaller species — a subadult moose and adult bull wapiti, for example. The identity of some hoof tracks cannot be established reliably. Physical dimensions of white-tailed deer and mule deer tracks in Alberta are not significantly different.

TABLE 2.2
WALKING GAIT DIMENSIONS FOR ADULT UNGULATES
(J. Halfpenny, personal communication)

	Stride Length (cm)		Straddle (cm)	
	Range	Mean	Range	Mean
Deer	90–110	104	14–20	17
Wapiti (Elk)	115–155	133	15–33	24
Moose	140–200	159	26–41	32
Pronghorn	75–85	80	12–20	15
Mountain Goat	75–80	78	17–23	20
Bighorn Sheep	88–94	91	8–12	11
Bison (Buffalo)	110–150	136	11–36	27

Position and measurement of a typical walking gait is illustrated in Figure 2.32. Typical adult tracks of each species are illustrated in Figures 2.33–35. Table 2.2 gives average stride length and straddle of a walking gait. When animals are moving across soft ground, they may splay their hooves considerably to provide improved traction.

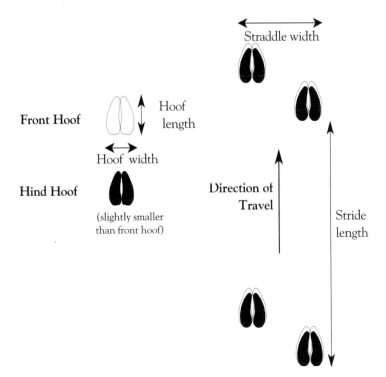

Figure 2.32
Hoof and gait measurements of ungulates.

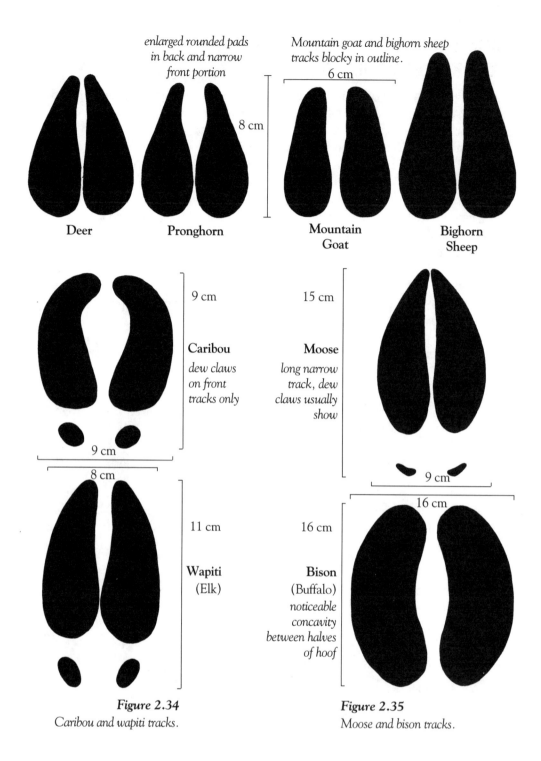

Figure 2.33
Deer, pronghorn, mountain goat and bighorn sheep tracks.

enlarged rounded pads in back and narrow front portion

Mountain goat and bighorn sheep tracks blocky in outline.

6 cm

8 cm

Deer

Pronghorn

Mountain Goat

Bighorn Sheep

9 cm

Caribou
dew claws on front tracks only

9 cm

15 cm

Moose
long narrow track, dew claws usually show

9 cm

8 cm

11 cm

Wapiti (Elk)

16 cm

16 cm

Bison (Buffalo) *noticeable concavity between halves of hoof*

Figure 2.34
Caribou and wapiti tracks.

Figure 2.35
Moose and bison tracks.

IDENTIFICATION OF DEER SPECIES

The most confusing hoofed mammals in Alberta to identify are mule deer and white-tailed deer. Although there are gross similarities between these species, a practised eye can pick out numerous differences in colouration, behaviour, and movement. Individual characteristics are not always reliable, however, so several features should be compared (Table 2.3, Figure 2.36). Individuals that share features of both species may be hybrids (see Chapter 5). Hybrid deer generally have an intermediate appearance with respect to skin glands, and ear and tail dimensions.

William Wishart (personal communication) has suggested that white-tailed deer and mule deer differ in the orientation of their eye sockets. Mule deer orbits are oriented laterally while white-tailed deer orbits are angled forward. Presumably, these differences reflect the advantages of increased peripheral vision of mule deer inhabiting open habitats versus improved depth perception of white-tailed deer frequenting thick cover.

Mule Deer

White-tailed Deer

Figure 2.36
Differences in antlers and rumps of mule deer and white-tailed deer. Drawings by Sarah Stelfox.

TABLE 2.3

DIFFERENCES BETWEEN MULE DEER AND WHITE-TAILED DEER

(based on Wishart, 1986)

Feature	Mule Deer	White-tailed Deer
Metatarsal glands	>10.0 cm long; surrounded with brown hairs	<5.0 cm long; surrounded with white hairs
Interdigital glands	Surrounded with brown hairs	Surrounded with white hairs
Tarsal glands	Usually brown or light tan	Usually whitish
Pre-orbital glands	Large, conspicuous and deep	Inconspicuous and shallow
Ears	20 cm with conspicuous black trim	16 cm with occasional black trim
Tail	Round and white with black tip, half naked on the underside	Long, bushy and brown with white fringe, white below and fully haired becoming a conspicuous flag when elevated
Rump patch	Conspicuous white at all times	White rear inconspicuous when covered by brown tail
Coat colour	Grey with black trimmings, dark chest, white belly	Brown with white trimmings, conspicuous white ventral strip from front to back
Antlers	Dichotomous branching (forked) with poorly developed brow tines and long back tines, wide tip to tip spread	Single branches from the main beam with well-developed brow tines and relatively short back tines; narrow tip to tip spread
Skull	Deep lacrimal pit, orbit directed laterally	Shallow lacrimal pit, orbit directed forward
Running gait	High vertical bounds	Low leaps and bounds

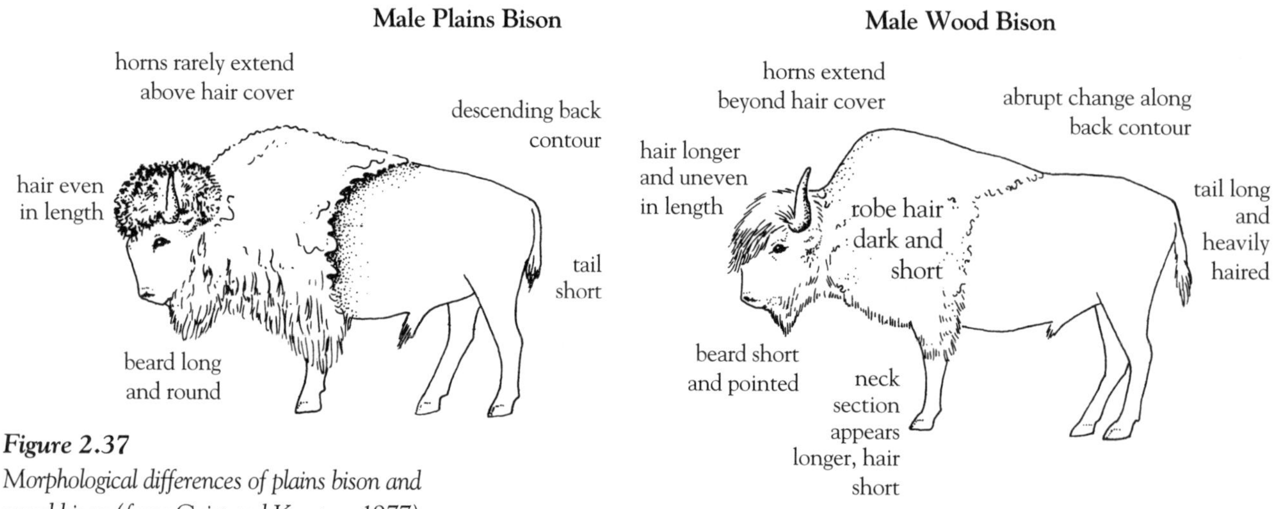

Male Plains Bison   Male Wood Bison

horns rarely extend
above hair cover

descending back
contour

hair even
in length

horns extend
beyond hair cover

abrupt change along
back contour

hair longer
and uneven
in length

robe hair
dark and
short

tail long
and
heavily
haired

tail
short

beard long
and round

beard short
and pointed

neck
section
appears
longer, hair
short

Figure 2.37

*Morphological differences of plains bison and
wood bison (from Geist and Karsten, 1977)
Drawings by Sarah Stelfox.*

TABLE 2.4

DIFFERENCES BETWEEN PLAINS BISON AND WOOD BISON

(based on Geist and Karsten, 1977; differences most pronounced in adult males)

Feature	Plains Bison	Wood Bison
Hair on head	Long and even	Uneven in length
Beard	Long and rounded	Short and pointed
Ventral mane	Very long	Very short
Hair on front leg	Very long "chaps"	Very short
Robe hair	Light and long	Dark and short
Robe contour	Distinct border along flank extends down to tarsals	Less distinct and extends down
Tail	Short	Longer than plains bison
Dorsal contour	Descending toward tail	Horizontal
Horns	Rarely extend above hair	Usually extends above hair
Hair tufts on penis sheath	Long hair	Short hair

IDENTIFICATION OF WOOD BISON AND PLAINS BISON

To assist in the identification of wood bison and plains bison, Geist and Karsten (1977) have
stereotyped a typical male specimen of each (Table 2.4 and Figure 2.37). Since individual characteristics are generally not reliable, several features should be compared. The differences among
immature and adult females are especially difficult to distinguish. To help you master the conformational differences of these "subspecies", visit Elk Island National Park east of Edmonton to view
plains bison on the north side of Highway 16 and wood bison on the south side.

IDENTIFICATION OF NEWBORN
AND YOUNG HOOFED MAMMALS

Although the species of newborn animals can generally be determined by the adult individuals
near them, it is worthwhile learning their distinctive features. Remember not to approach or touch
newborns, or to assume that they have been abandoned. Their mother is generally not far away.
For some species, such as the wapiti, moose, and bison, the mother may approach and attack
people if she perceives a threat to her offspring. Spring and early summer are the calving seasons
and provide the best opportunity to see newborns.

Motorists should be particularly cautious of newborns along roadways, as they are unaccustomed to vehicles and may behave unpredictably. The following descriptions and photographs (see pages 13–20) will assist the reader in identifying newborns.

- Diminutive size and relatively long legs are clear indications of a newborn. Young moose calves appear to have particularly lengthy legs.
- A spotted neonatal coat is found on white-tailed deer, mule deer and wapiti. This newborn coat, which provides camouflage, will be lost when the animal is 3–4 months of age.
- The neonatal coat of both bison and moose is reddish in appearance. This newborn coat will be lost when the calf is 3–4 months of age.
- The horns of bighorn sheep lambs, mountain goat kids, and pronghorn kids are either absent, hidden, or visible as small nubs.
- Moose calves do not have a distinctive throat bell.
- Moose calves are often seen as twins.
- Suckling is generally a newborn behaviour. Suckling may persist for the first several months of life, continuing on into the winter for some species.
- The neonates of the "hider" species — white-tailed deer, mule deer, wapiti, and pronghorn — are frequently hidden among vegetation during their first weeks of life.
- Generally, newborns that are not "hiding" are more playful than older individuals and may be observed frolicking and interacting with other newborns.
- Newborns often emit distinctive vocalizations. Refer to Chapter 3 (Communication) for details.

DICHOTOMOUS KEYS

How to Use a Dichotomous Key

To use the dichotomous keys presented in this chapter, begin with the first pair of statements. Read both options, and decide which more accurately describes the animal or its feature. The right-hand column either directs you to a new couplet or identifies the animal. If you are directed to a new couplet, read both statements and decide which of the two is correct. Proceed in this manner until you identify the animal. Where possible, examine the dichotomous keys for several different features (e.g., body shape, horns/antlers, skulls) to be sure you have properly identified the species.

Key to Antlers and Horns

1 If antlers present,* then .... go to 2
If horns present,* then 6

2 If palmate (palm-like) antlers, projecting horizontally at right angles to the skull, then .... **Moose**
If antlers not generally palmate, then .... go to 3

3 If shovel-like brow tine extends forward over face; other tines pointed; antlers often present on both males and females, then ....**Caribou**
If brow tine not shovel-like in appearance, then .... go to 4

4 If main antler beam sweeps back over shoulders; tips of tines may appear ivory coloured, then .... **Wapiti** (Elk)
If main antler beam projects upwards or forwards, then .... go to 5

5 If antler with single beam from which secondary unforked tines project upwards; brow tines generally long, then ....**White-tailed Deer**
If antler tines forked (y-shaped branches); brow tine usually short, then ....**Mule Deer**

6 If horns forked (forking uncommon in does); prong extending forward from main beam, then ....**Pronghorn**
If horns unforked, then .... go to 7

7 If horns curve outwards, then upwards, then ....**Bison** (Buffalo)
If horns otherwise, then .... go to 8

8 If horns smooth and black, curving upwards and slightly backwards, then ....**Mountain Goat**
If horns massive and spiralling in males; female horns shorter and less curved; horns of males commonly broomed (broken and shredded at tips from fights in the fall rut); at close range, the annual growth rings may be visible on ram horns, then ....**Bighorn Sheep**

* Note that the horns of male pronghorn are atypical in that they branch. The horns of female pronghorn generally do not branch.

Key to Body Conformation and Colour

1   If hair coat white or yellowish white; animal stocky in appearance; both sexes with a noticeable beard, then ..... **Mountain Goat**
    If hair coat colour not completely white, then .... go to 2

2   If massive animal with prominent shoulder hump and huge head; shaggy brown hair on shoulders and front legs; pelage of newborn calves reddish in appearance, changing to brown before winter, then ....**Bison** (Buffalo)*
    If not as above, then .... go to 3

3   If noticeable flap of haired skin (bell) suspended beneath throat; animal dark in colour and long-legged; appearance ungainly; upper lip thick and overhanging, then .... **Moose**
    If not as above, then .... go to 4

4   If two broad white stripes across throat; body generally rusty-brown in appearance; white rump hairs become erect when animal is alarmed; black cheek patch on males visible at close range, then .... **Pronghorn**
    If throat not white; or if white, not present as distinct stripes, then .... go to 5

5   If rump and upper side of tail brown or reddish; tail raised when alarmed, exposing white underside; white throat patch; body generally brown, grey, or reddish-brown, then ....**White-tailed Deer**
    If rump cream-coloured, not brown, then .... go to 6

6   If hair coat on neck and legs darker than on shoulders, then .... **Wapiti** (Elk)
    If hair coat on neck and legs not darker than on shoulders, then .... go to 7

7   If hair on neck cream or white in colour; pronounced mane of long white hair; hooves proportionally large then .... **Caribou**
    If hair on neck not cream or white in colour, then .... go to 8

8   If ears large; tail white with black tip; white throat patch; cream- or white-coloured rump patch; pelage is reddish-brown in summer and greyish-brown in winter, forehead dark, then .... **Mule Deer**
    If ears small; tail brown and not black tipped; muzzle white; appearance stocky; cream-coloured rump surrounding small brown tail, then .... **Bighorn Sheep**

A more detailed comparison of plains bison and wood bison is provided earlier in this chapter.

Key to Skulls

1   If horns or horn cores absent, then .... go to 2
    If horn or horn cores present, then .... go to 6

2   If upper canine tooth or tooth socket present, then .... go to 3
    If upper canine tooth or tooth socket absent, then .... go to 4

3   If maximum width of middle lower incisor less than 6 mm; premaxilla not in contact with nasals; a straight edge placed above orbits at right angle to the long axis of the skull is supported by the orbits and shows a gap between straight-edge and frontal bone, posterior nares divided by vomer, then ....**Caribou**
    If maximum width of middle lower incisor greater than 10 mm; premaxilla in contact with nasals; straight edge placed above orbits at right angle to the long axis of the skull can not generally touch both orbits simultaneously as the frontal bone is elevated, posterior nares not divided by vomer, then ....**Wapiti** (Elk)

4   If conspicuous depression in skull between orbits; nasal bones very short; premaxilla elongated, then .... **Moose**
    If no conspicuous depression in skull, then .... go to 5

5   If deep preorbital pits (>8 mm) in front of eye socket, then .... **Mule Deer**
    If shallow preorbital pits (<6.5 mm) in front of eye socket, then .... **White-tailed Deer**

6   If orbits projecting noticeably from skull; skull with flattened horn cores projecting nearly vertically (very small in females); antorbital pit absent, horn sheaths deciduous, then .... **Pronghorn**
    If orbits not projecting noticeably from skull; horn cores not noticeably flattened, then .... go to 7

7   If skull massive (>400 mm long), horns or cores projecting laterally outward, away from side of head, then .... **Bison** (Buffalo)*
    If skull otherwise, then .... go to 8

8   If horn cores oval or round, slender and erect; horn sheaths, if present, are smooth, black, slender, and curving vertically upward and backward, then .... **Mountain Goat**
    If horn cores spreading laterally, more or less triangular in cross-section; horn sheaths, if present, roughened by transverse ridges, then .... **Bighorn Sheep**

It is often difficult to distinguish skulls of bison and cattle. When a bison skull is placed on a flat surface, the zygomatic arch (postorbital bar) can not be seen from above because the frontal bone is greatly expanded behind the orbit. The zygomatic arch is visible from above in skulls of domestic cattle.

Key to Tracks (for adult ungulates)

1 If track length greater than 13 cm, then .... go to 2
   If track length less than 13 cm, then .... go to 3

2 If track 15–17 cm in length and round in outline; noticeable concavity between adjacent halves of hooves;
   dew claw impressions seldom visible, then ....**Bison** (Buffalo)
   If track 13–15 cm in length, greatly exceeding track width; dew claws often visible, then ....**Moose**

3 If track 10–12.5 cm, then ....**Wapiti** (Elk)
   If track length less than 10 cm, then .... go to 4

4 If large circular hooves that spread easily; each half of hoof with rounded tip and back; tips of hooves generally pointing
   inward; dew claw generally visible on front tracks; track 8–9 cm in length; track width generally
   exceeds track length, then ....**Caribou**
   If track not noticeably circular, generally less than 8.5 cm in length; track width less than track length, then .... go to 5

5 If overall shape of track blocky or square in outline, then .... go to 6
   If track pointed in front and not square in outline, then .... go to 7

6 If outer sides of track straight; overall track appearance wedge-shaped; track 7.5–9 cm in length; dew claws
   usually not visible, then ....**Bighorn Sheep**
   If tracks appear blocky; tips are wider and more rounded than those of bighorn sheep; track length 6.5–7.5 cm;
   dew claws usually not visible, then ....**Mountain Goat**

7 If rounded pads at back of track contrast with narrower front portion; track 6.5–7 cm in length; dew claw imprints never
   present; slight concavity along outer margin of hoof, then ....**Pronghorn**
   If tracks heart-shaped in outline and 6.5–7 cm in length; dew claws seldom visible, then ....**Deer**

ACKNOWLEDGMENTS

Dr. Jim Halfpenny of Gardner, Montana, offered valuable comments on track dimensions and illustrations.

3

Communication

Denis Chabot

Using communication signals based on sight, hearing, smell and touch, ungulates effectively convey information to others that helps ensure group cohesion, mother-calf bonds, predator detection and avoidance, and dominance or submission for access to food and mates. Following a brief explanation of the evolution and ritualization of communication signals, a classification scheme for communication is proposed. The advantages and disadvantages of communication channels (optical, acoustic, chemical, tactile) in different environments are briefly described with selected graphics that illustrate the importance of posture to communication, some vocalizations of wapiti in the form of spectrograms, and the location of skin glands which release communication chemicals. The chapter concludes with tables that document the various communication signals and displays used by each of Alberta's ungulates through sight, sound, smell and touch.

DEFINITION

One of the most important features of intra-specific interactions is that animals can affect the behaviour of other individuals without coercing them by brute force. In such cases, animals are said to communicate. Formally, there is communication when a *sender* initiates in some *channel* (i.e., the physical medium, such as optical, acoustic, chemical, or tactile) a physical signal that is detected by a *receiver*. For communication to take place, this signal must also affect the probability of subsequent behaviour or the physiological state or arousal level of the receiver (Hailman, 1977; Smith, 1977; Geist, 1978; Tavolga, 1983). Communication is more efficient energetically, but can be less reliable than mechanical influence (i.e., force) in affecting the behavioural or physiological state of the receiver (Wilson, 1975; Dawkins and Krebs, 1978; Walther, 1984).

This is a very broad definition, almost equating communication with social behaviour (Burghardt, 1977; Tavolga, 1983). Various attempts have been made to restrict the scope of the term "communication". Tavolga (1968) developed a hierarchy of six levels of communication. In the lower three levels, signals consist simply of the presence of an organism, or the by-products of its current activity or physiological state. Most researchers do not consider this real communication. In the other three levels, however, the signals are produced by structures or behaviours specialized for communication, often called *displays*. Displays are what most biologists mean by communication signals.

EVOLUTION OF COMMUNICATION SIGNALS

Animals are under strong selection pressures to efficiently monitor their environment, including conspecifics and other animals. Many aspects of other animals and their behaviour can be used to help predict their next actions, or to profit from their discoveries, such as food, a predator, etc. (Smith, 1977, 1985; Geist, 1978; Krebs and Dawkins, 1984). The cues used are by-products of animals' presence and activity, and have not been selected for any communication function. The behaviour changes induced in the receiver can be of some benefit to the individual being observed (the sender). Natural selection will increase the efficiency of cues that induce responses in the

*The raised lip and distinctive facial expression of many male ungulate species, as illustrated by this white-tailed deer buck, is **flehmen**— a behaviour used by males to biochemically analyze the urine of females for chemicals that indicate reproductive status.*
Photo by J. Nolan.

receiver that benefit the sender. If the necessary genetic variability is present, the cues will be modified for a communication function and become displays (Moynihan, 1970; Smith, 1977, Geist, 1978; 1985; Krebs and Dawkins, 1984). This process has been called *ritualization* (Manning, 1979).

WHO BENEFITS FROM COMMUNICATION?

It is clear that senders must benefit from communication signals for them to evolve into displays. The effect on receivers depends on the degree of compatibility in reproductive interest between sender and receiver. When the interests of both interactants are largely compatible, as in some courtship displays or group cohesion signals, receivers can benefit directly from communication, and natural selection favours increased sensitivity to the signals. The situation is less clear when the interactants are in direct conflict. For example, a wapiti stag that answers a dominance display by abandoning food or mate to the dominant without a fight does not gain a direct benefit in doing so (Dawkins and Krebs, 1978; Geist, 1978; Krebs and Dawkins, 1984). But such a submissive response increases its fitness (Smith, 1977), since the subordinate avoids a fight that it was unlikely to win and thereby saves energy and avoids injuries. In addition, it can remain near the dominant, which is advantageous in some circumstances (e.g., protection from predation, possibility to sneak some copulations later on, etc.). The receiver is therefore under selection to respond appropriately to dominance signals of larger conspecifics, but only to those signals that reliably predict the strength or condition of the opponent.

COMMUNICATION CHANNELS USED BY HOOFED MAMMALS

There is a "modality" corresponding to each medium of transmission. Thus, optical (i.e. visual) signals rely on sight, acoustic signals on audition, chemical signals on either olfaction or taste, and tactile signals on touch. The habitat in which a species lives will determine, in part, which types of signals are effective. For example, animals living in dense forest will not have much opportunity to use visual signals, and should rely on other channels to transfer information to conspecifics. Similarly, social systems affect signals: gregarious animals have more opportunities to use visual and tactile signals than do solitary animals. Herd animals usually require a more complex communication system to deal with the varied interactions they encounter daily. In very large groups, however, visibility may be obscured and, in some conditions, acoustic signals may be preferable to visual signals.

A complete study of communication systems involves the following: the examination of the sensory systems of the animal to determine usable communication channels and possible signals; behavioural observations leading to categorization of behaviours that seem to be involved in communication; observation of the reaction of the receiver; formulation of hypotheses as to the meaning of each signal; manipulations or playback experiments to demonstrate that the meaning of the signals is what was predicted. There are few species for which all levels of study have been undertaken, and in those cases, it is usually for a subset of the communication repertoire.

Biologists have some knowledge of wild hoofed mammals' sensory systems and their sensitivity, but most research has been limited to behavioural observations, with few controlled manipulations or playback experiments. Fortunately, ungulate communication signals appear quite stereotyped, and their effects are often obvious. Thus, the lack of controlled experiments is usually not a major problem in understanding ungulate displays, except for chemical signals.

CLASSIFICATION OF COMMUNICATION SIGNALS

There is no entrenched scheme for classifying communication signals. It is common practice to categorize signals according to the medium in which they are carried, and either the context in which they are used (e.g., courtship, aggression, mother-offspring interactions, etc.), or a presumed or demonstrated function (e.g., threatening opponent, courting mate, etc.). This system is not entirely satisfactory, however, because some communication signals are comprised of several components and channels. In fact, redundancy is often built in to minimize communication failures. Integrated displays may lose some meaning when defined by such artificial classifications (Walther, 1984). Another difficulty is that displays may be used in more than one context, or have more than one function. Walther (1984) suggests that a natural classification would focus on the message or meaning of displays.

The implementation of such a classification system for all nine species of Alberta hoofed mammals is beyond the scope of this chapter. Instead, I present lists of behaviours which are known or expected to have a communicative value, broken down by channel and broad contextual categories. Thus, one can quickly determine which behavioural elements to watch for in the field or compare the species for their use of the various behaviours. The tables are based on a review of the literature on the behaviour of hoofed mammals. It can be difficult to classify some of the behaviours found in the literature into the proper channel and behavioural category, and my interpretation may differ from that of the author(s) who described the behaviours.

Behaviours that are displays or elements of displays are in bold in the tables. The other behaviours also have communicative value, but I did not have enough evidence of specialization for communication to classify them as displays or display elements. The sources for each entry are given directly in the tables, to allow the reconstruction of complete displays (sometimes including elements from many channels) and details of the context in which they are used. The tables do not provide information on the frequency of use or the sequencing of the various behaviours, which is sometimes available from the sources cited. Because some species and some channels have been studied less than others, no distinction was made between behaviours that are not used by a species and behaviours that a species has not yet been observed to use. For a given channel and contextual category, there may be elements belonging to more than one display. Often ungulates have several displays that can be used in the same context, each conveying a different intensity level or a different message.

Some behaviours convey information in more than one channel. For instance, rustling horns or antlers in vegetation, a behaviour common to all species but the bison (Tables 3.3 and 3.4), is usually considered an acoustic display. It could also be a visual display when performed in open habitat or near a conspecific. The same could be said for stamping the ground with one foreleg. Digging dirt with horns or antlers, opening the preorbital glands, pawing and urinating in a pit, and urinating on the hind legs all involve the chemical channel (Tables 3.5 and 3.6), but could also be considered visual or acoustic signals. To minimize clutter, such behaviours were only included in the channel considered the most important by observers.

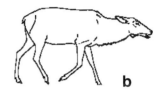

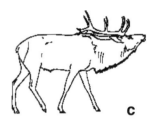

Figure 3.1
Some visual displays in wapiti. a) threat and b) submissive displays in cows; c) herding and d) courtship displays in bulls. Displays with opposite meanings are often very different, a phenomenon called "antithesis". Note especially the relative position of head, neck, eyes, ears, and antlers. Modified from Geist, 1982, with permission from the author.

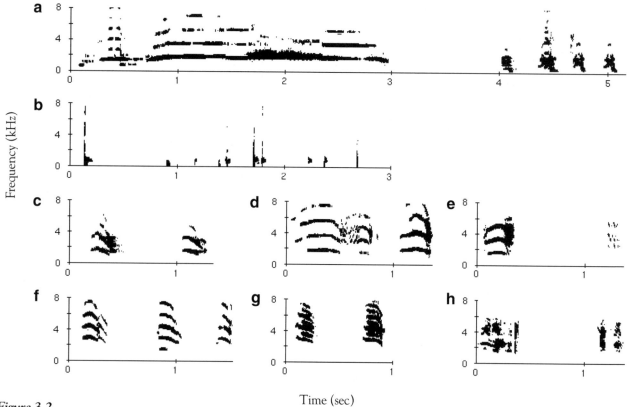

Figure 3.2

Common vocalizations of wapiti. Bull during rut: a) bugle followed by "yelps"; b) "clucking"; cow: (c) contact and (d and e) distress calls. Distress calls from (f) 1-day-old and (g) 45-day-old fawn. Cow submissive calls (h). Spectrograms produced on Kay Elemetrics Corp. Sona-Graph 6061B.

VISUAL SIGNALS

Visual communication involves stereotyped behaviours that can be seen by conspecifics (Tables 3.1 and 3.2). Hoofed mammals often exploit their shape, size, and ornaments (e.g., coat patterns, horns/antlers) to convey information. The relative position of horns or antlers, neck, head, eyes and ears are especially important. A few generalities can be made from Tables 3.1 and 3.2. Ungulates threaten each other by advertising which method of attack will be used in fighting. Thus, animals bring their weapons ready for use. In contrast, dominance displays emphasize body size and weapons but weapons are usually not readied for combat (Geist, 1971, 1981, 1982; Bromley, 1977; Walther, 1984). Finally, many species combine submission, dominance and even threat displays in their breeding behaviour. Threats are especially common while males herd or chase females, while dominance and submissive displays are used for courtship when the females are in or near estrus.

To improve communication efficiency and insure that the message is received, animals often use redundant displays. This is accomplished by using more than one display with the same message, repeating the display, or by combining display elements from different channels, (Geist, 1978). However, rarely used signals are often very effective. Secondly, using clearly different displays to communicate opposite meanings (antithesis) helps to prevent confusion in the receiver. Figure 3.1 illustrates this for the wapiti. Hinds (cows) threaten each other by lowering the ears, staring, grinding teeth, exposing canines, and raising head, chin and sometimes a foreleg (weapon threat, since hinds fight by striking with forelegs). The submissive display is almost the exact opposite: neck is stretched, with head and chin low, ears are along the neck, the animal makes rapid chewing motions and usually moves away. Stags (bulls) herd females by stretching the neck and holding the head parallel to the ground with antlers along the neck. This behaviour is directed at the female, and is often followed by a rush or by bugling. When courting, stags hold the head high, flick the tongue, and move slowly and gently about the female (Geist, 1982).

ACOUSTIC SIGNALS

Many vocalizations and sounds have been documented for Alberta's ungulates (Tables 3.3 and 3.4). It should be noted that this list is not exhaustive, as some faint sounds require close range observations to be detected. Contrary to studies in other species (especially birds), researchers have paid little attention to acoustic signals in ungulates. Brief qualitative descriptions of the sounds are usually provided, along with the context in which they are used. Rarely have quantitative descriptions, such as spectrograms been provided (exceptions are Struhsaker, 1967; Lent, 1974b; Gunderson and Mahan, 1980; Richardson *et al.*, 1983; Bowyer and Kitchen, 1987a). This makes it difficult to compare sounds across species. Spectrograms are graphic representation of sounds. They display the frequency content of sounds over time. Figure 3.2 depicts the spectrograms of some wapiti calls recorded at the Ministik Wildlife Research Station, Alberta. Generally, soft tonal sounds are used for mother-offspring interactions, as well as in some submissive and courtship displays. In contrast, aggressive signals are often loud, low-pitched and harsh.

CHEMICAL SIGNALS

Olfactory signals are less studied, in part because of the difficulty humans have in detecting and describing them. Often this form of communication is deduced from anatomical studies showing presence of glands, and from observations of behaviours that suggest odours are detected, or could be released. Figure 3.3 shows the epithelial glands identified for Alberta species (vestigial glands not included). Tables 3.5 and 3.6 describe behaviours that a) suggest that conspecific odours have been detected, and b) can release metabolites (secretions, urine, feces) onto the self or into the environment, or add environmental or conspecific odours to the body. An advantage of chemical signals over other signals is that they can persist. For this reason, in ungulates as in other species, they are often used for advertising reproductive, dominant or territorial status.

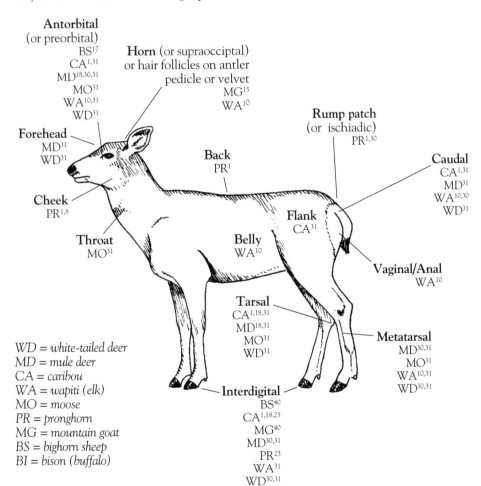

Figure 3.3
Location of epithelial glands on the body of ungulates, and species for which each gland has been reported. Sources are given in superscripts. Refer to Table 3.2 for references.

Velvet hanging from the freshly exposed antlers of a buck is a sure sign that the rut season is not far away. When engorged with blood, the warm velvet provides critical nutrients and minerals to the developing antler, but the velvet dies shortly after the antlers are fully formed. At this time, bucks rub their antlers on saplings to dislodge the drying velvet and to polish the bony material beneath.
Photo by J. Nolan.

TACTILE SIGNALS

Tactile signals are easy to describe, yet difficult to study. This is because they lie at the fringe of communication: most definitions of communication contrast communication signals with physical coercion. For the other senses this distinction is obvious. In the case of many tactile signals, it is a matter of degree, and the distinction is often blurred.

Tables 3.7 and 3.8 include behaviours that involve contact between conspecifics but fall short of full fighting or physical displacement of conspecifics. Many of these behaviours are quite obviously displays or part of displays: licking the dominant's face, for instance, does not coerce the dominant. The threat signals, however, are more difficult to deal with. For example, Geist (personal communication, 1989) considers the foreleg kick of the bighorn sheep a true display (it is very stereotyped, often executed in the air, without contact), but not the similar (but more variable) behaviour of deer, moose and wapiti. On the other hand, Walther (1984) gives the front kick of the latter species full display status. Following Geist's example, I did not consider them displays, but did classify them as signals because they usually result in displacing the recipient, but are less energetically costly than actually pushing it out of the way. Butting was included as a means of communication for the same reason. Sparring in many deer species, as well as clashing in bighorn sheep, is close to combat, but is very stereotyped. Thus I considered them to be displays. Real fights among deer and bighorn rams are different and occur in a different context (Geist, 1971).

ACKNOWLEDGMENTS

I thank Valerius Geist for discussing an early draft of this document with me. His first-hand experience with all nine species discussed here made for most helpful comments. I am also very grateful to Cyrille Barrette, Valerius Geist, Robert Hudson and Tim Toth for reviewing a later version of this chapter. I am very grateful to Ross Lein for kindly making the sound analyzing equipment available to me.

TABLE 3.1

VISUAL SIGNALS OF DEER, CARIBOU, WAPITI AND MOOSE
(in broad contextual categories)

Y = Young, F = Female, and M = Male
Numbers in superscript refer to the sources (see Table 3.2)
Entries in bold are display elements

Behaviour	White-tailed Deer	Mule Deer	Caribou	Wapiti (Elk)	Moose
Contact (mother-offspring or between herd members)					
head lowered then brought back up	—	—	F[25,34]	—	—
head kept horizontal, at calf height	—	—	F[25]	—	—
Submission					
exaggerated chewing motion	—	—	—	F[19,38]	—
head low, nose down	**FM**[18]	**FM**[18]	—	F[19,38]	YM[14]
head high	—	M[14,18]	—	—	YM[14]
head shake or twist	—	—	—	F[19,38]	—
direct gaze	FM[18,40]	FM[18]	—	—	—
averted gaze (turning head or body)	**FM**[18,22]	**FM**[18]	M[24]	YFM[19]	YM[14]
ears back along neck	**FM**[18,22]	**FM**[18]	—	F[38]	—
crouch	**FM**[18]	**FM**[18]	—	F[41]	—
lordosis	—	—	—	—	—
sham grazing	FM[22]	FM[18]	FM[3,40]	FM[40]	FM[40]
male urinating like a female	—	M[18]	—	—	—
Breeding behaviour (herding, courtship)					
averted gaze	M[18,22]	M[18]	M[3]	M[19]	—
looking at mate	—	—	M[24]	—	—
head down	—	—	M[3,24]	F[16]M[38]	—
head and chin at shoulder level, neck stretch	**M**[18]	**M**[16,18]	**M**[3,16,24,34]	**M**[16,19,38]	**M**[14,16]
same, with head twist	—	—	**M**[4]	—	—
same, with low crouch	**M**[18]	—	—	—	**M**[14]
head and horns/antlers high	—	**M**[18]	—	**M**[16,38]	**M**[27]
head waving from side to side	—	—	—	—	—
head suddenly swung upward	—	**M**[16,18]	—	—	—
tongue flicking	**M**[40]	**M**[18]	**M**[3]	**M**[19,38]	**M**[14]
foreleg kick (no contact)	—	—	—	—	—
piloerection	—	F[16]	—	—	—
rush	M[18]	M[18]	—	M[19,38]	—
raising tail	—	—	—	F[19]	—
lordosis	F[40]	F[18]	—	F[19]	—
bolting, circling around mate, frolicking	F[18]	F[18]	—	F[19]	—
stiff walk, swaying gait or prancing	—	—	M[34]	—	M[16,27]
Dominance and space claim					
eyes averted	—	M[18]	—	M[19]	—
sideward turn of head	—	—	—	—	—
head low or at shoulder level, antlers up	M[22]	M[5,18]	M[3,24,34]	M[19]	—
head and chin at shoulder level, neck stretch	**—**	—	—	**—**	—
same, with head twist	—	—	—	—	—
head and horns/antlers up	—	M[14,18]	—	—	M[40]
sudden head up	—	M[18]	—	—	—
arching back	—	M[16,18]	—	—	—
broadside presentation or parallel walk	M[15]	M[5,15,16,18]	M[16]	M[16,19]	M[16]
piloerection	—	M[5,16,18]	—	—	M[16]
tail up and/or moving	FM[40]	FM[11,16,18]	—	—	—
tail down	—	—	—	—	—
stiff movements or swaying gait	—	M[11,16,18]	M[16]	—	M[16,27]
Attention/Alarm					
piloerection	YFM[35]	YFM[18]	—	YFM[41]	YFM[14]
tail raised	YFM[35]	YFM[18]	YFM[1,25]	—	—
head high, ears up/frontward, staring	YFM[40]	YFM[18]	YFM[3,25]	YFM[19,38]	FM[12,14]
with one hind leg extended out to the side	—	—	FM[25,34]	—	—
head lowered then slowly brought back up	—	—	F[25,34]	—	—
stiff walk or trot, or stotting	YFM[35]	YFM[17,18]	F[25]	YFM[19,38]	—

TABLE 3.1

VISUAL SIGNALS *(continued)*

Behaviour	White-tailed Deer	Mule Deer	Caribou	Wapiti (Elk)	Moose
Threat					
direct gaze	FM[29,22]	FM[11,16,18]	YFM[25]	YFM[41]	YFM[2]
ears dropped down or backward	FM[29,22]	FM[11,16,18]	YFM[3,25,34]	YFM[2,38]	FM[14]
bite-threat, symbolic biting	FM[17]	—	—	F[41]	—
withdrawing upper lip, tongue protruding	—	—	—	FM[16,19]	—
nose licking	—	M[11]	—	—	—
head low, horns/antlers toward opponent	M[22]	M[5,11,16,18]	YFM[3,25,34]	FM[2,19,16,38]	M[14,39]
head low or at shoulder level, antlers up	—	—	—	—	—
head and chin at shoulder level, neck stretch	—	M[5,11]	FM[25,34]	FM[38]	—
same, with head twist	—	M[18]	—	FM[2]	—
head and nose up, horns/antlers high	M[22]	FM[16,18]	—	YFM[2,16,38]	FM[14,27]
head lowered and then swung upward	—	—	F[25]	—	—
symbolic rising on hind legs	M[22]	FM[18]	YFM[3,25,34]	YF[38]	FM[14,27]
tail raised	—	—	—	—	—
kick with stiff foreleg (no contact)	—	—	F[25]	YF[2,38]	—
hind leg raised or kicking at vegetation	—	—	—	—	M[14,15]
piloerection	M[22]	FM[11,18]	—	—	YFM[14]
rush threat (rapid approach)	FM[22]	FM[16,18]	F[25]M[3]	M[19,38]	FM[14]

TABLE 3.2

VISUAL SIGNALS OF PRONGHORN, MOUNTAIN GOAT, BIGHORN SHEEP AND BISON *(in broad contextual categories)*

Y = Young, F = Female, and M = Male
Numbers in superscript refer to the sources (listed below)
Entries in bold are display elements

Behaviour	Pronghorn	Mountain Goat	Bighorn Sheep	Bison (Buffalo)
Contact (mother-offspring or between herd members)				
head lowered then brought back up	—	—	—	—
head kept horizontal, at calf height	—	—	—	—
Submission				
exaggerated chewing motion	—	—	—	—
head low, nose down	F[9]	FM[15,40]	—	M[28]
head high	M[8,23]	—	M[14]	—
head shake or twist	F[9]	—	YF[17]	M[28]
direct gaze	—	FM[15,40]	—	—
averted gaze (turning head or body)	M[23]	—	FM[17]	M[28]
ears back along neck	—	FM[15,40]	—	—
crouch	F[9,23]	FM[15,40]	—	—
lordosis	—	—	M[17]	—
sham grazing	FM[40]	FM[40]	FM[40]	M[28]
male urinating like a female	—	—	—	—
Breeding behaviour (herding, courtship)				
averted gaze	M[9]	—	—	—
looking at mate	F[8,9]	M[15]	—	M[28]
head down	—	—	—	—
head and chin at shoulder level, neck stretch	—	—	FM[17]	M[40]
same, with head twist	—	—	M[17]	—
same, with low crouch	—	FM[15,17]	M[17]	—
head and horns/antlers high	M[8,9]	—	M[17]	—
head waving from side to side	M[8,9]	M[15]	—	—
head suddenly swung upward	—	—	—	M[28]
tongue flicking	M[9]	M[15]	M[17]	—
foreleg kick (no contact)	—	M[15]	M[17]	—
piloerection	M[8,9]	—	—	—
rush	—	—	—	—
raising tail	F[8,9]	M[15]	—	—
lordosis	F[9]	—	F[17]	F[28]
bolting, circling around mate, frolicking	—	—	F[17]	—
stiff walk, swaying gait or prancing	M[8,9]	M[14]	—	—

TABLE 3.2

VISUAL SIGNALS *(continued)*

Y = Young, F = Female, and M = Male
Numbers in superscript refer to the sources
Entries in bold are display elements

Behaviour	Pronghorn	Mountain Goat	Bighorn Sheep	Bison (Buffalo)
Dominance and space claim				
eyes averted	M[8]	—	M[17]	—
sideward turn of head	—	**YFM**[15]	—	**M**[28]
head low or at shoulder level, antlers up	—	—	—	—
head and chin at shoulder level, neck stretch	—	—	**FM**[17]	—
same, with head twist	—	—	**M**[17]	—
head and horns/antlers up	M[8]	—	**M**[17]	**M**[28]
sudden head up	—	—	—	**M**[28]
arching back	—	**YFM**[15]	—	—
broadside presentation or parallel walk	**M**[8,23]	**YFM**[15]	—	**M**[28]
piloerection	**M**[8,23]	—	—	—
tail up and/or moving	—	—	—	**M**[28]
tail down	M[23]	—	—	—
stiff movements or swaying gait	**M**[8,23]	**M**[15]	—	—
Threat				
direct gaze	**FM**[8]	—	**YFM**[17]	**M**[33]
ears dropped down or backward	**FM**[8,9,23]	**YFM**[15]	**M**[17]	—
bite-threat, symbolic biting	—	—	—	—
withdrawing upper lip, tongue protruding	—	—	—	—
nose licking	—	—	—	—
head low, horns/antlers toward opponent	**M**[8,9,23]	**YFM**[15]	**FM**[17]	**M**[28]
head low or at shoulder level, antlers up	**M**[23]	—	—	—
head and chin at shoulder level, neck stretch	—	—	—	—
same, with head twist	—	—	**M**[17]	—
head and nose up, horns/antlers high	—	—	—	—
head lowered and then swung upward	—	—	—	—
symbolic rising on hind legs	—	—	**YFM**[17]	—
tail raised	—	—	—	**M**[33]
kick with stiff foreleg (no contact)	—	—	**FM**[17]	—
hind leg raised or kicking at vegetation	—	—	—	—
piloerection	M[0]	—	—	—
rush threat (rapid approach)	**M**[8]	**FM**[15]	**M**[15,17]	**M**[28]
Attention/Alarm				
piloerection	**M**[8,9,23]	—	—	—
tail raised	—	—	—	—
head high, ears up/frontward, staring	M[23]	—	**YFM**[17]	—
with one hind leg extended out to the side	—	—	—	—
head lowered then slowly brought back up	—	—	—	—
stiff walk or trot, or stotting	**M**[8]	**M**[15]	**YFM**[17]	—

SOURCES:

1 Albone, 1984
2 Altmann, 1956
3 Bergerud, 1974
4 Bouckhout, 1972
5 Bowyer, 1986
6 Bowyer and Kitchen, 1987a
7 Bowyer and Kitchen, 1987b
8 Bromley, 1977
9 Bromley and Kitchen, 1974
10 Bubenik, 1982
11 Cowan and Geist, 1961
12 de Vos, 1958
13 Espmark, 1971
14 Geist, 1963
15 Geist, 1964
16 Geist, 1966
17 Geist, 1971
18 Geist, 1981
19 Geist, 1982
20 Gunderson and Mahan, 1980
21 Halls, 1978
22 Hirth, 1977
23 Kitchen and Bromley, 1974
24 Lent, 1965
25 Lent, 1966
26 Lent, 1974
27 Lent, 1974
28 Lott, 1974
29 Moore and Marchinton, 1974
30 Müller-Schwarze, 1974
31 Müller-Schwarze, 1987
32 Murie, 1932
33 Park, 1969
34 Pruitt, 1960
35 Richardson et al., 1983
36 Rideout, 1978
37 Spencer, 1943
38 Struhsaker, 1967
39 Walther, 1984
40 Geist, personal communication
41 Personal observation at Ministik Station

TABLE 3.3

ACOUSTIC SIGNALS OF DEER, CARIBOU, WAPITI, AND MOOSE
(in broad contextual categories)

Y = Young, F = Female, and M = Male
Numbers in superscript refer to the sources (see Table 3.2)
Entries in bold are display elements

Sound	White-tailed Deer	Mule Deer	Caribou	Wapiti (Elk)	Moose
Contact calls (mother-offspring or between herd members)					
soft bleat, bawl or whine	**YF**[21,35]	**YF**[30]	**Y**[25]	—	**Y**[12]
soft grunt or snort	**F**[35]	—	**F**[3,25]	—	**F**[12]
short, high-pitched, loud squeal	—	—	—	**YF**[6,19,32,38]**M**[37]	—
hoof click	—	—	**YFM**[15,18]	**YFM**[15,19]	—
Submission					
soft whine	—	—	—	**YF**[19,41]	**Y**[27]
loud squeal (during sparring)	—	—	—	**M**[6,19,38]	—
breeding behaviour (herding, courtship)					
humming, buzzing	—	**M**[18]	—	—	—
soft bleat, moan or whine	**M**[21]	**M**[18]	—	—	**FM**[40]
long, loud moan and/or roar	—	**M**[18]	—	**M**[6,19,38]	**FM**[27]
short, loud, harsh moan, grunt, roar	**M**[18,29,35]	**M**[16,18]	**M**[3,34]	**M**[6,19,38]	**M**[3,27]
snort followed by wheezing	—	—	—	—	—
guttural "clucking"	—	—	—	**M**[38]	—
tongue flicking	—	**M**[18]	**M**[3]	**M**[6,19,38]	**M**[14]
rustling horns/antlers in vegetation	**M**[29]	**M**[20]	**F**[3]	—	—
foot stamp	**M**[18]	**FM**[18]	—	—	—
Dominance					
loud moan or roar	—	—	**M**[3]	**M**[2,6,32,38]	—
short, loud moan ("yelps")	—	—	—	**M**[6,19,32,38]	—
snort followed by wheezing	**FM**[18,35]	**M**[18]	—	—	—
guttural "clucking"	—	—	—	**M**[32,38]	—
rustling horns/antlers in vegetation	**M**[18,29]	**M**[18]	**M**[3]	**M**[19,38]	—
Threat					
short, harsh bark, roar, grunt, snort	**FM**[21,35,11]	**FM**[16,18,11]	**M**[3,25]	**M**[19]	**FM**[27]
high-pitched moan	—	—	—	—	—
sneeze-like sound	**M**[29]	—	—	—	—
hissing	—	—	—	**YFM**[6,19]	—
grinding teeth	—	—	—	**YFM**[6,19]	**FM**[40]
stamping ground with foreleg	**M**[18]	**M**[16,18]	—	**M**[19]	—
Alarm, startle					
loud bleat or squeak	—	—	—	—	—
snort, blow or bark	**YMF**[18,21,35]	**YMF**[18,30]	**F**[25]	**FM**[2,19,32,38]	**FM**[12]
stamping ground with foreleg	**YFM**[21,35]	**YFM**[18]	—	—	—
distress					
loud bleat or bawl	**YF**[21,35]	**Y**[20]	—	**—**	—
loud squeal	—	—	**—**	**YF**[6,19,32]	—
loud harsh grunt	—	—	**YF**[13,25]	—	—
Other					
whine during nursing	**Y**[35]	—	—	—	—
long moan around parturition	—	—	—	**F**[32]	—

TABLE 3.4

ACOUSTIC SIGNALS OF PRONGHORN, MOUNTAIN GOAT, BIGHORN SHEEP AND BISON *(in broad contextual categories)*

Y = Young, F = Female, and M = Male
Numbers in superscript refer to the sources (see Table 3.2)
Entries in bold are display elements

Behaviour	Pronghorn	Mountain Goat	Bighorn Sheep	Bison (Buffalo)
Contact calls (mother-offspring or between herd members)				
soft bleat, bawl or whine	Y[8]	YF[26]	YFM[17,37]	Y[20]
soft grunt or snort	F[8]	—	—	—
short, high-pitched, loud squeal	—	—	—	YFM[20]
hoof click	—	—	—	—
Submission				
soft whine	—	—	—	—
loud squeal (during sparring)	—	—	—	—
Breeding behaviour (herding, courtship)				
humming, buzzing	—	**M**[15,36]	—	—
soft bleat, moan or whine	—	—	—	—
long, loud moan and/or roar	**M**[8,9]	—	—	—
short, loud, harsh moan, grunt, roar, snort	—	—	**M**[17]	**M**[28]
snort followed by wheezing	**M**[23]	—	—	—
guttural "clucking"	—	—	—	—
tongue flicking	**M**[9]	**M**[15]	**M**[17]	—
rustling horns/antlers in vegetation	—	—	—	—
foot stamp	—	—	—	—
Dominance				
loud moan or roar	—	**M**[40]	—	**M**[28]
short, loud moan ("yelps")	—	—	—	—
snort followed by wheezing	**M**[8,23]	—	—	—
guttural "clucking"	—	—	—	—
rustling horns/antlers in vegetation	**M**[8,23]	**FM**[15]	**YFM**[17]	—
Threat				
short harsh bark, roar, grunt, snort	**M**[8,9]	**YFM**[15,36]	**M**[13,37]	**FM**[20,28,33]
high-pitched moan	—	**M**[36]	—	—
sneeze-like sound	—	—	—	—
hissing	—	—	—	—
grinding teeth	**M**[8,23]	—	**M**[37]	—
stamping ground with foreleg	—	**FM**[40]	**M**[17]	**FM**[28,33]
Alarm, startle				
loud bleat or squeak	Y[8]	—	—	—
snort, blow or bark	FM[8]	—	YFM[17]	—
stamping ground with foreleg	—	—	YFM[16]	—
Distress				
loud bleat or bawl	—	—	—	—
loud squeal	—	—	—	—
loud harsh grunt	—	—	—	—
Other				
whine during nursing	—	—	—	—
long moan around parturition	—	—	—	—

TABLE 3.5

CHEMICAL COMMUNICATION OF DEER, CARIBOU, WAPITI AND MOOSE

(in broad contextual categories)

A) *Behaviour of conspecifics suggest a chemical signal being used*
B) *Behaviours associated with releasing chemical signals*
Y = Young, F = Female, and M = Male
Numbers in superscript refer to the sources (see Table 3.2)
Entries in bold are display elements

Behaviour	White-tailed Deer	Mule Deer	Caribou	Wapiti (Elk)	Moose
A)					
Individual or status identification, contact (mother-offspring, herd members)					
licking young after birth	F[17]	F[17]	F[25]	F[19]	F[17]
sniffing conspecific's anogenital region	—	F[30,31]	YFM[1,25]	YFM[38]	—
sniffing conspecific's nasal region	YF[22]	M[30]	F[1,25]	YFM[38]	M[14]
sniffing conspecific's tarsal gland	—	YFM[30,31]	—	—	—
sniffing trails left by conspecifics	M[25,29]	FM[30]	FM[3,25]	—	—
Breeding behaviour (herding, courtship)					
flehmen	M[22]	M[18]	M[3]	M[38]	M[14,27]
sniffing face/neck or back of mate	—	—	—	M[38]	—
sniffing mate's caudal/anogenital area	M[18]	FM[18,30]	FM[1,3]	M[38]	FM[14,27]
B)					
Submission					
licking or rubbing face/neck of dominant	—	—	—	**M[41]**	—
Breeding behaviour					
flaring of back gland hair	—	—	—	—	—
opening preorbital gland	—	—	—	**M[19]**	—
standing in front of mate, presenting cheek	—	—	—	—	—
waving head in front of mate	—	—	—	—	—
pawing and urinating, wallowing in pit	—	—	—	—	**FM[14,27]**
urination on hind legs (tramping)	—	—	**M[3,24]**	—	—
Dominance and space claim					
flaring of tarsal/metatarsal gland hairs	—	**FM[18]**	—	—	—
flaring of back gland hair	—	—	—	—	—
presenting cheek to opponent	—	—	—	—	—
urination on hind legs while sometimes rubbing hocks	**M[18,29,22]**	**YFM[18,30,31]**	**M[1,3,24]**	—	**M[14,18]**
urination on neck/belly and ground pawing	—	—	—	**M[7,19,38]**	—
defecating/urinating in pit	**M[18,29,22]**	**M[18]**	—	**M[7,19]**	**M[14,27]**
directing material on self while digging	—	—	—	—	—
laying or wallowing in pit	—	—	—	**M[7,19,38]**	**M[14,27]**
rubbing head glands on soil or vegetation	**M[29,22]**	**FM[18,30,31]**	—	**YFM[7,19,38]**	—
digging dirt with horns/antlers	**M[22]**	—	—	**M[19,38]**	**M[27]**
Threat					
opening preorbital gland	—	**M[11]**	—	**YFM[41]**	—
Attention/alarm					
flaring of tarsal/metatarsal gland hair	**YFM[18]**	**YFM[18,31]**	—	—	—
flaring of back gland/rump patch hair	—	—	—	—	—
raising on hind legs and making a sharp turn	—	—	**FM[25,34]**	—	—
Excitement					
opening of preorbital gland	—	**FM[18]**	—	**YFM[41]**	—
sometimes rubbing hocks	**YFM[18,29]**	**YFM[18,30]**	**FM[1,3,18]**	—	**FM[14,18]**

TABLE 3.6

CHEMICAL COMMUNICATION OF PRONGHORN, MOUNTAIN GOAT, BIGHORN SHEEP AND BISON

(in broad contextual categories)

A) Behaviour of conspecifics suggest chemical signal being used
B) Behaviours associated with releasing chemical signals
Y = Young, F = Female, and M = Male
Numbers in superscript refer to the sources (see Table 3.2)
Entries in bold are display elements

Behaviour	Pronghorn	Mountain Goat	Bighorn Sheep	Bison (Buffalo)
A)				
Individual or status identification, contact (mother-offspring, herd members)				
licking young after birth	F[8]	F[8]	F[17]	F[26]
sniffing conspecific's anogenital region	—	—	—	—
sniffing conspecific's nasal region	—	—	YF[17]	—
sniffing conspecific's tarsal gland	—	—	—	—
sniffing trails left by conspecifics	—	—	—	—
Breeding behaviour (herding, courtship)				
flehmen	M[9]	M[15]	YFM[17]	YFM[28]
sniffing face/neck or back of mate	F[1,8,9]	—	F[17]	—
sniffing mate's caudal/anogenital area	—	M[15]	M[17]	M[28]
B)				
Submission				
licking or rubbing face/neck of dominant	—	—	**FM[17]**	—
Breeding behaviour				
flaring of back gland hair	**M[9,23]**	—	—	—
opening preorbital gland	—	—	—	—
standing in front of mate, presenting cheek	**M[8,30]**	—	—	—
waving head in front of mate	**M[8,9]**	—	—	—
pawing and urinating, wallowing in pit	—	—	—	—
urination on hind legs (tramping)	—	—	—	—
Dominance and space claim				
flaring of tarsal/metatarsal gland hairs	—	—	—	—
flaring of back gland hair	**M[9,23]**	—	—	—
presenting cheek to opponent	**M[8]**	—	—	—
urination on hind legs and rubbing hocks	—	—	—	—
urination on neck/belly and ground pawing	—	—	—	—
defecating/urinating in pit	**M[8,9,23]**	**FM[15]**	—	**M[28]**
directing material on self while digging	—	**FM[15]**	—	**M[28]**
laying or wallowing in pit	—	—	—	**M[28]**
rubbing head glands on soil or vegetation	**M[8,23]**	**M[15]**	**YFM[17]**	—
digging dirt with horns/antlers	—	—	—	**M[28,33]**
Threat				
opening preorbital gland	**M[31]**	—	—	—
Attention/Alarm				
flaring of tarsal/metatarsal gland hair	—	—	—	—
flaring of back gland/rump patch hair	**M[8,9,23]**	—	—	—
raising on hind legs and making a sharp turn	—	—	—	—
Excitement				
opening of preorbital gland	—	—	—	—
sometimes rubbing hocks	**Y[1]**	—	—	—

TABLE 3.7

TACTILE COMMUNICATION SIGNALS OF DEER, CARIBOU, WAPITI AND MOOSE

(in broad contextual categories)

Y = Young, F = Female, and M = Male.
Numbers in superscript refer to the sources (see Table 3.2)
Entries in bold are display elements

Behaviour	White-tailed Deer	Mule Deer	Caribou	Wapiti (Elk)	Moose
Initiation of urination/defecation					
licking anogenital region of young	F[17]	F[17]	F[25]	F[19]	F[17]
Contact (mother-offspring or between herd members)					
nose touch	YF[22]	M[30]	F[1,25]	YFM[38]	—
allogrooming	YFM[22]	YFM[22]	—	YF[38]	—
nudging	—	—	F[25]	—	—
sparring	**M**[18,22]	**M**[5,18]	**YM**[3,25,34]	**M**[19,38]	—
Submission					
licking/rubbing on face or body of dominant	M[18]	—	—	—	—
allogrooming	M[22]	M[22]	—	F[40]	—
Breeding behaviour (herding, courtship)					
head/chin resting on mate's back	—	**FM**[18]	M[3]	M[38]	M[27]
licking/rubbing face/neck or back of mate	—	F[17]	F[3]	FM[19,38]	M[27]
licking mate's caudal/anogenital area	M[18]	M[18]	M[1,3]	FM[19,38]	FM[14,27]
foreleg kick	—	F[13]	—	—	—
nudging	—	M[18]	F[3]M[40]	F[19]M[40]	—
precopulatory mounts	M[18]	FM[18]	M[3]	FM[19,38]	—
Dominance and space claim					
foreleg kick	—	—	—	—	—
licking subordinate's caudal area	—	—	—	—	—
mounting	—	M[18]	YMF[3]	YFM[41]	—
clashing	—	—	—	—	—
Threat					
symbolic biting	M[18]	—	—	FM[41]	—
head lowered and then swung on opponent	—	—	F[25]	—	—
foreleg kick	M[39]	FM[4,39]	F[25]	YFM[38]	M[14]
butting	—	—	—	—	—

TABLE 3.8

TACTILE COMMUNICATION SIGNALS OF PRONGHORN, MOUNTAIN GOAT, BIGHORN SHEEP AND BISON

(in broad contextual categories)

Y = Young, F = Female, and M = Male
Numbers in superscript refer to the sources (see Table 3.2)
Entries in bold are display elements

Behaviour	Pronghorn	Mountain Goat	Bighorn Sheep	Bison (Buffalo)
Initiation of urination/defecation				
licking anogenital region of young	F[8]	—	—	—
Contact (mother-offspring or between herd members)				
nose touch	—	—	—	—
allogrooming	—	—	—	—
nudging	—	—	—	—
sparring	**M**[8]	—	—	**M**[40]
Submission				
licking/rubbing on face or body of dominant	—	—	**FM**[17]	—
allogrooming	—	—	—	—
Breeding behaviour (herding, courtship)				
head/chin resting on mate's back	—	M[15]	—	**M**[28]
licking/rubbing face/neck or back of mate	F[8,9]	M[15]	F[17]	**M**[27]
licking mate's caudal/anogenital area	M[40]	M[15]	**M**[17]	**M**[28]
foreleg kick	—	M[15,39]	**FM**[17]	—
nudging	—	M[40]	—	—
precopulatory mounts	—	—	M[17]	FM[28]
Dominance and space claim				
foreleg kick	—	—	**FM**[17]	—
licking subordinate's caudal area	—	—	**M**[17]	—
mounting	—	—	(YF)**M**[17]	**M**[28]
clashing	—	—	(YF)**M**[17]	—
Threat				
symbolic biting	—	—	—	—
head lowered and then swung on opponent	—	—	—	—
foreleg kick	—	—	**FM**[17]	—
butting	—	—	**M**[17]	—

Distribution

J. Brad Stelfox and
John G. Stelfox

Ungulates are not randomly distributed across Alberta, but rather they occupy habitat and exploit their environment in a predictable pattern that reflects their body size and shape, foraging habits, social structure, ability to cope with snow and terrain, and predator avoidance strategies. Species by species differences in habitat preferences, also referred to as "ecological separation", is the evolutionary result of competition between different species for resources. This chapter explores differences in resource requirements for cover, shelter, and forage of each species. Provincial distribution maps, complete with animal density estimates, are presented for each species. To offer recreationalists a better chance of seeing ungulates in wild settings, a list of selected viewing locations is provided. Many translocations of ungulates have been undertaken by governmental agencies during the last several decades. These movements have been chronicled to help unravel the confused ancestry of many of our contemporary populations.

INTRODUCTION

This chapter examines the distribution and abundance of Alberta's hoofed mammals in relation to ecological regions, habitat requirements, and the physical environment. Those occupational patterns that minimize interspecific competition, including ecological separation across environmental gradients such as topography, diet, and snow depth, are discussed. Historic and recent accounts of ungulate translocations are documented, and locations where hoofed mammals can be readily viewed are offered.

A fundamental objective of game biologists is to develop and maintain habitat—that complex association of plants, soil, water, topography and climate that provide a life support system for wildlife. All hoofed mammals have four basic habitat requirements that must be satisfied: food, water, escape or hiding cover, and shelter from inclement weather. Recently, a fifth requirement, protection from human harassment, has become evident as human activities expand and accelerate throughout the province. Incompatible human land-uses particularly affect caribou, wapiti and mountain goats, species that readily abandon otherwise suitable areas when subjected to various forms of harassment or stress.

ECOLOGICAL SEPARATION

Based on regional differences in elevation, soils, climate, and dominant vegetation, Alberta contains seven major biophysical ecoregions: lowland, mixed-wood, prairie, parkland, foothills, subalpine and alpine-barren (Figure 4.1). Relationships between elevation, plant communities and distribution of each hoofed mammal species are depicted in Figure 4.2. When distributions of these ecoregions and ungulate species (Figures 4.3–4.11) are compared, some measure of ecological separation within the ungulate community is apparent. Pronghorn are found primarily in the prairie region, bighorn sheep and mountain goat in the alpine-barren and subalpine, mountain caribou in the alpine-barren, subalpine and foothills, and bison of Wood Buffalo National Park frequent the lowland region. Woodland caribou are located primarily in the mixed-wood region. Greatest overlap in distribution occurs among wapiti, moose, mule deer and white-tailed deer. Elevationally, bison are not present above the parkland region while white-tailed deer, mule deer and wapiti are found from the low-elevation mixed-wood, prairie, and lowlands upwards throughout the foothills, with mule deer and wapiti extending further into the subalpine and lower alpine-barren regions.

Within each of Alberta's ecoregions, heterogeneous environments facilitate some measure of ecological separation among co-occurring hoofed mammals, mainly due to different preferences along biophysical gradients. Particularly important parameters are degree of vegetative cover, topography, exposure, forage type, plant association growth stage (early, mid, mature), and climate (especially snow depth, temperature, wind speed).

Pronghorn, bison, mountain caribou, bighorn sheep and mountain goats prefer open plant associations where they rely on keen eyesight, speed, or climbing ability to elude predators. Moose, woodland caribou and mule deer are primarily forest dwellers and use their surroundings for concealment. Wapiti and white-tailed deer are ecologically flexible and can adapt readily to both open and wooded habitats. Pronghorn, woodland caribou, bison and white-tailed deer prefer flat to rolling terrain while moose, mountain caribou, mule deer and wapiti inhabit flat, rolling or moderately steep terrain (Nietfeld *et al.*, 1985). Mountain caribou, wapiti, and mule deer may traverse steep slopes of 30° when moving between desirable habitats. Bighorn sheep and mountain goats generally prefer steep grasslands above 1300 m with slopes in excess of 45–50°.

Cover and Shelter Preferences

Escape cover offering concealment from humans and predators is normally tall grass, shrubs and/or trees for deer, moose and wapiti but may be rocky scree slopes for bighorn sheep and mountain goats. Broken, uneven terrain is important in that animals can position obstacles between themselves and predators. Cover is especially important for concealment of newborns. Shelter (thermal cover) is vital during winter, especially for the less hardy white-tailed and mule deer, wapiti and pronghorn. Winter shelter must provide shallow snow and minimum windchill conditions. Exposed, wind-swept grasslands facing prevailing westerly winds are unsuitable for winter range except for bighorn sheep and mountain goats which have thick insulative winter coats. Even so, during winter storms bighorn sheep and mountain goats usually move to areas where windchill conditions are less severe. Other species, excluding pronghorn, shelter in the protection of mature stands of spruce, pine or fir where windchill conditions and snow depths are lowest during severe winter conditions. The importance of mature stands of conifers for the winter survival of moose, wapiti, caribou, mule deer and white-tailed deer cannot be overstated. Pronghorn find refuge in valleys and coulees during winter storms or migrate further south where winter conditions are less severe. A converse situation occurs in summer as the more winter-hardy species (caribou, moose, bighorn sheep, mountain goats) strive to remain cool. Summer habitat for bighorn sheep and mountain goats includes cool, alpine pastures and occasionally caves. Mountain caribou seek snowfields, windy mountain ridges and forested north-facing slopes to keep cool, while moose spend hot days in dense, coniferous forests, lakes, streambanks, and wet willow or alder thickets. During hot summer conditions, upward migration by ungulates inhabiting the foothills and subalpine regions offers ameliorated climatic conditions.

Habitat Preferences and Foraging Strategies

Five forage types are available to hoofed mammals: grasses and sedges (often called graminoids), forbs (herbs or wild flowers), browse (trees and shrubs), aquatic plants, and lichens/mosses. Wapiti, bison and bighorn sheep are primarily "grazers" with a preference for grasses and forbs. Moose are characterized as "browsers", feeding on leaves and stems of trees and shrubs. Caribou, white-tailed deer, mule deer, pronghorn and mountain goats are mainly "mixed feeders" that forage on a variety of grasses, forbs and woody plants.

Pronghorn utilize forbs, low shrubs, grasses and agricultural crops in the prairie ecosystem. Deer and wapiti in mixed-wood, parkland and foothills regions are "mixed feeders" taking advantage of diverse browse, forbs, native grasses and cultivated forage and cereal crops. In subalpine and prairie regions, deer and wapiti consume more native grass species because of their greater abundance and nutritive value compared to grasses in mixed-wood and foothills regions. Predominant forages of moose are browse and, in summer, aquatic plants such as pond lily. During the last few decades, moose have fed extensively on cultivated hay, grain, and pasture forage as they extend their range into farmlands, and as human settlements encroach further into traditional moose range. Caribou are mixed feeders that consume substantial amounts of lichen, moss, leaves and the small stems of shrubs and forbs. On subalpine and alpine-barren ecoregions the amount of grasses and forbs in their diet increases.

Bighorn sheep and mountain goat have distinct foraging strategies that minimize competition in alpine-barren and subalpine ranges. Bighorn sheep forage primarily on fertile grassy slopes where they select grasses and lesser amounts of forbs and low shrubs. Mountain goats forage on less fertile, precipitous slopes where they favour forbs and browse. A detailed account of provincial plant species commonly used by Alberta's ungulates is provided in Chapter 12.

Although foraging preferences exist, changes in animal distribution, forage availability, and nutritive value lead to seasonal changes in forage selection. Whereas grasses are highly palatable and nutritious in spring and early summer, they become less nutritious in fall and winter. Reduced grass palatability is caused by loss of protein and increased fiber content. Similarly, forbs quickly decline in protein and energy levels in late summer but continue to provide a good source of phosphorus throughout the year. During fall and winter seasons, the higher protein, phosphorus and carotene (vitamin A) levels of woody forage encourage greater browsing.

Alberta's hoofed mammals are adept at selecting relatively nutritious forages during all seasons. In early spring, they seek out vegetation growing on low-elevation, southerly slopes where the ground thaws early and initiates new plant growth. Runoff snowmelt on lowlands draws out ground frost and initiates plant growth. For this reason, wapiti and caribou are seen feeding on new grass growth along the Maligne and Athabasca River floodplains in April and May. Similarly, in early spring, moose frequent muskeg lowlands, bison the Athabasca delta lowlands, and white-tailed deer the various river and lake lowlands. As this forage matures, hoofed mammals seek wooded pastures where forage remains green under the shade of trees and tall shrubs. By moving progressively upslope in the foothills and mountains, ungulates are able to track floral "green-up" in spring and early summer. Alpine forage is also more nutritious in summer than comparable low-elevation forage (Johnston, 1973). Mountain herbivores finding senescent forages on dry, exposed southerly slopes can move to woodlands and open northerly slopes where green forage, cool conditions and water prevail until fall.

The white-tailed deer is an agile jumper, a requisite skill for a species that prefers forested habitat to escape hunters and predators. Photo by J. Nolan.

Lowland habitats such as bogs, ponds and streams are preferred habitat of moose during the summer season. These areas provide abundant forages (aquaphytes and willow) and allow moose to cool themselves in water during times of heat stress. Photo by J. Nolan.

Instinctively, ungulates search out vegetation, soil and water that satisfies their mineral requirements. Mineral reserves become depleted in the spring when the physiological stresses of pregnancy, lactation, and new hair growth place large demands on calcium, phosphorus and copper reserves. A study by the Canadian Wildlife Service (McCrory, 1967) of mountain goats using soil licks along the Athabasca River in spring and early summer indicated that the major elements extracted were copper (essential for hair development, blood formation and bone development), calcium (essential for lactation and bone development of kids), and chlorine (important for acid-base balance and development of digestive enzymes). Consumption of water and soil from licks with high concentrations of sulfur may be due in part to its importance for hair growth during the molt and its vermicide qualities. Just as humans require salt for basic metabolism, hoofed mammals also have an appetite for salt. Forages growing on dry sites are frequently low in salt while those growing under wet or aquatic conditions are usually high in sodium and chlorine. Moose appear to obtain the majority of their yearlong salt requirements from pond lilies and other aquatic vegetation consumed during summer. Several natural mineral licks in Alberta have been found to be high in sodium (McCrory, 1967).

During winter when deep snow and severe windchill conditions make most high-elevation ranges unsuitable, hoofed mammals generally frequent lower, wooded or semi-wooded ranges. For those species that inhabit mountainous regions, winter ranges usually comprise 10 percent or less of the total yearlong range (Cowan, 1950). Availability and productivity of these small wintering areas set upper limits on population density, and thus are vital to the welfare of hoofed mammals in the mountains. Mountain goats, and to a lesser extent bighorn sheep, continue to use alpine and subalpine ranges unless snow depths and/or windchill conditions force them onto lower grasslands and semi-forested pastures. Wapiti and deer prefer semi-open, aspen woodlands during winter months, which supply a diverse selection of grasses, forbs, and browse, as well as the high-protein forage of fallen aspen leaves (Nietfeld, 1983).

DISTRIBUTION AND ABUNDANCE

Provincial distribution and abundance of Alberta's hoofed mammals are illustrated in Figures 4.3–4.11. Figures 4.3 and 4.4 indicate that prairie, parkland, and southern mixed-wood regions contain prime habitat for both white-tailed deer and mule deer. In addition, the foothills and river valleys of the northern mixed-wood regions contain high densities of mule deer. Average densities of 0.2–1.0 deer/km² occur on primary habitat for both deer species, though local densities can be much higher. Optimum habitat for white-tailed deer is aspen parkland where native vegetation is interspersed with farmland (Nietfeld *et al.*, 1985). Optimal mule deer habitat is found along river valleys where shelter from adverse weather, good escape terrain, and a variety of browse, forb and grass species occur (Nietfeld *et al.*, 1985).

Distribution of woodland caribou lies in the climax coniferous forest and muskeg habitats of the mixed-wood zone (Figure 4.5). These habitats provide an abundant supply of arboreal and ground lichens, mosses, forbs and dwarf shrubs. In northeastern Alberta and the Peace River regions, black spruce muskegs are important year long habitat, while in summer, jackpine ridges are also important (Nietfeld *et al.*, 1985).

Mountain caribou winter in coniferous forests of the subalpine and foothills ecoregions, preferring Englemann spruce/subalpine fir forests, wet shrublands and wet forb meadows. In summer, mountain caribou ascend to subalpine and alpine meadows dominated by heath, dwarf shrubs, Englemann spruce and subalpine fir. Glaciers, snowfields and windy ridges provide relief from summer heat and insect harassment. Within the mountains of Jasper National Park, caribou distributions are positively correlated to the presence of spruce/fir forests, alpine tundra with broad valleys, traversable passes and summer snowfields (Stelfox et al., 1978).

Wapiti are located in the foothills and subalpine regions, except for a few isolated populations in the mixed-wood and prairie ecoregions (Figure 4.6). Their varied diet and flexible distribution patterns enable wapiti to frequent stands of mixed-wood cover surrounded by cultivated fields, muskeg habitat during winter, and rugged subalpine and alpine barren ranges in summer. Most habitats in the mixed-wood and foothills regions are used throughout the year. Most populations are migratory, overwintering in foothills, grasslands and mixed-wood forests, then moving up-slope as grasses green-up in late spring and early summer. Early successional stages of pine forests following logging or fire, as well as grasslands, are prime habitats and may support densities of 0.3–2.0/km². Interspersed mature pine and aspen forests offer a favourable combination of shelter and forage during winter months. However, wapiti are particularly sensitive to human activities, and will abandon excellent habitat if incompatible land-uses occur.

Optimal moose habitat is found in the foothills and mixed-wood regions (Figure 4.7). Young, mixed-wood forests provide adequate forage and escape cover while mature conifer forests provide cool conditions during the hot summer and adequate thermal cover during winter. Where conditions are favourable, moose densities may achieve 0.5–1.5/km². Muskeg lowlands and well-drained valley bottoms offer prime habitats throughout the year. If available, moose utilize coniferous subalpine areas in summer to forage on subalpine fir.

In Alberta, pronghorn are restricted to rolling, open terrain of the prairie zone of southeastern Alberta (Figure 4.8). Highest densities (0.7–0.9/km²) occur in relatively undisturbed native grasslands where suitable forage, cover, water, and abrupt topography are proximal (Nietfeld et al., 1985). Sagebrush provides important food and cover in winter, although shrubby cover exceeding 60 cm in height is avoided. Specific habitat requirements include slough bottoms for summer range, slopes or crests of hills for fawning, and hilly rangelands with eroded coulees for escape terrain (Barrett, 1980).

Bighorn sheep and mountain goats are restricted to subalpine and alpine barren zones of the eastern slopes of the Rocky Mountains in south-western Alberta (Figures 4.9 and 4.10). Semi-open grassy slopes adjacent to precipitous terrain (1,300–2,625 m elevation), provide optimal escape cover and forage. Bighorn sheep densities on optimal range may reach 1.0/km². Following the arrival of deep winter snow, bighorn sheep congregate to feed on open windswept south/southwest facing slopes. However, lower elevation grasslands along valleys, benches and old burns also provide suitable range if rugged escape terrain is nearby. Lambing ranges are located along dry, sunny, secluded cliffs where suitable forage occurs nearby.

Distribution of mountain goats is more restricted than that of bighorn sheep. In summer, mountain goats inhabit steep colluvial or bedrock terrain above 2,250 m where patches of mountain avens prevail and caves and mineral licks are available. Winter and summer ranges are often similar, but during periods of deep snow, mountain goats may move to the transition zone between fir forests and open alpine slopes.

LOCATIONS TO OBSERVE HOOFED MAMMALS

Table 4.2 lists several locations where Alberta's hoofed mammals can be observed in their natural settings. These locations, accessible to the motorized public, are generally in federal and provincial parks where animals are less wary and easier to view, photograph and study. A few suggestions are offered which might improve your chances of successful sightings.

- **Late fall and winter** months are favourable seasons for viewing bighorn sheep, wapiti, moose, and deer in the foothills and mountains. During these seasons, wildlife are concentrated on low-elevation ranges along the Athabasca River, North Saskatchewan River, Bow River, Crowsnest River and Waterton Lakes. October, November, and December offer especially fruitful viewing, as animals are in excellent condition and are less wary due to the breeding season (rut).

- **Spring** (May–early June) is a period when new plant growth on low elevation grasslands attract wapiti, deer, bighorn sheep and bison onto open ranges where they are generally more visible than during the winter (January–April).

- **Early summer** (June–July) is suitable for viewing mountain goats as they descend to low-elevation mineral licks adjacent to the Yellowhead and Jasper-Lake Louise highways.

- **Summer** (August–September) is ideal for viewing pronghorn on the prairies of southeastern Alberta. They are banded together in large groups and are less wary due to the rutting season and low human harassment (the hunting season has not yet started.)

TRANSLOCATIONS

Table 4.1 is a compilation of historic and recent ungulate translocations that involved Alberta. Wapiti were most commonly transplanted, followed in incidence by bison, bighorn sheep, pronghorn, moose and mountain goats. The list includes those movements of native ungulates that were undertaken to establish wild populations in new areas. It does not include transplants involving commercial sale of wildlife to private landowners, game farms or zoos. A survey of the literature and knowledgeable "old-timers" found no evidence of caribou or deer translocations.

Wapiti transplants between 1900 and 1936 were from Montana and Manitoba into Alberta in an effort to replenish a depleted population (Stelfox, 1964). Thereafter, wapiti transplants were from overstocked ranges within the province to suitable ranges in Alberta, Saskatchewan, and British Columbia.

Most bighorn sheep transplanted from Alberta have gone to the United States. Plains bison were translocated into Alberta from the United States and Manitoba between 1897 to 1914 to re-establish viable provincial populations after the loss of historic herds in the 1800s. The major translocation of plains bison occurred during the period 1925–1928, when 6,673 were moved from Wainwright Buffalo Park to Wood Buffalo National Park.

Initial transplants of wood bison were from Wood Buffalo National Park to Elk Island National Park in 1965, and to the Mackenzie Bison Sanctuary, Northwest Territories in 1963 to protect and increase remnant herds of the wood bison strain. These two herds increased rapidly and several transplants were subsequently made from Elk Island National Park to northwestern Alberta, Jasper National Park, the Yukon Territories and Manitoba during the period 1978–1986.

Small numbers of mountain goats have recently (1972–1988) been translocated from the Grande Cache region into depopulated southern Alberta ranges between Nordegg and the Highwood range (Smith, 1986, 1987).

TABLE 4.1

UNGULATE TRANSLOCATIONS INVOLVING ALBERTA

Year	Origin	Destination	Number	Source(s)
Wapiti (Elk)				
1900	Mordan, Manitoba	Banff National Pk.	5	Lloyd, 1927
1902	Portage La Prairie, Manitoba	Banff National Pk.	1	Lloyd, 1927
1910	Banff National Pk.	Wainwright Buffalo Pk.	6	Lloyd, 1927
1911	Flathead Indian Res., MT	Wainwright Buffalo Pk.	7	Lloyd, 1927
1917	Yellowstone National Pk., MT	Banff National Pk.	63	Lloyd, 1927
1917	Yellowstone National Pk., MT	Waterton Lakes National Pk.	58	Dwyer, 1968
1920	Yellowstone National Pk., MT	Jasper National Pk.	88	Lloyd, 1927
1920	Yellowstone National Pk., MT	Banff National Pk.	194	Lloyd, 1927
1927	Wainwright Buffalo Pk.	Cookson, British Columbia	25	Lloyd, 1927
1933	Wainwright Buffalo Pk.	Adams Lake, British Columbia	25	Spalding, pers. comm.
1936	Yellowstone National Pk., MT	Hinton	27	Lands and Forest Ann. Report
1937	Elk Island National Pk.	Alberta; precise location unknown	200	Blyth and Hudson, 1987
1938	Wainwright region	Cypress Hills Provincial Pk.	~12	Redgate, 1978
1946	Elk Island National Pk.	north Kootenay Valley, B.C.	25	Elk Island National Pk. records
1949	Elk Island National Pk.	Birch River, Wood Buffalo National Pk.	24	Law, 1949
1949	Elk Island National Pk.	The Pas, Manitoba	??	Elk Island National Pk. records
1950	Canmore Corridor	Elbow River	50	Danielson, 1978
1950	Elk Island National Pk.	west of Whitecourt	21	Stelfox, 1964
1953	Elk Island National Pk.	Siebert-Marguerite Lakes	96	Wishart, 1964
1956	Elk Island National Pk.	Calling Lake	27	Govt. memorandum
1956	Elk Island National Pk.	Rat Lake	33	Wishart, 1964
1956	Elk Island National Pk.	Rourke Creek	29	Govt. memorandum
1956	Elk Island National Pk.	Cypress Hills Provincial Pk.	82	Elk Island National Pk. records
1960	Banff National Pk.	Spirit River	??	Banff National Pk. comm.
1964	Banff National Pk.	Saddle Hills	26	McFetridge, 1984
1965	Banff National Pk.	Saddle Hills	28	McFetridge, 1984
1970	Banff National Pk.	Paulson, B.C.	10	Banff National Pk. comm.
1971	Banff National Pk.	Deer Pk., B.C.	75	Banff National Pk. comm.
1972	Elk Island National Pk.	Meikle River	28	McFetridge, 1984
1972	Elk Island National Pk.	Lovet Creek	18	McFetridge, 1984
1973	Jasper National Pk.	Notikewin	14	McFetridge, 1984
1973	Jasper National Pk.	Notikewin	20	McFetridge, 1984
1973	Jasper National Pk.	Deer Creek	40	Redgate, 1978
1973	Elk Island & Jasper Nat Pks	87-3-W6	20	McFetridge, 1984
1973	Jasper National Pk.	British Columbia	120	Woody, 1973
1974	Jasper National Pk.	Sundre	44	Paulsen and Bruns, 1977
1977	Elk Island National Pk.	Clearwater Valley area	68	Paulsen and Bruns, 1977
1978	Elk Island National Pk.	Clearwater Valley area	29	Paulsen and Bruns, 1977
1979	Elk Island National Pk.	Clearwater Valley area	40	Paulsen and Bruns, 1977
1982	Elk Island National Pk.	Amadou Lake	25	Watson and Lynch, 1986
1982	Elk Island National Pk.	Pelican Mountains	21	Watson and Lynch, 1986
1982	Elk Island National Pk.	Pelican Mountains	29	Watson and Lynch, 1986
1982	Elk Island National Pk.	Thickwood Hills, Saskatchewan	30	Elk Island National Pk. records
1983	Elk Island National Pk.	Kikino Metis Colony	6	Elk Island National Pk. records
1983	Elk Island National Pk.	Blackstone River	32	Elk Island National Pk. records
1984	Elk Island National Pk.	Scoop Lake, B.C.	69	Elk Island National Pk. records
1984	Bob's Creek	Blackstone River	68	Clarkson *et al.*, 1984
1985	Priddis	Wandering River	19	Allen, 1985
1985	Ya-Ha-Tinda, Banff	Prospect Creek, Mountain Pk.	35	Smith, 1985
1985	Ya-Ha-Tinda, Banff	Smoky River, near Grande Cache	40	Smith, 1985
1985	Elk Island National Pk.	Prince Albert, Saskatchewan	39	Elk Island National Pk. records
1987	Elk Island National Pk.	Conklin, St. Paul region	22	Elk Island National Pk. records
1988	Elk Island National Pk.	Conklin, St. Paul region	91	Elk Island National Pk. records
1989	Elk Island National Pk.	Loon Lake, Saskatchewan	41	Elk Island National Pk. records
1989	Elk Island National Pk.	Loon Lake, Saskatchewan	71	Elk Island National Pk. records
1990	Elk Island National Pk.	Glaslyn, Saskatchewan	59	Elk Island National Pk. records
1991	Elk Island National Pk.	Stoney Cr., west of Whitehorse, YK	18	Elk Island National Pk. records
1991	Elk Island National Pk.	Bradburn Lake, north of Whitehorse, YK	17	Elk Island National Pk. records
1991	Elk Island National Pk.	Woodshire Lakes, Yukon	18	Elk Island National Pk. records
1991	Elk Island National Pk.	Blackfoot Recreational Area	25	Elk Island National Pk. records
Moose				
1947	Elk Island National Pk.	Alberta; precise location unknown	45	Blyth and Hudson, 1987
1948	Elk Island National Pk.	Saskatchewan	100	Elk Island National Pk. records
1948-52	Elk Island National Pk.	Cape Breton Highlands Pk., N.S.	25	Blyth and Hudson, 1987
1956	Elk Island National Pk.	Cypress Hills Provincial Pk.	4	Government memorandum
1987	Elk Island National Pk.	Blackfoot Grazing Reserve	6	Elk Island National Pk. records
1987	Elk Island National Pk.	Rocky Mountain House area	1	Elk Island National Pk. records

TABLE 4.1

UNGULATE TRANSLOCATIONS INVOLVING ALBERTA *(continued)*

Year	Origin	Destination	Number	Source(s)
Pronghorn				
1900	Brooks area	Banff National Pk.	12	Lothian, 1981
1909	Brooks area	Banff National Pk.	7	Lothian, 1981
1910	Brooks area	Wainwright Buffalo Pk.	9	Lothian, 1981
1911	Banff National Pk.	Wainwright Buffalo Pk.	4	Lothian, 1981
1911	Blazier	Wainwright Buffalo Pk.	8	Lothian, 1981
Mountain Goat				
1924	Banff National Pk.	Shaw Creek Game Reserve, Vanc. Island	4	Spalding, pers. comm.
1972	Grande Cache	Shunda Mountain	7	Quaedvlieg *et al.*, 1972
1986	Caw Ridge, near Willmore	Picklejar Lakes, Highwood	2	Smith, K., 1986
1987	Caw Ridge, near Willmore	Livingstone Range, Kananaskis	9	Smith, K., 1987
1988	Caw Ridge, near Willmore	Livingstone Range, Kananaskis	2	Smith, K., pers. comm.
Bighorn Sheep				
1927	Banff National Pk.	Spences Bridge, Thompson River, B.C.	49	Spalding, pers. comm.
1927	Banff National Pk.	Squilax, near Chase, B.C.	50	Spalding, pers. comm.
1928	Banff National Pk.	Wichita Mtn., Oklahoma	14	Banff National Pk. comm.
1939	Banff National Pk.	Sandia Mtns., New Mexico	9	Ramey, R.R., pers. comm.
1961	Sheep River Sanctuary	South Dakota	12	Wishart, W., pers. comm.
1964	Banff National Pk.	Gila River, New Mexico	10	Ramey, R.R., pers. comm.
1970	Jasper National Pk.	Fraser Canyon, B.C.	12	Bradford, W., pers. comm.
1970	Banff National Pk.	Challis National Forest, Idaho	24	Banff National Pk. comm.
1970	Banff National Pk.	Utah	20-25	Ramey, R.R., pers. comm.
1971	Jasper National Pk.	Hell's Canyon Dam, Oregon	20	Ramey, R.R., pers. comm.
1971	Jasper National Pk.	Lostine Range, Oregon	20	Woody, 1971
1973	Waterton Lakes National Pk.	New Mexico and Utah	20	Watt, R., pers. comm.
1974	Waterton Lakes National Pk.	Washington State	8	Watt, R., pers. comm.
1975	Waterton Lakes National Pk.	Washington State	2	Watt, R., pers. comm.
1989	Cadomin region	New Mexico	~30	Wishart, W., pers. comm.
Plains Bison (Buffalo)				
1897	Texas	Banff National Pk.	3	Lothian, 1981
1898	Winnipeg, Manitoba	Banff National Pk.	13	Lothian, 1981
1904	Newport, New Hampshire	Banff National Pk.	2	Lothian, 1981
1907	Pablo Herd, Montana	Elk Island National Pk.	190	Blyth and Hudson, 1987
1907	Pablo Herd, Montana	Elk Island National Pk.	206	Blyth and Hudson, 1987
1909	Pablo Herd, Montana	Wainwright Buffalo Pk.	218	Lothian, 1981
1909	Elk Island National Pk.	Wainwright Buffalo Pk.	325	Blyth and Hudson, 1987
1910	Pablo Herd, Montana	Wainwright Buffalo Pk.	28	Lothian, 1981
1910	Pablo Herd, Montana	Wainwright Buffalo Pk.	28	Lothian, 1981
1910	Pablo Herd, Montana	Wainwright Buffalo Pk.	46	Lothian, 1981
1911	Pablo Herd, Montana	Wainwright Buffalo Pk.	7	Lothian, 1981
1911	Banff National Pk.	Wainwright Buffalo Pk.	77	Banff National Pk. comm.
1912	Pablo Herd, Montana	Wainwright Buffalo Pk.	7	Lothian, 1981
1914	Pablo Herd, Montana	Wainwright Buffalo Pk.	10	Lothian, 1981
1925	Wainwright Buffalo Pk.	Wood Buffalo National Pk.	1,634	Lothian, 1981
1926	Wainwright Buffalo Pk.	Wood Buffalo National Pk.	2,011	Lothian, 1981
1927	Wainwright Buffalo Pk.	Wood Buffalo National Pk.	1,940	Lothian, 1981
1928	Wainwright Buffalo Pk.	Wood Buffalo National Pk.	1,088	Lothian, 1981
Wood Bison (Buffalo)				
1963	Wood Buffalo National Pk.	Mackenzie Bison Sanctuary, N.W.T.	18	Novakowski, 1963
1965	Wood Buffalo National Pk.	Elk Island National Pk.	24	Blyth and Hudson, 1987
1978	Elk Island National Pk.	Jasper National Pk.	28	Elk Island National Pk. records
1980	Elk Island National Pk.	Nahanni National Pk., Yukon	28	Elk Island National Pk. records
1981	Elk Island National Pk.	Banff National Pk.	5	Elk Island National Pk. records
1984	Elk Island National Pk.	Hay/Zama Lakes	30	Elk Island National Pk. records
1984	Captive herd Alberta/Saskatchewan	Waterhen, Manitoba	34	Elk Island National Pk. records
1986	Elk Island National Pk.	Nisling River, Yukon	34	Elk Island National Pk. records
1988	Elk Island National Pk.	Waterhen, Manitoba	28	Elk Island National Pk. records
1990	Elk Island National Pk.	Nisling River, Yukon	50	Elk Island National Pk. records
1991	Elk Island National Pk.	Hanging Ice Bison Ranch, N.W.T.	97	Elk Island National Pk. records

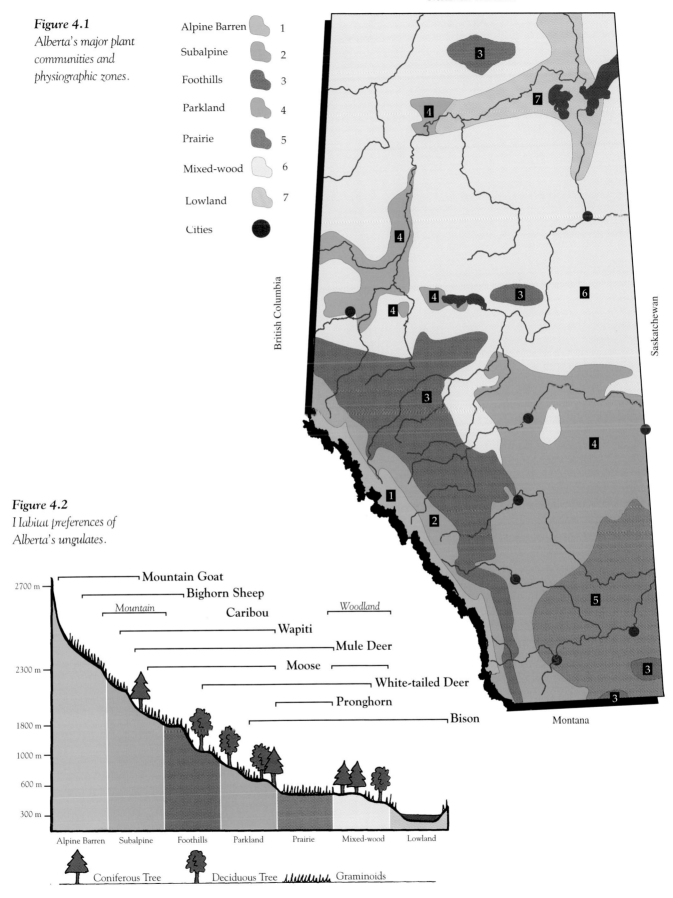

Figure 4.1
Alberta's major plant communities and physiographic zones.

Alpine Barren	1
Subalpine	2
Foothills	3
Parkland	4
Prairie	5
Mixed-wood	6
Lowland	7
Cities	

Northwest Territories

British Columbia

Saskatchewan

Montana

Figure 4.2
Habitat preferences of Alberta's ungulates.

Mountain Goat
Bighorn Sheep
Mountain   Caribou   *Woodland*
Wapiti
Mule Deer
Moose
White-tailed Deer
Pronghorn
Bison

2700 m
2300 m
1800 m
1000 m
600 m
300 m

Alpine Barren   Subalpine   Foothills   Parkland   Prairie   Mixed-wood   Lowland

Coniferous Tree   Deciduous Tree   Graminoids

Habitat Rating	Animals/km^2	
Primary	0.2 - 1.0	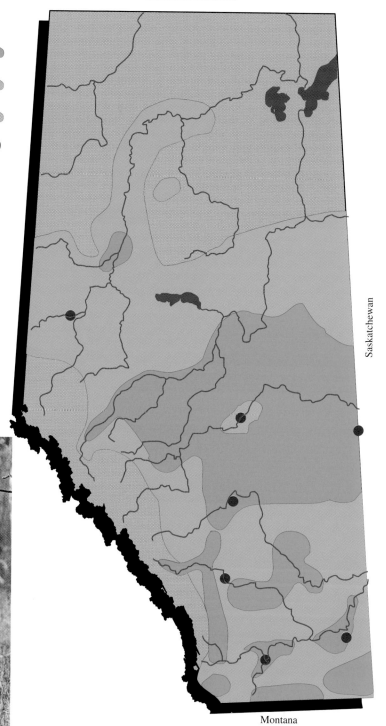
Secondary	0 - 0.2	
Inadequate or Poor		
Cities		

Figure 4.3
Distribution and abundance of
white-tailed deer *in Alberta*
(modified from AFWD, 1992).

White-tailed deer
*are often secretive, preferring to
withdraw to heavy brush during
the day and to emerge along
forest edges during evenings and
night to forage.
Photo by Dan and Sue Foley.*

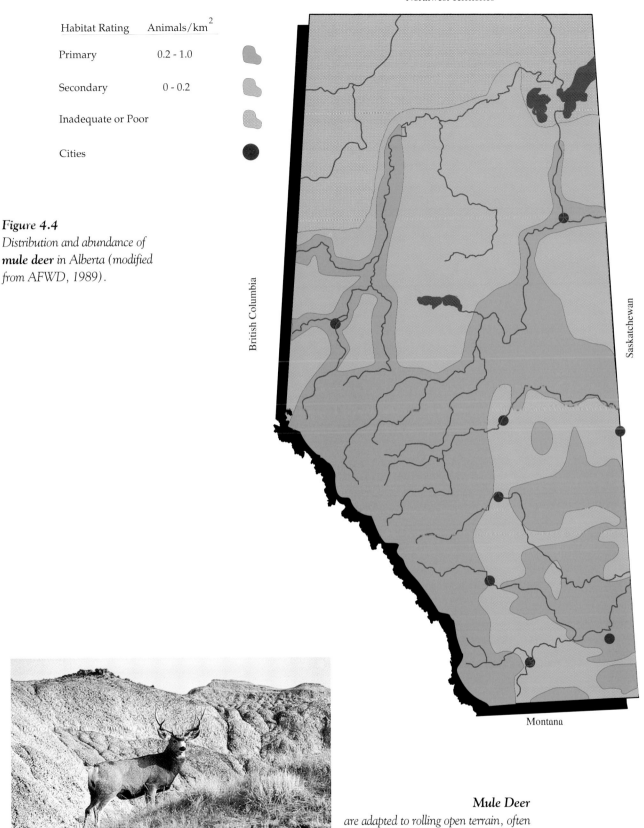

Habitat Rating	Animals/km^2
Primary	0.2 - 1.0
Secondary	0 - 0.2
Inadequate or Poor	
Cities	

Northwest Territories

British Columbia

Saskatchewan

Montana

Figure 4.4
Distribution and abundance of
mule deer *in Alberta (modified*
from AFWD, 1989).

Mule Deer
are adapted to rolling open terrain, often
preferring river breaks. Their bounding
gait is well suited to broken terrain.
Photo by G. Rowan.

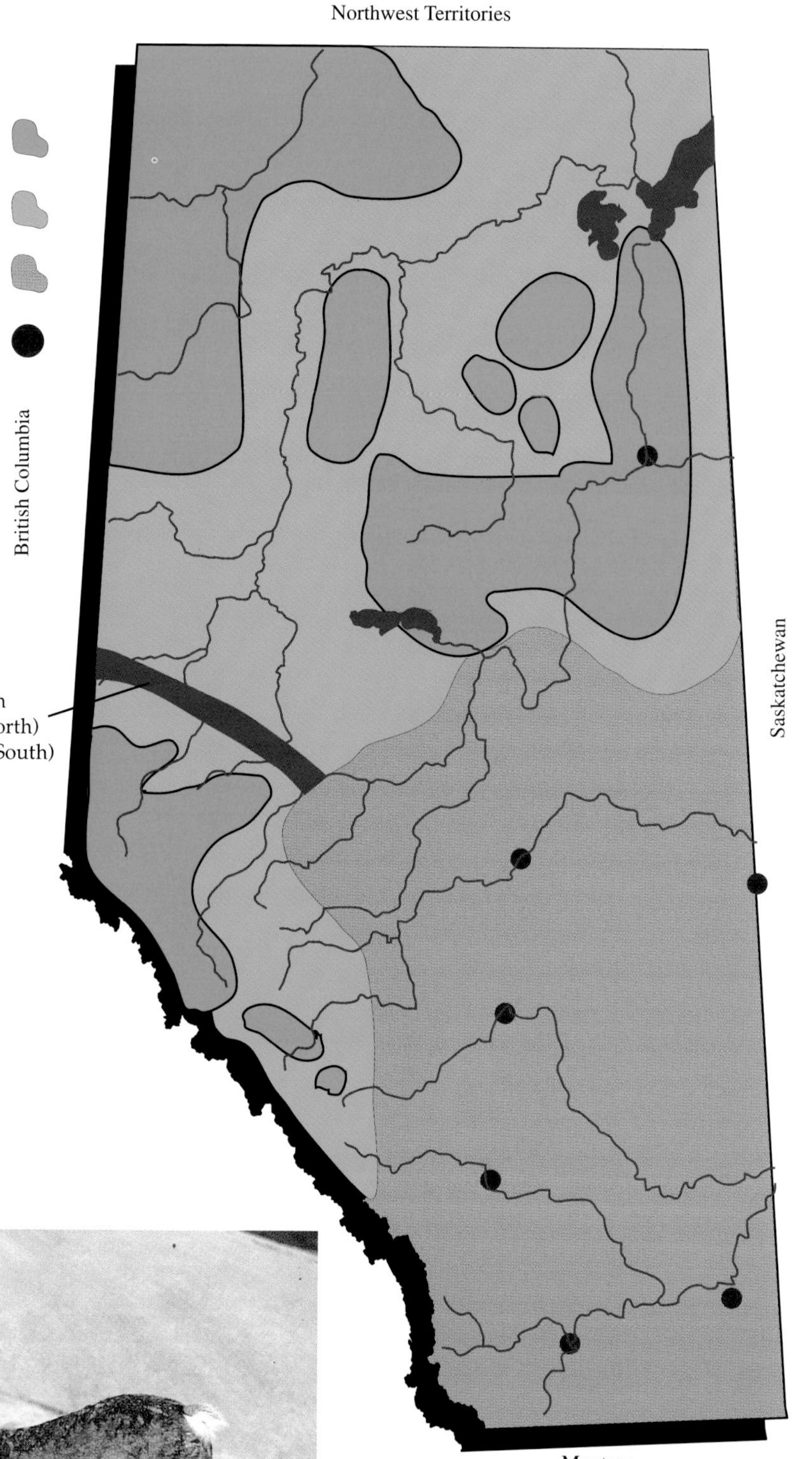

Northwest Territories

Habitat Rating	Animals/km^2
Primary	
Mountain Caribou	~0.02
Woodland Caribou	~0.01-0.05
Secondary	< 0.01
Inadequate	
Cities	

British Columbia

Saskatchewan

Figure 4.5
Distribution and abundance of **caribou** *in Alberta (based on comments of Jan Edmonds and Blair Rippin).*

Approximate division
between woodland (to north)
and mountain caribou (to South)

Montana

Caribou
are found in Alberta's subalpine and mixedwood communities. The mountain caribou subspecies seek out snowfields in the summer to remain cool and to avoid insects.
Photo by D. On.

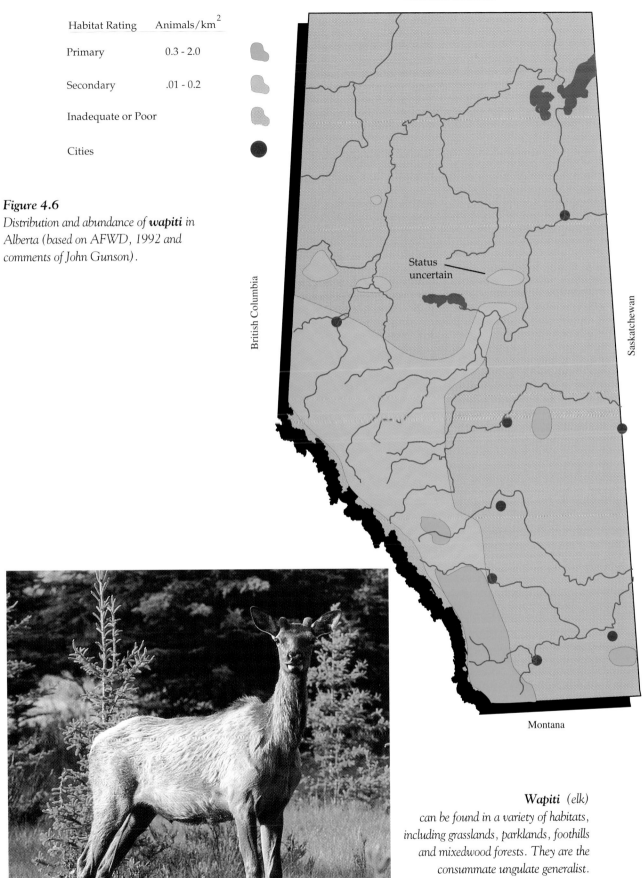

Habitat Rating	Animals/km^2
Primary	0.3 - 2.0
Secondary	.01 - 0.2
Inadequate or Poor	
Cities	

Figure 4.6
*Distribution and abundance of **wapiti** in Alberta (based on AFWD, 1992 and comments of John Gunson).*

Northwest Territories

British Columbia

Saskatchewan

Status uncertain

Montana

Wapiti *(elk)*
*can be found in a variety of habitats, including grasslands, parklands, foothills and mixedwood forests. They are the consummate ungulate generalist.
Photo by Dan and Sue Foley.*

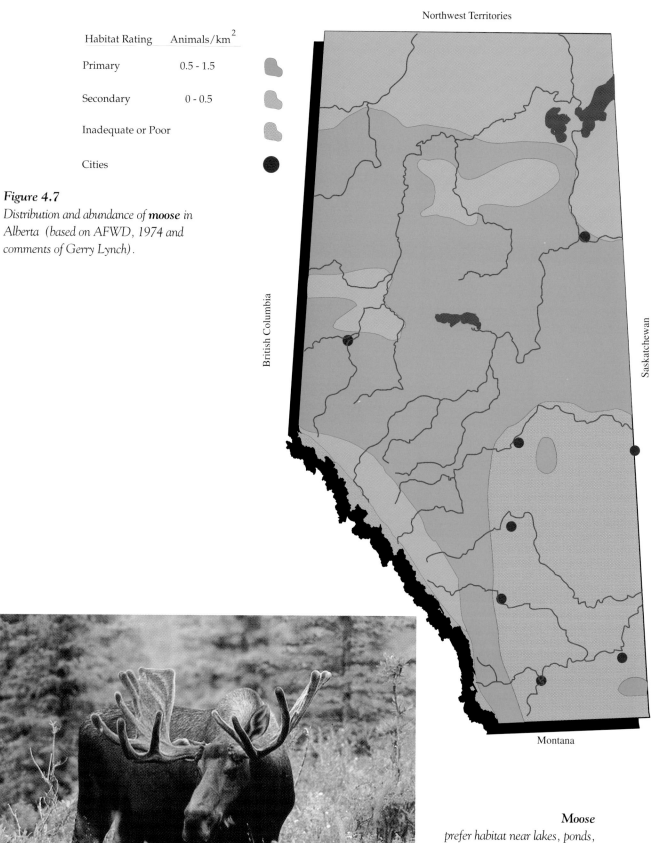

Habitat Rating	Animals/km^2
Primary	0.5 - 1.5
Secondary	0 - 0.5
Inadequate or Poor	
Cities	

Figure 4.7
Distribution and abundance of **moose** *in Alberta (based on AFWD, 1974 and comments of Gerry Lynch).*

Moose
prefer habitat near lakes, ponds, creeks, and muskeg during the summer, where they find abundant browse and can cool themselves in the water on hot days.
Photo by D. On.

Figure 4.8

*Distribution and abundance of **pronghorn** in Alberta (based on AFWD, 1990, and comments of Morley Barrett).*

Habitat Rating	Animals/km^2
Primary	0.6 - 0.9
Secondary	0.3 - 0.6
Marginal	< 0.3
Important Wintering Areas	
Cities/Towns	

Stettler

Drumheller

Brooks

Medicine Hat

Lethbridge

Manyberries

Montana

Saskatchewan

Pronghorn
prefer grassland communities where they find can abundant grasses and forbs.
Photo by G. Rowan.

Smoky River

Grande Cache

Athabasca River

Pinto Creek Herd

Jasper

Brazeau River

Shunda Mountain Transplant Herd

N. Saskatchewan River

Rocky Mountain House

Red Deer

Clearwater River

British Columbia

Bow River

Banff

Calgary

Kananaskis River

Highwood River

Livingstone Range Transplant

Oldman River

Lethbridge

Castle River

Montana

Figure 4.9

*Distribution and abundance of **mountain goats** in Alberta (based on comments of John Stelfox and Kirby Smith).*

Habitat Rating	Animals/km^2
Primary	0.1 - 0.4
Secondary	0.0 - 0.1
Inadequate	
Cities/Town	

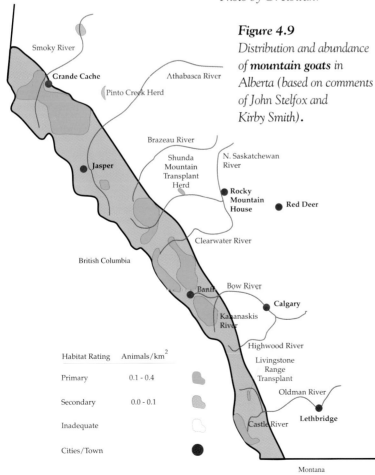

Mountain goats
prefer steep mountain cliffs during all seasons. Massive shoulders, thick coats, and secure footing are all critical to occupying this severe habitat.
Photo by B. Smith.

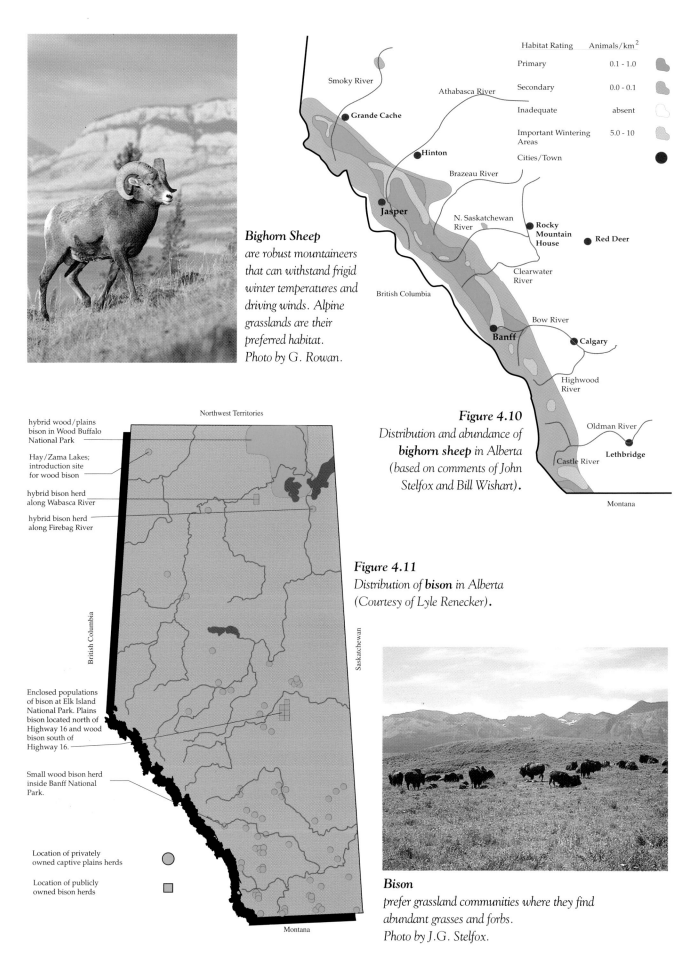

Bighorn Sheep
are robust mountaineers that can withstand frigid winter temperatures and driving winds. Alpine grasslands are their preferred habitat. Photo by G. Rowan.

Habitat Rating	Animals/km^2
Primary	0.1 - 1.0
Secondary	0.0 - 0.1
Inadequate	absent
Important Wintering Areas	5.0 - 10
Cities/Town	

Smoky River

Athabasca River

Grande Cache

Hinton

Brazeau River

Jasper

N. Saskatchewan River

Rocky Mountain House

Red Deer

Clearwater River

British Columbia

Bow River

Banff

Calgary

Highwood River

Oldman River

Lethbridge

Castle River

Montana

Figure 4.10
*Distribution and abundance of **bighorn sheep** in Alberta (based on comments of John Stelfox and Bill Wishart).*

Figure 4.11
*Distribution of **bison** in Alberta (Courtesy of Lyle Renecker).*

Northwest Territories

hybrid wood/plains bison in Wood Buffalo National Park

Hay/Zama Lakes; introduction site for wood bison

hybrid bison herd along Wabasca River

hybrid bison herd along Firebag River

British Columbia

Saskatchewan

Enclosed populations of bison at Elk Island National Park. Plains bison located north of Highway 16 and wood bison south of Highway 16.

Small wood bison herd inside Banff National Park.

Location of privately owned captive plains herds

Location of publicly owned bison herds

Montana

Bison
prefer grassland communities where they find abundant grasses and forbs. Photo by J.G. Stelfox.

TABLE 4.2

SELECTED LOCATIONS WHERE RECREATIONALISTS CAN VIEW UNGULATES IN NATURAL SETTINGS

Species	Location	Spring	Summer	Fall	Winter
White-tailed Deer	Cypress Hills Provincial Park	•			
	Wainwright	•			
	Waterton Lakes National Park	•	•	•	•
	Elk Island National Park	•		•	
	Strathcona County	•	•	•	•
	Parkland County	•	•	•	•
Mule Deer	Waterton Lakes National Park	•	•	•	•
	Jasper National Park	•		•	•
	Blue Creek		•	•	
	Porcupine Hills	•	•	•	•
	Boundary of Suffield Military Base	•	•	•	•
Caribou	Skyline Trail, Jasper National Park		•	•	
	Maligne/Medicine Lake vicinity	•			•
	Muskeg-Huckleberry Township Road, Hwy 40				•
Wapiti (Elk)	Elk Island National Park	•		•	•
	Athabasca Valley, Jasper National Park	•	•	•	•
	Ya-Ha-Tinda Ranch, east of Banff National Park	•		•	•
	Porcupine Hills	•			•
	Cypress Hills Provincial Park	•	•		•
	Immediately north of Black Diamond				•
Moose	Elk Island National Park	•	•	•	•
	Porcupine Hills	•		•	•
	Cypress Hills Provincial Park				
	Chip Lake-Whitecourt-Valleyview	•		•	•
Pronghorn	Pinhorn Grazing Reserve		•	•	
	Highway 36 (Hanna-Brooks)		•	•	
	Highway 1 (Suffield)		•	•	
Mountain Goat	Mt. Kerkeslin, Jasper National Park		•		
	Caw Ridge near Grande Cache	•	•	•	•
	Mt. Hamell near Grande Cache	•	•	•	•
	Spray Lakes area, Kananaskis Provincial Park	•			
	Mt. Coleman, Banff National Park	•	•	•	•
Bighorn Sheep	Disaster Point, Jasper National Park	•	•	•	•
	Cinquefoil Mtn., Jasper National Park	•	•	•	•
	Columbia Icefields, Jasper National Park	•	•	•	•
	Canmore Corridor, Exshaw, Hwy 1A	•	•	•	•
	Sheep River Wildlife Sanctuary	•			
	Cadomin-Luscar area of Coalbranch	•	•	•	•
	Mount Norquay, Banff National Park	•		•	•
	Waterton Lakes National Park	•	•	•	•
Plains Bison (Buffalo)	North enclosure, Elk Island National Park	•	•	•	•
	Bison enclosure, Waterton Lakes National Park	•	•	•	•
Wood Bison (Buffalo)	South enclosure, Elk Island National Park	•	•	•	•
	Bison enclosure, Banff National Park	•	•	•	•

5

Population Dynamics and Reproduction

J. Brad Stelfox and
John G. Stelfox

Alberta's hoofed mammals have experienced significant changes in their provincial populations in the last 100 years: some have increased, such as white-tailed deer, while others have decreased, such as mountain caribou. This chapter attempts to reconstruct, using illustrations and tables, the population dynamics of Alberta's hoofed mammals over the last several decades and explores some of the causes of population increases and declines. The population graphs emphasize the historical importance of habitat loss, "bad" winters, predator control, market hunting in the late 1800s and sport hunting. Hoofed mammal populations for each of Alberta's national parks are estimated. Reproductive features of each species, such as age of sexual maturity, length of breeding season, and number and weight of offspring are documented for each species.

INTRODUCTION

Alberta has neither lost nor acquired native ungulate species during the last few thousand years, however, there have been some drastic changes in relative abundance. Large-scale climatic change and its effect on plant communities is undoubtedly partly responsible for population fluctuations, yet its influence is dwarfed by the impact of humans. The advent of horses and firearms to local Indian tribes, particularly the Blackfoot, greatly increased hunting proficiency of aboriginal people in the 1700s. The emergence of market hunters, who provisioned a growing settler community with meat and hides in the 1800s, rapidly depleted wildlife in areas surrounding settlements. Elimination of ungulates over vast tracts of Alberta was inevitable in light of the burgeoning human population, intensifying hunting pressure, extensive land cultivation, competition with livestock, and introduction of livestock diseases that were transmissible to wild herbivores. It was not until the late 1800s, when moose, wapiti, bison and caribou had been removed from most of their traditional range, that steps were taken to protect remnant populations. These measures included the appointment of game guardians, a moratorium on shooting bison, the first bag limits, restricted hunting seasons, and a ban on market hunting.

POPULATION DYNAMICS

Although accurate estimates of provincial ungulate populations are fundamental to the establishment of biologically meaningful hunting seasons, they are not easily obtained. Many factors limit efforts to accurately count ungulate populations, and these include the sheer immensity of Alberta, the rugged and remote habitat of such species as bighorn sheep and mountain goat, the concealment of forest-dwelling species, inadequate money, equipment and manpower to properly census populations, and the vagaries associated with extrapolating provincial estimates from small surveys. In trying to construct figures depicting provincial population size since the turn of the century (Figures 5.1–5.7), it became obvious that for three species (white-tailed deer, mule deer, mountain goat), historical records were inadequate to construct even crude population trends. For caribou, wapiti, moose, bighorn sheep and bison, the figures reflect general trends only. It is only for pronghorn, a conspicuous and gregarious species inhabiting open grasslands of southeast Alberta, that we have accurate, long-term population estimates. It must also be noted that the low populations at the turn of the century for wapiti, pronghorn and bighorn sheep reflect primarily the decimating effects of market hunters. Population estimates in Alberta since 1900, where available, are compiled in Tables 5.1 and 5.2. Given the constraints under which wildlife biologists operate to collect this information, readers must appreciate the difference between a "population estimate" and "population size". Quantifying ungulate populations is seldom an exact science.

Numerical change in animal populations is important to wildlife biologists as it indicates much about the dynamic nature of the biophysical environment and the way animal populations respond to changes in their surroundings. For example, many indicators of reproductive performance, such as age of sexual maturity, number of offspring, and birth rate reflect environmental quality. Biologists can monitor these parameters and examine the causes and effects of population change. To illustrate the complex array of population, environmental, and human factors that affect changes in ungulate populations, a simple model is presented (Figure 5.8). Most important, the impact of humans and their land uses on environmental quality and ultimately on ungulate body condition should be acknowledged. Illustrations of changes in provincial population sizes (Figures 5.1–5.7) attempt to identify those factors that have increased or decreased ungulate population levels.

REPRODUCTION

Any evaluation of a change in population numbers must consider reproductive performance, for it is the population's ability to produce a healthy calf crop that will offset animals lost to mortality factors such as predators, hunters, roadkills, disease, poachers and winterkill. Reproductive performance can be assessed by many criteria, including age of sexual maturity, age of first breeding, cow/calf ratio, calf survivorship and calving interval. Close monitoring of these parameters is of value to the wildlife biologist, for changes indicate how populations respond to human or environmental influences, such as a skewed sex ratio caused by a sex-selective hunt, or poor body condition caused by a severe winter. The reproductive performance of hoofed mammals is also critical to the economic viability of the game farmer, who strives to have females breed young and as frequently as possible thereafter.

Reproductive isolation among co-occurring populations is often used as a convenient measure of a biological species. In Alberta, the validity of this statement is muddled, however, by occasional sightings of deer that exhibit characteristics of both mule deer and white-tailed deer (Wishart, 1980). In an effort to clarify possible reproductive ties between mule deer and white-tailed deer, Bill Wishart and Bob McClymont of the Alberta Fish and Wildlife Division have conducted a deer hybridization study during the past several years. Although the study is not yet complete, the following patterns have emerged. First, hybrids do occur in Alberta and generally represent the offspring of a mule deer doe and a white-tailed buck. Val Geist of the University of Calgary believes the willingness of female mule deer to receive courting bucks of either species explains this pattern. White-tailed deer females, in contrast, are more elusive and are less easily approached by males. Whereas male 50:50 hybrid offspring are sterile, female hybrids are reproductively viable. Not surprisingly, external body features such as ear length, tail length and colour, and epithelial glands may be intermediate in appearance or size to the purebred forms. Examination of muscle protein by electrophoresis indicates that hybrids possess characteristics of mixed parentage.

In a chronologically meaningful order, values for reproductive categories are provided for each ungulate species in Table 5.3. Since reproductive characteristics can be influenced by a host of factors, it must be recognized that these values represent averages.

TABLE 5.1

PROVINCIAL POPULATION ESTIMATES

(excluding National Parks and privately owned herds)

	White-tailed Deer	Mule Deer	Caribou	Wapiti (Elk)	Moose	Pronghorn	Mountain Goat	Bighorn Sheep
1902	NA	NA	NA	~400	NA	NA	NA	NA
1906	NA	NA	NA	NA	NA	1,000	NA	NA
1907	NA	NA	NA	300–1,000	NA	1,200	NA	NA
1908	NA	NA	NA	NA	NA	1,600	NA	NA
1910	NA	NA	NA	NA	NA	1,000	NA	2,000
1914	NA	NA	NA	NA	NA	1,000	NA	3,000
1916	NA	NA	NA	175-365	NA	NA	NA	NA
1919	NA	NA	NA	NA	NA	2,000	NA	NA
1920–1923	NA	NA	NA	NA	NA	<2,000	NA	NA
1924	NA	NA	NA	2,000	NA	1,100	NA	4,000
1925–1926	NA	NA	NA	NA	NA	<2,000	NA	NA
1930	NA	NA	2,000+	NA	NA	NA	NA	NA
1932	NA	NA	NA	NA	NA	1,000	NA	NA
1945	NA	NA	NA	NA	NA	15,000	NA	NA
1948	NA	NA	NA	NA	NA	4,000	NA	NA
1950	~60,000	~175,000	NA	NA	NA	NA	NA	2,000
1952	NA	NA	NA	NA	NA	4,000	NA	3,000
1953	NA	NA	NA	NA	NA	5,000	NA	NA
1954	NA	NA	NA	NA	NA	8,000	NA	NA
1955	NA	NA	NA	NA	NA	10,000	NA	NA
1956	NA	NA	NA	NA	NA	15,000	NA	NA
1957	NA	NA	NA	NA	NA	12,500	NA	NA
1958	NA	NA	NA	NA	NA	NA	(3,000–	NA
1959	90,000	175,000	NA	20,000	45,000	11,000	4,000)	NA
1960	NA	NA	NA	NA	NA	12,000	NA	NA
1961	NA	NA	NA	NA	NA	13,000	NA	NA
1962	NA	NA	NA	NA	NA	11,500	NA	6,000
1963	NA	~60,000	NA	NA	NA	19,040	NA	NA
1964	NA	~60,000	NA	NA	NA	20,177	NA	NA
1965	NA	~60,000	NA	NA	NA	14,231	NA	NA
1966	NA	NA	(7,000-	NA	NA	12,428	NA	NA
1967	NA	NA	9,000)	NA	NA	10,037	NA	NA
1968	NA	NA	NA	NA	NA	10,000	~1,000	NA
1969	NA	NA	NA	NA	NA	8,500	NA	NA
1970	NA	57,000	NA	NA	NA	11,000	NA	NA
1971	NA	NA	NA	NA	NA	10,000	NA	4,000
1972	NA	NA	NA	19,000	NA	10,500	NA	4,000
1973	NA	NA	5,000	20,000	NA	10,500	1,000	4,500
1974	NA	100,000	4,500	20,000	250,000	11,000	1,000	4,500
1975	138,130	NA	4,500	20,000	250,000	12,000	1,000	4,500
1976	NA	NA	4,500	20,000	250,000	18,000	1,200	4,500
1977	NA	NA	4,500	20,000	250,000	18,000	1,200	5,000
1978	NA	NA	(1,500-	NA	NA	10,919	NA	NA
1979	NA	NA	3,500)	NA	NA	15,330	NA	NA
1980	118,000	73,000	4,000	15,000	118,000	18,637	(1,500-	5,400
1981	NA	NA	NA	NA	120,000	20,707	2,000)	NA
1982	NA	100,000	NA	NA	120,000	21,202	NA	NA
1983	NA	73,000	NA	18,000	120,000	NA	(1,500-	6,000
1984	130,000	94,000	NA	20,000	118,000	32,071	2,000)	NA
1985	118,000	85,000	<2,500	19,000	120,000	24,174	NA	NA
1986	82,050	64,000	<1,900	18,000	118,000	25,098	(1,500-	NA
1987	NA	NA	NA	NA	NA	NA	2,000)	NA
1988	NA	NA	NA	17,000	100,000	28,624	2,000	6,500
1989	NA	NA	NA	NA	NA	NA	NA	NA
1990	146,000	94,000	3,500	17,000	90,000	20,000	1,700	5,200

NA = Data not available

REFERENCES
(in addition to Alberta Fish and Wildlife Division Annual Reports):

White-tailed Deer
Webb, 1959

Mule Deer
Webb, 1959; Glasgow, 1987

Caribou
Edmonds, 1986

Wapiti (Elk)
Webb, 1959; Carr, 1976; Gunson, 1988

Moose
Webb, 1959; Stelfox, 1966; Lynch, 1975

Pronghorn
Mitchell, 1965; Armstrong, 1967

Mountain Goat
Webb, 1959; Quaedvlieg et al., 1973; Hall, 1977

Bighorn Sheep
Stelfox, 1971; Hebert et al., 1985

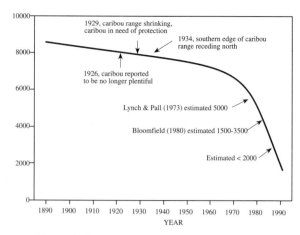

Figure 5.1
*General trend of caribou populations in Alberta
(modified from Edmonds, 1986).*

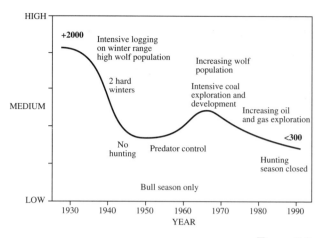

Figure 5.2
*General trend of mountain caribou populations
in Willmore/Grande Cache region
(modified from Gunson and Edmonds, 1987).*

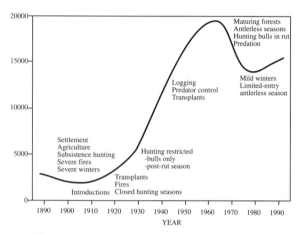

Figure 5.3
*General trend of wapiti (elk) populations in Alberta
(modified from Gunson, 1988).*

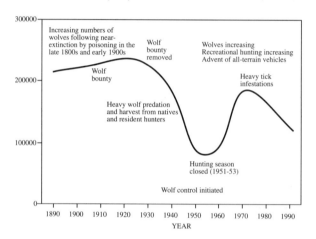

Figure 5.4
*General trend of moose populations in Alberta
(modified from Lynch, 1986).*

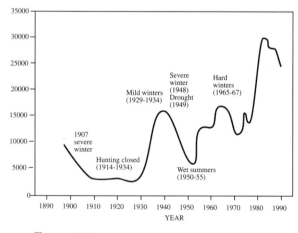

Figure 5.5
*General trend of pronghorn populations in Alberta
(modified from Mitchell, 1980; and Watson, 1988).*

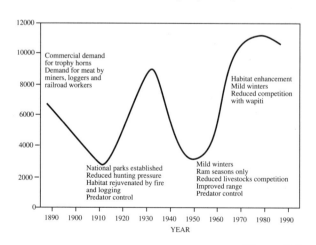

Figure 5.6
*General trend of bighorn sheep populations in Alberta
(modified from Stelfox, 1992).*

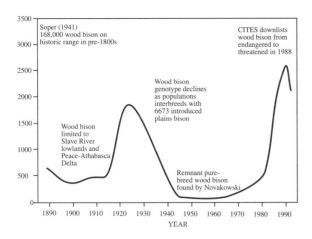

Figure 5.7

General trend of wood bison (buffalo) populations in western Canada (modified from the 1987 wood bison COSEWIC status report).

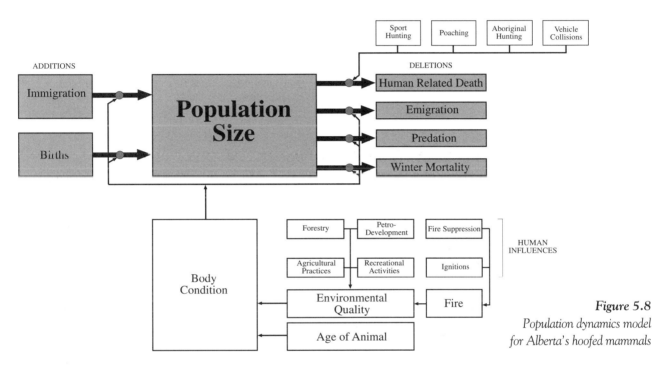

Figure 5.8

Population dynamics model for Alberta's hoofed mammals

TABLE 5.2

1993 OVERWINTERING UNGULATE POPULATIONS IN ALBERTA'S NATIONAL PARKS

	Waterton Lakes	Banff	Jasper	Elk Island	Wood Buffalo
White-tailed Deer	50–100	300–350	400–500	400–425	< 150
Mule Deer	300–400	850–950	400–600	<50	0
Caribou	0	20–25	250	0	< 200
Wapiti (Elk)	800–900	2,600	800–1000	1,566	0
Moose	20–40	80–120	250–300	393	NA
Pronghorn	0	0	0	0	0
Mountain Goat	40–60	1200	NA	0	0
Bighorn Sheep	200–250	2,350–2,450	2,500	0	0
Bison (Buffalo)					
Plains	12–20	0	0	557	0
Wood	0	9–12	0	284	0
Hybrid	0	0	1	0	3,000

SOURCES:

Waterton Lakes National Park
Robb Watt, Warden, personal communication

Banff National Park
Rick Kunelius, Warden, personal communication

Jasper National Park
Wes Bradford, Warden, personal communication

Elk Island National Park
Wes Olson, Warden, personal communication

Wood Buffalo National Park
Janet Mercer, Warden, personal communication

TABLE 5.3

REPRODUCTIVE PARAMETERS*

	White-tailed Deer	Mule Deer	Caribou	Wapiti (Elk)	Moose
Female Sexual Maturity (months)	6/18	18	30	18	18
Male Sexual Maturity (months)	18	18	30	18	18
Male First Breeding (months)	18/30	18/30	30/42	40	48/60
Breeding Season	November–early Dec.	mid-Nov.–mid-Dec.	early/mid-October	early Sept.–early Oct.	late Sept.–mid-Oct.
Breeding Strategy	Dominance Hierarchy	Dominance Hierarchy	Dominance Hierarchy	Mobile Harem	Pair Tending
Gestation (days)	200	203	229	256	245
Calving Season	June	mid-June	late May/early June	late May/early June	mid-May/early-June
Number of Offspring	2(1-3)	2(1-3)	1(1-2)	1(1-2)	1(1-2)
Newborn Weight (kg)	3-4	2.7-3.9	5-9	9-20	11-16
Neonate Strategy	Hider	Hider	Follower	Hider	Hider
Period of Lactation (months)	3	3	4–5	4–5	6
Important References	Hesselton & Hesselton, 1982; Wishart, 1986	Mackie et al., 1982; Halls, 1984; Wishart, 1986	Miller, 1982	Flook, 1970; Peek, 1982	Coady, 1982

TABLE 5.3

REPRODUCTIVE PARAMETERS (continued)

	Pronghorn	Mountain Goat	Bighorn Sheep	Bison (Buffalo)
Female Sexual Maturity (months)	16	30	18/30	30
Male Sexual Maturity (months)	16	30	18	30/42
Male First Breeding (months)	60	60	48	84
Breeding Season	mid/late Sept.	mid-Nov.–mid-Dec.	Nov.–Dec.	late July–late Aug.
Breeding Strategy	Territorial Harem	Dominance Hierarchy	Dominance Hierarchy	Dominance Hierarchy
Gestation (days)	250	180	175	285
Calving Season	late May	late May–mid-June	May–June	May
Number of Offspring	2(1–3)	1(1–2)	1(1–2)	1
Newborn Weight (kg)	3.8	2.3	3.6–4.5	14–18
Neonate Strategy	Hider	Follower	Follower	Follower
Period of Lactation (months)	3.5–4	2	3.5–4	3.5–4
Important References	Mitchell, 1967; Mitchell, 1980	Wigal and Coggins, 1982	Geist, 1971; Shackleton, 1985 Festa-Bianchet, 1988	Reynolds, Glaholt & Hawley, 1982

* These values are averages, since the timing of reproductive events can be affected by such factors as latitude, body condition, weather, age and population density.

6
Predation

John R. Gunson,
Martin Jalkotzy,
Ludwig N. Carbyn and
Laurence D. Roy

Many societal attitudes towards predators and the effects of carnivores on ungulate prey populations are based on emotions, myths and historical biases. This chapter explores the detailed life history, predatory strategies and distribution of each of the major predators in Alberta (coyote, wolf, black bear, grizzly bear and cougar) and examines evidence (mostly provincial in origin) for the complex relationships between populations of predator and prey. This chapter concludes by presenting a framework for evaluating the biological and social need for predator control.

INTRODUCTION

Few aspects of ungulate management receive as much public attention as do considerations involving predators. Public impressions of carnivores, both favourable and unfavourable, are often based on scant factual information and are steeped in myths and mistruths, many of which can be traced to a European heritage. Alberta has witnessed a history of mercurial public opinion, with distinct phases of predator condemnation up to the 1950s and protection in the 1970s and 1980s. Polarized and heated sentiments manifested themselves as a province-wide predator eradication program (1952–1956) for rabies control and, conversely, a moratorium on limited, specific predator control that had been intended to relieve an endangered mountain caribou population of wolf predation (1980s).

In Alberta, the wolf (*Canis lupus*), coyote (*Canis latrans*), cougar (*Felis concolor*), black bear (*Ursus americanus*), and grizzly bear (*Ursus arctos*) are considered primary predators in terms of their effects on specific hoofed mammal populations. Secondary carnivores are bobcat (*Lynx rufus*) and occasionally lynx (*Lynx lynx*), wolverine (*Gulo gulo*), and golden eagle (*Aquila chrysaetos*). This chapter examines the predator/prey interface and uses the wolf, coyote, cougar and bear to illustrate the effects, patterns and processes of predation.

PATTERNS AND PROCESSES

Predation, by shaping the physical appearance and behaviour of prey species, has played an important role in the evolution of Alberta's hoofed mammals. Acting collectively, such mortality factors as predation, disease, parasites, harsh winter conditions and seasonally reduced forage availability greatly affect survivorship, and hence the genetic composition of ungulate populations.

An examination of behaviour and life history offers fascinating insight into how both predators and prey attempt to maximize genetic fitness and prolong survival. Given the importance of the predation event (a sustaining meal for the predator, death for the hoofed mammal), it is not surprising that numerous adaptations have evolved, and are continually fine-tuned, in this race-like struggle that has no winner and no end. Predators employ diverse tactics to capture hoofed mammals, and their strategies are closely tied to social structure, habitat preferences and body size. Solitary carnivores inhabiting forested and broken terrain, such as the cougar, must rely on stealth to stalk closely, and they must possess explosive speed to overcome their quarry in a short distance. Others, such as the wolf, rely on the collective strength of the pack and on an ability to run long distances to exhaust and bring down their large prey. Bears, both black and grizzly, are generalist foragers and take advantage of vulnerable ungulates.

Predators possess finely-tuned senses of sight, smell and hearing to detect prey, and they utilize massive jaw musculature and robust dentition to quickly dispatch and consume their prey. Hoofed mammals are not idle players in the predator/prey game, but exploit a variety of adaptations to reduce the likelihood of being detected or killed by predators. Like the predators that pursue them, hoofed mammals are endowed with acute sight, hearing and smell. For those smaller species that reside in forests, crypsis (camouflage) is important. The combination of slow, careful movement, body colour similar to surroundings, and obscured body outlines against background objects provides effective concealment. Herbivores inhabiting open habitat may rely on exceptional speed (pronghorn) or rugged terrain (bighorn sheep, mountain goat) to escape predators. Others, such as deer and wapiti, may avoid predation by entering bodies of water. Larger species such as the bison and moose may utilize their physical prowess (sheer immensity or sharp hooves) to discourage predators and to protect young. Gregarious species such as wapiti and bison have security in numbers and their many ears, eyes, and noses are likely to detect approaching predators. When one considers all the precautions and strategies available to hoofed mammals, it is not surprising that many studies indicate that old, diseased, and very young individuals are most frequently killed by predators.

The evolutionary impact of predation is well exemplified by the deer fawn. Immediately following birth, the placental remains may be eaten by the doe to reduce smell. The altricial fawn is covered by a neonatal spotted coat, and is carefully concealed in similar-colored vegetation. In this bed it will lay prostrate and still for countless hours each day during the first several weeks of its life. The doe only returns for short periods to nurse, and often consumes the fawn's urine and feces, presumably to reduce scent.

Responses by predators to changes in prey density are either functional or numerical. A functional response occurs when the number of prey eaten per predator in a specific time varies directly with the number of prey available. A numerical response is one where the predator population increases or decreases with available food. Numerical fluctuations are mediated through dietary changes that affect birth rates, survival, litter size, and movements. Both functional and numerical responses may occur simultaneously.

It is the response of predators to the dynamics of prey availability that determines whether predators can control their prey populations. This relationship can be illustrated by a hypothetical system containing one predator species (the wolf) and one prey species (caribou). If caribou forage conditions improve, and non-predation mortality (e.g., hunting) remains minimal, one would expect their numbers to increase to a new level concomitant with forage availability. Although increased caribou numbers might result in greater kill rates per wolf (functional response), an increase in wolf densities (numerical response) may or may not occur. Unlike herbivores, whose numbers are generally limited by availability of forage and protective cover, territoriality and social constraints may prevent an increase in wolf density (Pimlott, 1970). Behaviours that place an upper limit on pack membership and number of breeding females discourage a numerical response in wolves. Some researchers (see Keith, 1983), however, believe wolf densities are also regulated by food availability. Let us now examine a second scenario where wolves prey on several ungulate species, of which one is caribou. If caribou numbers gradually decline because of overhunting, loss of critical habitat and harassment, the contribution of caribou to the wolves' diet is reduced. This trend does not mean a reduced impact of wolves on caribou, however. The wolf pack may not decline in numbers since it is maintained nutritionally by a diverse prey base. It is the combination of diverse prey diet for wolves, loss of critical habitat and diminished ungulate populations that allows the caribou population to decline further. Buoyed by alternate prey sources, but still exploiting caribou when they are found, the wolf now controls caribou numbers. This theoretical model may have a real counterpart in the case of mountain caribou and wolves in west-central Alberta. Long-term studies by the Alberta Fish and Wildlife Division indicate that loss of habitat, increased wolf numbers and hunting may have precipitated an observed decline in mountain caribou numbers (Edmonds and Bloomfield, 1984). Responding to alarming census results, hunting of caribou was discontinued in 1980. Despite low caribou numbers, it is believed that wolves and bears continue to prey on this endangered population. Of particular concern is the low survivorship of caribou calves, which seem particularly vulnerable to predation. Proposals by government biologists to conduct a selective cull of wolf packs that occupy particular caribou ranges (Edmonds, 1988) was met with heated public disapproval.

Deciphering predator/prey population dynamics can be difficult, especially when searching for causes and consequences of changes in population size. A good example is provided in Figure 6.1, which illustrates the relative abundance of wolves and moose in Alberta during the last several decades (Gunson, 1984; AFWD, 1991). At first glance, it appears that some population cyclicity is occurring and that peak wolf populations are lagging behind the moose population by several years. Furthermore, rapid increases in moose populations coincide with sharp declines in wolf numbers, and vice versa. It would seem logical, and may be correct, to assume that wolves are controlling moose populations and that predator control programs, by removing wolves, would lead to greater numbers of moose. A closer examination of the system has revealed to biologists that habitat quality, number of hunting licenses, amount of hunter access, and tick (*Dermacentor albipictus*) infestations also clearly affect moose abundance. This example stresses the importance of identifying and quantifying as many variables as possible.

No matter how hard we search for unified, simplistic theories of predation, few, if any, are universally applicable. For example, scientists once believed that predation was generally "compensatory" in nature: death from predation simply replaced other inevitable mortality (Errington, 1946). This can be rephrased: Individuals in excess of the carrying capacity constitute a doomed surplus, which can be lost without affecting population levels. Many predator ecologists now consider predation to be non-compensatory, or additive, in which deaths caused by predators are not

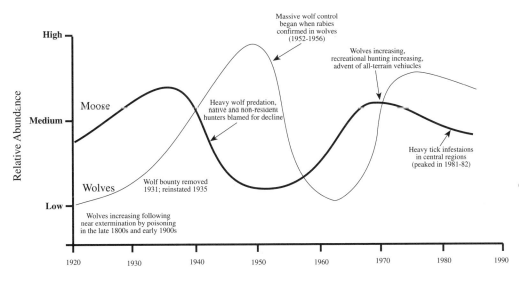

Figure 6.1
Changes in wolf and moose populations in Alberta (based on Stelfox, 1969; Gunson, 1984).

TABLE 6.1

CURRENT MORTALITY SOURCES FOR ALBERTA'S NATIVE UNGULATES

	Proximal Factors		Ultimate Factors*
	Major Predator	Others	
White-tailed Deer	coyotes on neonates, cougar, feral dogs	hunting, starvation, road kills	loss of protective habitat during severe winter conditions
Mule Deer	wolves, cougar, coyotes on neonates	hunting, starvation, road kills	susceptibility to hunting, loss of open habitat resulting from fire suppression
Caribou	wolves	illegal hunting, aboriginal hunting, road kills along Hwy. 40	recreation-based disturbance of mountain populations, habitat loss from logging and fires
Wapiti (Elk)	wolves, cougar, bears on neonates	hunting, road kills	resource development and recreation-based harassment, habitat loss from fire suppression, agricultural land clearing
Moose	wolves, bears on neonates, cougar	hunting, road kills, hair loss caused by winter ticks	habitat loss from fire suppression along foothills, agricultural land clearing
Pronghorn	coyotes and bobcats on neonates	hunting, severe winter blizzards, road kills	habitat loss from expanding cultivation, fences prevent access to resources and interfere with traditional movements
Mountain Goat	golden eagle on neonates, wolves, cougar	hunting, high angle falls, rock fall	improved access of goat ranges for hunters and recreationalists
Bighorn Sheep	cougar, wolves, coyotes, eagles on neonates	hunting, pneumonia-lungworm complex, road/train kills	harassment from recreationalists and resource development, forest encroachment on winter range
Bison (Buffalo)	wolves	brucellosis, anthrax, tuberculosis, occasional mass drownings	introduction of diseased plains bison into Wood Buffalo National Park, forest encroachment on boreal prairie habitat

* *Those factors which indirectly increase mortality by 1) adversely affecting activity patterns, 2) reducing critical biophysical resources or 3) predisposing animals to disease or predation.*

offset by other causes of mortality. If the magnitude of that mortality is significant, then predation can depress rates of population growth in ungulate populations. Under these circumstances, hunters and predators are in direct competition for the same resources.

Although predators kill a substantial number of Alberta's hoofed mammals, there are many other sources of mortality. Table 6.1 documents various proximal and ultimate causes of death for ungulates in Alberta.

WOLVES

Wolves are the most important predator of ungulates in northern forested regions of Alberta and have been the subject of extensive provincial research (Cowan, 1947; Stelfox, 1973; Carbyn, 1975; Fuller and Keith, 1980; Clarkson, Schmidt and Gunson, 1984; Oosenbrug and Carbyn, 1985; Schmidt and Gunson, 1985; Dekker, 1986; Carbyn and Trottier, 1987, 1988; Bjorge and Gunson, 1989).

Early explorer accounts of wolves in Alberta (Anthony Henday, David Thompson, Alexander Henry) indicated an abundant predator that enjoyed a province-wide distribution (AFWD, 1991). Since the arrival of settlers to Alberta, the wolf has experienced two pronounced cycles of abundance and scarcity (see Gunson, 1992). From the late-1800s to the 1920s, wolves were largely extirpated from the prairies, parklands, and mountain parks of Alberta. The decline was caused by an impoverished ungulate prey base (largely from market hunting, intentional decimation of bison herds and severe winters), and public and government persecution through bounty-induced shooting, trapping, snaring and poison (strychnine) campaigns. Wolf numbers subsequently recovered in the 1930s and 1940s in response to moderate ungulate numbers and relaxed persecution. A second wave of predator control occurred in the 1950s in response to public perceptions relating to livestock depredation, rabies and adverse effects on ungulate populations. During the next several years, Stelfox (1969) estimated that wolves were reduced from 5000 to between 500 and 1000. During the last few decades, enlightened public attitudes towards predators in general, and wolves specifically, have permitted a recovery in both numbers and distribution. It would appear that wolf numbers are now limited by available habitat and prey numbers. Trends in provincial wolf numbers (1920–1990) are graphically presented in Figure 6.1. Figure 6.2 illustrates current distribution. Observed wolf densities in Alberta during the last few decades varied from 1 wolf/40 km² to 1 wolf/225 km² (Gunson, 1992).

Wolves are cursorial (they run down prey) and usually hunt in packs. Packs generally consist of 9–12 individuals and appear to be positively related to the size of the principal prey species. Wolf packs preying on white-tailed deer were of 2–9 individuals (Pimlott *et al.*, 1969; Mech, 1973), whereas those preying on moose (Peterson, 1977; Fuller and Keith, 1980) consisted of 6–22 wolves. The fundamental unit of the pack is a pair of breeding adults; these individuals will be accompanied by varying numbers of pups, yearlings, and non-breeding adults.

The prey's rump is the preferred target, but the head and other body parts may also be attacked. Although some prey are caught and killed quickly, it is not unusual for "open habitat" prey (such as caribou) to be pursued unsuccessfully for several kilometers. Once the prey is brought down, pack members quickly rip the carcass apart and consume large quantities of meat. After an initial feeding, wolves generally leave the carcass and rest nearby, returning for subsequent feedings if the carcass was not completely consumed.

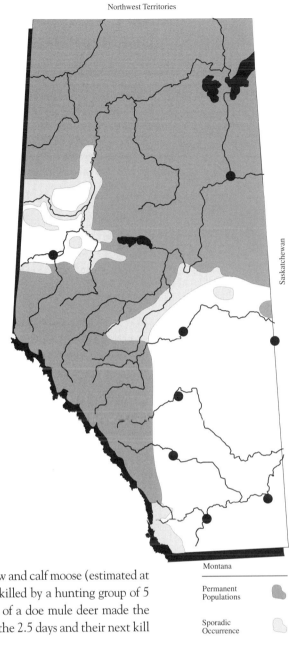

Figure 6.2
Distribution of wolves in Alberta (modified from AFWD, 1991).

Near the Brazeau River in 1985, a pack of 11 wolves consumed a cow and calf moose (estimated at 95% consumption in each case) in 2.5 days. These 2 moose were killed by a hunting group of 5 wolves while the other 6 wolves of the pack remained at the kill of a doe mule deer made the previous evening. Each wolf consumed about 40 kg of meat during the 2.5 days and their next kill was not observed for another 9 days.

Ungulates are the staple food of wolves in Alberta, although beaver are frequently killed if available during summer months. In Alberta, wolves have been documented to kill native ungulates (white-tailed deer, mule deer, caribou, wapiti, moose, mountain goat, [occasionally] bighorn sheep, and bison), and domestic ungulates (horses, sheep, cattle). Wolves are opportunistic foragers, and will kill and feed on any prey species (including beaver, snowshoe hare, and microtines) that are vulnerable.

Kill rates of wolves are generally measured by radio-tracking collared individuals during winter by aircraft. North American studies suggest that kill rates are influenced by pack size, prey size and abundance. In north-eastern Alberta where moose are the primary prey, Fuller and Keith (1980) documented one moose kill/pack of 9-10 wolves every 4.7–5.4 days. In the central foothills where wolves also feed on several small-bodied ungulates, Schmidt and Gunson (1985) recorded average kill rates of 1 ungulate/pack every 2.6 days. Consumption of moose (by wolves during winter) at

0.12 kg/kg wolf/day was identical in two studies in northern Alberta, i.e., Simonette River (Bjorge and Gunson, 1989) and Muskeg River (Fuller and Keith, 1980).

Competition for ungulates between wolves and hunters was studied in the headwaters of the Brazeau River on the Eastern Slopes (Schmidt and Gunson, 1985; Gunson, 1986). Wolf predation by one pack was the major limitation to an unproductive, declining wapiti herd. Hunters killed an average of 15 wapiti annually over a five-year period within the territory of the Blackstone wolf pack, compared to an estimated 60 wapiti killed annually over two years by wolves. In a boreal forest area in northern Alberta, an area with fewer prey species, Fuller and Keith (1980) observed that hunters and wolves killed an equal number of radio-marked yearling and adult moose. The study revealed that wolves preferentially killed young, old or debilitated individuals.

Recent studies of wolves by the Canadian Wildlife Service in Wood Buffalo National Park indicate that packs in winter kill an average of one bison per week and that the young and old age classes are most vulnerable to predation (Oosenbrug and Carbyn, 1985; Carbyn and Trottier, 1987, 1988). Daily meat consumption per wolf in winter varied from 2.5–6.4 kg (average = 4.3 kg/day). At times, calves are particularly vulnerable to predation. Observations of wolf/bison interactions indicated that older bison, particularly bulls, attempt to protect young calves from wolves. Most wolf attacks were directed at bison herds with calves, and one encounter between wolves and a herd with a young calf lasted 11 hours (Carbyn and Trottier, 1988). Another series of summer observations documented extensive predation on calves (Carbyn, in prep.). Kill rates of one pack averaged one calf per day in mid-June and was as high as three calves per day.

In Jasper National Park during the 1950s and 1960s, an intensive predator control program greatly reduced wolf numbers. During this period of low wolf density, studies by Cowan (1947) and Carbyn (1975) indicated that wapiti populations were not significantly affected by wolves. In recent years, warden surveys have documented general declines in wapiti herds and increased wolf sightings. Most wardens and biologists attribute wapiti herd attrition to loss of critical winter habitat (the result of fire suppression), to mortality during the severe winter of 1973-74, and to wolf predation. The impact of sport hunting along the boundaries of Jasper National Park may also play an important role in reduction of herd size.

Numerous studies have shown that wolf predation, particularly in northern regions, is an important limiting factor on ungulate populations. Following most episodes of wolf control, hoofed mammal populations increase (Gasaway et al., 1983; Atkinson and Janz, 1986; Farnell and McDonald, 1987). Increases in ungulate numbers following wolf control may in turn lead to an imbalance between herbivore populations and the vegetation that supports them.

Wolves have frequently been accused of surplus killing (the act of killing more prey than are eaten). Although surplus killing by wolves has been substantiated on caribou calving grounds in the arctic (Miller et al., 1985) and in other locations, studies by Carbyn (1987) and Schmidt and Gunson (1985) in the boreal forests of Alberta indicate that wolves generally do not underutilize the carcasses of their prey. Less efficient use of carcasses may occur when deep snow conditions increase prey vulnerability and therefore predation rate.

COYOTES

Coyotes occur throughout Alberta and have increased their numbers continentally during the last century in response to expansion of agriculture, deforestation, extermination of red wolves, and reduction of the range of gray wolves (Nowak, 1978). Although coyotes are carnivores, their food habits are varied and include numerous vertebrate species (consumed as either prey or as carrion), insects and fruit (Todd et al., 1981).

Food habit studies based on stomach contents or scats are unable to distinguish predation from carrion feeding. Studies based on snow tracking (Ozoga and Harger, 1966) and radio-telemetry (Hamlin *et al.*, 1984) have more clearly distinguished the predatory role of coyotes on ungulate populations. Predation does occur but coyotes rely heavily on carrion as a food source at all times of the year. Because of their small size, coyotes generally prey on smaller animals. Mice, voles, ground squirrels, hares, other small mammals and birds are important food sources for coyotes, but they can and do prey on larger species. Coyote predation on domestic sheep in Alberta shows a dramatic selection for smaller size not only towards lambs over ewes but towards smaller lambs (Roy and Dorrance, in prep.), though adult ewes (>100 kg) and even adult cattle have been killed by coyotes in Alberta (Dorrance, 1982). Predation by coyotes on wild ungulates is directed towards neonates, though many documented examples of predation on larger adults exist. Predation on larger mammals usually involves cooperative hunting by groups of coyotes. Coyotes kill deer by bites to the throat and head region (Ozoga and Harger, 1966) with the death resulting from either crushing of the skull or occlusion of the trachea resulting in asphyxiation (Simons, 1988). Some cases of predation on large healthy prey involve long chases by coyote packs with biting to all parts of the prey's body. Ungulate neonates are killed by bites to the head.

In Alberta coyotes are known to kill pronghorn, bighorn sheep and deer (Bruns, 1970; Shank, 1977; Barrett, 1984; Ashcroft, 1986). Predation on larger Alberta ungulate species like wapiti or moose is minimal and likely limited to neonates or to injured animals. Although Barrett (1984) determined that at least 21 of 62 marked pronghorn fawns were killed by coyotes and that coyotes were the main predator of pronghorn fawns in Alberta, they were not limiting pronghorn population growth. No major studies on the effect of coyote predation on deer have been conducted in Alberta. However, information from Montana indicated that coyotes were the major cause (90%) of summer mortality of mule deer fawns (Hamlin *et al.*, 1984). Although they concluded that coyote predation could reduce fawn survival on a nutritionally healthy deer population, they hypothesized that alternate prey availability could buffer the effects on deer populations. Similarly, Messier *et al.* (1986) concluded that coyotes numerically affected white-tailed deer populations in southern Quebec. They noted winter predation directed towards fawns and older deer, but not necessarily towards individuals in poor physiological condition. In this study, deer congregating in winter yards during deep snow conditions were more vulnerable to coyote predation. Fawns constituted 40% of the food consumed by coyotes in June and July, suggesting a significant effect on neonate survival. Predation on bighorn sheep usually involves coyotes cutting off ewes or lambs from rugged escape cover (Shank, 1977; Ashcroft, 1986). Similar tactics are likely used for predation on mountain goats. Coyotes are unlikely to affect bighorn sheep and mountain goat populations if adequate escape terrain is available.

Connolly (1978) cited 12 studies where removal of coyotes increased survival of ungulate offspring, and another 12 studies where control of coyotes had little effect on deer and bighorn sheep populations. Since few studies implicated predators as the sole controlling factor on ungulates, he concluded that predators acting together with weather, disease and habitat change affect prey numbers. Some authors have concluded that coyotes do have a severe effect on deer numbers while others have concluded that although coyotes kill many deer, they do not control populations. Teer *et al.* (1991) examined the effect of coyotes on an unhunted white-tailed deer population over a 35-year period and could only conclude that predation acting together with other environmental perturbations was an important factor in population stability.

Although in some local situations coyote predation affects ungulate populations, coyotes in general do not control ungulate populations in Alberta. Situations where effects of coyote predation on ungulates may be severe include winter predation on deer or pronghorn in poor condition in deep, crusted snow or situations of neonate predation in suboptimal habitats resulting from environmental factors (*e.g.*, drought) or landscape alteration by humans.

COUGARS

Cougars, whose distribution is illustrated in Figure 6.3, prey primarily on ungulates in Alberta. In an ongoing study in the foothills and mountains southwest of Calgary (Ross and Jalkotzy, 1989; Ross and Jalkotzy, 1990; Jalkotzy and Ross, 1991), ungulates were represented in 90% of over 200 kills discovered between 1981 and 1991. Major prey identified in this study were mule deer, moose, wapiti, and white-tailed deer. Bighorn sheep were also killed occasionally. Other prey identified in the study included porcupine (*Erethizon dorsatum*), beaver (*Castor canadensis*), coyote, domestic dog (*Canis familiaris*), snowshoe hare (*Lepus americanus*), and grouse (*Dendragopus canadensis, Bonasa umbellus*). Since kills were located by tracking radio-collared cougars, and since small prey are more quickly consumed, the sample is probably biased towards larger prey. However, continuous snow tracking of radio-collared cougars in 1990 and 1991 support the notion that small mammals make an insignificant contribution to the winter diets of cougars in Alberta. These results are similar to those determined from analyses of cougar scats and stomachs collected during the study. Of 63 stomachs collected from hunter-killed cougars throughout their provincial distribution, 69% contained cervids, predominantly mule deer. Biomass of prey consumed by cougars emphasized the importance of larger ungulates. Although they were killed less frequently than deer, wapiti and moose represented 25% and 33% of meat consumed, respectively. Mule deer and white-tailed deer comprised 39% of cougars' diets. The importance of moose as cougar prey has not been documented to the same degree elsewhere. This may reflect greater availability of moose to cougar in Alberta.

The cougar's diet in Alberta is generally similar to cougar diets studied elsewhere in North America. Most studies indicated that deer were the most important prey item, usually representing over 50% of kills, followed by some combination of wapiti, porcupine, beaver, hares, small carnivores, and domestic stock (Anderson, 1983).

Bighorn sheep do not appear to be vulnerable to cougar predation at the Sheep River study area (Ross and Jalkotzy, 1989; Ross and Jalkotzy, 1990; Jalkotzy and Ross, 1991). Similar findings were found west of the continental divide in the East Kootenays of British Columbia. However, bighorn sheep were killed by cougar along the Fraser River in the Junction area (Harrison and Hebert, 1988). These differences may be related to the complexity of the ungulate community. Both the Sheep River and East Kootenay study areas contain ungulates other than deer and bighorn sheep. In the Junction study area, only bighorn sheep, and occasionally mule deer, occur.

Among wapiti and moose killed by cougars in the Sheep River area, certain sex/age classes were preferentially taken. For moose, calves were selectively killed and adults ignored. Among wapiti, cows and calves were taken most frequently. These observations presumably reflect the difficulty of cougars preying on large-bodied individuals and the risk of injury from hooves and antlers. Both sexes and all age classes of mule deer were represented in the kill sample from the Sheep River area, demonstrating the proficiency of cougars in preying on smaller cervids.

The condition of prey killed by cougars at Sheep River was assessed by determining femur marrow fat levels of prey carcasses. Fifteen of 19 (79%) moose calves had fat levels below 25% and were probably suffering from nutritional stress. Eight of those were severely stressed, since marrow fat levels were below 10%. From these data, it appears that moose calves in poor condition are more susceptible to cougar predation than healthy calves. However, since the general condition of the moose calf population in the study was not known, the level of selectivity cannot be established. All wapiti killed by cougars had high percentages of marrow fat, while mule deer kills had marrow fat values ranging from very low to high. The overall body condition of wapiti and deer with high marrow fat cannot be determined because of the limitations of the marrow fat technique (Mech and Delgiudice, 1985).

A strong relationship was revealed between cougar sex class and ungulate prey selection at Sheep River. Male cougars selected moose calves, whereas females killed primarily mule deer and wapiti. When represented as biomass, moose comprised 89% and 16% of the males' and females' diet, respectively. Conversely, wapiti and mule deer together comprised 80% of the female cougars' diet. Reasons for these apparent dietary differences are not clear, though males, being 60% heavier than females, are better physically equipped to kill larger prey. However, an adult wapiti is larger than a moose calf, and females kill more cow wapiti than males do. Since home ranges of resident males are several times larger than those of resident females, and often overlap with female territories, similar prey should be available to both sexes. Male and female cougars may have different hunting techniques or may hunt in different habitats. By doing so, the availability and/or susceptibility of different prey may differ for each sex class. In addition, female cougars are required to kill more frequently to provision their offspring. This probably forces them to hunt more abundant prey species, even though they may be more difficult to catch because of their gregarious nature. This additional practice may improve their killing efficiency. Male cougars, on the other hand, do not have to deal with the demands of raising young and can afford to specialize on a larger prey animal which they encounter less frequently.

Research in progress at Sheep River is shedding some light on prey requirements of cougars. Cougars kill prey at varying rates dependent upon size of prey, and the cougar's sex and reproductive status, and size and age of litters. A solitary female that had not yet bred killed mule deer, principally fawns, once every 13 days. The consumption rate for this female was 2.5 kg/day over a three-month period. When travelling with two small kittens, an adult female killed a mule deer every 10 days. This rate increased to one kill/seven days when litters of two kittens were over a year old. If these older kittens are eating 50 to 100% of their mother's intake, then the adult female is consuming meat at a rate of between 2.4–3.9 kg/day. One female travelling with three dependent kittens over 18 months old made five kills including a branch-antlered bull wapiti and a moose calf over 27 days, or one kill every 5.2 days. Conversely, a solitary adult male killed four moose calves in 52 days, one calf every 13 days or about 6.3 kg/day. These kill and consumption rates are similar to those estimated in Idaho (Hornocker, 1970), Arizona (Shaw, 1977), Utah (Ackerman, 1982, Robinette *et al.*, 1959) and Nevada (Robinette *et al.*, 1959).

Cougars are stalking predators that generally require cover, either vegetative or topograhical, to kill successfully. Cougar kills at Sheep River were most frequently located in pine- and/or spruce-dominated forests with understories of alder, willow, and deadfall. In addition, most kills were on hillsides averaging a 15° to 20° slope, and which most often were facing a northerly or easterly direction. Snow tracking of cougars indicated that habitats in which kills were found were also those most frequently hunted. Typically, cougar tracks crossed south and west-facing slopes in

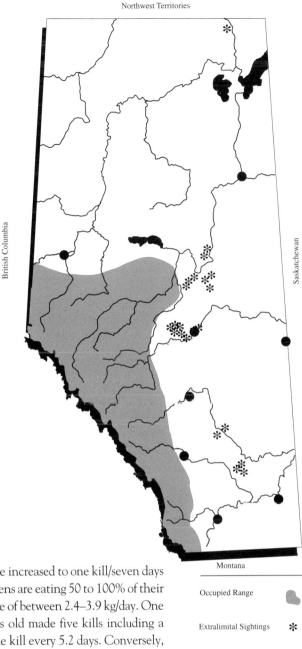

Occupied Range

Extralimital Sightings

Cities

Figure 6.3
Distribution of cougar in Alberta (modified from AFWD, 1992).

direct lines, but on north and east-facing slopes in heavy cover they often went back and forth across the hill. Cougars also walked ridges and the tops of steep slopes, where they could launch attacks downhill.

Reconstructions of successful attack sequences at Sheep River provide a glimpse of what few people have seen: a cougar bringing down a large ungulate. Most chases led downhill, particularly during the terminal phase. Successful attack distances (distance between the initiation of the attack and the point of first contact between predator and prey) varied depending on the species of prey. Typically, attacks on moose covered shorter distances on average than those on deer: 19 m and 52 m, respectively. The killing distance (the distance between the point of first contact and the kill site) followed a similar pattern. Moose were brought down most quickly, while wapiti and mule deer took longer to subdue. Longer attack distances are probably less successful on larger ungulates because cougars have more difficulty bring them down.

Death usually resulted from a combination of suffocation and loss of blood. By clamping down on the throat area from below, a cougar's long canines often damaged major blood vessels in the neck, while at the same time the trachea was collapsed. A smaller percentage of ungulates died from broken necks.

If kills occurred in open areas, the carcass was often dragged to nearest cover. Although cougars are capable of dragging their largest prey, smaller prey such as deer were dragged more often than were wapiti and moose. Recent cougar kills can usually be identified by debris that is raked over the prey, hiding it to make it more difficult for scavengers to find.

Cougars are probably the principle source of mortality to ungulate populations in the foothills and mountains of southwestern Alberta, a region where wolves are rare. Cougars are relatively abundant in these habitats (2.5–5 cougars/100 km^2), and exert a powerful influence on the anti-predator strategies of ungulates living in the same areas.

BLACK AND GRIZZLY BEARS

The fact that black bears and grizzly bears hunt and kill ungulates in Alberta is undisputed, but the extent of this predation is poorly documented. Spring bear hunters, trappers, and other experienced woodsmen have reported observations of black bears trailing cow moose in the spring.

The importance of black bear predation of ungulate calves was first demonstrated in the Coolwater/Glover Ridge complex in north-central Idaho (Schlegel, 1976). Predation by bears accounted for the deaths of at least 47% of 53 radio-collared and bonded wapiti calves between parturition and early July. Following translocation of 65% (n=75) of the area's black bear population in 1976, calf survival increased from 20% to 61% in 1977. By 1979, recurrence of low calf survival (27%) was attributed to a high return rate of transplanted black bears. Predation by different carnivores may be compensatory since mountain lion kills of wapiti calves increased from 9% to 17% when bear numbers were reduced. Schlegel's work had profound implications to bear-ungulate management throughout their range of sympatry in North America, and other studies soon followed.

On the Kenai National Moose Range in Alaska, researchers from the Kenai Moose Research Centre monitored 47 radio-collared, bonded moose calves in 1977 and 1978 (Franzmann et al., 1980). Predation by three species accounted for about one-half of the calf mortality through late July. Black bears killed 16 of the 47 calves, brown bears (grizzly) three, wolves three, and an unknown predator, one. In this study, predation by black bears occurred when the moose calves were very small (0–2 months), whereas predation by brown bears and wolves occurred throughout the year. In another Alaskan study, 55% of 120 neonatal, radio-collared moose calves died during the first six weeks of life (Ballard *et al.*, 1981). Predation accounted for 86% of the natural deaths in the Nelchina Basin with predation by brown bears responsible for 91% of these deaths.

In Canada, studies in Saskatchewan, the Yukon and Alberta were patterned after pioneering American work. Moose managers implicated black bears in declining moose populations in the Cumberland Delta of east-central Saskatchewan. Black bears were removed in 1983 with a resulting increase in calf survival from 20–30 to 77 calves/100 cows (Stewart *et al.*, 1985). In the southern Yukon, grizzly bears killed moose calves at greater rates than wolves or black bears (Larsen and Gauthier, 1985). Eighty-six percent of 76 radio-collared moose calves died within 1 year. Of the total mortality, 63% was due to grizzlies, 26% to wolves, 5% to non-predators, 2% to black bears, and 4% to unknown predators.

Efforts to evaluate bear predation of ungulates in Alberta have been preliminary. Black bears killed at least three of eight radio-collared moose calves in the Lakeland and Fort McMurray regions of the northeast (Nolan and Barrett, 1985). Wielgus (1986) observed grizzly bear predation of wapiti in Kananaskis Country and suggested that most predation was by adult bears. He further speculated that grizzly bears hunted selectively in mature coniferous habitats where dense cover provided a greater visual screen and more successful predation.

It is obvious that bear predation, either singularly or in combination, can be a major source of mortality to ungulate populations. Black bears are abundant in Alberta; the estimated provincial population is 40,000. Bear predation of moose and other wild ungulates should be more intensively evaluated considering Ballard and Larsen's (1987) prediction that "where black bears are the most numerous predator, they will also be the most significant neonate mortality factor".

MANAGEMENT

Social and political interests dictate the outcome of predator management programs as commonly as do biological realities. In areas where carnivore, human, and hoofed mammal populations co-exist, one of three management options exist (see Figure 6.4).

Scenario 1: Carnivores as exclusive predators of hoofed mammal resource. Human influence is minimized and free rein given to natural processes. This is the scenario that applies in Alberta's national parks.

Scenario 2: Humans and carnivores share the hoofed mammal resource. Management decisions relating to offtake of ungulates by predators and humans are driven by government agency priorities as influenced by public sentiment. This scenario best describes most of Alberta's green zone.

Scenario 3: Humans assume dominant role as predator of hoofed mammal resource. Large predators are reduced or eliminated and ungulates are managed primarily for hunters. This is the scenario that best describes Alberta's agricultural landbase.

A conceptual framework that considers predator control is provided in Figure 6.5. Predator control measures need not be incompatible with maintaining viable carnivore populations in Alberta. Regulated control of predators represents a management option if based on such considerations as predator and prey densities, the diversity of the prey base, and the need for both predators and man

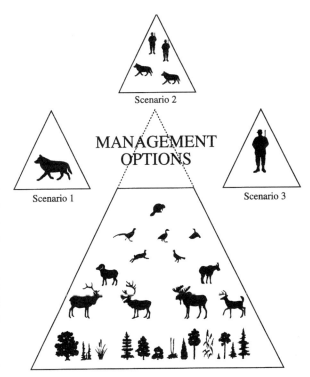

Figure 6.4
Predator management options (Carbyn, 1983; adapted from drawing by A. Raszewski).

to utilize prey populations. Obviously, the equation is variable and will be affected by land tenure (private versus public) and land-use (agricultural, recreational, or conservation).

Justifications for or against wolf control have increasingly become a philosophical rather than biological debate. Growing interest in non-consumptive use of wildlife has lead to greater societal sympathy for large predators. While recreationalists cherish the possibility of seeing a wolf or cougar, there is growing discontent among East Slope outfitters who are finding it progressively more difficult to show their clients abundant hoofed mammals.

Wolf populations in Alberta have in recent years taken on international significance. This profile may affect management of Alberta's predators, since our wolves represent populations from which the U.S. mountain states might repopulate, either through natural immigration or releases. For example, movements of wolves from southwestern Alberta and southeastern British Columbia into the U.S. have been welcomed by conservationists (Ream *et al.*, 1985).

Figure 6.5
Model of predator management options (modified from Connolly, 1978; and Theberge, 1985).

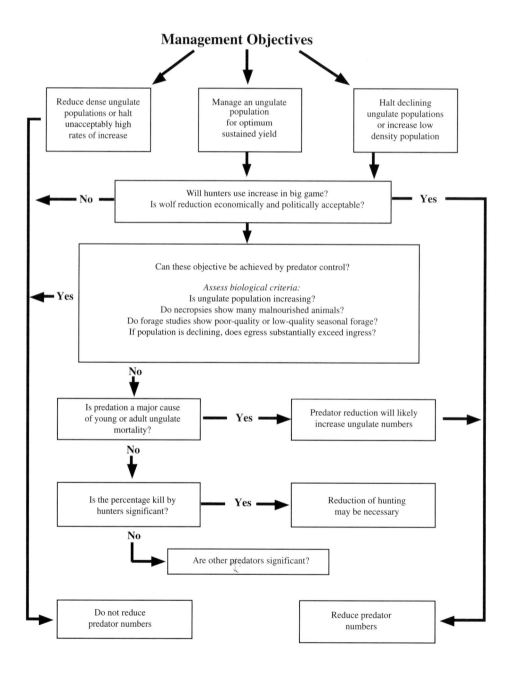

Parasites and Disease

William M. Samuel

Although confronted by and supporting a diverse community of diseases and parasites, Alberta's hoofed mammal populations, for the most part, are not harmed by these organisms. Parasites generally complete their life history in and on ungulates without causing death to their host, suggesting a long co-evolutional history. There are notable exceptions to this rule, however, and some are reviewed in this chapter. Descriptions of the life cycle and effects of selected viruses, bacteria, roundworms, flukes, tapeworms and ticks are presented. A comprehensive list of parasites and diseases found in and on Alberta's ungulates has been assembled, and graphics illustrating selected parasites and diseases are provided.

INTRODUCTION

Only a few of the many parasitic and disease agents reported from the wild ungulates of Alberta are pathogens. In certain situations the following are good examples: epizootic hemorrhagic disease (white-tailed deer), soremouth (bighorn sheep and mountain goat), pasteurellosis and lungworm (bighorn sheep), liver fluke (wapiti and moose), and winter tick (moose and, perhaps, mule deer, wapiti, and woodland caribou). These and other parasites and diseases of Alberta's hoofed mammals are reviewed.

Virtually every wild or captive ungulate becomes infected with some disease or parasite at one time or another during its life. Most of these organisms are small, live in inconspicuous places in the body and occur in small numbers. Seldom is the host harmed by these parasites. The parasites remain in fairly low numbers during the life of the host causing no or few detectable problems. In rare instances, usually when ungulates are stressed by severe winters or an overused food supply, parasites can become pathogens, robbing the host of processed food or body fluids, depositing their wastes or toxins, or invading critical body tissues.

What follows is a brief and general overview of the types of parasites and diseases found in wild, free-ranging hoofed mammals of Alberta with emphasis on several agents considered to be the most pathogenic. Since 1970, research conducted by the Department of Zoology, University of Alberta, or by colleagues in various places in Alberta has included the necropsy of several hundred hoofed mammals for parasites and diseases. Results from these necropsies, some of which have been published (e.g., Samuel *et al.*, 1976, 1978; Samuel, 1987a), provided the data base for this chapter.

Tables 7.1 and 7.2 identify those parasites and diseases documented in native hoofed mammals within Alberta.

GENERAL TYPES OF PARASITES AND DISEASES

Examples from six types of parasitic/disease organisms, including viruses, bacteria, roundworms, flukes, tapeworms and ticks, will be covered.

Viral Examples

Epizootic hemorrhagic disease is an important disease that primarily affects white-tailed deer. The first documented outbreak in North America occurred in 1955. Transmission between deer apparently occurs via biting gnats. Deer experimentally infected with the virus become ill within 10 days of exposure and die shortly thereafter. Varying degrees of hemorrhages can occur in virtually any tissue or organ. The only documented important outbreak in Alberta occurred in 1962 when approximately 450 white-tailed deer, 20 mule deer, and 15 pronghorns were found dead in southern Alberta (Chalmers *et al.*, 1964). A minor outbreak may have occurred in southern Alberta in 1970–1971.

Soremouth or contagious ecthyma is a common viral disease of domestic sheep and goats around the world. It also occurs in humans (called "orf") resulting in crusty lesions on the hands and lower arms. In Alberta, it is fairly common in bighorn sheep (Figure 7.1; Blood, 1971; Samuel *et al.*, 1975). It has been reported from mountain goats of British Columbia and Alaska. Outbreaks in Alberta and

Figure 7.1
Severe case of soremouth (contagious ecthyma) in a bighorn sheep.
Photo by W.M. Samuel.

elsewhere have occurred in bighorn sheep, mountain goats, muskoxen and Dall's sheep. Transmission between animals is by direct contact. The prevailing belief is that soremouth is a stress-precipitated disease reflecting crowding through high population levels or disruption of the habitat. Little factual information is available.

Bacterial Example

Pasteurellosis is an infectious bacterial disease of wild and domestic animals. A pasteurellosis-involved pneumonia (the principal agent is *Pasteurella haemolytica*, but *Pasteurella multocida* may also be involved), along with other agents such as lungworm and viruses, has been recognized for many years as an important, though poorly understood, component of major die-offs in bighorn sheep populations. However, thanks to recent research conducted in Alberta by Onderka and Wishart (1984, 1988) and Onderka *et al.* (1988) following a recent die-off of sheep in southwestern Alberta, and related studies elsewhere (Schwantje, 1988a, 1988b; Foreyt, 1989), we now have a better idea of how the pasteurella bacteria and lungworm operate.

A pneumonia-related die-off of bighorn sheep occurred in southeastern British Columbia in 1981. The only significant agent recovered was *Pasteurella haemolytica*. The dying sheep had mixed with a domestic sheep herd, but the pasteurella organisms probably did not originate from domestic sheep (for background information on bighorn die-offs associated with proximity to domestic livestock, see discussion below and Foreyt and Jessup, 1982; Onderka *et al.*, 1988; and Foreyt, 1989). The die-off spread into southern Alberta and northern Montana. Affected animals displayed bouts of coughing, laboured breathing, difficulty in standing or holding up the head, and nasal discharge.

A workshop was held in Cranbrook in May, 1983 (Schwantje, 1983) where bighorn sheep experts from throughout North America discussed this and other die-offs. The feeling was that multiple stress-related factors appeared to predispose bighorn sheep to pneumonia by acting on the immunity or resistance level of each sheep. Potential exacerbating factors that could have led to the die-off include contact with domestic sheep, other disease, inclement weather, harassment by man or other animals, etc.

Onderka and Wishart began research to determine the triggering mechanism that started the die-off. Because domestic sheep often are carriers of *Pasteurella* spp., they housed bighorn lambs with domestic sheep. One month later the bighorn lambs had an extensive bronchopneumonia caused by *Pasteurella haemolytica*. Foreyt (1989), in a separate similar experiment, produced acute pasteurellosis in bighorns after they had contact with domestic sheep that were carriers of *P. haemolytica*.

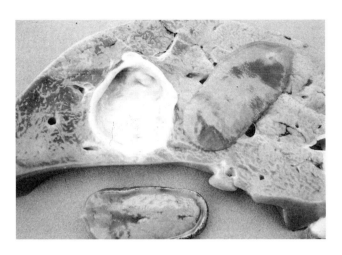

Figure 7.2
*The large American liver fluke found in the white "cyst" in the liver of a white-tailed deer.
Photo by W.M. Samuel.*

These results do not indicate that all pasteurella-related die-offs of bighorns result from contact with domestic sheep. This is because Onderka and Wishart have discovered that bighorn sheep have a serotype of *P. haemolytica* (biotype T) that is common in Alberta bighorns and less common in domestic sheep. The 1981–82 die-off was probably caused by the "bighorn" strain of *P. haemolytica*. When the bighorn strain is inoculated into domestic sheep, no disease results (Onderka *et al.*, 1988).

The strain of *P. haemolytica* (biotype A) that is common in domestic sheep killed two captive bighorn sheep within two days following inoculation (Onderka *et al.*, 1988), indicating that bighorn sheep are extremely susceptible to both the domestic livestock strain and the bighorn strain of *P. haemolytica*. It implies that managing these species in close proximity to one another is potentially a threat to bighorns.

Helminths (roundworms, flukes and tapeworms)

As with hoofed mammals in other parts of North America, the ungulates of Alberta are host to a variety of internal helminth parasites (and other disease agents) that live throughout the body (Tables 7.1 and 7.2). The roundworms or nematodes are the internal parasites most commonly found. Many (approximately 90% of those in Alberta's ungulates) have direct life cycles. That is, the parasites are transmitted directly from one animal to another. Adult worms in the mammal host lay eggs that exit with the feces. On the ground these eggs hatch and develop into small, worm-like larvae. The larvae migrate from the feces onto the surrounding vegetation where they develop to the infective stage and are swallowed accidentally by the next host while it is feeding. The adult worms live a short time in this host, usually only a few weeks, and the cycle is repeated. Obviously, the direct-life-cycle nematodes have the potential to increase their numbers significantly when host density is high.

A few nematodes have indirect cycles requiring an intermediate host such as a snail or some other invertebrate for development of the larvae to the infective stage. The famous lungworms of bighorn sheep (see next paragraph), thought by many to cause the massive die-offs we hear about from time to time, utilize very small snails as part of their life cycle. These snails are ingested accidentally by sheep during feeding on vegetation.

TABLE 7.1

COMMON AND SCIENTIFIC NAMES OF PARASITIC WORMS RECOVERED FROM HOOFED MAMMALS OF ALBERTA AND THE LOCATION OF THESE PARASITES IN THE HOST

Common Name	Scientific Name (Genus only)	Location of worm in host
Nematodes (Roundworms):		
Capillary worm	*Capillaria* spp.	Small intestine/liver
Trichostrongyle	*Cooperia* spp.	Small intestine
Lungworm	*Dictyocaulus* sp.	Bronchioles
Thread-necked worm	*Nematodirella* sp.	Small intestine
Thread-necked worm	*Nematodirus* sp.	Small intestine
Large stomach worm	*Marshallagia* sp.	Abomasum
Legworm	+*Onchocerca* sp.	Under skin
Lungworm	+*Orthostrongylus* sp.	Bronchioles
Medium stomach worm	*Ostertagia* spp.	Abomasum/Small intestine
Muscleworm	+*Parelaphostrongylus* sp.	Muscles
Lungworm	+*Protostrongylus* spp.	Lungs
Trichostrongyle	*Pseudostertagia* sp.	Abomasum
Pinworm	*Skrjabinema* spp.	Caecum
Trichostrongyle	*Teladorsagia* sp.	Abomasum
Stomach hair worm	*Trichostrongylus* spp.	Abomasum/Small intestine
Whipworm	*Trichuris* spp.	Caecum
Abdominal worm	+*Setaria* spp.	Abdominal cavity
Cestodes (Tapeworms):		
Tapeworm	+*Avitellina* sp.	Small intestine
Hydatid tapeworm	+*Echinococcus* sp.	Lung
Common tapeworm	+*Moniezia* spp.	Small intestine
Thin-necked bladderworm	+*Taenia* spp.	Liver/Lung/Muscle
Fringed tapeworm	+*Thysanosoma* sp.	Small intestine
Trematodes (Flukes):		
Large American liver fluke	+*Fascioloides* sp.	Liver
Rumen fluke	+*Paramphistomum* sp.	Rumen
Fluke	+*Zygocotyle* sp.	Caecum

* Parasites with direct life cycles

+ Parasites with indirect life cycles

Lungworms of bighorn sheep

Most bighorn sheep of Alberta have lungworms; two species are present (*Protostrongylus stilesi* and *Protostrongylus rushi*). These parasites have been incriminated in one way or another in virtually every die-off of bighorn sheep in Alberta and throughout North America for the last 50 years. *Protostrongylus stilesi* and *P. rushi* have only been reported from bighorn sheep and mountain goats, not domestic livestock. Because lungworms and pasteurella organisms are two more-or-less typical features of most sheep die-offs, the pneumonic condition is often called lungworm-pneumonia complex.

Lungworms are thought to be important to bighorn sheep primarily because: 1) they can be transmitted to the fetus *in utero* and 2) they cause extensive damage to lung tissue. Transplacental transmission of lungworm has been reported in bighorn sheep populations of Alberta. Spraker and

Hibler (1982) differentiate three types of die-off patterns in bighorn populations. Type 1 is a mass mortality affecting all animals in the population. This type of die-off is regarded as being stress-induced, and caused by bacteria or viruses. The second type is a summer loss of lambs following a Type 1 die-off. It also appears to be stress-related. The third type of die-off is a summer mortality of lambs. This type of die-off is closely tied to transplacental transmission of lungworm, but it is also possibly stress-related and depends "on reduced resistance of lambs due to stress or malnutrition" (Samson et al., 1987). Affected lambs suffer bouts of coughing, have rough, shaggy, yellowish hair coats, and are small in size and light in body weight.

An all-age Type 1 die-off occurred in the Sheep River Wildlife Sanctuary of southwestern Alberta in 1985–1986 when an estimated 60–65 bighorn sheep died (Festa-Bianchet, 1988). Stress-related factors in that die-off included harassment by man, dogs, and livestock in the form of extensive livestock grazing on bighorn winter range, road construction, and recreational use.

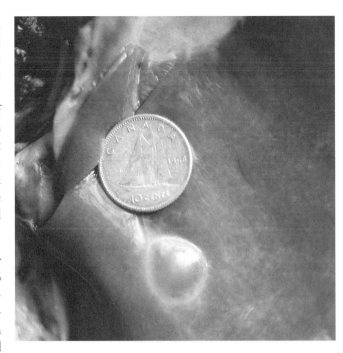

Figure 7.3
Bladderworms on the liver of a moose.
Photo by W.M. Samuel.

Festa-Bianchet suggests that the die-off was precipitated by "an increase in sheep numbers and abuse of the winter range". He also suggests that to ideally manage bighorn sheep, one has to control bighorn sheep populations (only necessary when mortality caused by predation and other natural sources is low) and protect habitat. An important question is how much stress do we, the source of most problems on the face of our planet, think that a bighorn sheep can take?

Liver fluke of deer, wapiti and moose

The large American liver fluke (*Fascioloides magna*) is one of the best known parasites of North American hoofed mammals (Figure 7.2). This is because it is large (several centimeters long), easy to see in the liver, has a broad geographic distribution in North America, and is very common particularly in white-tailed deer and wapiti. This parasite was described in Italy in 1875 after having been introduced there with American wapiti by the king of Italy in 1865.

Members of the family Cervidae, particularly wapiti and white-tailed deer, were long considered the normal or usual host for liver fluke because 1) the parasite completed its life cycle in these hosts, and 2) both hosts appeared to tolerate the parasite reasonably well. However, results of recent research in Alberta and British Columbia by Dr. Margo Pybus of the Alberta Fish and Wildlife Division suggest that wapiti and moose are susceptible to massive infections and some individuals succumb to the infection.

Liver flukes are common in deer, wapiti and moose that live in river-bottom, coastal or lake regions throughout much of North America. It is a particular nuisance along the Atlantic and Gulf coasts from the Carolinas to Texas, the Pacific Northwest (Vancouver Island, Washington, Oregon), around the Great Lakes (Minnesota, Wisconsin, Michigan, Manitoba, and Ontario), in the Rocky Mountains of British Columbia and Alberta from Calgary south into Montana, and in lake regions of the far northern forests (e.g., Saskatchewan, Quebec). In Alberta, smaller foci include Cypress Hills (Alberta-Saskatchewan border), Elk Island National Park, and a captive population of wapiti near Lac La Biche.

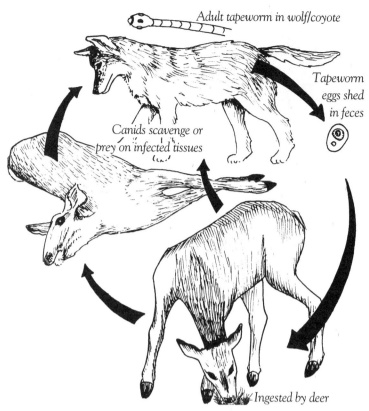

Adult tapeworm in wolf/coyote

Tapeworm eggs shed in feces

Canids scavenge or prey on infected tissues

Ingested by deer

Figure 7.4
Life cycle of liver- or muscle-inhabiting larval tapeworms transmitted to carnivores, particularly coyotes and wolves. Tapeworm eggs are shed in the feces and later, when the feces have disappeared, ingested accidentally by ungulates such as deer. Carnivores become infected by eating liver or muscle tissue with tapeworm larvae (see Figures 7.3 and 7.5) during predation or scavenging.

Adult flukes occur in fibrous capsules in the liver. The capsule walls are whitish-yellow, thick and fibrous, often filled with a brownish-black fluid. The surface of the liver is often pitted and contains white fibrous scars.

Prevalence of infection in many surveys varies considerably (from <1% to 73%) in white-tailed deer, the most studied host. Prevalence in other hosts includes: 58% (woodland caribou, Labrador), 88% (moose, Minnesota), 86% (wapiti, Alberta-British Columbia), 14% (mule deer, Alberta-British Columbia), and 37% (cattle, Texas). A total of 1.1 million of 31 million cattle livers federally inspected in the United States in 1973 were condemned due to presence of either giant liver fluke or its close relative found only in domestic livestock.

Liver flukes can become established in new areas when wild ruminant hosts are transplanted (see Samuel 1987b); thus, preventive measures and/or treatment are important areas of concern. Elimination of snails (aquatic snails are needed to complete the life cycle of this parasite) in vegetated small ponds or prevention of access to such ponds by ruminants will break the cycle. A field trial against liver flukes in wild wapiti has been completed in Alberta using a new compound called triclabendaxole.

One of the main reasons that this parasite is such a nuisance is because infection in deer/wapiti spills over into domestic sheep and cattle. Domestic sheep are very susceptible to liver fluke infection and the resulting disease is serious in them. Cattle show some resistance, but their infected livers are condemned.

In Alberta in the early 1900s, Buffalo National Park was founded near Wainwright as a refuge for plains bison brought there from Elk Island National Park, Banff, and two areas of Montana (Lothian, 1981). The Park was fenced and by the 1920s, there were 7,000 bison, numerous wapiti, moose, deer, yak (to cross with bison) and a few pronghorn. The wapiti were heavily infected with *F. magna*. Just before World War II, when the park was being transformed to the army camp it is today, 2,918 bison, 1,806 wapiti, 113 moose and 242 deer were killed because of the high levels of tuberculosis and liver flukes (Lothian, 1981). Apparently owing to this drastic decrease in host density, the parasite disappeared from that region and is no longer present in Camp Wainwright.

Some wapiti were shipped to the Cypress Hills for release (and liver flukes have recently been discovered there) and to Ontario where they became involved in a liver fluke outbreak in wapiti, bison, cattle and sheep.

Tapeworms

One of the most visible parasites in Alberta's ungulate fauna is a juvenile stage of a tapeworm found on/in the liver (Figure 7.3). The scientific name of the parasite is *Taenia hydatigena*. The young tapeworms, called bladderworms or water blisters by hunters, and "cysticerci" by parasitologists, will grow into a fairly harmless adult in the gut of a carnivore, usually a coyote, wolf or dog.

Thus, to complete the life cycle, the carnivore must eat the cysticercus-infected tissues from cervids (Figure 7.4, and see Samuel, 1988a).

Taenia hydatigena bladderworms are present in (and usually harmless for) virtually all of our deer-like ungulates in Alberta including white-tailed deer, mule deer, moose, wapiti, bighorn sheep, mountain goat, pronghorn and woodland caribou. Anywhere coyotes or wolves are found, one will find this cyst-like parasite in the livers of ungulates.

This parasite is not infective for man. In addition, freezing or cooking will kill it. The meat and the liver of infected deer are completely safe for human consumption. Bladderworms are usually only aesthetic problems that are easily removed from the liver during processing. Admittedly, a liver with numerous "cysts" may be undesirable for table use.

Figure 7.5
Muscle-inhabiting "cysts" of larval tapeworm, Taenia ovis krabbei, in heart muscle of a moose. Photo by W.M. Samuel.

It is well known that a hunter may abandon the entire deer carcass when bladderworms are encountered in the liver during the evisceration process. When a carcass is discarded and left to rot in the woods because of a harmless tapeworm cyst in the liver, not only are game laws violated, but the anti-hunting factions have some costly evidence of abuse.

A close relative of *Taenia hydatigena* is *Taenia ovis krabbei*. It lives as a young tapeworm in "cysts" about 5 mm in diameter in the musculature of moose, mule deer and caribou (Figure 7.5). It occurs in no other ungulates of Alberta. Hunters call the parasite "measles" or "blisters". The young tapeworm grows to an adult stage in the gut of carnivores such as coyotes, dogs and wolves, and the occasional bear or mountain lion.

When this parasite is discovered in the meat during the butchering process, the natural inclination is to either feed the "measly" meat to the dogs or discard it with the garbage. Neither alternative is wise because this parasite can complete its life cycle in dogs, does not infect man, and is killed by normal cooking or freezing. In addition, the cysts are easily removed during butchering. In Alberta, it occurs in small numbers in mule deer, but is very abundant in moose.

So, what are the take-home messages regarding these tapeworm parasites? Avoid feeding your dog (or allowing it to feed upon) offal from hoofed mammals unless the offal is first cooked or frozen. Also, be careful when discarding viscera, bones with some meat on them, etc. Even though these worms are usually benign infections in dogs, why infect your trusty canine companion with unwelcome tapeworms? And remember, the tapeworm cysts seen in muscle or liver of ungulates are not infective for man.

Winter Ticks

The winter tick, *Dermacentor albipictus*, is a common parasite of moose, wapiti, mule deer and white-tailed deer throughout Alberta; the moose is the primary and most susceptible host for this pest (Figure 7.6). It is found throughout the northern and western United States and southern Canada. In western Canada, it ranges north into the Yukon Territory and the Northwest Territories.

Clinical signs of tick-induced disease include loss of winter hair (first appears on neck, shoulders, and perianal region [Figure 7.7]), emaciation, loss of fear of man, weakness and death (Glines and

Samuel, 1989). These signs (seen in winter, particularly March and April) are common for moose, less common for wapiti and mule deer, and very rare for white-tailed deer. The skin of moose shows extensive rubbed areas, broken and/or lost winter hair, scabbing, and local inflammation at the point of the tick bite. Affected moose suffer from anemia, malnutrition, and loss of body heat.

Factors involved in decreasing the size of the winter tick population include cold weather, snow, fire and magpies. Snow buries the larval "seed tick" stage that is found on vegetation in the autumn waiting for a host to come along. Snow and cold kill the adult blood-engorged female tick that drops from the moose in late winter-early spring. Fire kills both these life stages. Magpies eat many blood-fed female ticks often when they are still on moose in March-April (see review by Samuel, 1987c).

Because the life cycle is so predictable, examination of a moose hide for ticks can be used to determine when the moose died. Thus, determination of the ages of ticks on moose has been used as evidence in a moose-poaching legal case (Samuel, 1988b).

Figure 7.6
Winter ticks and associated lesions on a moose.
Photo by W.M. Samuel.

TABLE 7.2

DISEASES AND PARASITES REPORTED FROM ALBERTA'S WILD UNGULATES

Common or Scientific Name	Site*	White-tailed Deer	Mule Deer	Caribou†	Wapiti (Elk)	Moose	Prong-horn	Mountain Goat	Bighorn Sheep	Bison (Buffalo)
Viral Diseases:										
Bovine viral diarrhea	LU				+	+	+			
Contagious ecthyma	MO/HO							+	+	
Chlamydial group	MT						+			
Encephalitis	BR					+	+			
Epizootic hemorrhagic disease	SC	+	+				+			
Infectious bovine rhinotracheitis	LU				+					
Parainfluenza type 3	LU				+	+	+			
Fibroma	SK		+			+				
Bacterial Diseases:										
Anthrax	MU									+
Black leg	MU					+				
Brucellosis	MT				+					+
Foot rot	SC						+			
Leptospirosis	KI					+				
Lumpy jaw	MO								+	
Pasteurellosis	LU								+	
Tuberculosis	LU		+		+	+				+
Fungal Diseases:										
Ringworm	SK		+							
Protozoa:										
Coccidia *Eimeria* spp.	SI	+	+		+			+	+	+
Sarcocystis (many spp.)	MU	+	+		+	+		+	+	+

TABLE 7.2

DISEASES AND PARASITES (continued)

Common or Scientific Name	Site*	White-tailed Deer	Mule Deer	Caribou†	Wapiti (Elk)	Moose	Prong-horn	Mountain Goat	Bighorn Sheep	Bison (Buffalo)
Nematodes (Roundworms):										
Gastrointestinal worms:										
Marshallagia marshalli	AB							+	+	
Ostertagia (6 spp.)	AB/SI	+	+		+	+	+	+	+	+
Pseudostertagia bullosa	AB						+			
Teladorsagia davtiani	AB							+	+	
Trichostrongylus spp.	AB/SI	+	+		+	+				+
Capillaria (1 sp.)	SI/LI						+	+		
Cooperia (4 spp.)	SI		+		+		+			+
Nematodirella (2 spp.)	SI		+		+	+	+			+
Nematodirus (7 spp.)	SI		+		+			+	+	+
Skrjabinema (2 spp.)	CA	+	+				+	+		
Trichuris (~4 spp.)	CA	+	+		+	+	+	+	+	
Lungworms:										
Orthostrongylus macrotis	LU	+	+		+	+	+			
Dictyocaulus viviparus	LU	+	+		+	+				+
Parasites of miscellaneous organs:										
Parelaphostrongylus odocoilei	MU		+	+				+		
Setaria (2 spp.)	AC	+	+		+	+	+			+
Onchocerca cervipedis	SC	+	+			+				
Cestodes (Tapeworms):										
Avitellina sp.	SI							+		
Echinococcus granulosus	LU		+		+	+				
Moniezia (2 spp.)	SI				+	+	+	+	+	+
Taenia hydatigena	LI	+	+		+	+	+	+	+	+
Taenia ovis krabbei	MU		+			+				
Taenia omissa	LU		+							
Thysanosoma actinioides	SI	+	+		+	+	+	+		
Trematodes (Flukes):										
Fascioloides magna	LI	+	+		+	+				
Paramphistomum sp.	R					+				
Zygocotyle lunata	CA	+			+	+				
Arthropods (External):										
Ticks:										
Dermacentor albipictus	SK	+	+	+	+	+			+	
Dermacentor andersoni	SK		+		+		+	+	+	
Otobius megnini	SK							+	+	
Insects:										
Botfly larvae										
Cephenemyia spp.	NC	+	+		+					
Chewing lice										
Tricholipeurus spp.	SK	+	+							
Bovicola spp.	SK				I					I
Sucking lice										
Solenopotes spp.	SK	+	+							

* AB = abomasum; AC = abdominal cavity; BR = brain; CA = caecum and large intestine; HO = hooves; KI = kidneys; LI = liver; LU = lungs; MO = mouth; MT = ? or many tissues; MU = muscle; NC = nasal cavity and pharyngeal region; R = rumen; SK = skin; SI = small intestine; and SC = under skin.

† There is very little information on the parasites and diseases of woodland caribou of Alberta.

Much recent discussion of the winter tick problem on Alberta's moose has centred on treating moose with a chemical to rid them of ticks. This sort of approach could best be termed a waste of time and taxpayers' money. Unlike wapiti, moose are not social animals: they tend to remain in small groups far removed from one another. Thus, it would not be feasible to capture them for treatment or to try and put a topical treatment in the environment. Actually, the best treatment is probably preventive in nature. That is, maintain their range in good condition through proper management of moose numbers so that surviving animals remain in good nutritional condition.

Figure 7.7
An Alberta "ghost" moose. This condition is induced by winter ticks that cause moose to groom and hence prematurely lose their winter hair coat. Photo by M.L. Drew.

SUMMARY

Only a few disease and parasitic agents have been reviewed here. Examples chosen include forms assumed or proven to be serious pathogens to our hoofed mammal populations. Some of the examples are probably well known to the hunting/outdoor fraternity in Alberta. A few examples of non-pathogenic parasites easily observed by the hunter during processing of the carcass were also reviewed.

8

Hunting and Harvest

*J. Brad Stelfox and
Shawn Wasel*

To many Albertans, it is not possible to think of ungulates without discussing a favourite autumn activity: sport hunting. To these recreationalists, the fall hunt is an important and anxiously awaited season. This chapter begins with a brief examination of the history of hunting, then describes Alberta's hunting community in terms of its abundance, age, gender and landbase constituency (urban vs. rural). Specific attention is paid to the causes and consequences of the reduced numbers of hunters in this province. The likelihood of hunters killing their quarry is quantified for each ungulate species and the geographic origin of the largest 20 trophy heads are mapped. For those who wish to rough score their trophies, Boone and Crockett scoring forms are provided here and in Appendix 7.

The colourful history of the outfitting and guiding community in Alberta is chronicled and recent changes in the regulation of this industry are discussed. Tables detailing numbers of hunting tags, estimated sport harvest and identity of hunters of top trophies are provided. A table comparing the "yield" of large trophies of all provinces and states concludes the chapter.

INTRODUCTION

Hunting of big game was an integral part of the lifestyle of native Indian and early European migrant communities in Alberta. Although there must have been some element of sport, the main purpose of hunting was to provide meat for sustenance, hides for clothing and shelter, and bones for tools and implements. In the mid to late 1800s, widespread exploitation of hoofed mammals by market hunters provisioned a rapidly growing human population. As agriculture and livestock practices became established, however, reliance on wild ruminants dwindled, and today only a small proportion of Albertans use game meat extensively. Reduced dependence on game meat as Albertans switched to agricultural products (grains, beef, pork, and poultry), however, did not result in expansion of game numbers. Rather, the incompatibility of wild ungulates with emerging agricultural practices led to widespread loss of habitat.

With 1) the recognition that ungulates were vulnerable to overhunting; and 2) a shift from subsistence to recreational hunting, provincial government agencies (now Alberta Fish and Wildlife Services) were established in the early 1900s to steward wildlife resources. The history and mandates of these agencies are described in Chapter 9.

Excellent historic accounts of hunting in Alberta have been published. Ondrack's (1985) *Big game hunting in Alberta* provides a thorough review of sport hunting in Alberta, which has long been recognized as a hunting paradise. Fall seasons on white-tailed deer, mule deer, wapiti, moose, pronghorn, bighorn sheep and, until recently, caribou and mountain goat, have attracted local, out-of-province and international hunters. From a trophy standpoint, Alberta has a reputation for

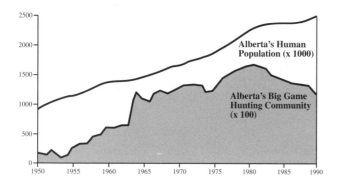

Figure 8.1

Trend in human population and big game hunting in Alberta. Size of big game hunting community based on wildlife certificate sales.

large white-tailed deer, wapiti, moose and bighorn sheep. The world-record bighorn sheep and non-typical mule deer were taken in Alberta.

ALBERTA'S HUNTERS

Hunting license sales and the estimated provincial harvest are presented in Tables 8.1 and 8.2, respectively. Although the number of hunters in Alberta generally increased with the provincial human population from the 1950s to the late 1970s, there has been a noticeable decrease since 1980 (Figure 8.1). Several explanations account for this recent downward trend, including reduced disposable incomes caused by a faltering petrochemical economy, loss of hunting tradition as fewer parents introduce their children to hunting, continued urbanization, and a growing and more vocal anti-hunting community.

Men represent the dominant (~95 percent) though apparently declining gender of Alberta's hunting community. From 1974 to 1984, women increased from 3.1 to 5.7 percent (Boxall and Smith, 1986) of all residents purchasing big game hunting certificates. One might expect that this trend has continued during the last several years, but recent studies (Todd and Lynch, 1992) indicate that women represent two and four percent, respectively, of individuals hunting wapiti and moose in 1991.

Alberta's hunting community has aged in recent decades faster than the provincial population and clearly has a problem recruiting acceptable numbers of young hunters. The proportion of hunters in the 15–19 and 20–24 year-old age-classes declined significantly from 1974 to 1984 (Boxall and Smith, 1986). When these authors compared the ages of hunters and the provincial human population, they found that individuals less than 35 years of age were under-represented in the hunting community and that the contribution of this age-class to hunting is declining (Figure 8.2).

Figure 8.2

Age of Alberta's hunting community (modified from Boxall and Smith, 1986).

Although the majority of Albertans live in large urban centres, ~60 percent of Alberta's hunting community come from rural settings or small towns (Figure 8.3). Urbanites from Edmonton, Calgary, Red Deer and Lethbridge represented ~40 percent of Alberta's resident hunters in 1984, and have declined by 8 percent since 1974 (Boxall and Smith, 1986). The importance of rural Alberta to hunting is once again emphasized. Continued urbanization of Alberta's population, and the apparent growing disinterest of young rural people for hunting (Boxall and Smith, 1986) suggest that hunting will continue to decline in the province.

In comparison to other provinces, a greater percent of Albertans hunt than residents of central Canada and British Columbia, but not as high a percent as most Maritime provinces (Figure 8.4).

Perhaps the most disturbing trend concerning hunting in Alberta today is the growing disfavour the public holds for hunters. As society's interest in non-consumptive use of wildlife grows, greater concern about the merits of sport

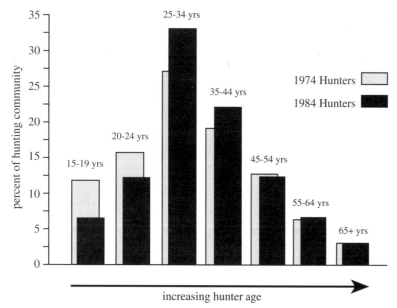

hunting has been expressed. Discontent with sport hunting has been fuelled by well-publicized incidents of unethical hunter behaviour. The legitimate sport-hunting community should be alarmed about the future of their recreation, and take strong steps to reduce hunter/landowner conflict and educate the general public about the biological value of sustained-yield recreational harvest.

Possible Consequences of the Loss of Alberta's Hunters

If hunting acceptance and involvement continues to dwindle, societies can expect to observe consequences directly related to the loss or reduction of the autumn harvest of wildlife. These consequences are diverse but most stem from increased ungulate densities as populations respond to the removal of an important autumn mortality factor, the sport hunter.

The following changes can be expected in areas where natural predators (wolves, bears, cougars) are not common.

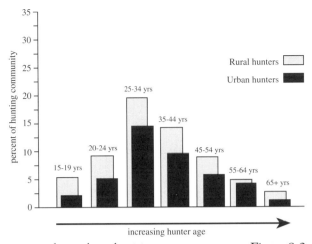

Figure 8.3
Rural and urban wildlife certificate holders by age in 1984 (modified from Boxall and Smith, 1986).

Winter Die-Offs

Ungulate populations may generally become more unstable numerically and witness more pronounced "die-offs" during winters due to poor body condition. During winters of deep snow, mortality can be severe and elicit public outcry. This outcome arises from the significant difference in forage availability and quality in spring/summer (birth season) and winter seasons (nutritional impoverishment). Put simply, ungulate habitats can support far greater numbers during the summer than during the winter. If surplus animals entering the population from birth are not offset by animals lost to predation, disease or hunting, ranges will become overstocked, forages will be overused, and loss of body condition will inevitably occur. Since healthy populations of predators are not found throughout much of Alberta, the importance of hunting as a mechanism to remove the harvestable surplus cannot be overstated. There will be winters where society will be confronted by the relative merits of killing wild ungulates by hunting rather than by starvation. Well-studied and publicized overpopulations and die-offs of ungulates occurred following removal of sport hunting or restricted hunting seasons on the Kaibab Plateau of Arizona (1920s), in Pennsylvania

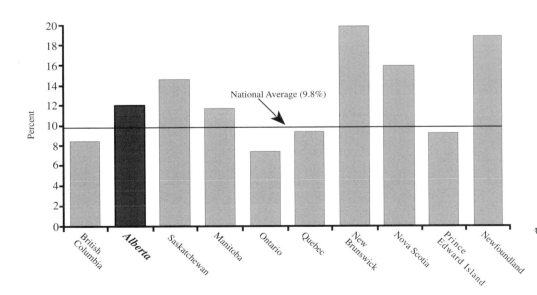

Figure 8.4
Percentage of Canadians participating in hunting wildlife in 1986 (modified from Filion et al. 1989).

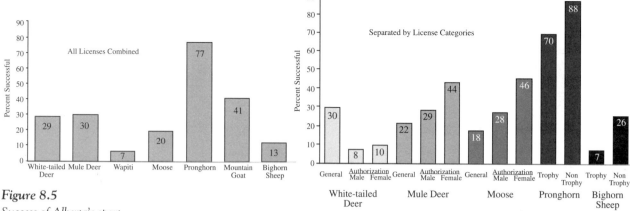

Figure 8.5

Success of Alberta's sport hunters (1985–1987).

Hunting big game in Alberta's mountains can offer a lifelong memory, complete with stunning scenery, challenging weather, long days, sore legs and seat, and, with luck, a trophy to bring home on horseback.

Photo by S. Crites.

(1920-1930s), and in Utah (1940-1950s). These scenarios emphasize the importance of hunting to maintaining a desirable balance between herd size and environmental quality.

Conflicts with Agriculturalists

Increased conflicts between agriculturalists and ungulates relating to damage to haystacks, forage crops and fences may occur. Native ungulates unable to locate suitable amounts of forage in wildlands will turn to agricultural alternatives.

As herds raid haystacks and agricultural fields, and subsequently die of starvation during cold, deep-snow winters, society will exert pressure on government agencies to provide supplementary forage. Government agencies are likely to respond by implementing translocation programs and by strategically planting forage crops and positioning hay stacks to mitigate this problem. These provisioning programs may not be successful if implemented on a crisis basis, and may only serve to place additional pressure on a limited natural food supply. The reader is directed to further discussion of ungulate depredations in Chapter 9, Management.

Conflicts with Urban-dwellers

Increased numbers of ungulates, particularly deer, may occur in urban areas. This trend will be in response to inadequate forage in rural and wilderness settings, and to fewer hunter/wildlife interactions that maintain a fear of humans. Even small woodlots in towns and cities may attract deer searching for forage.

Ungulate/Vehicle Collisions

As ungulate populations increase, particularly in areas of dense human populations, increased ungulate/vehicle collisions and associated injuries and deaths may occur. This trend may be accompanied by inflated insurance premiums for drivers living in high risk areas. Records from Strathcona County (820 km²) east of Edmonton show a steady increase in reportable vehicle collisions (>$1000 damage) involving ungulates from 88 in 1982 to ~155 in 1992 (Corporal Frank Dunn, Sherwood Park Highway Patrol, pers. comm., 1992). Most collisions involved white-tailed deer and caused ~$4,000–5,000 damage to the vehicle. These numbers are undoubtedly small in comparison to those involving minor damage and near-misses. In the Strathcona County area during this time, several injuries and two fatalities were caused by vehicle collisions involving white-tailed deer or moose.

Economic Implications

If hunting declines in Alberta, so will hunting-related expenditures. Drawing from data presented in Table 10.1, approximately 38.4 million dollars were spent by sport hunters in Alberta during 1986 (1986 dollars). To differing levels, loss or reduction of expenditures by hunters will be felt by the outfitting, taxidermy, sporting goods, travel and accommodation industries.

Managing Hunters

Alberta's hunting community, approximately 114,000 strong in 1992, is represented provincially by the Alberta Fish and Game Association. The Association serves as a political lobby for hunting, land use and conservation issues, and it funds various projects supportive of wildlife and its habitat.

Management of hunting in Alberta is the responsibility of the Alberta Fish and Wildlife Division. All of Alberta's first-time hunters must complete a hunter training course before being eligible to purchase a wildlife certificate. This program is intended to educate young hunters in the proper skills, equipment, safety and etiquette.

Hunting Success

Hunting success in Alberta (1985–1987) is provided for each species (Figure 8.5 and Table 8.3). Greatest success was experienced by those hunting pronghorn and mountain goat, while the most difficult species to take were wapiti and bighorn sheep. As indicated by tag sales during the late 1980s and early 1990s (resident and non-resident hunters combined), the most frequently hunted ungulates were white-tailed deer, mule deer and moose, followed by wapiti, pronghorn, bighorn sheep and mountain goat.

ALBERTA'S TROPHIES

Trophy Locations and Scores

Locations of the 20 highest-scoring antlers or horns in Alberta are illustrated in Figures 8.6–8.9. In addition to sport hunters curious about trophy location, these maps are of interest to the wildlife biologist, for they suggest areas where optimal habitat conditions have allowed animals to achieve their genetic maxima. Drawing from *Alberta wildlife trophies: Official records of the Alberta Fish and Game Association* (Anonymous, 1986), and updated (1992) records, the rank, year, hunter/owner, hunt location and score of Alberta's top 20 antlers or horns are described for each species in

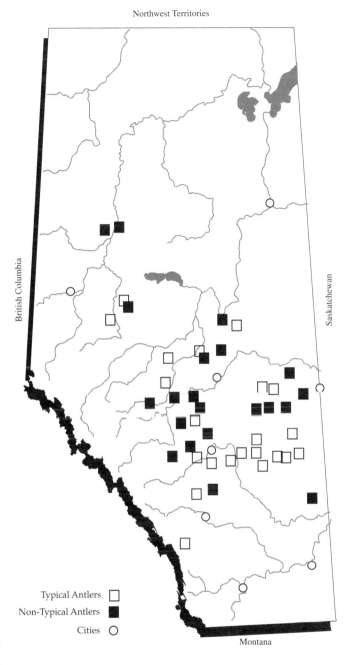

Figure 8.6
Location of Alberta's top 20 white-tailed deer antlers. Some symbols are missing because hunters have not disclosed specific trophy location.

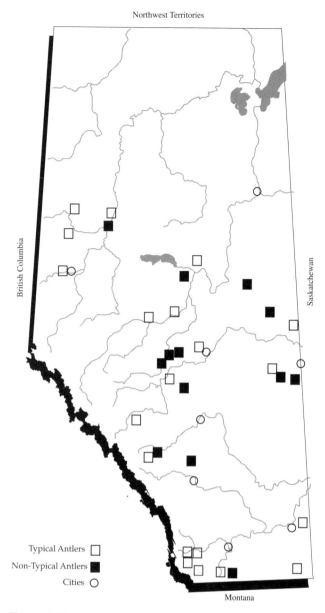

Northwest Territories

British Columbia

Saskatchewan

Typical Antlers ☐
Non-Typical Antlers ■
Cities ○

Montana

Figure 8.7
Location of Alberta's top 20 mule deer antlers. Some symbols are missing because hunters have not disclosed specific trophy location.

Tables 8.4–8.12. Scoring details for the top antlers and horns from Alberta are included in the Boone and Crockett scoring forms (Figure 8.10 and Appendix 7). To gain an appreciation of the geographic origins of large trophies in North America, and how Alberta compares, the location of the top 100 antlers and horns are presented in Table 8.13.

From the standpoint of trophies, the most encouraging provincial news concerns white-tailed deer. Their emerging prominence probably stems from a series of mild winters, the increase in agricultural fringe areas, and the compatibility of white-tailed deer with agricultural "edge" and human activities. Recent promotional campaigns have attracted nonresident hunters pursuing this wary ungulate. The Koberstein and McGarvey bucks shot in Alberta in 1991 have accelerated the "whitetail" hype significantly.

Scoring Trophies

To assist those wishing to "rough score" their trophy antlers and horns, scoring sheets for each species are included (Figure 8.10 and Appendix 7). For those hunters needing a registered scoring of their trophy antlers or horns, a list of official scorers can be obtained from the Alberta Fish and Game Association (6924–104 Street, Edmonton, 437–2342).

THE BIG GAME OUTFITTING AND GUIDING COMMUNITY

History of Outfitting

The first white men to venture into the Canadian Rockies were fur traders attempting to cross the Cordillera to establish trade with the Pacific slopes region and the Oregon country. Explorers and missionaries arrived next and were followed by men associated with the survey and construction of the Canadian Pacific Railroad (CPR) through the Canadian Rockies. The earliest outfitters in Alberta arose as a direct result of the CPR and to a lesser extent such scientific expeditions as the Geological Survey of Canada. Outfitters were employed by the CPR to pack supplies for survey expeditions searching for a suitable pass to extend the CPR line to the Pacific ocean. The railway provided easy access to the scenic Alberta Rockies, and in an effort to help subsidize the enormous construction costs, the CPR encouraged people to travel by rail into the heart of the Canadian Rockies. Scientists, alpinists, and sportsmen were lured to Banff, which provided a staging area to the wild and unexplored mountains of the west. By 1897 several large outfits had arisen in Banff to meet the increasing demands for outfitting services and to allow adventurers to explore these wildlands, which were only accessible by foot. The length of the expedition and any special equipment that was brought along dictated the number of horses, wranglers, cooks, and guides required. Pack strings often exceeded five horses per person.

Following this era of exploration, a new demand for outfitters developed for hunting and fishing expeditions. Bighorn sheep were very alluring to the wealthy hunter. Greater demand for hunting expertise encouraged many guides employed by the earliest outfitters to branch off and establish their own outfits. Jim Simpson, Jim Brewster and Bill Brewster were some of the more colourful and famous of these early big game outfitters. The boundaries of Banff and Jasper National Parks—established in 1885 and 1914, respectively—enveloped much of the better sheep-hunting country. An understaffed warden service did not permit rigid enforcement of Park borders, and many outfitters hunted wherever bighorn sheep were abundant. In 1909, however, improved warden boundary patrols, tighter hunting regulations, licensing of guides, and registration of all hunting parties helped to curtail hunting within the mountain parks.

As access to Alberta's non-mountainous game country improved, outfitting opportunities expanded to the aspen parklands and boreal forests of central and northern Alberta. The abundance of trophy moose, black bear, white-tailed deer, and grizzly bear proved to be attractive to both American and European hunters. In time, Alberta developed a reputation for record-class moose, bighorn sheep, mountain goat, white-tailed deer, grizzly bear and wapiti.

Regulation of the Outfitting Industry

As the demand for guiding and outfitting services in Alberta increased, so too did the number of licensed guides and outfitters. All that was required to begin outfitting was to pass a government examination and pay the fee. Once the license was issued, the guide could ply his service anywhere in Alberta. During those early decades when big game supply exceeded demand, this system served well, and few problems of overharvest occurred. The first legislation controlling the number of animals that could be harvested by non-resident (NR) or non-resident alien (NRA) hunters (those who most commonly hire outfitters) applied to bighorn sheep. High trophy value of this species and the great demand for guided hunts made bighorn sheep the most lucrative species to outfit for.

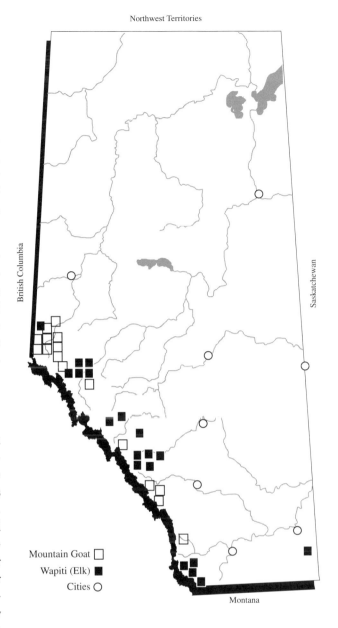

Mountain Goat □
Wapiti (Elk) ■
Cities ○

Figure 8.8
Location of Alberta's top 20 wapiti antlers and mountain goat horns. Some symbols are missing because hunters have not disclosed specific trophy location.

In 1972, bighorn sheep permits sold to NR/NRA hunters were limited to 80 rifle-hunting permits and 8 bowhunting permits. A further restriction was applied to sheep outfitters, who were required to hold $500,000 liability insurance, a fidelity bond and enough equipment to provision four hunters in the field for two weeks. Each sheep outfitter was issued four NR/NRA sheep permits that were valid for a specific area and entitled him to guide not more than 4 NR/NRA sheep hunters each season. Guiding opportunities for all other big game species remained unrestricted at this time. From 1970–1988 Alberta became well known by Danish, German, Norwegian and Swedish hunters for its outstanding black bear and moose hunting. In the same period, trophy white-tailed deer and black bear made Alberta increasingly popular among American hunters. The wapiti in Alberta have not been generally abundant, as improved hunter access associated with logging and exploration roads, intensive use of all-terrain vehicles, increasing loss of habitat,

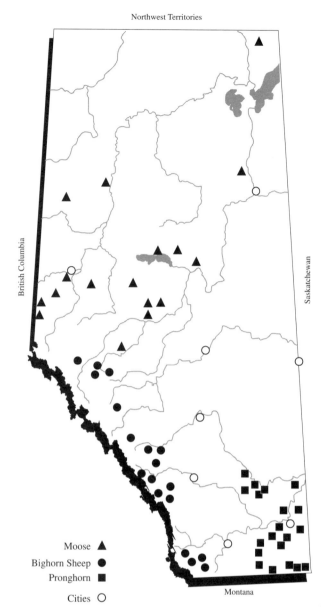

Northwest Territories

British Columbia

Saskatchewan

Montana

Moose ▲
Bighorn Sheep ●
Pronghorn ■

Cities ○

Figure 8.9
Location of Alberta's top 20 moose antlers and bighorn sheep and pronghorn horns . Some symbols are missing because hunters have not disclosed specific trophy location.

and predation by wolves have limited wapiti numbers. However, the outstanding size of bull wapiti in Alberta have made it a popular region for NR/NRA hunters seeking an exceptional trophy.

The high demand for guiding services, relatively low operating cost, and ease of entering the outfitting business saw the back-country become a crowded place during hunting seasons. In an effort to improve the quality of the outfitting/guiding industry, the Alberta Government passed legislation in 1988 requiring individuals providing outfitting services to NR/NRA hunters to have an outfitter-guide permit. Two classes of outfitter-guide permits were made available: Class S permits are required by outfitters who own NR/NRA sheep permits, and class T permits are required by outfitters who do not contract NR and NRA sheep hunters. Regulations were established to help protect clients and increase the standards of the industry. In order to be eligible for a guide-outfitter permit the candidate must have held a valid guide license for at least one year, have a valid emergency first-aid certificate, hold a fidelity bond of $10,000 or more, carry public liability insurance of $500,000 or more, and be able to provide field accommodation for clients.

As stricter controls on the licensing of outfitters emerged, the problems of controlling harvest by NR/NRA hunters and re-stricting areas where outfitters could operate were addressed. Controlling harvest of big game by NR/NRA hunters ensured hunting opportunities for residents, and geographically restrict-ing outfitters minimized conflicts between resident and nonresident hunters. Four methods of distributing allocations were initially proposed: 1) grandfathering, 2) draws, 3) self-allo-cation, and 4) point systems. Grandfathering, or the one-time granting of allocations to outfitters based on past use, was ini-tially proposed. This method was employed to distribute NR/NRA sheep permits to outfitters in 1972 and was an effective and acceptable means of distribution. The rapidly changing composition of Alberta's outfitting industry in the 1970s and 1980s made distri-bution of allocations based on grandfathering unacceptable. Grandfathering grants a public resource to a fortunate few based entirely on their historic share of the market. Furthermore, if grandfathering was allowed and allocations were transferable, those granted allocations could become instantly wealthy if their permits were sold.

Draws, which are frequently used to distribute resident hunting licenses in Alberta, would not be feasible for NR/NRA hunters because of the short notice given to successful applicants. The potential uncertainty among outfitters and their clients concerning permits was considered an unacceptable business practice and the draw system was scrapped.

A self-allocation strategy proposing that outfitters divide amongst themselves all allocations for a specific area was rejected because of the inevitable disputes it would cause among outfitters.

A fourth allocation strategy considered was a points system that would grant allocations to outfitters based on the size of the operation. It was felt however, that this system was more suitable for areas that had fixed assets such as permanent base camps and lodges, and it too was rejected.

In November, 1989, the Minister of Forestry, Lands and Wildlife announced the implementation of the new outfitter-guide policy for Alberta. One of the main goals of the policy was "the protection of the wildlife resource such that viable populations are maintained in perpetuity for the benefit of all Albertans". The new policy involved the introduction of an allocation system as a means of restricting the number of NR/NRA hunters. Ownership of allocations gives the outfitter the right to purchase specific NR/NRA hunting licenses for clients hunting with the outfitter. In order to ensure maximal hunting opportunities for residents, NR/NRA harvest in each wildlife management unit (WMU) is limited such that harvest by NR hunters will not exceed 10% of the total provincial harvest. In WMUs where residents are on draw the number of NR/NRA allocations could not exceed 10% of the allowable harvest.

Once the number of NR/NRA allocations for each WMU was established, allocations were initially made available to licensed outfitters through a sealed bid system in 1990. Remaining and additional allocations were distributed through open auctions where all licensed outfitters could bid for species-specific allocations in each WMU. Allocations distributed during sealed bid and open auctions were retained by the highest bidder until the end of the 1992 hunting season. At the close of the 1992 season all allocations were relinquished to the Minister. In August, 1992, all allocations (except bighorn sheep) were resold at an open auction. These allocations were issued for an initial five-year term with an option to renew for a second five-year term. Two types of allocations were offered for sale. Type "O" allocations can be used during the rifle and archery season, and type "B" allocations which can only be used during the archery season. Allocations not used by the outfitter for two consecutive years will be forfeited to the Minister. Retention of these allocations by outfitters are subject to payment of the annual allocation fee ($75.00 for pronghorn and mule deer, $100 for moose, $125 for white-tailed deer and $150 for wapiti). The Minister reserves the right to cancel allocations at any time for "conservation or resident use considerations".

Increasing numbers of hunters in Alberta are giving up their modern rifles in favour of primitive weapons such as bows (above) and black-powder rifles (below). These weapons generally require greater skill on behalf of the hunter, as the hunter must approach their quarry more closely to ensure a killing shot.
Photos by J. Nolan.

Economic Contribution and Resource Use

The outfitting industry remains a very significant contributor to the Alberta economy. In 1991, 2,330 NR/NRA outfitted big game hunters spent $11,676,600 in Alberta and the total economic contribution of the outfitted hunting industry in Alberta for 1991 was $23,082,400 (Exceleration Corp., 1992). There has been considerable concern voiced by resident hunters that outfitters are significantly decreasing resident hunting opportunities. Analysis of big game hunting licenses sold in Alberta in 1990 indicate that 2.7% of 229,785 licenses were purchased by NR/NRA hunters. Of the estimated 61,471 big game animals harvested in 1990, NR/NRA hunters accounted for 1.9 percent (Exceleration Corp., 1992).

The Future

Overall, the recent changes in the guiding and outfitting industry in Alberta have resulted in a transition from a subsistence lifestyle or income supplement to a big-business industry. Policy and regulation changes have resulted in the loss of small-scale operations and their replacement by large-volume full-time outfitters able to meet the requirements of the new legislation. A reduced number of licensed outfitters (April 1992,

226 licensed outfitters) has created a more manageable industry in comparison to the uncontrolled situation that existed in the past.

The arrival of more business-oriented outfitters and guides in Alberta has not resulted in the loss of the colour, character or tradition that early outfitters embodied. Their passion and respect for wild places and wild things is unmatched, and the thrill of the hunt flows strong in their veins. Tales of past hunts and future prospects still dominate their thoughts, and a wet cold day in the bush is preferred to a day spent book-keeping in the office. Like guides of old, they are driven to seek that trophy lying just beyond the next rise or around the next turn.

TABLE 8.1

HUNTING TAGS SOLD IN ALBERTA

SOURCES: Alberta Fish and Wildlife Division Annual Reports.

	White-tailed Deer	Mule Deer	Caribou	Wapiti (Elk)	Moose	Pronghorn	Mountain Goat	Bighorn Sheep	Total Tags	Certificate Sales
1950	—NA[1]—		NA	NA	NA	NA	—NA[2]—		NA	12,732
1951	—14,532—		NA	NA	NA	NA	—NA—		NA	14,340
1952	—NA—		NA	NA	NA	NA	—962—		NA	19,862
1953	—NA—		NA	NA	6,628	NA	—1,121—		NA	NA
1954	—NA—		NA	NA	8,853	NA	—1,099—		NA	NA
1955	—NA—		NA	NA	25,068	NA	—1,055—		NA	24,924
1956	—NA—		NA	NA	28,697	NA	—620—		NA	28,528
1957	—NA—		NA	NA	33,590	NA	—268—		NA	33,356
1958	—NA—		NA	NA	45,576	NA	—772—		NA	45,379
1959	—NA—		NA	NA	47,250	NA	—805—		NA	46,986
1960	—NA—		NA	NA	62,398	NA	—1,036—		NA	62,116
1961	—NA—		NA	NA	59,504	NA	—NA—		NA	59,227
1962	6,057		NA	NA	67,915	NA	—NA—		NA	67,566
1963	7,022	5,621	NA	NA	65,302	3,007	439	1,099	NA	64,809
1964	13,803	9,367	NA	NA	59,111	5,255	NA	1,055	NA	118,843
1965	23,736	32,263	120	NA	42,373	4,191	NA	NA	NA	109,593
1966	28,087	34,318	360	NA	48,756	4,519	NA	NA	NA	106,132
1967	23,294	38,835	380	NA	62,029	1,004	NA	NA	NA	124,028
1968	37,713	38,125	554	26,181	48,729	2,385	NA	NA	NA	119,978
1969	43,953	41,738	655	27,869	53,631	SC	59	1,432	129,337	117,408
1970	37,167	33,204	507	25,541	57,406	798	SC	1,519	156,142	128,708
1971	42,113	32,541	302	25,859	59,699	1,001	SC	1,582	163,097	132,451
1972	41,928	32,421	471	18,448	44,661	1,102	75	1,460	131,837	131,837
1973	42,443	33,371	414	19,189	54,353	1,080	50	1,636	152,544	132,476
1974	28,219	23,600	264	15,489	41,960	1,130	53	1,302	111,991	121,409
1975	31,871	26,842	371	15,509	41,758	1,474	55	1,910	119,776	124,804
1976	38,911	30,905	323	14,701	44,052	1,722	48	2,269	132,903	136,497
1977	50,117	39,339	347	15,786	45,258	2,721	50	2,616	156,217	150,107
1978	60,967	52,290	451	28,995	59,606	975	56	2,932	205,836	155,749
1979	70,338	57,760	121	30,990	65,482	1,159	47	3,218	228,997	161,117
1980[3]	86,525	72,800	56	29,627	63,635	2,491	42	2,564	257,740	166,191
1981[3]	74,603	58,726	SC	32,671	65,106	1,904	45	3,170	236,225	164,527
1982[3]	77,442	59,969	SC	34,009	63,971	3,426	44	3,655	242,243	162,573
1983[3]	78,049	61,663	SC	35,936	63,662	4,175	46	3,987	247,518	162,304
1984[3]	77,711	56,161	SC	35,888	53,677	8,026	36	4,415	235,914	149,838
1985[3]	80,660	60,065	SC	37,330	56,148	5,136	32	4,289	243,660	146,413
1986[3]	83,255	58,792	SC	37,107	59,893	6,781	35	4,599	250,462	151,708
1987[3]	80,661	57,568	SC	32,278	59,196	9,521	16	3,374	242,614	148,621
1988[3]	81,009	46,109	SC	26,605	58,920	6,731	SC	2,903	222,277	144,738
1989[3]	81,167	46,650	SC	25,887	56,919	5,680	SC	2,661	218,964	140,115
1990[3]	77,674	44,697	SC	22,469	48,586	5,229	SC	2,524	221,446	128,783
1991[3]	64,978	36,948	SC	18,750	36,785	1,859	SC	2,465	161,785	113,928

[1] White-tailed deer and mule deer tag sales combined for period 1950–1961

[2] Mountain goat and bighorn sheep tag sales combined for period 1950–1962

[3] Values based on General License Sales only

NA Not available

SC Season closed

Records of North American
Big Game

BOONE AND CROCKETT CLUB

Old Milwaukee Depot
250 Station Drive
Missoula, MT 59801

TYPICAL
WHITETAIL AND COUES' DEER

Kind of Deer __Whitetail__

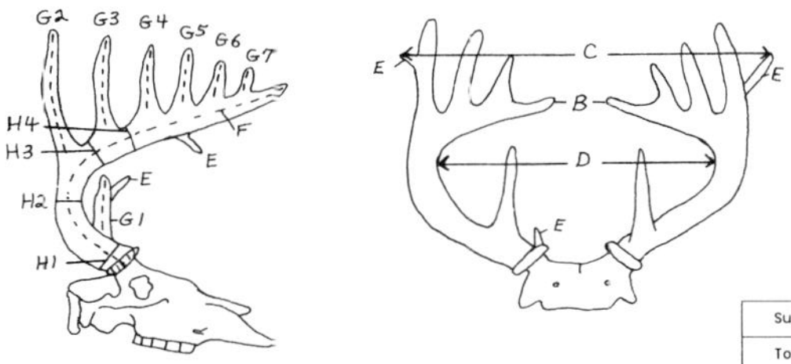

Minimum Score: Awards All-time
Whitetail   160   170
Coues'   100   110

DETAIL OF POINT MEASUREMENT

	Abnormal Points	
	Right Antler	Left Antler
Subtotals		
Total to E.		

	Column 1 Spread Credit	Column 2 Right Antler	Column 3 Left Antler	Column 4 Difference
A. No. Points on Right Antler				
No. Points on Left Antler				
B. Tip to Tip Spread	20⁴⁄₈			
C. Greatest Spread	24⁷⁄₈			
D. Inside Spread of Main Beams (Credit May Equal But Not Exceed Longer Antler)	22⁵⁄₈			
E. Total of Lengths of Abnormal Points				
F. Length of Main Beam		24³⁄₈	25¹⁄₈	6⁄₈
G-1. Length of First Point, If Present		7¹⁄₈	6¹⁄₈	1
G-2. Length of Second Point		12⁴⁄₈	13	4⁄₈
G-3. Length of Third Point		11²⁄₈	11³⁄₈	¹⁄₈
G-4. Length of Fourth Point, If Present		8⁴⁄₈	8³⁄₈	¹⁄₈
G-5. Length of Fifth Point, If Present		2⁶⁄₈	3⁶⁄₈	1
G-6. Length of Sixth Point, If Present		–	–	–
G-7. Length of Seventh Point, If Present		–	–	–
H-1. Circumference at Smallest Place Between Burr and First Point		5	5	–
H-2. Circumference at Smallest Place Between First and Second Points		4²⁄₈	4²⁄₈	–
H-3. Circumference at Smallest Place Between Second and Third Points		4⁵⁄₈	4⁴⁄₈	¹⁄₈
H-4. Circumference at Smallest Place Between Third and Fourth Points		4⁶⁄₈	4⁷⁄₈	⁷⁄₈
TOTALS		85¹⁄₈	86³⁄₈	3⁶⁄₈

Column 1	22⁵⁄₈
ADD Column 2	85¹⁄₈
Column 3	86³⁄₈
Subtotal	194⁴⁄₈
SUBTRACT Column 4	3⁶⁄₈
FINAL SCORE	190³⁄₈

Exact Locality Where Killed:

Date Killed: By Whom Killed:

Present Owner:

Owner's Address:

Guide's Name and Address:

Remarks: (Mention Any Abnormalities or Unique Qualities)

SEE OTHER SIDE FOR INSTRUCTIONS

I certify that I have measured this trophy on _____ 19___
at (address) _____ City _____ State _____
and that these measurements and data are, to the best of my knowledge and belief, made in
accordance with the instructions given.

Witness: _____   Signature: _____
                           B&C OFFICIAL MEASURER

B&C OFFICIAL MEASURER   I.D. Number

INSTRUCTIONS FOR MEASURING TYPICAL WHITETAIL AND COUES' DEER

All measurements must be made with a 1/4-inch wide flexible steel tape to the nearest one-eighth of an inch. Wherever it is necessary to change direction of measurement, mark a control point and swing tape at this point. (Note: A flexible steel cable can be used to measure points and main beams only.) Enter fractional figures in eighths, without reduction. Official measurements cannot be taken until the antlers have air dried for at least 60 days after the animal was killed.

A. Number of Points on Each Antler: To be counted a point, the projection must be at least one inch long, with the length exceeding width at one inch or more of length. All points are measured from tip of point to nearest edge of beam as illustrated. Beam tip is counted as a point but not measured as a point.

B. Tip to Tip Spread is measured between tips of main beams.

C. Greatest Spread is measured between perpendiculars at a right angle to the center line of the skull at widest part, whether across main beams or points.

D. Inside Spread of Main Beams is measured at a right angle to the center line of the skull at widest point between main beams. Enter this measurement again as the Spread Credit if it is less than or equal to the length of the longer antler; if greater, enter longer antler length for Spread Credit.

E. Total of Lengths of all Abnormal Points: Abnormal Points are those non-typical in location (such as points originating from a point) or from bottom or sides of main beam) or extra points beyond the normal pattern of points. Measure in usual manner and enter in appropriate blanks.

F. Length of Main Beam is measured from lowest outside edge of burr over outer curve to the most distant point of what is, or appears to be, the main beam. The point of beginning is the center of the burr where the beam centerline along the outer curve of the beam intersects the burr, then following generally the line of the illustration.

G-1-2-3-4-5-6-7. Length of Normal Points: Normal points project from the top of the main beam. They are measured from nearest edge of main beam over outer curve to tip. Lay the tape along the outer curve of the beam so that the top edge of the tape coincides with the top edge of the beam on both sides of the point to determine the baseline for point measurements. Record point lengths in appropriate blanks.

H-1-2-3-4. Circumferences are taken as detailed for each measurement. If brow point is missing, take H-1 and H-2 at smallest place between burr and G-2. If G-4 is missing, take H-4 halfway between G-3 and tip of main beam.

FAIR CHASE STATEMENT FOR ALL HUNTER-TAKEN TROPHIES

FAIR CHASE, as defined by the Boone and Crockett Club, is the ethical, sportsmanlike and lawful pursuit and taking of any free-ranging wild game animal in a manner that does not give the hunter an improper advantage over such game animals. Use of any of the following methods in the taking of game shall be deemed UNFAIR CHASE and unsportsmanlike:

I.   Spotting or herding game from the air, followed by landing in its vicinity for the purpose of pursuit and shooting;

II. Herding, pursuing, or shooting game from any motorboat or motor vehicle;

III. Use of electronic devices for attracting, locating, or observing game, or for guiding the hunter to such game;

IV. Hunting game confined by artificial barriers, including escape-proof fenced enclosures, or hunting game transplanted solely for the purpose of commercial shooting;

V.   Taking of game in a manner not in full compliance with the game laws or regulations of the federal government or of any state, province, territory, or tribal council on reservations or tribal lands;

VI. Or as may otherwise be deemed unfair or unsportsmanlike by the Executive Committee of the Boone and Crockett Club.

I certify that the trophy scored on this chart was taken in FAIR CHASE as defined above by the Boone and Crockett Club. In signing this statement, I understand that if this entry is found to be fraudulent, it will not be accepted into the Awards Program and all of my prior entries are subject to deletion from future editions of Records of North American Big Game and future entries may not be accepted.

Date: _____   Signature of Hunter: _____
                   (Have signature notarized by a Notary Public.)

Figure 8.10

An example of the Boone and Crockett scoring forms.
See Appendix 7 for the complete set for Alberta's ungulates.

TABLE 8.2

ESTIMATED PROVINCIAL SPORT HARVEST[1]

REFERENCES

General
Schneider, 1983; Ondrack, 1985; Stelfox et al., 1991; Alberta Fish and Wildlife annual reports.

White-tailed Deer
Armstrong, 1966; Schurman and Hall, 1976–1977

Mule Deer
Armstrong, 1966; Schurman, 1977, 1978, 1979; Schurman and Hall, 1976; Anonymous, 1989

Caribou
Burgess, 1970; Edmonds, 1986

Wapiti
Schurman, 1979; Gunson, 1987

Moose
Anonymous (in prep.)

Pronghorn
Mitchell, 1965; Wishart and Hall, 1967; Wishart, 1969; Barrett, 1970–1973; Hofman, 1974; Schurman, 1976- 1979; Schurman and Hall, 1976; Anonymous, 1990

Mountain Goat
Quadvlieg, Gunderson, and Cook, 1973

Bighorn Sheep
Wishart, 1968; Quadvlieg, Gunderson, and Cook, 1973; Schurman and Hall, 1976; Schurman, 1976

Year	White-tailed Deer[2]	Mule Deer[2]	Caribou	Wapiti (Elk)	Moose	Pronghorn	Mountain Goat	Bighorn Sheep[3]
1906	—NA—		NA	NA	NA	NA	NA	NA
1907	—59—		NA	SC	14	49	NA	NA
1908	—125—		NA	SC	37	45	NA	NA
1909	—299—		5	SC	86	89	38	40
1910	—540—		8	SC	184	126	46	54
1911	—619—		30	SC	305	101	56	49
1912	—768—		40	SC	425	105	58	90
1913	—908—		56	SC	865	119	42	65
1914	—1,388—		78	SC	1,335	SC	61	78
1915	—692—		34	SC	1,116	SC	40	110
1916	—560—		28	SC	849	SC	26	83
1917	—705—		43	SC	1,026	SC	37	57
1918	—828—		45	SC	900	SC	43	76
1919	—851—		52	SC	974	SC	33	77
1920	—1,047—		55	SC	1,080	SC	35	76
1921	—1,120—		68	SC	1,018	SC	47	108
1922	—1,180—		~40	SC	913	SC	44	92
1923	—1,083—		~40	SC	816	SC	41	61
1924	—1,541—		~40	SC	1,031	SC	42	62
1925	—NA—		~40	SC	~1,000	SC	NA	NA
1926	—NA—		~40	SC	NA	SC	NA	NA
1927	—NA—		~40	SC	NA	SC	NA	NA
1928	—NA—		~40	SC	NA	SC	NA	NA
1929	—season closed—		~40	SC	NA	SC	NA	NA
1930	~500	2,931	~40	SC	2,434	SC	NA	NA
1931	~500	NA	~40	SC	2,599	SC	NA	NA
1932	~500	NA	~40	SC	NA	SC	NA	NA
1933	~500	NA	~40	SC	NA	SC	NA	NA
1934	~500	NA	~40	NA	NA	NA	NA	NA
1935	~500	NA	~40	NA	NA	NA	NA	NA
1936	~500	NA	~40	NA	NA	NA	NA	NA
1937	~500	NA	~40	NA	NA	243	NA	NA
1938	~500	NA	~40	NA	NA	161	NA	NA
1939	~500	NA	~40	NA	NA	SC	NA	NA
1940	~700	NA	~40	NA	NA	NA	NA	NA
1941	~700	NA	~40	NA	NA	NA	NA	NA
1942	~700	NA	~40	NA	NA	NA	NA	NA
1943	~700	NA	~40	NA	NA	NA	NA	NA
1944	~700	NA	NA	NA	NA	NA	NA	NA
1945	~700	NA	NA	NA	NA	NA	NA	NA
1946	~700	NA	NA	NA	NA	NA	NA	NA
1947	~700	NA	NA	NA	NA	NA	NA	NA
1948	~700	NA	SC	NA	NA	NA	NA	NA
1949	~700	NA	SC	NA	NA	1,036	NA	NA
1950	~1,000	NA	40	1,578	NA	SC	150	190
1951	~1,000	NA	NA	NA	NA	110	90	110
1952	2,940	NA	4	940	2,740	SC	82	140
1953	~1,000	NA	10	1,060	514	SC	110	90
1954	~1,000	NA	20	2,295	684	SC	167	140
1955	4,572	NA	17	2,312	5,540	SC	128	144
1956	~1,000	NA	9	~1,200	2,173	1,923	233	70
1957	~1,000	NA	7	~4,300	2,554	2,178	116	NA
1958	3,218	NA	12	2,343	3,538	2,094	157	NA
1959	3,274	NA	16	2,717	3,496	SC	210	NA
1960	4,585	NA	25	2,050	4,465	1,440	225	NA
1961	3,543	NA	80	3,268	4,486	2,169	188	215
1962	3,920	NA	30	~1,800	5,129	2,308	258	216
1963	2,996	10,957	35	5,581	4,975	2,422	254	237
1964	3,500	NA	13	~5,000	4,527	4,308	211	223
1965	6,000	7,500	63	~4,600	3,313	3,170	194	228
1966	6,320	7,731	76	~4,000	9,483	3,478	195	376
1967	8,000	NA	NA	~3,500	7,427	496	126	335
1968	9,500	12,614	100	4,918	17,318	955	85	281
1969	11,000	10,818	NA	3,834	20,161	SC	55	269

TABLE 8.2

ESTIMATED PROVINCIAL SPORT HARVEST (continued)

	White-tailed[2] Deer	Mule[2] Deer	Caribou	Wapiti (Elk)	Moose	Pronghorn	Mountain Goat	Bighorn[3] Sheep
1970	9,000	NA	NA	~3,200	13,686	481	SC	201
1971	10,000	NA	26	~2,600	14,291	628	SC	199
1972	10,500	NA	46	2,156	10,764	665	22	215
1973	11,000	10,957	24	2,014	12,948	798	14	223
1974	4,356	3,594	21	1,600	7,432	739	13	196
1975	5,912	5,097	20	1,600	8,488	1,122	29	323
1976	8,100	7,154	24	1,400	9,339	1,260	29	286
1977	11,000	NA	20	1,415	10,547	1,995	16	308
1978	13,000	12,920	NA	1,645	14,387	674	23	315
1979	28,900	13,000	9	~1,500	12,930	914	24	293
1980	NA	NA	SC	1,457	14,200	1,935	24	419
1981	NA	NA	SC	1,357	14,846	2,364	32	347
1982	17,000	NA	SC	1,899	14,506	2,640	23	500
1983	NA	NA	SC	1,803	14,410	3,309	26	476
1984	24,542	15,783	SC	2,726	8,622	6,757	10	649
1985	20,210	17,837	SC	3,104	9,839	3,950	11	482
1986	24,678	15,728	SC	2,843	14,151	4,735	24	513
1987	22,891	16,230	SC	1,810	14,110	7,783	13	473
1988	27,769	13,755	SC	1,667	14,371	4,487	SC	314
1989	28,331	14,506	SC	1,944	13,233	4,075	SC	271
1990	26,847	15,409	SC	2,011	11,796	3,658	SC	278
1991	29,887	14,386	SC	2,125	10,463	1,266	SC	306

SC – Season Closed, NA – Data Not Available

[1] These values are estimates of numbers of animals killed by sport hunters (resident and non-resident). They do not include mortality arising from bullet wounding, poaching or other causes of death. There are no economical techniques for estimating sport harvest During the 1950s and 1960s, hunter check stations were used to get a sample of success. These values were then extrapolated to the total number of hunters (determined by hunting tag sales) to estimate provincial harvest. Check stations have been largely replaced by telephone surveys made by either Alberta Fish and Wildlife Division or the Alberta Fish and Game Association. These surveys are comparatively economical, but suffer from low sample size and human qualities like boastfulness and loss of memory.

[2] White-tailed deer and mule deer harvest combined for period 1906–1929

[3] Harvest of bighorn sheep after 1965 includes non-trophy individuals

TABLE 8.3

HUNTING SUCCESS AND HUNT CHARACTERISTICS (1985–1990) IN ALBERTA

Sources: Alberta Fish and Wildlife Division Annual reports

Species	1985	1986	1987	1988	1989	1990	Average
Wapiti (all permits combined)							
Percent Successful	8.0	9.0	6.0	6.0	7.0	9.0	7.5
Mean Hunting Days/Hunter	5.3	5.5	6.0	7.7	7.7	7.5	6.6
Number Hunter Days/Animal	57.7	77.6	115.5	102.6	84.0	65.6	83.8
Moose (all permits combined)							
Percent Successful	16.0	25.0	22.0	22.0	22.0	22.0	21.5
Mean Hunting Days/Hunter	5.2	5.4	5.5	7.7	7.3	7.3	6.4
Number Hunter Days/Animal	30.5	28.4	33.6	28.2	28.3	27.6	29.4
Pronghorn (all permits combined)							
Percent Successful	83.0	69.0	76.0	67.0	72.0	69.0	72.7
Mean Hunting Days/Hunter	1.9	2.0	2.0	1.8	1.8	1.8	1.9
Number Hunter Days/Animal	2.1	2.4	2.6	2.1	2.2	2.3	2.3
Mountain Goat							
Percent Successful	NA	73.0	81.0	no season	no season	no season	77.0
Mean Hunting Days/Hunter	NA	5.7	3.8	no season	no season	no season	4.8
Number Hunter Days/Animal	NA	7.6	4.5	no season	no season	no season	6.1
Bighorn Sheep (Trophy)							
Percent Successful	7.0	7.0	8.0	8.0	8.0	8.0	7.7
Mean Hunting Days/Hunter	5.5	5.6	5.9	6.2	8.8	7.8	6.6
Number Hunter Days/Animal	72.1	77.5	91.5	92.5	98.7	78.3	85.1
Bighorn Sheep (Non-Trophy)							
Percent Successful	38.0	23.0	30.0	27.0	31.0	28.0	29.5
Mean Hunting Days/Hunter	4.0	4.0	3.9	4.6	4.1	3.5	4.0
Number Hunter Days/Animal	10.7	11.1	9.1	11.2	8.8	8.4	9.9

TABLE 8.4

ALBERTA'S TOP 20 WHITE-TAILED DEER TYPICAL ANTLERS

Sources: Alberta wildlife trophies. Official records of the Alberta Fish and Game Association *(Anonymous, 1986), Records of North American big game (Boone and Crockett, 1988)*, and *Boone and Crockett Club's 21st big game awards (Sitton and Reneau, 1992)*

Rank	Year	Hunter/Owner	Location of Hunt	Score
1	1967	Stephen Jansen	Beaverdam Creek	202 6/8
2	1991	Don McGarvey	Edmonton	199 5/8
3	?	Morris Kimball*	Alberta	198 4/8
4	1969	Eugene Boll	Buffalo Lake	190 5/8
5	1984	Glen Davis	Westlock	190 3/8
6	1977	Norman Salminen	Czar	188 4/8
7	1986	Colin Letawsky	Vermilion	184 7/8
8	1988	Gregory Graff	Paddle River	184 5/8
9	1984	Dave Baker*	Sylvan Lake	184 0/8
10	1986	Kevin Scheeler*	WMU 230	183 7/8
11	1985	Albert Huber*	Sunset House	183 3/8
12	1966	Ovar Uggen (Pick-Up)	Red Deer River	183 0/8
13	1990	Dennis Urban	Evansburg	182 5/8
14	1972	Robert Hebert*	Pine Lake	182 3/8
15	1990	Alan Bell	Czar	182 1/8
16	1989	Dave Seitz	Inisfree	181 7/8
17	1977	Robert Crosby	Pine Lake	181 4/8
18	1985	Lorne Napier (Pick-Up)*	High Prairie	181 2/8
19	1980	Bob Trefiak*	Alberta	181 1/8
20	1962	Archie Smith	Stettler	180 7/8
20	1981	Norman Steinwand	Castor	180 7/8

*Not entered in Boone and Crockett Records of North American Big Game *(1988)*

TABLE 8.5

ALBERTA'S TOP 20 WHITE-TAILED DEER NON-TYPICAL ANTLERS

Sources: Alberta wildlife trophies. Official records of the Alberta Fish and Game Association *(Anonymous, 1986), Records of North American big game (Boone and Crockett, 1988)*, and *Boone and Crockett Club's 21st big game awards (Sitton and Reneau, 1992)*

Rank	Year	Hunter/Owner	Location of Hunt	Score
1	1991	Neil Morin	Whitemud Creek	279 6/8
2	1976	Doug Klinger	Hardisty	277 5/8
3	1984	Jerry Froma	Barrhead	267 7/8
4	1973	Leo Eklund	Pigeon Lake	255 4/8
5	1989	David Rogers (Pick-Up)	Drayton Valley	244 1/8
6	1984	Dean Dwernychuk	East Cochrane	241 1/8
7	1990	Doug Fossheim	Edson	239 5/8
8	1973	Jim Niwa	Acadia Valley	233 2/8
9	1986	Harry Hueppelsheuser	Winfield	232 1/8
10	1990	Richard Nelson	Provost	230 7/8
11	1973	Del Johnson	Red Deer	230 6/8
12	?	Lloyd McMahon*	Alberta	230 4/8
13	?	Murray Gibbs*	Hardisty	225 5/8
14	1964	Russell Thornberry	Edgerton	222 5/8
15	1984	Robert Dickson	High Prairie River	221 6/8
16	1970	Reg Dean*	Caroline	219 2/8
16	1970	Hank Stainbrook*	Caroline	219 2/8
18	?	Kim Kimball*	Edgerton	218 5/8
19	1990	Craig Miller	Flagstaff	217 5/8
20	1979	Harold Roth*	Leslieville	217 0/8

*Not entered in Boone and Crockett Records of North American Big Game *(1988)*

TABLE 8.6

ALBERTA'S TOP 20 MULE DEER TYPICAL ANTLERS

Sources: Alberta wildlife trophies. Official records of the Alberta Fish and Game Association *(Anonymous, 1986), Records of North American big game (Boone and Crockett, 1988)*, and *Boone and Crockett Club's 21st big game awards (Sitton and Reneau, 1992)*

Rank	Year	Hunter/Owner	Location of Hunt	Score
1	1981	Duncan Baldie	Medicine Hat	199 4/8
2	1960	Charles Lundgard	Hines Creek	198 6/8
3	1983	Orin Alsager*	Battle River	195 2/8
4	1988	Gerald Carter	Peace River	194 5/8
5	1989	Jeff Reichert	Teepee Creek	193 6/8
6	1976	Malcolm Wynne	Alberta	193 4/8
7	1980	Scott Roberts	Devon	193 1/8
8	1985	Gavin Craig	Webley	193 0/8
9	1930	George Cairns	Blind Canyon	192 6/8
10	?	Ryan Magnussen	Burnt Timber	192 0/8
11	1977	Bruno Dams	Judy Creek	191 7/8
12	1962	Gordon Bisgrove	?	191 2/8
13	1983	Metro Eliuk	Buck Lake	190 7/8
14	1958	George Griffiths	Milk River	189 7/8
15	1990	R.W. Sinclair	WMU 204	189 5/8
16	1989	Randy Norton	Fort Assiniboine	189 4/8
17	1984	Larry Scriba	Wanham	189 2/8
18	1940	John Kropinak	Pincher Creek	189 0/8
19	1958	George Cairns	Yarrow Creek	188 4/8
19	1989	Jim Kent	?	188 4/8

*Not entered in Boone and Crockett Records of North American Big Game *(1988)*

TABLE 8.7

ALBERTA'S TOP 20 MULE DEER NON-TYPICAL ANTLERS

Sources: Alberta wildlife trophies. Official records of the Alberta Fish and Game Association *(Anonymous, 1986), Records of North American big game (Boone and Crockett, 1988)*, and *Boone and Crockett Club's 21st big game awards (Sitton and Reneau, 1992)*

Rank	Year	Hunter/Owner	Location of Hunt	Score
1	1926	Ed Broder	Chip Lake	355 2/8
2	1960	Philip Pearman*	Rimbey	272 7/8
3	?	Derold Erickson*	Amisk	262 3/8
4	1930	Otto Schmalzbauer*	Maloy	254 4/8
5	?	Jack Frey*	Alberta	250 2/8
6	1941	Eric Westergreen	Waterton Park	247 5/8
7	1945	Julius Hagen	Lac LaBiche	245 2/8
8	?	Darren Larose	Rocky Mtn. House	244 7/8
8	?	Jim Boland*	Alberta	244 7/8
10	1930	R.W.H. Eben - Ebenau	Slave River	243 5/8
11	1990	Glen Sawchuk	Virginia Hills	242 5/8
12	1963	Mel Johnson	Rumsey	238 6/8
13	1987	Rick MacDonald	WMU 148	235 6/8
14	1956	James Tauh	Viking	231 7/8
15	1984	Terry Rehaume	Rat Creek	230 5/8
16	?	Ted Baier	P200	229 7/8
17	1961	Gordon Cole	Milk River	228 0/8
18	1951	George Pitman	Alberta	226 6/8
19	1932	Ray McLaughlin	Carrot Creek	225 5/8
20	1966	M. Karbonik	?	225 4/8

*Not entered in Boone and Crockett Records of North American Big Game *(1988)*

TABLE 8.8

ALBERTA'S TOP 20 WAPITI (ELK) ANTLERS AS OF 1990

Sources: Alberta wildlife trophies. Official records of the Alberta Fish and Game Association (Anonymous, 1986), Records of North American big game (Boone and Crockett, 1988), and Boone and Crockett Club's 21st big game awards (Sitton and Reneau, 1992)

Rank	Year	Hunter/Owner	Location of Hunt	Score
1	1977	Clarence Brown	Panther River	419 6/8
2	1971	Bruce Hale	Muddy Water River	418 0/8
3	1946	Henry Folkman	Red Deer River	402 5/8
4	?	Ray Hindmarsh	Berlin	401 7/8
5	1963	Ray Hindmarsh	Rock Lake	400 7/8
6	1952	Ralph A. Fry	Ram River	399 2/8
7	?	Ray Hindmarsh	Beck Lake	399 0/8
8	?	Monty Adams	Waterton Park	398 0/8
8	1979	Pat Adams	Pincher Creek	398 0/8
10	1968	Harold R. Vaughn	Rock Lake	396 1/8
11	1938	George Brown (Pick-Up)	Panther River	394 2/8
11	1976	Roy Crawford	Granbirn Gap	394 2/8
13	1952	Allan Foster	Waterton Park	393 2/8
14	1986	Joe A. Riviera	Cut Off Creek	393 1/8
15	?	Ray Hindmarsh	Rock Lake	393 0/8
16	1955	Bill Brooks	Panther River	392 5/8
17	1955	Bob Dial	Clearwater	390 6/8
18	1986	Doug Wolson	Sundre	390 1/8
19	1970	Doug Belyea	Yarrow Creek	387 5/8
20	1977	Leonard L. Hengen	Panther River	386 5/8

* Not entered in Boone and Crockett Records of North American Big Game (1988)

TABLE 8.9

ALBERTA'S TOP 20 CANADA MOOSE ANTLERS

Sources: Alberta wildlife trophies. Official records of the Alberta Fish and Game Association (Anonymous, 1986), Records of North American big game (Boone and Crockett, 1988), and Boone and Crockett Club's 21st big game awards (Sitton and Reneau, 1992).

Rank	Year	Hunter/Owner	Location of Hunt	Score
1	1978	Tim Harbridge	Whitecourt	226 7/8
2	1960	Carl J. Buchanan	Driftwood River	225 0/8
3	?	Gordon Klebe*	Ft. McMurray	224 0/8
4	1947	Manuel Dominguez	Clearwater River	222 0/8
5	1984	Bob Bugera*	Whitecourt	220 7/8
6	1977	Frank Baldwin	Firebag River	217 2/8
7	1986	Ed Sikorski	Slave Lake	217 0/8
8	?	Gordon Klebe*	Ft. McMurray	215 5/8
9	1960	Russell Watts*	Fox Creek	215 3/8
9	1971	Artie G. Brown	Latornell River	215 3/8
11	1988	Nick Denecky	Manning	215 0/8
12	1986	Duane Haub	WMU 518	214 6/8
12	1956	Karl Weber	Narraway River	214 6/8
14	1975	Al Baird	Hines Creek	213 0/8
15	1966	O. Neilson*	Alberta	212 6/8
16	1937	R.W.H. Eben-Ebenau	Slave Lake	212 5/8
17	1968	Heino Moora*	Whitecourt	211 0/8
17	1972	Lester C. Hearn	Grande Prairie	211 0/8
19	1967	H. Wiese*	Edson	210 4/8
20	1964	R.V.D. Goltz	Sheep Creek	210 1/8

* Not entered in Boone and Crockett Records of North American Big Game (1988)

TABLE 8.10

ALBERTA'S TOP 20 PRONGHORN HORNS

Sources: Alberta wildlife trophies. Official records of the Alberta Fish and Game Association (Anonymous, 1986), Records of North American big game (Boone and Crockett, 1988), and Boone and Crockett Club's 21st big game awards (Sitton and Reneau, 1992)

Rank	Year	Hunter/Owner	Location of Hunt	Score
1	1913	S. Prescott Fay	Brooks	86 2/8
2	1964	Oliver Ost	Seven Persons	85 6/8
3	1964	H.M. Stephens*	Bow City	85 2/8
3	1987	Bill McKenzie	?	85 2/8
5	1988	Vern McIntosh	Brooks	84 6/8
5	1964	J.E. Edwards*	Jenner	84 6/8
7	1990	Cameron Owen	Cutbank Creek	84 4/8
8	1966	G. Vandervalk	Milk River	84 0/8
9	1988	Brian Gathercole	Foremost	83 4/8
9	1983	Robert Romnek*	Brooks	83 4/8
9	1989	Ralph Cervo	Wildhorse	83 4/8
12	1975	Dennis Andrews	Rolling Hills	83 2/8
12	1975	Roger H. Stone	Medicine Hat	83 2/8
14	1989	Rae Cervo	B.G.Z. 8	83 0/8
14	1979	Allan Brown*	Empress	83 0/8
16	1975	Dennis Deboer	Medicine Hat	82 6/8
16	1975	Dennis Andrews	Medicine Hat	82 6/8
18	1963	N. Mandryk	Medicine Hat	82 4/8
18	1975	N. Dale Lucas*	Alberta	82 4/8
18	1977	Ken Meredith*	Etzicom	82 4/8
18	1977	Randy Collins*	Nemiscan	82 4/8

* Not entered in Boone and Crockett Records of North American Big Game (1988)

TABLE 8.11

ALBERTA'S TOP 20 MOUNTAIN GOAT HORNS

Sources: Alberta wildlife trophies. Official records of the Alberta Fish and Game Association (Anonymous, 1986), Records of North American big game (Boone and Crockett, 1988), and Boone and Crockett Club's 21st big game awards (Sitton and Reneau, 1992)

Rank	Year	Hunter/Owner	Location of Hunt	Score
1	1907	Indian; L.K. Luxton, owner	Bow Summit	54 0/8
2	1962	Dick Dollman*	Sulphur Mountain	52 0/8
3	1967	Russel A. Fisher	Sheep Creek	51 2/8
3	1937	Justus Von Lengerke	Hard Scrabble Pass	51 2/8
5	1942	Walter B. McClurkan	Brazeau River	50 4/8
5	1965	Terry Thrift, Jr.	Smoky River	50 4/8
7	?	Bob Mascarin	Alberta	49 4/8
8	1961	Jim Kerr	Mt. Hamell	49 2/8
9	1983	Duane Young	Eagles Nest Pass	49 0/8
10	1964	R. Pechanec	Alberta	48 4/8
11	1977	Stanley Simpson	Dutch Creek	48 1/8
12	1944	Alfred Erdman	Smoky River	47 7/8
13	1973	Ralph Hope	Smoky River	47 4/8
13	1978	Ken Nowicki	Willmore Wilderness	47 4/8
15	?	George Vandervalk	Alberta	47 2/8
15	1963	A. Cyr	Highwood River	47 2/8
15	1966	A. Lalonde	Smoky River	47 2/8
18	1957	Joe F. Kubasek	Kananaskis River	47 0/8
18	1967	R. Cervo	Kananaskis River	47 0/8

* Not entered in Boone and Crockett Records of North American Big Game (1988)

TABLE 8.12

ALBERTA'S TOP 20
BIGHORN SHEEP HORNS

Sources: Alberta wildlife trophies. Official records of the Alberta Fish and Game Association (Anonymous, 1986),
Records of North American big game (Boone and Crockett, 1988), and Boone and Crockett Club's 21st big game awards (Sitton and Reneau, 1992)

Rank	Year	Hunter/Owner	Location of Hunt	Score	Rank	Year	Hunter/Owner	Location of Hunt	Score
1	1911	Fred Weiller	Blind Canyon	208 1/8	11	1965	Bob Woodward	Castle River	197 0/8
2	1924	Martin Bovey	Oyster Creek	207 2/8	12	1968	George Biron	Yarrow Creek	196 7/8
3	1955	Roy C. Stahl (Pick-Up)	Burnt Timber Creek	206 3/8	13	1924	Donald S. Hopkins	Brazeau River	196 5/8
4	1918	Tom Kerquits	Panther River	202 2/8	13	1938	Bill Foster	Alberta	196 5/8
5	1932	A.H. Hilbert (Pick-Up)	Jasper	201 1/8	15	1953	J.F. Kubasek	Highwood	196 2/8
6	1937	Norman L. Lougheed	Brazeau River	200 1/8	16	1962	Al Leary	Cadomin	196 0/8
6	1955	Otis Chandler "Picked Up"	Alberta	200 1/8	17	1890	Indian	Bow River	195 4/8
8	~1947	Bill Foster	Alberta	198 6/8	18	1961	Jim Neeser	West Sundre	195 3/8
9	1965	Herb Klein	Saskatchewan Lake	198 1/8	19	1985	Alta. Fish and Wildlife (confiscated)	Canmore	195 1/8
10	~1947	Bill Foster	Alberta	197 5/8	20	1944	G.M. DeWitt	Ram River	194 7/8

*Not entered in Boone and Crockett Records of North American Big Game (1988)

TABLE 8.13

TOP 100 TROPHIES IN NORTH AMERICA — HOW DOES ALBERTA COMPARE?*

Ranking	White-tailed Deer		Mule Deer		Mountain Caribou	Wapiti
	Typical	Non-Typical	Typical	Non-Typical		(Elk)
1	Minnesota (11)	Saskatchewan (12)	Colorado (48)	Colorado (19)	British Columbia (61)	Wyoming (19)
2	Texas (10)	Wisconsin (10)	New Mexico (14)	Utah (17)	Yukon (23)	Montana (18)
3	Wisconsin (9)	Minnesota (8)	Wyoming (10)	Idaho (14)	N.W.T. (14)	Alberta (17)
4	Montana (6)	Alberta (8)	Utah (10)	Arizona(12)	-	Idaho (13)
5	Missouri (7)	Ohio (6)	Idaho (9)	Montana (7)	-	Colorado (9)
6	Iowa (7)	Montana (5)	Arizona (4)	New Mexico (6)	-	Oregon (7)
7	Saskatchewan (6)	Texas (5)	Oregon (3)	Oregon (5)	-	Arizona (6)
8	Alberta (5)	Kansas (5)	Nevada (2)	Wyoming(4)	-	New Mexico (5)
9	Kansas (4)	Washington (4)	-	Saskatchewan (4)	-	Saskatchewan (3)
10	Ohio (3)	Nebraska (3)	-	Alberta (1)	-	Washington (2)
Boone & Crockett Maximum Score	206 1/8	333 7/8	225 6/8	355 2/8	452 0/8	442 3/8
Alberta Maximum Score	204 2/8	279 6/8	199 4/8	355 2/8	below standard	419 6/8

Ranking	Canada Moose	Pronghorn (Antelope)	Mountain Goat	Bighorn Sheep	Bison (Buffalo)
1	British Columbia (50)	Wyoming (42)	British Columbia (58)	Alberta (59)	N.W.T. (28)
2	Alberta (23)	Arizona (20)	Alaska (22)	British Columbia (18)	Wyoming (22)
3	Saskatchewan (10)	Montana (7)	Washington (10)	Montana (17)	Alaska (14)
4	Ontario (6)	New Mexico (7)	Montana (6)	Wyoming (4)	South Dakota (13)
5	Quebec (4)	Nevada (7)	Idaho (4)	Colorado (2)	Montana (10)
6	Manitoba (3)	Oregon (4)	Nevada (3)	North Dakota (1)	Arizona (5)
7	Maine (2)	Alberta (3)	Alberta (2)	South Dakota (1)	Utah (3)
8	-	California (3)	-	-	Alberta (2)
9	-	Colorado (3)	-	-	Manitoba (1)
Boone & Crockett Maximum Score	242 0/8	93 4/8	56 6/8	208 1/8	136 4/8
Alberta Maximum Score	226 7/8	86 2/8	54 0/8	208 1/8	133 4/8

* *Rankings of provinces, territories, and states indicate geographic contribution of trophy antlers and horns to the Boone and Crockett trophy records. Numbers in brackets indicate the number of horns or antlers which score in the top 100. Data collated from Records of North American big game (1988) and Boone and Crockett Club's 21st big game awards (1992).*

9

Management

William D. Wishart,
John G. Stelfox,
Edmund S. Telfer and
John R. Gunson

Earliest efforts at managing Alberta's hoofed mammals were directed at preventing excessive harvest by commercial and sport hunters by establishing bag limits, restricted seasons, and offering protection to females. As the science of wildlife management became established and more sophisticated, managers began using hunters as tools to maintain ungulate populations within bounds set by available habitat and socio-political pressure — not an easy task when you throw in such unmanageable variables as bad winters and, occasionally, disease.

A condensed history of ungulate management eras in Alberta is chronicled in both narrative and table form. The principle of "sustainable offtake" is described, for it is the basis from which harvest by hunters is calculated. The problems confronting wildlife biologists trying to count ungulate populations in different habitats are identified, as are time proven census methods.

Habitat management is the foundation of ungulate management, for without adequate resources to provide food, shelter and water, no ungulate population will prosper. There are many human land-uses (agriculture, petro-chemical, mining, forestry, recreation) that affect our provincial ungulate populations – specific attention is given to the rapidly expanding forest industry and the way it alters wildlife habitat. Other controversial management topics addressed in this chapter include poaching, aboriginal hunting, crop depredation, and the wolf/caribou conundrum in west-central Alberta.

INTRODUCTION

The first attempt to manage wildlife in Alberta was to introduce hunting regulations for the protection of plains bison in 1877. Regardless of hunting seasons, however, it was too late, and the plains bison was doomed to be replaced by the cow and the plow. Closed seasons from February to September were introduced in 1883 for pronghorn and deer, but no bag limits were established. Annual bag limits of six each for pronghorn, bighorn sheep, mountain goat and both deer species were introduced in 1892. In 1899 it became illegal to kill more than three deer of either species in any year, and by 1903 females were protected. Once hunting seasons were established, management efforts emphasized the creation of parks and sanctuaries. During the early 1900s, Wainwright Buffalo Park and Elk Island Park were established for plains bison and wapiti, followed by Nemiscam and Wawaskesy for pronghorn, and finally Wood Buffalo National Park for wood bison. During the same period, our mountain parks were established for their scenic beauty and to protect threatened wildlife. This pattern of setting restrictive hunting seasons, protecting females and establishing game preserves was the general approach to wildlife management adopted throughout North America in the early 20th century.

In 1933, Aldo Leopold introduced the world to the scientific approach to wildlife management. The basis of his treatise revolved around the growth potential of populations and the identification and regulation of the factors that limit population growth. To gain a quick insight into modern big game management, imagine an isolated island with habitat capable of supporting 100 deer every winter. The objective of a wildlife manager would be to sustain this population of 100 animals in perpetuity by removing the annual surplus. In other words, the manager would attempt to maintain the population numbers within the carrying capacity of the island. This goal is subject to four basic steps in wildlife management:

1. Obtain a census or inventory of the population, preferably before and after the removal program.

2. Quantify the annual production of young and the percentage increase in the population from the previous year.

3. Determine which factors limit the rate of increase of the population (usually habitat loss or modification).

4. Based on the above, determine what actions are necessary to sustain the population in a healthy and highly productive state.

The annual process of determining annual production and harvest rates is illustrated in Figure 9.1.

CENSUS TECHNIQUES

In Alberta, pronghorn serve as a good example of how the four steps of wildlife management are applied. Pronghorn are easily counted by aerial surveys on sunny mornings and evenings during the summer months. Aerial block transects of pronghorn habitat provide estimates of density as well as of fawn production for the year prior to the fall hunting season. Based on population surveys and information on hunting success gathered from questionnaires, hunter check stations, and incisor bar returns, the manager can determine the number of permits to issue so that hunters will regulate the pronghorn population.

Since the introduction of wildlife management units (WMUs) into the Alberta hunting regulations in 1964, biologists have been able to manage pronghorn more specifically. For example, where severe weather conditions or high predation rates have adversely affected herds, the WMUs and the limited-entry permit system allow managers to schedule restricted or male-only seasons specifically in those units affected. Prior to the arrival of management units and limited-entry systems, pronghorn hunting seasons throughout Alberta were based solely on the status of herds in preferred hunting areas. As a result, there were many years of closures. Today, pronghorn are one of the most successfully managed and hunted ungulate species in western North America.

Another readily visible species for summer census is the mountain goat. Nursery herds of adult nannies and kids are easily located and classified during the month of August. Adult males are solitary and less visible, so accurate adult sex ratios are difficult to obtain. In Alberta, the four management steps outlined earlier have been applied with token seasons under a very restrictive draw system for the past several years. However, mountain goat management has not been very successful, as some unknown factors limiting mountain goat production have yet to be determined. Consequently, the limited goat season was closed in 1988.

Bighorn sheep are most easily censused on winter ranges (approximately 100 ranges have been identified outside Alberta's national parks) during the breeding season. Unfortunately, as with the remaining ungulate species, these winter surveys are post-hunting or "after the fact" surveys. In other words, the survey is too late to take into account what the population status was prior to the hunting season and too early to account for how the winter will affect survival and productivity for the next hunting season. However, in the case of bighorn sheep, there are presently a number of herds that have been marked and monitored throughout the spring, summer, and fall seasons. These herds assist managers by providing an annual index to survival and production. Bighorn sheep were the first ungulate species in Alberta to have a trophy size restriction placed on males. In 1956, the 3/4 curl law was introduced and in 1968 the horn size restriction was increased to 4/5 curl. It is not possible to maintain a stable, healthy, highly productive bighorn population by simply removing older rams. As a consequence, in 1966 a draw system for harvesting ewes and lambs was introduced. Questionnaires and lower jaw (incisor bar) returns indicated that hunters avoid shooting lambs and ewes with lambs. Wildlife man-agers have had to take these preferences into account along with different rates of hunting success for each WMU when setting quotas and permits for non-trophy sheep or other female seasons.

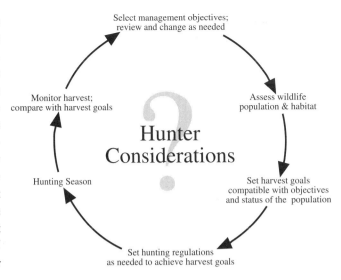

Figure 9.1
Ungulate harvest model (modified from Connolly, 1981)

Alberta's hunters also shoot proportionally few young mule deer and moose, preferring older individuals. In contrast, white-tailed deer hunters apparently do not have sufficient time to distinguish fawns from adult does and are more likely to shoot the first deer seen. Deer and moose are censused using aerial transects in blocks of suitable habitat to estimate densities, which are then applied to similar habitats to extrapolate population estimates of each WMU. There are other indirect methods of obtaining population estimates. For example, by obtaining pre- and post-hunting season sex and age ratios along with the number, sex, and age ratios of the harvest, it is possible to estimate population levels before and after the harvest.

Wapiti inhabiting forests during winter are very difficult to survey. Consequently, most wapiti surveys are made during the winter in areas where they graze on open slopes and valleys of foothill and mountain regions.

Both wapiti and mule deer males were given trophy status in many WMUs during the 1980s, requiring hunters to shoot only males that possess a minimum number of antler tines. In both cases the purpose was to allow the more vulnerable yearling males to attain a more respectable antler size.

The most difficult ungulate to survey and manage is the woodland caribou, since most of its life cycle is spent in or near dense conifer forests. The mountain subspecies, however, is relatively easy to survey in alpine habitat during the fall rut. At that time, herd size and sex and age ratios can be readily obtained. A recent radio-tagging study of the mountain caribou herd in the Willmore Wilderness Area indicated that annual predation rates can exceed annual calf production. In addition, winter habitat has been depleted and is declining rapidly due to pulp and paper forest clearing projects. Although some key areas are to be left untouched for travel corridors and winter feeding sites, the caribou is already on the threatened species list in Alberta. Accordingly, the hunting season for caribou in Alberta has been closed for several years.

Today the main focus of wildlife management is not so much the numbers game as it is the habitat game. Most wildlife managers are busy directing their efforts toward the cornerstone of wildlife, that is, habitat retention and improvement. The challenge today for all Albertans who are interested in retaining our diverse ungulate populations in respectable numbers is to be certain that these species are represented by professional wildlife managers at the bargaining tables on all major land-use decisions.

Table 9.1 chronicles major events in the history of hoofed mammal management in Alberta.

TABLE 9.1

DEVELOPMENTS IN THE MANAGEMENT HISTORY OF ALBERTA'S UNGULATES

Year	Management Event
1877	An Ordinance for the Protection of the Buffalo – Alberta's first game law.
1883	An Ordinance for the Protection of Game – passed by the Northwest Territories Government.
1887	First Game Guardian appointed in Alberta.
1889	Killing of bison prohibited.
1892	First bag limits established for big game.
1903	Hunting not permitted on Sundays.
1907	Alberta receives the first game act (The Act of 1907). Residents required to purchase license to hunt big game ($2.50). Hunting seasons closed for bighorn sheep, mountain goat and wapiti and shortened for pronghorn. Rocky Mountain Parks and Elk Island Park set aside as reserves to protect game. Sale of game heads required government brands.
1909	Buffalo Park near Wainwright established.
1922	New Game Act passed, incorporating revisions of the Act of 1907. Wood Buffalo National Park established to protect remnant population of wood bison.
1925–28	Approximately 6670 plains bison from Wainwright Park sent by rail and barge to Wood Buffalo National Park. These animals were known to be infected with tuberculosis and brucellosis. Relocation conducted despite a warning by biologists concerning disease transmission and genetic contamination.
1932	Wild mammals and non-migratory birds proclaimed provincial property, having been transferred from federal ownership. Scarlet clothing required for big game hunting. Non-resident hunters required licensed guides or residents. Lieutenant-Governor in Council (Cabinet) empowered to make hunting regulations.
1941	New prohibitions include loaded firearms in vehicles and the shooting of swimming big game.
1946	Game Act of 1946 recognizes right of aboriginal peoples to hunt and trap wild animals for food during all seasons on all unoccupied Crown lands and on any lands on which Indians have right of access. Metal tags required to be placed on all big game by hunters.
1959	Title of Director of Fish and Wildlife and Game Officers recognized.
1961	Titles of Game Officers changed to Wildlife Officers. Hunters prohibited from filling big game tags of other hunters. Hunting while impaired by alcohol or drugs becomes an offence. Outfitters legally responsible for the actions of their clients, and liable to any penalties.
1965	24 pure wood bison captured at Nyarling River in Wood Buffalo National Park sent to Elk Island National Park as part of a program to develop several separate herds of wood bison.
1968	Blaze orange a legal substitute for scarlet hunting clothing.
1974	Fish and Wildlife Habitat Fund established, funded by the sale of habitat stamps on licenses.
1980	Hunting season for caribou closed indefinitely. Those possessing suspended hunting licenses must pass hunter test to be eligible to hunt.
1984	Committee on the Status of Endangered Wildlife in Canada (COSEWIC) recognizes that western Woodland Caribou are "Rare".
1985	Alberta's Policy for Management of Threatened Wildlife designates woodland caribou as "Threatened". Wildlife Act designates woodland caribou as "Endangered". Wood Buffalo National Park declared a World Heritage Site by UNESCO. A major reason for this declaration was the world's largest herd of bison residing in the park. Hunting colours (blaze orange) no longer required.
1986	Government White Paper discusses the merits of legalizing game ranching in Alberta.
1987	Mandatory first-time hunter test. New Wildlife Act and Regulations. Bison reclassified as a domestic animal south of the 22nd baseline.
1988	CITES downlists wood bison from "Endangered" to "Threatened" category. Mountain goat hunting season closed.
1990	Heated debate among federal and provincial agencies, native peoples, agricultural community, and biologists concerning the merit of removing entire population of brucellosis-infected hybrid bison from Wood Buffalo National Park.
1991	Livestock Industry Diversification Act (LIDA) ratified, allowing meat sales from game farms. Native species were permitted on game farms under auspices of the Alberta Agriculture Division.
1993	Wildlife Identification Number (WIN) cards issued to all hunters. As an important part of the Client Licensing and Survey System (CLASS), WIN cards will assist the Alberta Fish and Wildlife Service to assign priority to hunters applying for special licenses and draws.

MANAGEMENT HISTORY OF ALBERTA'S UNGULATES

1670–1870: Alberta was administered by the Hudson Bay Company. The fur industry was the prime resource, though big game animals, in particular bison, were harvested for food in the prairies and foothills. In forested regions, moose and caribou provided the majority of food for aboriginal and the few whites and metis. There were no game laws.

1870–1905: Wildlife resources were managed primarily by the federal Department of the Interior. Management consisted mainly of developing administrative structures to facilitate resource development, especially agriculture, timber harvesting and mining. Big game populations declined drastically or disappeared in the prairie and parkland ecoregions. Big game continued to provide sustenance to people in forested regions. The earliest game laws in Alberta were devised.

1906–1929: The Forest Reserves Act was established to preserve water and reserve timber, and exclude homesteading from unsuitable areas. Protection of declining wildlife populations was evident in federal and provincial legislation. Near the end of this period the provincial government initiated an inventory of provincial resources including minerals, timber and agricultural resources. The federal government maintained ownership of natural resources. Wildlife was administered under the Commission of Conservation constituted under the Conservation Act in 1909. The federal Committee on Fisheries, Game, and Fur-bearing Animals provided advice to provincial agencies who administered game laws. Both federal and provincial governments cooperated in establishing national and provincial parks and wildlife harvest regulations. The Wainwright Reserve was established to protect the bison from extinction while the Alberta Act gave all Dominion parks game preserve status. The Forestry Branch of the federal Department of the Interior examined the entire East Slopes south of the Athabasca River, including a detailed study of big game, their habitat requirements and reasons for decline in numbers. This inventory resulted in the delineation of four proposed game preserves of which three would be contiguous to the three mountain parks. Game management within these preserves and throughout the Forest reserves was the mandate of the Forestry Branch, especially after the creation of the Rocky Mountains Forest Reserve (Crowsnest, Bow River, Clearwater, Brazeau, and Athabasca Forests) in 1911.

1930–1945: In 1930, Alberta became responsible for its natural resources, and the Alberta Forest Service oversaw the management of forest, wildlife and watershed resources. Resources outside the forest reserves were the responsibility of the Land Branch until 1932, when all operations with respect to timber, haying, grazing, wildlife, homesteading and fire protection came under the auspices of the Alberta Forest Service.

1946–1969: In 1948, the Crowsnest, Bow River and Clearwater Forest Reserves were placed under the Eastern Rockies Forest Conservation Board, a joint federal-provincial environmental conservation body. Also, Alberta was divided into three major land-use zones, namely: the White Zone of heavy settlement area of the southeast; the Yellow Zone of crown land set aside for eventual settlement; and the Green Zone to be retained as forest land not to be developed. Provincial forest rangers in the Yellow and Green Zones assumed all wildlife management responsibilities until 1952. The Superintendent of Game and a small staff of game wardens were responsible for establishing big game seasons and for enforcing game laws, primarily in the White and Yellow zones. In 1952 the Department of Lands, Forests and Wildlife hired its first wildlife biologist, who was responsible to the Director of Wildlife (who was also the Director of the Alberta Forest Service). More wildlife biologists and wildlife officers were hired and in 1966 the complete responsibility of wildlife management throughout the province, excluding federal lands, was transferred to the Fish and Wildlife Division. The dominant resource management philosophy was conservation or wise use of a single resource. Road access increased greatly with the building of the Forestry Trunk Road (initiated in 1948), logging roads, and seismic lines. Although this allowed a dispersion of hunting pressure, it also resulted in excessive harvesting of big game populations from non-aboriginal poachers and from indiscriminate, year-long hunting by aboriginals.

Road-kill deer are an all too common sight in those parts of Alberta where high concentrations of deer and motorists coincide.
Photo by J. Nolan.

1970–1990: Resource management, including fish and wildlife management, reflected an increased awareness of the complex relationships among diverse resources and resource uses, due mainly to the environmental movement. Recreation became a major industry in the 1970s, and facilities for recreationalists increased at a controlled level. Especially evident was the increased interest in downhill and cross-country skiing, the use of over-snow and all-terrain vehicles, canoeing, hiking, mountain climbing, fishing and hunting. The Alberta population became more urban, and attitudes toward wildlife changed. The media "personalized" wildlife, and various organizations were formed to lobby against hunting, trapping and inhumane treatment of wildlife. Predator control, trapping and the wearing of fur garments were opposed by vociferous, urban societies. By 1985 these concerns, along with aboriginal hunting treaty rights, became sensitive issues with the result that traditional wildlife management practices declined and began to shift towards preserving islands of wildlife habitat for non-consumptive use.

HABITAT MANAGEMENT

Hoofed mammals are affected both directly and indirectly by a multitude of human land-use practices in Alberta (Figure 9.2). Most significant are the loss and modification of those habitat components needed to ensure a healthy population: namely forage, protective cover and water. If any one of these three components is in short supply, ungulate populations will either decline or fail to achieve optimal densities. For example, large forest clearcuts may create an abundance of herbaceous forage for a few decades, but may not be used by hoofed mammals because of inadequate cover from predators, human harassment or inclement weather.

Under most natural conditions, variations in elevation, topography, aspect, and fire history create complex mosaics of habitat types (meadows, shrublands, deciduous forests, coniferous forests) that collectively provide ideal hoofed mammal habitat. Practices such as agriculture and forestry, and many decades of fire suppression, have replaced many of these heterogeneous community assemblages with vast tracts of uniform plant communities such as grain crops, even-age stands of forest regrowth and overmature conifers. Although agricultural fringelands may provide good habitat for the secretive white-tailed deer, loss of local wapiti, moose and mule deer populations generally occurs. If ungulate populations are to be maintained in a healthy state, or are to rebuild in areas that supported historic populations, agriculturalists, foresters and others must include wildlife habitat requirements in their land management plans. An example of this new multiple-use approach to land tenure is being seen by progressive logging companies that have replaced large-block clearcuts with small, irregularly bordered cuts that leave unmerchantable snags standing and retain blocks of mature forest for protective cover.

A major thrust in effective habitat conservation is instilling an understanding of what constitutes "wildlife habitat" among those who manage or affect private and public wildlands. This responsibility lies to a large extent with the successful "Buck for Wildlife" program of the Alberta Fish and Wildlife Division. Launched in the 1970s, this program directs monies collected from game license fees back to habitat protection, development and purchases. In essence, it is a tax levied on sport hunters to ensure that their big game resources are perpetuated. Specifically, these funds are used to fence livestock from valuable wildlife habitat, conduct prescribed burns, purchase threatened wildlands and encourage farmers to maintain tree shelterbelts.

Not all areas with adequate forage, water, and protective cover from predators and weather, however, support healthy ungulate populations. A common factor in many of these deficient areas

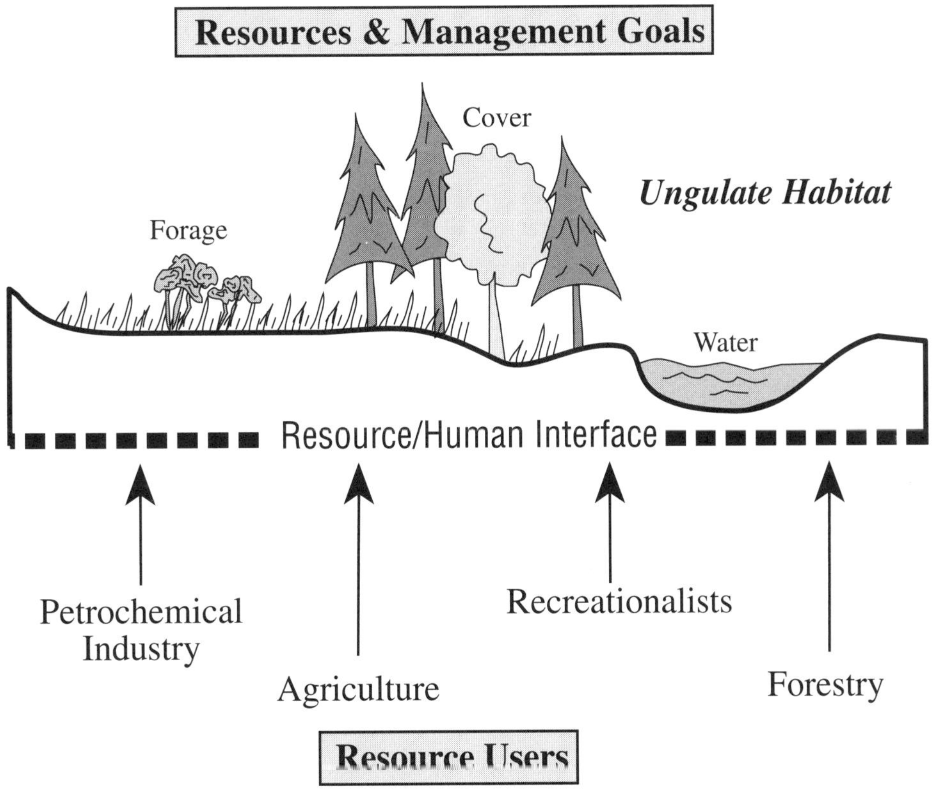

Resources & Management Goals

Cover

Forage

Ungulate Habitat

Water

Resource/Human Interface

Petrochemical
Industry

Recreationalists

Agriculture

Forestry

Resource Users

Figure 9.2
Ungulate/land-use conflicts.
Human land uses
practices such as agriculture,
recreation, forestry and the
petrochemical industry can
alter ungulate habitat and its
ability to provide adequate
levels of forage, cover
and water.

appears to be excessive human harassment. The combination of a growing human population and a network of roads and seismic lines criss-crossing Alberta now allows recreationalists access to previously remote areas. Wildlife biologists are beginning to recognize the subtle negative effects of noise arising from snowmobiles, ATVs, etc. Numerous studies have examined the general impacts of recreational pursuits on wildlife (Dorrance *et al.*, 1975; Stace-Smith, 1975; Ferguson, 1980; Yarmaloy, 1984). MacArthur *et al.* (1982) and Stemp (1983) have documented significantly elevated heart rates in bighorn sheep associated with various human activities.

In those situations where conflict between ungulates and humans is acute and long term, drastic alterations to wildlife habitat may be warranted. Such is the case along Highway 1 east of Banff townsite, where a long game-proof corridor has been erected along the highway. Although the cost of fencing and underground passageways has been considerable, the number of vehicle/ungulate collisions has been greatly reduced.

By altering availability of forage, emergency winter feeding of ungulates is a form of habitat mangement. During the winter of 1984–85, deep snow and recurrent cold spells in the Eastern Slopes and central portions of the province created widespread concern for ungulate survival. The Alberta Fish and Wildlife Division in cooperation with landowners and ~400 volunteers initiated a feeding program in February. At a cost exceeding $325,000, the program fed about 7,000 deer, 600 wapiti, and 200 pronghorn at 222 sites (Millson, 1985).

The majority of feeding sites were intercept locations for depredation control, but some were solely to prevent starvation. Although high winter mortality did not occur, perhaps because spring arrived early, the program did demonstrate that supplemental feeding can be an effective strategy for ungulate management in Alberta.

TABLE 9.2

FREQUENCY OF OCCURRENCES OF VARIOUS TYPES OF DAMAGE BY UNGULATES IN ALBERTA (1982/83–1991/92)

Type of Damage	Deer	Wapiti	Moose	Pronghorn	All Species[a]	Percent
Stacked feed	1,487	825	115	6	2,434	38
Other crops	1,172	368	69	89	1,705	27
Gardens	726	17	7	2	755	12
Trees [b]	423	3	49	36	512	8
Harass People	31	5	36	0	78	1
Harass Livestock	26	10	42	1	85	1
General Property Damage	316	41	100	5	464	7
Miscellaneous	193	27	48	15	380	6
Totals					6,413	100

[a] includes bison, caribou, mountain goat, bighorn sheep and unknown as well as those species shown

[b] includes orchards, shelterbelts, others

DEPREDATIONS BY UNGULATES

Wild ungulates commonly damage agricultural crops and other private property in Alberta: 6,423 such complaints were recorded by Alberta Fish and Wildlife Division from 1982-1991. White-tailed deer and mule deer accounted for 68% of these occurrences, followed by wapiti (20%), moose (7%), pronghorn (2%), and other species (~2%). Annual trends in complaints peaked during 1984/85—the last severe winter. Wapiti and deer damage occurrences have increased in frequency each year since 1987.

Table 9.2 lists major types of ungulate damage and nuisances. Damage to stacked forages (38% of complaints) are related to winter severity with a doubling or tripling of complaints during severe winters. Depredations by ungulates occur throughout the year but most frequently in January and February (31% of 5,382 complaints). Wapiti damage haystacks more frequently than other species, generally scattering and trampling hay. Crops damaged in gardens (12% of complaints) including strawberries, lettuce, carrots and turnips. Other crops damaged include cereal grains, pasture, and hay in fields. Standing, swathed, or combined crops (mostly cereal grains) represented 61% of complaints other than haystacks and gardens. Harassment of people (1% of complaints) and livestock or pets (1%) occur rarely. Damage to vehicles (84% caused by deer) was 45% of general property damages. Moose were responsible for 67% of 78 incidents of damage to fences.

The full extent of economic loss to ungulates in Alberta is unknown because of unreported damages, difficulty in measuring losses to certain types of crops like pasture and hay in fields, and poor estimates of loss for crops that are not included in compensation programs. The Alberta Hail and Crop Insurance program investigates claims and has records of ungulate damage back to 1964. Their data show average losses of $1,100 each on 10 pronghorn claims, $1,800 each on 80 deer claims, and $3,300 each on 30 wapiti claims during 1980-1983. Farmers that experience damage to haystacks are not compensated, but annual provincial losses range from $100,000 to several million dollars. Other crops not compensated include grazing lands, orchards, and stored crops.

Management options to reduce damage by ungulates in Alberta include compensation, animal removal, and preferentially, prevention. Tactics include cattle/ungulate AUM (animal unit month) management, enhancement of wapiti foods on winter public lands, and purchase or lease of winter ranges on private lands. To date, these tactics have received little use in Alberta.

Alberta's government has cost-shared the construction of fences for haystacks and will scare depredating ungulates from damage sites with noise-making devices. Intercept feeding (feeding ungulates at sites between their shelter and the crop) has been used: 600 wapiti were intercept fed from 1980–1985.

Translocation of offending ungulates can be used to stock ranges elsewhere. For example, 107 wapiti were moved from two damage sites during 1981–1985. Hunting seasons can be designed to reduce over-wintering populations of ungulates in depredation areas (e.g., special antlerless seasons, extended seasons, split seasons). Specific depredation hunts can effectively reduce ungulate populations, but remain publicly controversial.

UNGULATES AND FOREST MANAGEMENT: THE ROLE OF FIRE AND LOGGING

Forests occur extensively throughout the northern half of Alberta and along the province's foothills and mountains. Most of these areas belong to the Boreal Forest Region (Rowe, 1972) and the closely-related Subalpine Forest Region at higher elevations. Small areas of the "Montane Forest Region" occur in the major foothills valleys. Collectively, these forested biomes provide large-scale and important habitat to Alberta's hoofed mammal fauna.

The principal factor controlling occurrence, structure, and composition of Alberta's forests since the Ice Age has been fire (Tande, 1979; Heinselman, 1981; Murphy, 1985). The causes of these fires have been both natural (lightning strikes) and anthropic (both aboriginal and European man (Lewis, 1982), with many prehistoric fires set to improve ungulate forage production). There is not much doubt that dry summers, flammable vegetation, and plentiful ignition sources led to frequent fires in the days before European settlement. Van Wagner (1978) and Murphy (1985) suggest that the fire return interval (period of time within which the area burned equals the total area of the region) may have been as short as 40–50 years. With the frequent fires of pre-settlement Alberta, the proportion of old-growth forest (more than 150 years old) would have been on the order of five percent, and early successional forest stages would have prevailed. With the arrival of Europeans in the 19th century, burning rates increased dramatically for two or three decades then decreased markedly in areas near settlements. Reasons for the decline of fire prevalence included the advent of fire suppression techniques and equipment, and the emergence of the timber industry. Large-scale fires continued to be a common feature of Alberta's remote northern frontier.

During the early development of the forest industry the major products were lumber and railroad ties, and to a lesser extent firewood, mine props, and fence posts (Clark, 1988). Logging covered substantial areas adjacent to settlements but selectively sought larger conifer trees. This cutting strategy created extensive, patchy, partially-cut areas that produced excellent forage and cover for ungulates. A new era of forest management began in 1954 with the negotiation of a Forest Management Agreement (FMA) that leased vast forests for the production of pulp wood to Alberta's first pulpmill at Hinton. Subsequently, many other areas of Alberta have been leased to large forest companies. In the 1980s, new technology and risk capital became available for manufacture of hardwoods (primarily trembling aspen) into pulp. Collectively, the wide-scale commercial harvest of softwoods (conifers) and hardwoods (deciduous trees) by forest companies in Alberta has replaced wildfire as the major instrument shaping forests and resetting the ecological clock back to early successional communities.

The principal forest-dwelling ungulates in Alberta are white-tailed deer, mule deer, woodland caribou, wapiti and moose. In pre-settlement times, ungulate populations fluctuated with the fire regime; deer, wapiti and moose increased significantly following fire as they utilized abundant forage in the early successional communities. Woodland caribou were adversely affected, as they depended on lichens from older-aged forests for winter forage. With the emergence of the pulp industry, the forestry/ungulate interface changed drastically. Following 1954, timber harvest no longer selectively removed large trees, but adopted an indiscriminate approach to harvesting that clear-cut trees of all size classes. New silvicultural approaches to reforestation now encouraged the removal of any remaining patches of unmerchantable trees. The typical pattern of clear-cutting has been to log rectangular blocks in an alternating checkerboard pattern. The agreement negotiated with the early pulp companies stipulated that uncut residual blocks be left for 10 years to permit natural seeding of the cut-over areas. The residual blocks were then cut and regenerated by seeding or planting. More recently, forest leases have abandoned the time requirement before second cuts and now stipulate that the first-cut areas must achieve a specified post-cut tree height. Under both harvesting systems, extensive early successional stands are created. Although such areas provide good forage for deer, wapiti and moose, they often lack cover from predators, humans and meteorological stress (Tomm and Beck, 1981). While the residual uncut blocks remain to provide cover, the harvesting of 50% of the general area in staggered blocks of 16 ha offers excellent winter habitat for most ungulate species (Stelfox et al., 1976). When the residual blocks are cut, however, the area often becomes unproductive for ungulates for a few decades until adequate protective cover regrows. In areas of mature and old forest, excellent ungulate habitat can be maintained by delaying removal of residual blocks for 20+ years after initial cutting.

To keep the impact of logging in perspective, one must remember that about 1% of the land area covered by each FMA is logged annually. A forest company in operation for two or three decades will generally have less than 20% of its FMA logged and converted to young forests. The proportion of the FMA that can be logged is usually less than 80% because of such unproductive areas as muskegs and areas such as riparian habitat along streams, rivers, and lake shores where government rules prohibit logging.

As the forest industry in Alberta becomes more intensive, silvicultural treatments such as thinning have become more prevalent. Production of ungulate forage is often higher in such thinned stands as the post-logging burst of high browse production may be extended from 20 years to between 35 and 40 years. It should also be noted that thinning generally reduces protective cover for ungulates.

An emerging stand-tending treatment (still experimental in Alberta) that will affect ungulates is the use of herbicides by foresters to control herbaceous vegetation that competes with conifer seedlings. More research is required to determine whether herbicide applications can foster healthy conifer seedling growth without seriously reducing ungulate forage.

The woodland caribou, dependent on mature and old forests, presents a special management problem to foresters. Effective caribou management requires that a substantial proportion of mature and old forest be maintained at all times in localities used by caribou in winter. Recognition of this dependence is leading to modification of harvest schedules and layout of cutting blocks so that suitable winter habitat and travel lanes are maintained (Edmonds and Bloomfield, 1984).

Timber harvest requires an extensive road network. Although a road system was put in place throughout many forested areas of Alberta by the petroleum industry, it has been expanded greatly for forestry purposes. These roads have undoubtedly affected ungulates greatly by improving access for hunters, poachers, recreationalists, and humans engaged in other activities that perturb wildlife or their habitat. These problems can be mitigated by locating roads distant from critical ungulate wintering and calving habitat and by bulldozing barriers across spur roads and skid trails after they have been retired.

In general, forestry operations in Alberta maintain the mosaic of habitats that were available to ungulates under the pre-settlement fire regime, with the exception that early successional communities have increased at the expense of older forests. This shift in habitat composition is often beneficial to deer, wapiti and moose provided there is an adequate representation of protective cover. The same favourable picture cannot be painted for woodland caribou. Fortunately, there is increasing integration of planning and operations between managers of all land-based resources in Alberta in concert with the worldwide trend toward sustainable development.

POACHING

Empirical knowledge of the illegal harvest of big game is both an important and an evasive component of modern wildlife management. It is not possible for game managers to formulate sustained-yield hunter offtake rates unless the impact of all population-limiting factors, including poaching, is considered. Unfortunately, the illegal harvest of wildlife is difficult to quantify, since most infractions are neither observed nor reported. Although many acts of poaching are not observed, citizens who do witness violations often fail to notify authorities presumably because witnesses are unfamiliar with game laws, have negative attitudes toward wildlife, are related to or acquainted with the violators, or do not consider poaching to be a significant offence (Boxall and Smith, 1987).

A fascinating approach to quantifying the illegal harvest of Alberta's deer population was a 1985 violation simulation study described by Boxall and Smith (1987). In this study, Alberta Fish and Wildlife Division hired an individual to commit approximately 650 simulated acts of deer poaching. Of these staged infractions, only 7 were reported, even though 139 of the incidents were observed by landowners or the public. Based on the results of this study, Boxall and Smith estimate that approximately 1% of actual poaching incidents are reported. Accordingly, illegal offtake of deer in 1985 was estimated at 25,716 animals ± 17,495 (95% confidence interval). This level of harvest could approximate one illegal deer harvested for every two taken within the law.

Smith *et al*. (1989) clearly demonstrated the misleading potential of violation-simulation techniques where violations have been improperly defined and size of simulated violations are low. Despite these limitations, Boxall and Smith's study remains instructive about the unwillingness of Albertans to report violations of hunting regulations

THE ABORIGINAL PEOPLES ISSUE

Treaty 8 and the Natural Resources Transfer Act 512 allow Indian people in Alberta to hunt and fish wherever they have access to unoccupied Crown lands. Until oil and gas exploration became extensive in the late 1950s, the Alberta Government received few complaints about Indians over-harvesting big game populations. One exception was excessive harvest of ungulates, particularly bighorn sheep, along the East Slopes from 1880–1920, when Indians provisioned thousands of miners, railway workers, fur trappers and lumberjacks with meat. During 1913–1915, about 500 resident Stoney Indians shot 2,000 to 3,500 wild ungulates annually (Millar, 1915). Depletions of bighorn sheep along mountain valleys served by Transcontinental Railways in the late 1800s and early 1900s were blamed on liberal game laws and a general disregard for the laws (Hornaday, 1923). The Stoney Indians were annually shooting 650 to 1,000 bighorn sheep between 1913 and 1915 and selling trophy rams for $25–50 to big game hunters (Millar, 1915; Stelfox, 1971). These authors believed that the annual harvest of big game animals by Indians and Caucasians was largely responsible for a major decline in hoofed mammal populations within the foothills and mountains during the period 1880–1920.

Access to the foothills, subalpine, and mixed-wood regions increased rapidly after 1955 due to oil and gas exploration and timber harvest activities. By the 1960s the provincial government was receiving numerous complaints about Indians overharvesting big game during late winter and spring periods. Associated with improved road access to the foothills region, some local herds of bighorn sheep were allegedly extirpated by Indians during the period 1965–1988. The Alberta Fish and Game Association has frequently complained to the Alberta Fish and Wildlife Division and politicians about excessive aboriginal harvesting of wildlife and has passed numerous resolutions condemning this practice. The Alberta Fish and Wildlife Division recognizes that the annual harvest of big game by Indians and poachers is at least equivalent to the licensed fall harvest by hunters and can render sustained yield management efforts ineffective.

Between 1913 and 1915 Stoney Indians were annually shooting 650 to 1000 bighorn sheep. Photo from Conservation Fish, Birds and Game *(1915).*

The Aboriginal Resources Development Group (ARDG) recommends that access to Forest Management Agreement areas be managed to prevent non-aboriginal hunters from causing declines in game populations while not impeding aboriginals from exercising their treaty rights to hunt. Non-aboriginal hunters recommend that access management be designed to disperse hunting pressure and that seasonal access to specific areas (e.g., big game winter ranges) be denied to prevent overexploitation and harassment of wildlife in these critical areas.

The politically sensitive nature of this issue, and the somewhat conflicting involvement of two levels of government (provincial and federal) have resulted in no resolution of the problem. Both native and non-native hunters believe the solution lies in education, dialogue, and joint planning among aboriginal peoples, government, industry, and conservation organizations.

THE CARIBOU/WOLF ISSUE

During recent decades, biologists of the Alberta Fish and Wildlife Division have documented a pronounced caribou decline in west-central Alberta. Similar trends are feared for the caribou ranging widely across the vast boreal forests of northern Alberta (see Figures 5.1 and 5.2). Despite a moratorium on sport hunting of caribou initiated in 1980 and attempts to reduce poaching, the population has continued its downward slide. Similar trends have been documented in several other regions of Canada, noticeably British Columbia, Quebec and Ontario.

Although the causes of these population declines are not fully understood, there is ample evidence from radio-telemetry studies that survivorship of caribou calves is dangerously low. The prime culprit appears to be excessive levels of predation by wolves. Studies conducted in Alberta and British Columbia indicate that less than 10% of calves may be surviving their first year, a recruitment level far too low to maintain healthy population levels. One might expect wolf populations to decline along with caribou and become less of a factor. Such appears not to be the case, however, as high wolf densities appear to be maintained by alternative prey species such as moose. Increasing moose populations may be contributing to an expanding wolf population to the detriment of caribou. Population ecologists describe this system as a "predator-pit", whereby caribou cannot recover as they are preyed on frequently by an abundant predator (wolf) that is maintained by an alternative prey species (moose). Although other factors such as habitat fragmentation caused by the forestry industry are undoubtedly involved in the caribou story, many biologists believe that selective wolf control programs would place caribou back on a recovery track. Much of the public considers all forms of wolf culling to be either unethical or unjustified, however, and is presently unwilling to tolerate proposals to reduce wolf densities. This caribou/wolf scenario clearly illustrates the conflicts that can exist between biologists and citizen groups when recommended biological practices are socially and politically inexpedient. As concern for dwindling caribou populations intensifies, an intriguing conflict occurs between wolf and caribou preservation groups lobbying for the prosperity of their chosen wildlife species.

As forestry practices expand throughout old-growth conifer and mixed-wood forests in Alberta, biologists must remain vigilant to the effects of logging, particularly on the lichen forage so critical to caribou. The combined negative effects of forestry, habitat fragmentation, predation and human harassment may collectively prove too large a burden for Alberta's precarious caribou population to withstand.

10
Economic Aspects

*Wiktor L. Adamowicz
and Peter C. Boxall*

Few Albertans perceive wildlife in terms of dollar value to our provincial economy or to themselves, but this chapter may change their view. Our provincial ungulate populations are the source of significant income and provide valuable benefits from a variety of consumptive and nonconsumptive resource users. Sport and subsistence hunters, wildlife viewers, photographers and tourists are just some of many who spend money on activities directly related to hoofed mammals. Beneficiaries of expenditures include the accommodation, travel and photography industries, sporting goods stores, taxidermists, big game outfitters and a host of spin-off industries. This chapter explains that the basis for an economic evaluation of a natural resource goes far beyond expenditures, and estimates the consumptive, non-consumptive and non-use value of hoofed mammals in Alberta. The authors present a convincing argument that managers must consider the economic impacts of those land use practices (eg., agriculture, mining, forestry) that affect wildlife habitat and wildlife populations, and therefore availability and value of ungulates to consumptive and nonconsumptive users. As our provincial human population continues to increase and wildlands shrink, economic factors will become more important to management decisions, as will the public's interest in ungulate-based activities, and their willingness to pay for these opportunities.

INTRODUCTION

The hoofed mammals of Alberta are a prized and valuable natural resource, providing economic benefits to many sectors of the Alberta economy. As a renewable natural resource, hoofed mammals are a major source of economic value and regional income generation. In this chapter we explore the economic aspects of this resource. The concept of economic valuation for wildlife resources is presented along with some estimates of economic value for various hoofed mammal species in Alberta.

The importance of hoofed mammal species in Alberta is easily recognized by the number of hunting licenses sold and the expenditures on hunting these species. However, hoofed mammals also play a significant role in non-consumptive (or non-hunting) resource use. Large-mammal sightings enhance the experiences of non-consumptive users, and a significant proportion of non-consumptive users seek out contact with large mammals. Even individuals who never visit the wildlands (non-users) place values on the existence of hoofed mammals. In this chapter, we will examine the activity and values of consumptive users, non-consumptive users, and non-users, and explore some management issues in a socioeconomic context.

ECONOMIC COMPONENTS OF WILDLIFE RESOURCES

Just as any natural resource has value, wildlife resources also have value. A parcel of land has value because of its potential use for crops, its location, its scenic amenities, and its potential to provide future benefits. Similarly, wildlife resources have value in that they are associated with human

ACTIVITY
(Hunting, Viewing,
Commercial Use)

QUALITY
(Resources, Habitat,
Experience, Regulations)

EXPENDITURES

Support Industries
-tourism and travel
-guiding and outfitting
-taxidermy
-meat processing
-retail

Regional
Economic
Impact

VALUE
(See Figure 10.2)

Figure 10.1
Economic components.

wants and needs. In particular, wildlife is associated with hunting activities, meat products, viewing, photography and the maintenance of a diverse ecological structure. Different individuals have different priorities or preferences among values provided by wildlife. In this section we define the type of values for various products or services involving wildlife.

Most people consider economics to be a study of dollars and cents moving through the economy. In fact, economics is the study of the allocation of scarce resources. In the case of wildlife resources, we have a resource which is owned by the public, yet is not freely available: one must often pay licence fees and incur travel costs to enjoy the wildlife resource. Wildlife resources are renewable, yet they are fragile and in high demand.

The allocation of these scarce resources is a concern for management. The allocation of most resources is based on value. In a market system, values are determined by the consumers and producers in the marketplace. Prices serve as a common measure of value and are determined by the interaction of supply and demand. However, wildlife resources are not so easily valued, because most of the products and services of wildlife are not traded in markets. Values for this resource must be determined in a different fashion.

Wildlife resources compete with other natural resource industries (e.g., agriculture, forestry, petrochemical) for land area. Because these other natural resources have values that are clearly defined in the market, corresponding values must be determined for wildlife so that proper resource allocation decisions can be made. In the past, wildlife resources and other resources without market prices have been undervalued because of the lack of a standard of comparison, and they have suffered losses to market-based resources (e.g., timber). With improved valuation, the role of wildlife resources in land allocation and management can be properly recognized. The economic components of wildlife resources are summarized in Figures 10.1 and 10.2. The basis of the economic component is the activity, whether it be hunting, viewing, or even non-use. The degree of satisfaction from an activity depends on a variety of factors, including the quality of the resource, the quality of the habitat or hunting experience, and the type of experience permitted within the regulatory system. The quality of the experience influences value, which in turn influences future activity levels and types. For example, poor-quality hunting experiences due to resource, habitat, or regulatory problems may result in fewer hunting trips and a lower value on the activity.

Recreation activity generates both expenditure and economic value. This may seem confusing, because many individuals consider expenditure to represent value. This is not the case. Individuals who live adjacent to prime wildlife habitat will spend little in travel and lodging to enjoy the resource. Their personal values of the wildlife resources, however, may be many times greater than the value held by an individual who incurs great expense in travelling to enjoy the resource. While expenditures are not appropriate as a measure of value, they often provide a mechanism by which we can infer value. Also, expenditures are important for determining the regional economic impact of activities involving wildlife resources.

Expenditures on wildlife-related activities affect several industries within the province, including the tourism industry, retail and service sectors, and guiding and outfitting. Areas in Alberta that derive important income from recreation associated with hoofed mammals include the town of Wainwright, which benefits from the special deer hunt, and Jasper and Banff, which gain income from tourists who view bighorn sheep, wapiti and mountain goat.

Regional economic impact is a measure of the generation of economic activity in a region stimulated by the injection of external funds. Several businesses within a small town near the Willmore Wilderness, for example, may benefit from the money brought in by wildlife-oriented tourists. The income generated in these businesses is spread throughout the community. While these economic impacts are important on a regional scale, however, they are likely not significant on a provincial or national level. If an area is closed to hunting, individuals will still spend their money, either by hunting in different places or by spending it in some other activity (e.g., professional sporting events). The regional economic impact may also change location. The economic value for the resource, however, always remains with the resource.

In Table 10.1 we provide some estimates of the amount of money spent on recreational hunting of selected hoofed mammals in Alberta. Note the large amount spent by non-resident hunters. As a source of regional economic impact these hunters are quite significant; however, not many licences are sold to non-residents. The impact of resident hunters may be even more significant than that of non-residents in some regions because the number of hunters, especially for moose and wapiti, is quite large.

Expenditures presented in Table 10.1 should be interpreted carefully. These are not the specific amounts spent on wapiti hunting, moose hunting, etc. These amounts are the average seasonal expenditures on all hunting trips by individuals holding a particular licence. Of course, most hunters hold multiple licences, therefore many moose hunters may also be wapiti hunters. Thus, expenditure for each species cannot be added to obtain a total expenditure. The interesting aspect of Table 10.1 is the fact that holding a bighorn sheep licence increases the average expenditures per season, and holding a mountain goat licence increases this amount even more.

Hunting, however, is not the sole source expenditure on wildlife-related activities. As shown in Figure 10.1, the results of the 1987 *National Survey on the Importance of Wildlife to Canadians* (see Filion *et al.*, 1989) indicate that the average Albertan who took non-consumptive wildlife-related trips primarily to enjoy large mammals spent $942.78 during 1987. This indicates the large monetary impact of the non-hunting users on wildlife resources.

A significant amount of money is spent in the enjoyment of wildlife resources. However, these expenditures are not the only values that are important for public policy. In fact, direct estimates of expenditures can do little to determine the allocation of scarce resources. This is where we must turn to the estimation of economic value.

WILDLIFE VALUES

Values for wildlife can be categorized as **use** or **non-use** values. As shown in Figure 10.2, non-use values are values related to the preservation of the resource, independent of its use. Use values are related to activities such as hunting, viewing, and commercial use (direct use), or they can be related to the enjoyment of wildlife's role in other activities such as zoos and television programs (indirect use). Direct use values can be categorized as either consumptive use values or non-consumptive use values. Consumptive use includes those activities that have a direct impact on wildlife populations. Non-consumptive uses include all activities that do not directly reduce the supply of the resource. Non-use values are based on either potential future consumption or current satisfaction from the knowledge that a resource exists.

Consumptive Values

Consumptive values apply to situations such as recreational hunting, commercial use, and some ranching operations that involve wildlife. Commercial values for wildlife are realized when private ownership ventures (e.g., game farms) are permitted within the legislative framework. These commercial values would reflect supply of, and demand for, the wildlife resource and would result in a market value or price for wildlife not unlike the value of livestock in a feedlot. The more important issue is the value of the publicly owned wildlife resource, which can suffer over-harvesting or extirpation due to competing land uses. The determination of value of the wildlife resource is

Figure 10.2
Wildlife values. Modified from Asafu-Adjaye et al., 1989.

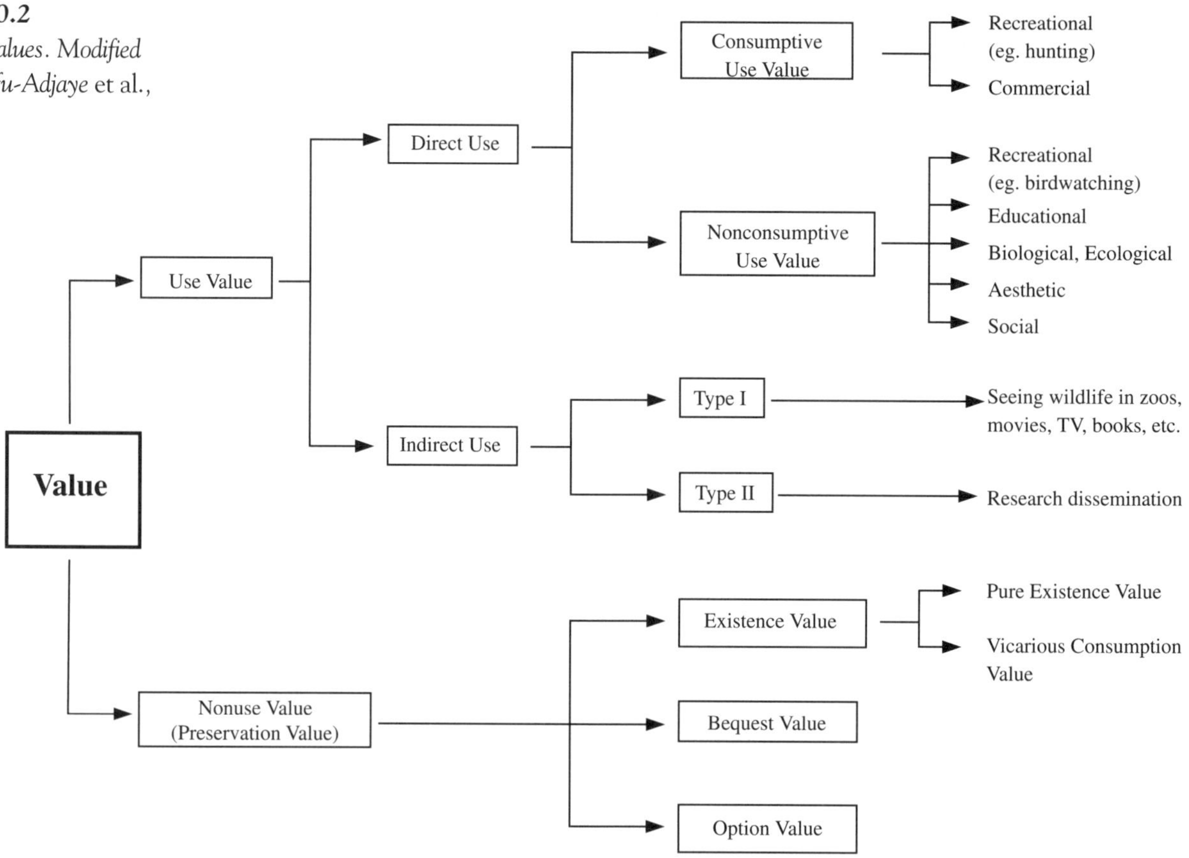

Value

- Use Value
  - Direct Use
    - Consumptive Use Value
      - Recreational (eg. hunting)
      - Commercial
    - Nonconsumptive Use Value
      - Recreational (eg. birdwatching)
      - Educational
      - Biological, Ecological
      - Aesthetic
      - Social
  - Indirect Use
    - Type I → Seeing wildlife in zoos, movies, TV, books, etc.
    - Type II → Research dissemination
- Nonuse Value (Preservation Value)
  - Existence Value
    - Pure Existence Value
    - Vicarious Consumption Value
  - Bequest Value
  - Option Value

necessary for comparison of values with other forms of resource use. Allocation of resources should occur through the determination and comparison of these societal values.

The value of wildlife to a recreational hunter can be reflected in the value of a recreational hunting day or trip. North American societies regulate access to the resource such that participation in hunting wildlife is not to be limited by personal income. In other words, license fees are kept artificially lower than what could actually be collected from individuals. Hunters would be **willing to pay** more for the privilege of their sport despite incurring expenditures to participate. **Willingness to pay** is one measure of economic value. The same principles hold for non-consumptive uses where no fees are collected for their recreational use but some benefit is achieved by involvement. Measures of the economic values for non-market resources are called **extra-market** values (or non-market values).

Several techniques exist for the determination of the maximum willingness to pay for a hunting day. These techniques can be classified into two groups, inferential and direct. The inferential approach uses market data to impute a maximum willingness to pay. The most commonly used inferential approach is the "travel cost" model. This model values the recreation site based on the number of visits that individuals make to the site (see McConnell, 1985). Several inferential models are designed to value changes in site characteristics and quality (see Mendelsohn, 1987). The direct techniques essentially ask the individuals how much they would be willing to pay, over and above all other hunting expenses, to hunt. Both the direct and inferential approaches have been criticized for a variety of reasons. The inferential approach has been criticized on the grounds that it makes a variety of assumptions about the behaviour of the recreationalist. The direct approach suffers from the fact that a hypothetical question is being asked and the people never actually have to pay these amounts. A number of useful references explain the two approaches, including McConnell (1985), Brookshire and Smith (1987), and Cummings *et al.* (1986). Considerable testing of these techniques has refined the measures and has shown that when appropriately applied, reasonable values for wildlife-related activities can be obtained.

In Table 10.2 we provide examples of extramarket values for the recreational hunting of some hoofed mammals. The values, collected by Adamowicz (1983), are results from a 1982 survey of Alberta hunters using the direct approach. The values from Sorg (1982), and Sorg and Nelson (1986) are for wapiti hunting in the western United States. The Sorg and Nelson results are based on the inferential travel cost model. The Sorg results are based on the direct approach. The mean willingness to pay of around $70, over and above all other costs, is a measure of the economic value of the activity. This figure can be tied to the land base in order to determine the value of the wildlife resource to consumptive users. The value of hunting as measured by the National Survey on the Importance of Wildlife to Canadians shows that large mammal hunting in total has an economic value of $211.10 (1987 dollars) per hunter per season in Alberta (Filion *et al.*, 1990). While there are several different techniques for estimating the extramarket value for various uses of wildlife resources, there is considerable consistency between estimates of value for these activities. There has also been considerable use of these values in land-use and related policy decisions involving conflicts between wildlife and other natural resource industries across North America.

Non-consumptive Values

Individuals who use the wildlife resource but do not affect the populations directly also have values relating to their activities. Non-consumptive values are commonly measured using the direct approach. Some results of direct-valuation questions asked of non-consumptive users are presented in Table 10.2. The value of wildlife to each non-consumptive user in Alberta in 1987 averages about $163 per season for general recreationalists and about $225 for those interested specifically in large mammals (Filion *et al.*, 1990; and unpublished data from the 1987 National Survey). Two aspects of these figures are worth noting. First, these non-consumptive values apply to a much larger portion of the total population of Alberta than do the consumptive values. Second, the non-consumptive values from specialized users (those who specifically sought out wildlife) are not very different from the values provided by hunters.

Additional information on the non-consumptive use of wildlife resources is presented in Figure 10.3. The number of individuals actively involved in non-consumptive use of wildlife is quite large (about 1.4 million in Alberta in 1987). Nearly one-third of all non-consumptive trips were specifically taken for the purpose of viewing or studying wildlife, and over two-thirds of those trips were taken for viewing or studying large mammals. The average expenditures of these individuals are quite comparable to the expenditures of consumptive users. Among those users not specifically interested in wildlife or large mammals, nearly all reported an increase in the enjoyment of their trip after an encounter with wildlife.

The importance of non-consumptive value is only now being recognized. The large number of individuals who participate in the non-consumptive use of wildlife, plus the significant value of encounters with wildlife, indicate that considerable effort should be spent in studying the activities and behaviour of this group. Management techniques in the past have concentrated on managing the resource for hunting. The importance of non-consumptive use may imply a significant change in the attitudes of Albertans, and this should be reflected in the management of the wildlife resource in the future.

Non-use Values

Non-use values can be broken into three categories: existence, bequest and option value. Existence value is a value assigned to the knowledge that a resource (wildlife species, for example) exists, regardless of whether the individual uses or consumes the resource today or will desire it in the future. Existence value is difficult to quantify, yet there is strong evidence that existence value is positive and may be significant. Individual donations to wildlife funds, societies and preservation groups, are evidence of existence value. Individuals who may never see a mountain goat or mountain caribou are willing to pay for the preservation of these species.

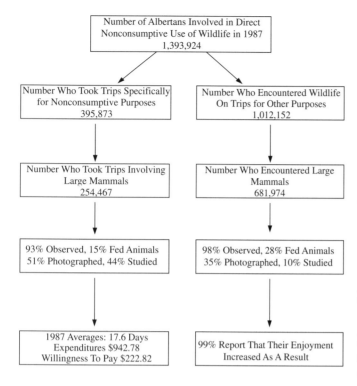

```
┌─────────────────────────────────┐
│ Number of Albertans Involved in Direct │
│ Nonconsumptive Use of Wildlife in 1987 │
│              1,393,924               │
└─────────────────────────────────┘
```

| Number Who Took Trips Specifically for Nonconsumptive Purposes 395,873 | Number Who Encountered Wildlife On Trips for Other Purposes 1,012,152 |

| Number Who Took Trips Involving Large Mammals 254,467 | Number Who Encountered Large Mammals 681,974 |

| 93% Observed, 15% Fed Animals 51% Photographed, 44% Studied | 98% Observed, 28% Fed Animals 35% Photographed, 10% Studied |

| 1987 Averages: 17.6 Days Expenditures $942.78 Willingness To Pay $222.82 | 99% Report That Their Enjoyment Increased As A Result |

Figure 10.3
Nonconsumptive wildlife use in Alberta during 1987.
Source: 1987 National Survey on the Importance of Wildlife to Canadians (*Filion* et al., *1989*).

Bequest value is a value that is based on the potential use of the resource by an individual's descendents. Often people are willing to pay into a fund in order to preserve a resource for their children. Bequest value is also difficult to estimate. However, efforts in this area are continuing.

Option value is a value derived from the fact that future supply and/or demand for the resource are uncertain. Option value will vary depending on the resource's value or activity and depending on the risk preferences of the individual. Some enjoy taking a gamble, but others do not. While option value is a component of economic value, it may be negative, dependent on risk-taking behaviour and the preference over wildlife services. Research is currently attempting to quantify this element of economic value.

An example of non-use value is presented in Table 10.2. The existence value of bighorn sheep in Colorado was elicited using a direct questioning approach by Brookshire, Eubanks and Randall (1983). The technique used in this study was to derive the willingness to pay for wildlife habitat for both users and non-users of the resource. While the value may seem small relative to other values in the table, this value is for a single species and reflects an average value per person per year. If aggregated over the entire population, this amount may be quite large. Other estimates of non-use values and a review of the theory can be found in Brookshire, Eubanks, and Sorg (1987).

Non-use values for wildlife in Alberta have been estimated by Adamowicz et al. (1991). Preservation values were obtained by administering a questionnaire to a random sample of Alberta households. This questionnaire asked respondents how much they were willing to donate annually to a hypothetical trust fund to be used solely for preserving wildlife in Alberta. The results indicated that respondents would donate an average of $80.90 (1987 dollars) to this fund. Aggregating over all households, these donations can be considered an estimate of preservation value totalling approximately $68 million per annum. Although these figures do not refer specifically to hoofed mammals, ungulates are certainly included in these values. Further research on partitioning preservation values by wildlife species group is clearly indicated. Preservation values have been identified as a priority for future National Surveys on the Importance of Wildlife to Canadians (see Filion et al. [1989] for a summary of the most recent survey).

Changes in Environmental Quality and Values

One of the most challenging issues facing economists and resource managers at the present time is the evaluation of the impact of changes in environmental quality. When habitat is lost or changed, what is the effect on the resource base and its users? Are users (consumptive or non-consumptive) willing to pay for improvements in wildlife habitat, increases in population numbers, or other quality improvements? Do the benefits of such quality improvements justify their costs? Economists are currently developing approaches to examine the benefits of environmental quality to consumptive and non-consumptive recreation activities. For example, Coyne and Adamowicz (1992) examined the benefits of reductions in crowding and increases in bighorn sheep population numbers for recreational bighorn sheep hunting in Alberta. They discovered that the benefits vary widely across bighorn sheep hunting sites in the province. The results of studies such as these may be useful in justifying intensive management of habitat in certain sites.

Changes in environmental quality also affect the site choice and recreational intensity level of participants. For example, Coyne (1990) presents a statistical model which shows where sheep hunters will likely go if an existing site is closed for the season. Such information is useful to resource managers in evaluating the impact of regulations.

Research on the impact of quality changes must proceed quickly. Most resource development (forestry, mining, etc.) will affect wildlife habitat. An assessment of the impact of such alterations is a necessary step in the economic analysis of the desirability of these projects.

MANAGEMENT ISSUES

Although on the surface one may not expect economic variables to affect wildlife management, in fact they do. Since the recognition by Aldo Leopold of the importance of the natural environment, including wildlife, in the lives of North Americans, resource managers have increasingly emphasized environmental considerations when evaluating land use decisions. In Alberta, we are only just beginning to face crucial decisions in resource allocation that our southern neighbours in the United States faced decades ago. This is particularly true for the hoofed mammal species in the province. The following points summarize some of the areas where we believe socioeconomic variables will play an important role in the management of hoofed mammals in Alberta.

1. The continuing encroachment onto wildlands through expansion of forestry, agriculture and oil and gas exploration will affect many hoofed mammals in the eastern slopes and boreal forest regions. Determination of the economic value of these species to Albertans will prove critical in decisions to reduce, enhance, or mitigate the effects that these industrial activities have on their well-being. Research must explore how these effects change the quality of wildlife-related recreational experiences.

2. The emerging importance of "preservation value" will have an important effect on regulatory processes surrounding the consumptive use of many hoofed mammal species, as well as on land-use activities involving resource allocation. This is illustrated by the closing of the mountain caribou and mountain goat seasons in the 1980s. In fact, hunter participation rates are declining throughout most of North America, including Alberta (Boxall and Smith, 1986, see Chapter 8). Studies of the reasons for the decline will prove useful in determining future management decisions involving hoofed mammals.

3. The significance of hoofed mammals in the traditional way of life of Alberta Treaty Indians and Metis will increasingly conflict with contemporary views of wildlife (recreation and preservation) held by other Albertans.

4. Increasing costs of wildlife management will result in new and innovative ways to collect funds from society to ensure that they are directed into priority areas (Brusnyk et al., 1990). The prioritization will be done on the basis of economic value.

As human populations continue to grow and wildlife habitat continues to decrease in size and quality, the use of economic values in selecting management options for hoofed mammals could prove significant to the long-term welfare of these species in Alberta. Hoofed mammals played a vital role in the lives of the early settlers of this province. Their role in modern Alberta society is less essential for survival, but people still possess strong concerns for the resource. The importance of wildlife to the quality of life in Western Canada is emerging as a significant issue in wildlife management.

SUMMARY

Hoofed mammals are important to the consumptive and non-consumptive use of wildlife by Albertans. Consumptive uses include recreational and subsistence hunting, as well as commercial uses of these resources. Non-consumptive uses include photography, viewing, and studying these mammals. The value of these activities is reflected in the number of participants and the willingness to pay of each participant. Economic impacts due to the existence of these resources are important to a number of regions in the province. The management of these resources and the maintenance of habitat depends on the use of true economic values in allocation decisions. In this chapter we have presented estimates of economic value for wildlife resources as well as some implications of socio-economic issues in the future management of hoofed mammal species.

ACKNOWLEDGMENTS

The authors would like to thank John Asafu-Adjaye and Michael Melnyk for their comments. The authors would also like to thank John Asafu-Adjaye for providing Figure 10.2.

TABLE 10.1

AVERAGE ANNUAL EXPENDITURES (IN DOLLARS) ON HUNTING BY RESIDENT AND NON-RESIDENT HUNTERS (1981–1982)

Category	Resident: Moose[2]	Wapiti (Elk)	Mountain Goat	Bighorn Sheep	Non-resident[1]: Moose	Wapiti (Elk)	Bighorn Sheep
Travel	179.29	199.91	652.29	333.58	251.39	286.81	480.61
Lodging	19.97	18.15	96.63	32.89	77.86	109.70	182.23
Food	76.49	84.28	312.95	168.58	95.92	104.53	132.11
Beverages	17.72	21.37	55.03	30.17	31.19	28.53	50.13
Rentals	3.70	0.69	56.33	8.69	5.08	11.57	15.87
Guiding	5.14	7.85	170.30	37.56	501.84	835.02	4,717.04
Ammunition	26.09	28.74	63.48	41.86	4.64	13.07	9.17
Services	24.98	34.65	312.43	121.12	34.68	118.50	393.66
Other	22.71	33.08	169.79	66.12	21.48	19.56	178.84
Total	376.09	428.72	1,889.23	840.57	1,024.08	1,527.29	6,159.66
Total (1986 $)[3]	497.94	567.62	2,501.34	1,112.91	1,355.88	2,022.13	8,155.39
Licenses Sold (81–82)	65,106	31,831	45	3,170	1,495	397	88
Licenses Sold (86–87)	59,915	32,790	16	3,230	561	777	85

[1] Amount spent in Alberta

[2] Species divisions are based on surveys of licence holders

[3] Expenditures adjusted by the consumer price index to 1986 values

TABLE 10.2

EXTRAMARKET VALUES

Activity	Species	Value	Source
Resident Hunting	Moose[1]	$72.01/day	Adamowicz, 1983
	Wapiti[1]	$63.00/day	Adamowicz, 1983
	Mountain Goat[1]	$68.04/day	Adamowicz, 1983
	Bighorn Sheep[1]	$72.94/day	Adamowicz, 1983
Non-resident Hunting	Moose[1]	$93.38/day	Adamowicz, 1983
	Wapiti[1]	$61.50/day	Adamowicz, 1983
	Bighorn Sheep[1]	$246.53/day	Adamowicz, 1983
Resident Hunting	Wapiti	$22.57/day	Sorg and Nelson, 1986
Resident Hunting	Wapiti	$92.00/day	Sorg, 1982
Change in Bighorn Sheep population[3]	Bighorn Sheep	$3.14/hunter	Coyne and Adamowicz, 1992
Loss due to site closure[4]	Bighorn Sheep	$3,300–$26,000	Coyne and Adamowicz, 1992
Existence Value (Non-users)	Bighorn Sheep	$7.00/year	Brookshire et al., 1983
Hunting	Large mammals	$224.27/season	N.S.I.W[2]
Non-consumptive trips	All trips	$165.22	N.S.I.W[2]
Non-consumptive trips	Large mammals	$224.75/year	N.S.I.W[2]

[1] Species categories based on samples of licence holders; these respondents hunt other species as well

[2] 1987 National Survey on the Importance of Wildlife to Canadians (Filion et al., 1989; 1990) and unpublished data on file at Alberta Fish and Wildlife Division

[3] The estimated willingness to pay, by Albertan sheep hunters, for a 10% increase in the bighorn sheep population

[4] The loss of benefits to resident bighorn sheep hunters associated with closing a sheep hunting site for one season. The values differ across sites

11
Commercialization

J. Brad Stelfox

*In recent years in Alberta, more public attention has been given to commercializa-
tion of wildlife, or "game farming", than any other aspect of hoofed mammal
management. The public appears split on this issue: conservationists, sport hunters
and wildlife managers view it with skepticism if not contempt, and are fearful
of genetic contamination, disease transmission, poaching and reduced access
of hunters to wildlife on private lands. Support for game farming comes from
certain sectors of academia and an agricultural community desperate to diversify,
who argue that it will conserve natural landscapes and is economically rewarding.
Improved economic performance of game farms over conventional livestock
stem from exploiting wildlife adapted to local environs, diversified foraging
strategies, high market value of velvet and reduced veterinary requirements.
This chapter attempts to lay out the facts (or suppositions), with the help of game
farming advocates (Drs. Robert Hudson and Lyle Renecker) and opponents
(Alberta Chapter, The Wildlife Society). A major theme of this chapter is that
Alberta must find some mechanism to economically reward those private
landowners who support wildlife. Without such an incentive, Alberta will
continue to lose wildlands, and therefore wildlife.*

INTRODUCTION

Until recently, Alberta's ungulates have been exclusively a public resource: owned, used, and arguably abused as public property. The importance of this long-standing relationship should not be understated, since many Albertans' ancestors originated from parts of Europe where average citizens neither owned nor had access to wildlife. Descendants of such "classist" systems hold dearly their right to experience and hunt public wildlife. Attendant with this "public wildlife" legacy have been several trends which are disturbing to the conservation community. As Alberta's human population has increased and expanded over the last several decades, so has the amount of wildland that has been radically altered by cultivation and livestock practices. Each year more pristine wilderness is lost to industry, agriculture and other incompatible land uses. Not surprisingly, loss of wildlife habitat results in loss of wildlife.

It has been argued that the major cause of habitat and wildlife loss in Alberta is the absence of sufficient incentives to those landowners who support our natural resources. Since western society is driven by monetary considerations, it has been suggested that financial incentives are required to ensure the survival of wildlife. Therefore, wildlife resources may need to be profitable to justify their existence. Responding to this new perception, economists are busy quantifying the direct and indirect economic benefits of wildlife in provincial and national parks, wilderness areas, and privately-owned wildlands (see Chapter 10). Specifically, the landowner must have a profit motive to maintain healthy wildlife habitat. In practice, however, owners of wildlands often suffer fiscal penalties. These penalties take many forms and may include:

- higher taxes for maintaining land in a non-agricultural state;

- loss of forage, both planted and in stacks, that is consumed by wildlife;

- inconveniences (e.g., responding to hunter inquiries, repairing damage, possible livestock loss) caused by those who hunt on private property; and

- forgoing of revenue that would have been generated if wildland had been brought into conventional agricultural production.

Given the financial burdens placed on private landowners who support wildlife habitat, and the absence of legal means for financial remuneration, it is surprising that wildlands are not disappearing more quickly. Prior to game farming, the primary economic beneficiaries of native ungulates were the big game outfitting community, taxidermists, the hunting equipment retail market, and the tourism industry associated with national and provincial parks. For those private landowners who support a significant percentage of Alberta's hoofed mammals, these revenues do not apply.

Given the tenuous economic climate of Alberta's agricultural community, many farmers are now exploring ways of reducing operating costs while increasing revenue. In this light, traditional wildlife and wildlands may not appear attractive to cost-conscious farmers. The draining of wetlands and the clearing of "marginal" bush has proceeded all too commonly in a failing attempt to harness all available land and swing the economic balance in favour of traditional agricultural practices.

During the past decade, new ideas about wildlife/landowner roles have arisen and been met with heated controversy. The most notable are game ranching/farming and fee hunting. Both would allow landowners to generate money from wildlife on private property. Although few would argue the need to financially assist landowners who support wildlife, many Albertans and conservation agencies are concerned about the potential abuses that both systems may encourage.

GAME FARMING AND RANCHING

Game ranching is the sustained commercial use of wild populations of hoofed mammals for production of meat and possibly sport-hunting opportunities. Arguments favouring game ranching initially emphasized an extensive system focusing on multi-species communities inhabiting mixed-wood forests where conventional agricultural practices are economically poor or marginal. Although the productivity and net revenue of this system would be modest, low operating costs would ensure a reasonable profit. In theory, it was argued, game ranching would preserve natural ecosystems while providing a healthy economic return.

Unlike game ranches, game farms manipulate distributions of animals, provision herds with forage during winter months, "improve" herds through selective breeding, provide medical attention in the form of vaccines and antibiotics, and typically raise a single "most rewarding" ungulate species. Because of the high operating costs of this system, game farmers must adopt an intensive approach to animal husbandry. Animals are concentrated into paddocks, handled frequently, and pushed to their reproductive maxima. In practice, game ranching and game farming represent different extremes of the same spectrum: one extensive and one intensive.

Since commercial utilization of wild ungulates became topical in the late 1970s, entrepreneurs lobbied successfully to have the Wildlife Act modified to permit this new industry. During this era, the merits and structure of the fledgling industry were debated both in political and public arenas. Readers are directed to numerous articles by Robert J. Hudson (1981, 1983, 1984, 1985, 1987, 1990) and Lyle A. Renecker (1988a,b, 1989a,b) for excellent treatments of the potential advantages of commercial utilization of hoofed mammals. Equally valuable are several articles by Valerius Geist (1983a,b, 1985a,b) that express serious reservations about the development of this industry.

Many species have been evaluated for their economic performance on game farms, with the wapiti emerging as the most suitable ungulate. Their general habitat requirements, flexible foraging strategies, gregarious social structure, rapid antler growth and tractable qualities together make the wapiti an ideal choice for game farmers. Photo by R.J. Hudson.

In 1991, Alberta's game farming community received formal recognition with the proclamation of the Livestock Industry Diversification Act (LIDA). This Act transferred most jurisdictional responsibilities associated with game farms from Alberta Fish and Wildlife Division to Alberta Agriculture. One of the major changes adopted by this Act was the legal slaughter of wapiti for meat at designated abattoirs in Alberta.

Although unrestricted forms of wildlife commercialization are not permitted in Alberta, game farming is permitted under the following restrictions:

1. a game farming permit must be obtained;
2. the game farm operation must be located on private property; and
3. all animals must be inspected and tagged in compliance with the Act.

The second and third conditions necessitate an intensive form of game utilization, since few private landholdings are large enough to support an extensive game ranch, and only the tractable animals of domestication operations can be approached, inspected and tagged.

Although several ungulate species have been examined for their potential in game farms (white-tailed deer, mule deer, moose), only the bison and wapiti have emerged as proven producers following logistical and economic considerations. Although wapiti game farms must conform to the above government regulations, the reclassification of bison as domestic animals in the early 1970s permits farmers to raise, kill, and market plains bison in a fashion similar to cattle.

Over the last several years, Alberta's game farming industry has experienced healthy growth. The provincial organization that represents this industry, the Alberta Venison Council, has grown since its inception in 1985 to a membership of ~300 in 1992. Although more time is required to substantiate the economic rewards of game farming, estimates by Renecker suggest that fully stocked wapiti game farms can generate a profit margin of $1000–1100/hectare compared to $225–300/hectare for a cattle operation at full production.

Major market products of game farms in Alberta are velvet, females sold for brood stock, large adult males sold as breeders, and immature males sold for meat. Although a small domestic market exists for velvet, the majority is shipped to the Orient where it enters the medicinal industry.

Much of the favourable economic returns of wapiti farms can be traced to the high market value of live animals and prime velvet. The following values typify auction sales during 1992 in Alberta (Norm Moore, personal communication, 1992): yearling females, $7,000–10,500; pregnant adult females, $12,000–17,000; open adult females, $9,000–12,000; male calves $2,000–3,500; male yearlings $2,500–3,000; breeding quality mature bulls, $5,000–8,000, and average mature bulls, $3,000–4,000. During recent years, approximately 75–80% of revenue from wapiti farms has been generated from live sales, the balance being produced from velvet. High grade wapiti velvet prices have generally increased since 1987 and now fluctuate from $200–250/kg. A single large bull can produce up to 8 kg of velvet annually.

1992 live sales of plains bison in Alberta (Norm Moore; personal communication, 1992) averaged $2,000–2,500 for pregnant adult females, $1,200–1,400 for female calves, and $700–900 for bull calves .

Existing regulations prohibit the commercial slaughter of native hoofed mammals, except bison and wapiti, in Alberta. White-tailed deer, mule deer, and moose must presently be shipped outside of Alberta for slaughter. The requirement for ante-mortem inspection of animals at a government licensed slaughterhouse strongly favours game farming and obviates the development of extensive game ranches stocked with wary animals.

As of July 1993, 154 game farms were registered in Alberta, supporting a combined population of approximately 4,323 wapiti, 600 white-tailed deer, 296 mule deer, and 17 moose (not including calves and fawns). In 1993, a provincial population of ~12,000 domesticated plains bison were being raised on ~120 ranches. Locations of privately owned herds of plains bison are illustrated in Figure 4.11.

From January, 1991 to July, 1993, approximately 2,700 wapiti were destroyed by Alberta Agriculture because of concerns relating to bovine tuberculosis, and over 90 game farms were placed under quarantine.

Opponents of game farming represent a vocal community in Alberta, and include the Alberta Fish and Game Association. Several reservations have been expressed, especially that game farming will:

1. reduce opportunities for recreational sport hunting;

2. increase poaching and illegal trafficking of venison;

3. contaminate genetic stock of wild-ranging ungulate populations;

4. introduce disease agents to Alberta when live game farm animals are imported.

In an attempt to mitigate the concerns of both lobby groups, the government has compromised by restricting game farming to private property. This ensures that sport hunting on public land will not be threatened.

The Disease Factor

Recently, a new concern about game ranching has surfaced in academic, public, and government circles. It addresses the possible introduction of undesirable diseases and parasites into Alberta as the result of inter-provincial and international movement of wild hoofed mammals. Of particular concern are the disastrous consequences that could befall Alberta if the meningeal worm Parelaphostrongylus tenuis were to become established in our white-tailed deer populations. This parasite, which does not adversely affect its natural host, the white-tailed deer, kills moose and other ungulate species by causing an acute neurologic disorder. To prevent the arrival of P. tenuis in Alberta, the importation of white-tailed deer has been prohibited. What is of present concern is the possibility that wapiti, or other ungulates, may survive infections long enough to serve as carriers. If transmission by this route is occurring, the widespread translocation of wapiti into

Alberta during the 1980s could spell trouble for our important and substantial moose population. Recognizing the severity of this situation, the provincial government has since placed a moratorium on importation of all Cervidae into Alberta. Recent studies by the University of Alberta and Alberta Fish and Wildlife Division (Samuel *et al.*, 1992) have shown that wapiti infected with moderate levels of *P. tenuis* larvae can survive the infection and shed viable larvae. Until reliable detection techniques and control measures for *P. tenuis* are devised, it would appear unwise for managers to permit the translocation of native hoofed mammals into Alberta from regions where white-tailed deer have meningeal worm.

FEE HUNTING

On the horizon may be yet another strategy intended to financially reward landowners who maintain wildlife and their habitat. Like game farming, fee hunting is being tried elsewhere in North America and stands to generate considerable resentment. The theory is simple: it provides a direct mechanism for landowners to charge hunters and recover their costs of supporting wildlife. Although fee hunting is illegal in Alberta, it still occurs to some extent, particularly by those who hunt white-tailed deer in areas producing trophy bucks. Nowadays, it is not uncommon to hear of hunters paying parking fees to enter private land. A somewhat analogous, though legal, arrangement occurs in parts of the United States, where successful hunters record the name of landowners on whose property big game animals were killed. These landowners are then eligible for remuneration from the state government. There is little doubt that Alberta's hunting community would object to any government-authorized plan to allow landowners to charge hunting fees. Their primary fears are that hunting privileges would be determined by supply and demand and that wealthy hunters would usurp preferred hunting areas.

HUNTING LICENSE FEES

Another possible strategy is to increase the cost of hunting licenses. The additional monies earned would be distributed to landowners who wisely steward their wildlife resources. As simple as this strategy sounds (hunters ultimately paying for the resources and activities they desire—not an uncommon idea in a free enterprise economy), it seems unpalatable to Alberta's hunters. Previous modest increases in hunting licenses have met with strong disapproval, as have the considerable fee increments applied to hunting licenses for 1991/92. License sales declined by 12% from 1989/90 to 1990/91 as hunters complained vociferously about license increases. Most hunters fail to recognize, however, that fees represent only a small percentage of the total costs of hunting big game in Alberta. More realistic estimates of the true costs of hunting to sport hunters in Alberta are provided in Table 10.1. For example, the cost of licenses to an average resident hunter in Alberta in 1986 represented less than 5% of total costs for hunting moose and wapiti, and less than 3% for hunting mountain goat and bighorn sheep.

Similarly, tax breaks for landowners who maintain wildlife habitat would be met with opposition from municipal taxation departments which would forgo considerable revenue.

A consensus is emerging that wildlife habitat is being lost at an alarming rate because of the economic plight of Alberta's landowners. Of the various people at whom we point an accusing finger, private landowners are relatively guiltless. As with any other component of contemporary society, it is the resource user who should pay the lion's share to propagate a resource — why should wildlife habitat on private land be any different? As Geist has accurately pointed out, there are many potential abuses of wildlife commercialization. It should be the mandate of our provincial government to devise creative ways of rewarding those who support our wildlife resource, while discouraging management systems that unfairly favour wealthy hunters and the illegal trade in wildlife and wildlife products. No one should question, however, that our present course of non-action is a poor alternative that will lead to further loss of wildlife and its habitat.

ADVANTAGES OF GAME FARMING

by Lyle A. Renecker and Robert J. Hudson

Few would argue that game farming provides much needed diversification for a failing agricultural economy and the rural communities which depend upon it. Game farming opens new niche-markets and offers an opportunity to develop efficient production systems that capitalize on the adaptations of indigenous wild ruminants (Telfer and Scotter, 1975; Renecker and Kozak, 1987; Renecker, 1989). World-wide, deer farming has been a significant industry for 25 years, experiencing phenomenal growth projected to continue well into the next century (Hudson et al., 1989). Canada was a late-comer with the first commercial farms established in the late 1970s. Fifteen years later and after several inevitable set-backs, the industry has persisted if not flourished. Game farming seems to be here to stay.

For the audience this book addresses, the question is less whether game farming is good for agriculture than whether it is good for wildlife. These concerns are articulated in the next section of this chapter. We argue here that it is possible to develop safeguards that will protect wild populations and that the benefits of landscape conservation accrue to all wildlife of the agricultural zone where game farming can be practised. On balance, game farming can be a positive force in nature conservation.

Landscape conservation

The greatest challenge facing government agencies is wildlife conservation on productive agricultural lands. Western Canada faces a crisis of habitat loss as the productive prairies and parklands are appropriated for crop production or commercial development. From pre-settlement to 1985, about 40% of the prairie wetlands disappeared (Millar, 1986). In 1984–85, habitat lost in western Canada was calculated to approach 32 ha/hr. During the open winter of 1986–87, an estimated 405,000 ha of topsoil were subject to severe wind-erosion.

In some cases, it would be in the farmer's self interest to keep land under a permanent plant cover. In others, where it simply pays with current prices and subsidies, it is difficult (if not hypocritical) to convince a farmer that he should forego draining a wetland, clearing a forest, or plowing a grassland. Since there are few economic incentives to retain wildlife habitat, the balance of existing land uses depends on the relative prices and input costs of crops and livestock. Crop diversification, for example into oilseeds, shifted the balance toward cultivation. Animal diversification should shift it in the other direction.

Although genetically-engineered cattle, llamas and other exotic livestock may provide the needed incentive, there is special appeal to adopting native species which have been displaced from the agricultural landscape.

The benefits of this shift away from croplands are improved sustainability of agriculture (stabilization of soils and maintenance of clean groundwater) and the provision of habitat for other species that inhabit these pastures, wetlands, and forests (for example, rodents, ducks, game birds, shore birds, etc.). Because wild ruminants can forage through snow, the tendency is to stock pastures longer but lighter
to the benefit of range condition. Also, the diverse diets of wapiti and their behavioural preference for cover encourage farmers to maintain more natural vegetation than they would for beef cattle.

It is important to understand the choices. Wild ungulates may indeed be "better" than farmed ones, but farmed ungulates on permanent pasture are arguably better than cultivated fields and drained wetlands.

Gene conservation

Commercial game production has mixed effects on genetic conservation. Commercial interest in bison in the 1800s played an important role in conserving the species. Commercial herds provided essentially all bison used to restock parks and reserves in the United States and Canada. There are several other examples world-wide where game farms have provided a genetic refuge and certain species under siege in their native lands may yet be saved on Texas game ranches. Most of the world's population of Indian blackbuck are in the United States. Grevy's zebra or even black rhinos may make their last stand on commercial ranches. Because ranches are able to maintain larger breeding populations and keep animals on range, they offer greater hope than the world's zoos.

Of course, genetic refuges are only a stop-gap measure. A species must be maintained under natural selective pressures. In time, wild and domestic stocks start to diverge even without purposeful selection for production traits. However, this results from accumulation of traits in domestic stocks which are maladaptive in the wild. So the domestic forms can hardly be considered potential sources of genetic contamination unless, of course, the flow of farm game to the wild is so great that a shift in gene frequency is maintained despite selective disadvantage.

Although indigenous captive stocks of wapiti are unlikely to shift the genetic makeup of wild populations, the introduction of red deer could and measures have been implemented to prevent introduction of red deer and hybrids.

Poaching

Use of market incentives to control environmental impacts of industry is an underlying theme of the Bruntland Commission Report "Our Common Future" and a major thrust of the National Round Table on the Environment. However, the market for wildlife products is considered by some to be too fierce to explore similar incentives in wildlife management.

For certain rare species and hence extremely valuable products (e.g., rhino horn), the market is almost impossible to control. Only total bans offer even a glimmer of hope. However, more common species, especially those which can be easily propagated, offer an opportunity to seize and regulate the market rather than scramble to limit damage caused by a market controlled by others.

Such is the case with venison and velvet antlers. Although average market values have continued strong, this has been achieved by providing high-grade product. In the case of antlers, there has been an encouraging trend to discount poor product such as would come from field-killed animals. Probably because of tagging and inventory requirements, velvet has been marketed in Alberta for many years without creating an obvious incentive to poachers. More animals are poached for trophies than for velvet.

There is an instructive inadvertent experiment underway. The velvet market is being served by domestic production and there already are indications that supply has caught up with demand. The demand for bear gall bladders is not so served (and for other reasons probably should not) and restrictive policies are reducing supplies from sport hunting. We suspect that the gall bladder market will ultimately be much more difficult to control.

Diseases and parasites

As with any livestock industry, there is need to develop comprehensive disease control programs. Some of these apply equally to all species and are already in place. But every new species on farms presents new special requirements. The challenge is to anticipate and deal with them.

For many decades, Agriculture Canada has conducted massive campaigns to control Tb (tuberculosis) in livestock. Except for outbreaks of infection in cattle in Manitoba and bison in Wood Buffalo National Park, the program was successful. However, in 1991, bovine Tb was detected in farmed wapiti and a program of traceback and slaughter began. Fortunately, because of the registration systems implemented by the industry, the destinations of the suspect animals were easily traced.

The inability to identify Tb reactors in the controversial wapiti shipment from the United States probably resulted from using the caudal fold test, the standard for cattle but inadequate for deer. Cervical and/or comparative cervical skin tests are more sensitive but false positives are common leading to needless destruction of animals. The higher sensitivity and specificity of the blood Tb test (BTB) should allow the problem to be more efficiently controlled (Griffin et al., 1991) and should, in time, allow the borders to be reopened. The industry has already adopted the newer techniques for animals offered at auction.

Although the problem is serious and must be cleaned up, the threat to wild populations is probably overestimated. Bovine Tb maintains itself in wild bison but seems not to maintain itself in native deer. Although Tb has been diagnosed in wild wapiti (including a recent case in Manitoba which is unrelated to game farming), the disease has not established despite the prevalence of Tb in farm livestock across Canada for many decades. The susceptibility of farmed wapiti seems related to high stocking densities.

Meningeal worms are another important consideration recognized early enough to prevent spread of the parasite west of the Manitoba-Saskatchewan border. Importation of wapiti and other potential patent carriers of the worm into Alberta is banned until efficient tests or anthelminthic treatments are developed.

The game farming industry has responded to these challenges responsibly and has contributed to knowledge of wildlife parasites and diseases through their support of scientific research. The problem of "moving the zoo" is not peculiar to game ranching. Game ranching simply has focused attention on the even more risky translocations which have been practised since the turn of the century to re-establish wild populations and repatriate pristine ranges.

Denigration

One of the most curious oppositions to game ranching is the denigration of wildlife and attenuation of public interest in wild populations. Presumably, people are reassured or even numbed by the abundance of wapiti or bison on farms and no longer care about wild populations. We believe the evidence does not support this view. The public shows intense interest in the fate of bison in Wood Buffalo National Park, in feral horses in Suffield, and in wild reindeer in Scandinavia. Interest in wildlife as a public resource has never been greater than when game ranching challenged the notion that it could never be any other way. People may tire of ice-cream and television—books and wildlife probably not.

Summary

Commercial game production offers a sound method of agricultural diversification for farmers and ranchers in Alberta. With appropriate controls, the industry can also serve the aims of nature conservation on agricultural lands both by encouraging retention of natural habitats and permanent pastures and by restoring species such as bison and wapiti that have been absent for over a century. For these species, the question may be less whether we want them domestic or wild than whether we can have them at all.

DISADVANTAGES OF GAME FARMING

Position Paper of the Alberta Chapter of The Wildlife Society

Introduction

Throughout Alberta's history, our abundant and diverse wildlife resources have played an important role; from the early fur trade days through provision of subsistence to Native people and early settlers to modern times where in 1989 Albertans spent about $660 million on wildlife-related recreational activities. Substantial commercial and domestic benefits are also derived from our wildlands in the form of trapping, tourism, guiding and native subsistence hunting.

Conservation and protection of our wildlife resources and provision of public opportunity to use them is given high priority in land-based plans and projects. However, the recent establishment of a big game farming industry in the province constitutes a significant threat to continued efforts to conserve and protect wildlife and their habitats. In addition, traditional public use of these resources is also in jeopardy.

From its early developmental stages in the mid-1980s, big game farming has been a controversial issue in Alberta. Opposition to the practice has come from sportsmen, conservation groups, livestock organizations and concerned individuals from a wide variety of backgrounds.

Arguments in opposition to big game farming have highlighted a number of potential problems. Experience over the past five years has shown that many of the concerns are legitimate and deserving of serious consideration at this time.

This paper summarizes and discusses the relevant issues and concerns and provides the reader with a factual basis upon which to reach a well-informed opinion on big game farming in the province.

Background

Rapid development of the big game farming industry in Alberta began in the mid-1980s as a result of encouragement from various sectors to explore options for agricultural diversification. Big game farming was touted as an economical and environmentally viable alternative to conventional agriculture on large tracts of marginal grazing land. As well, it was viewed as a more culturally adaptable form of agriculture on Indian Reserves and Metis Colonies.

Wapiti and deer were considered desirable species for game farming because of their ability to utilize naturally occurring range without expensive and environmentally objectionable habitat destruction. Minimal winter feeding requirements, adaptable grazing capabilities, and high-priced products were seen as attractive economic incentives.

Relaxation in legislation governing wildlife in captivity provided for private ownership of wildlife and was an important catalyst contributing to the rapid development of the industry. This resulted in numerous operators erecting big game containments and handling facilities which was the legal prerequisite to acquiring breeding stock. By mid-1991 there were about 150 licensed big game farmers in the province, most of whom raised wapiti as their primary species.

Original legislative changes in 1986 permitted use of specified indigenous species including black bear, pronghorn, mountain goat, bighorn sheep and cougar in addition to moose, wapiti and deer for big game farm purposes. Currently only moose, wapiti, white-tailed deer and mule deer are permitted.

The following is an outline of relevant issues and concerns regarding big game farming and the impact on wildlife and traditional wildlife use in the province.

Poaching

Concern:

The potential use of big game farms to launder wild ungulates or parts thereof which were acquired illegally was a fear very vocally expressed by hunting groups and the public in general.

An apparent lucrative market for wild meat and wild animal parts exists in North America and in eastern Asia. As a result of public concern in this area, efforts to combat poaching have recently been bolstered by numerous government wildlife agencies, including Alberta. The legal market for wild meat and parts of game farm animals was seen as providing an easy outlet for poachers.

Related to the issue of poaching is the expressed concern that Alberta big game farms may be used as paid sport hunting grounds as in some U.S. states. Such practice is viewed as unethical and distasteful by most organized hunting groups and many sectors of the general public. Also it was feared by hunting groups that such activity would further provoke the ire of the powerful anti-hunting lobby.

Evidence:

In an effort to curb potential illegal activity, a relatively rigorous system of animal identification, registration and monitoring was invoked early in the development of game farming in Alberta. Births, deaths, acquisition, sales, movements, importation and exportation must be documented. The system also included identification and registration of animal products. Recent suggestions of reducing the requirements for documentation of game farm animals pose a renewed threat of increased opportunity for illegal activities.

The system was tested and found to be relatively effective when it became necessary to trace individual animals through various owners in efforts to control an outbreak of bovine tuberculosis (see below).

Existing legislation prohibits sport hunting on licensed big game farms at present.

Conclusion:

The identification and reporting system is elaborate and requires considerable monitoring and enforcement by regulatory agents. There are opportunities for operators to circumvent the requirements and perhaps the easiest method of breaching is in the procedure of reporting births on the farms. Neonatal deer, moose and wapiti are relatively easily captured in the wild and can be registered subsequently as farm-born animals. This is made easier by the fact that operators are not expected to register animals immediately upon birth because the design of most facilities does not permit the early detection of calves or fawns until weeks or months after birth. A case involving an operator attempting to illegally add to his stock in this manner has been tried and resulted in a substantial penalty.

With increasing numbers of big game farms and game-farmed animals, monitoring and enforcement requirements likely will outstrip the capability of regulatory agents and it is unlikely that government will increase their capability to keep pace.

Legislation change in 1985 prohibited the sale of meat from game farm animals but permitted the sale of products such as antlers. In spite of considerable public concern, regulatory jurisdiction was transferred from the Alberta Fish and Wildlife Division to Alberta Agriculture in mid-1991. Regulation changes permitting the sale of wapiti meat were included in the new legislation. This provides even greater incentive and opportunity for poaching to occur.

The issue of sport hunting on big game farms is of concern relative to public access but is of little consequence to the viability of the wildlife resource in general.

Diminished Access to Wildlands by the Public and by Wildlife

Concern:

From the outset of rapid big game farm development in the mid-1980s, hunters and environmental lobbyists expressed fear that large tracts of high quality wildlands would be dedicated to big game farming or ranching. It was speculated that access to wildlife for hunting or viewing would be significantly reduced. Further, it was feared that access to critical wintering ranges by wild ungulates could be seriously reduced.

Evidence:

Legislative changes to accommodate big game farming contained two sections relevant to this concern:
1. the definition of big game "farming", the practice being legalized, was determined to be different from big game "ranching" in that the intent of "farming" permitted the private ownership of live wildlife and maintenance in a husbandry sense without the sale of meat as a product of the farm. "Ranching" was defined as the practice of raising specific wildlife for meat markets; and
2. big game farming was restricted to private land.

Conclusion:

Although these restrictions were reassuring, there are presently two related issues which affect public access to wildland as well as wildlife access to habitat on private lands dedicated to big game farming.
1. Ungulate-proof fences prohibit the use of habitat on game farms by wild ungulates and other larger wildlife species which previously could use the area while it was either unfenced or fenced in a conventional manner.
2. The practice of grazing bison (an indigenous Alberta species which is considered domestic under existing legislation) on public land leases is now permitted. This requires perimeter fencing which presents an effective barrier to larger wildlife species. Wildlife use of those lands is seriously affected as is public access to the wildlife resources contained therein.

Recent legislative change permitted the sale of wapiti meat raised on big game farms. This negated the distinction between big game "farming" and big game "ranching". Successful lobbying by big game farmers could result in the extension of crown land bison grazing to include big game farm animals. This would further reduce wildlife use and public access to public lands in the province.

Loss of Wildlife

Concern:

Opponents of big game farming expressed concern that collection of game farm stock from the wild would reduce the abundance of wildlife or substantially reduce the opportunity for traditional consumptive users.

Evidence:

Legislative changes in the mid-1980s included provision for wild capture of up to six of each big game farm species once in the lifetime of each licensed big game farmer.

Relatively limited wapiti stocks in the wild and the high demand for hunting and viewing in Alberta resulted in a ban in 1986 on live capture of that species for big game farm purposes. However, in 1987 and 1988 several deer were live-captured and placed on game farms. Public opposition and problems in subsequent survival and containment resulted in a general ban on live capture of white-tailed deer and mule deer in 1989. Capture of a very limited number presently is conducted on two military bases as a method of reducing a safety hazard on airstrips.

Stock acquisition is a critical issue among big game farmers. In an attempt to circumvent the lifetime limit, several operators split their facilities and registered each portion under a separate name (usually a relative) thus doubling the lifetime limit for the farm unit. Following the recent bovine Tb outbreak and subsequent depopulation efforts, operators have suggested that wapiti should be taken from National Parks to replenish lost big game farm stock.

The Alberta Fish and Wildlife Division maintains a list of various agencies, institutions and game farmers that are willing to accept orphaned and abandoned wildlife. However, the number of animals received is often small and game farmers are the lowest priority. As a result, many operators acquired breeding stock in the U.S. and other Canadian provinces. This action resulted in numerous concerns and consequences discussed below under genetics and disease.

Direct loss of wildlife resulting from big game farms has recently surfaced in another form. Wild ungulates (moose, wapiti and deer) are attracted to the perimeters of big game farms, particularly during the breeding period. Attempts to enter have resulted in fence damage and/or damage to game farm animals which sparred with wild cohorts. In at least three cases attempts to discourage these intruders have been unsuccessful and wild stock was destroyed.

Some free-ranging animals successfully entered perimeter fences and were subsequently destroyed because the farms were under quarantine for Tb control purposes.

Conclusion:

Big game farms are being established within wild ungulate range and attraction of wild stock will become an increasing problem with disastrous results for the intruding animals.

With the ban on importing coupled with the loss of stock in Tb control efforts, operators will be lobbying for stock from wild sources in the province thus reducing the availability to traditional consumptive users.

Genetic Contamination

Concern:

Husbandry of wapiti on big game farms in other parts of the world has resulted in efforts to produce desired characteristics via cross-breeding with red deer. This closely-related European species breeds readily with wapiti, producing viable offspring.

Early opposition to Alberta's big game farming initiative identified a concern that red deer/wapiti hybrids would likely be imported to Alberta as big game farm stock. Subsequent escape to the wild could allegedly result in genetic contamination of wild wapiti in the province. Genetic mixing was deemed undesirable by concerned groups since our wild populations could be seriously affected by ill-adapted and genetically inferior red deer stock.

Evidence:

This concern resulted in two efforts to address the potential problem of genetic contamination.
1. Importation restrictions and prior genetic testing were imposed to assure only "pure" wapiti would enter the province.
2. Big game farmers were encouraged to construct facilities to adequately contain their stock.

A significant number of hybrids did enter the province in the early years of game farming. A test slaughter or neuter program was established to remove the undesired genetic stock.

The effectiveness of the genetic test as well as the elimination procedure was plagued with problems and game farm stock in the province still contains some red deer genetic material.

Efforts to assure containment of stock on big game farms were ineffective. Relevant legislation enacted in 1986 did not contain standards for fence quality nor design. Prerequisite for obtaining a big game farm licence was and is at present contingent upon acceptance by the regulatory agent of a game farm design proposal. The onus is largely on the operator to contain his stock and adequate fence height, etc., but is only encouraged via policy. Adequate containment continues to be a problem as about 50 animals have been recorded as escaped over the past few years. Most of these were subsequently recovered or destroyed.

Concern about containment is also relevant to discussions above under the topic of loss of wildlife and below under disease concerns.

Conclusion:

In Alberta the environmental threat of introducing red deer hybrids to wild wapiti population via game farming is presently a moot point as importation occurs in the future, identification and prohibition of red deer and their hybrids will be a renewed concern. In addition, other jurisdictions should be encouraged not to move untested animals into the range of wild wapiti.

Introduction of Disease

Concern:

Wild ungulates are susceptible to a number of diseases of cattle, sheep, and goats as well as several parasites unique to wildlife. The potential for game farm animals to introduce disease to domestic and wild stock is a worldwide concern. Rapid growth of the game farming industry in Alberta necessitated the importation of many animals to meet the demand for breeding stock. Fears were expressed about the potential introduction of diseases or parasites that do not exist presently in Alberta. Traditional livestock diseases include tuberculosis, brucellosis, anaplasmosis, and bluetongue. Wildlife parasites of concern include the meningeal worm (*Parelaphostronglylus tenuis*), the carotid artery worm (*Elaeophora schneideri*), and giant liver flukes (*Fascioloides magna*) (the latter is established in a small portion of the province at present). These parasites could be transmitted to and become established in free-ranging wildlife populations.

The agricultural, economic, and human health concerns regarding the above livestock diseases are well documented. The wildlife parasites are less well-known.

Mule deer in the western U.S. can be infected with the carotid artery worm. Although the worm causes few problems in mule deer, it is very pathogenic to wapiti. Similarly, many white-tailed deer in eastern North America are infected with the meningeal worm. It too causes little damage in its normal host, white-tailed deer, but can cause fatal neurologic disease in most other cervid species. Neither of these parasites occurs in Alberta.

Some wapiti survive infections of meningeal worm and pass infective larvae in their feces. Importation of such animals could result in importation of meningeal worm into Western Canada and subsequent infection of white-tailed deer. The consequences of infecting free-ranging white-tailed deer are undetermined, but could include extensive mortality of indigenous ungulates, especially moose, mule deer and caribou.

Evidence:

Current regulations prohibit the importation of mule deer and white-tailed deer in an attempt to prevent the introduction of carotid artery worm and meningeal worm, respectively.

In 1988, Alberta imposed a moratorium on the importation of wapiti until their potential role as a carrier of meningeal worm could be determined.

Recent investigations at the University of Alberta in conjunction with Alberta Fish and Wildlife Division have shown that meningeal worm could be imported with wapiti. There is presently no reliable method of detecting wapiti infected with meningeal worm and no reliable treatment.

All animals imported from outside Canada are subject to quarantine and testing for Tb, brucellosis, anaplasmosis, and bluetongue. However, often the tests used were those known to be effective in identifying infected agricultural livestock. As a result infected wapiti have inadvertently been brought into Canada. Several other serious diseases have occurred in wapiti on game farms in western Canada. In 1986, bluetongue was detected on a Manitoba game farm. Subsequently, 51 wapiti were destroyed and the disease apparently was eradicated.

In December, 1990 bovine tuberculosis was confirmed in a game farm wapiti in Alberta. As a result, an extensive and exhaustive effort was made by provincial and federal disease specialists to control and eradicate the disease. About one half of the 4,200 wapiti along with numerous deer and other species on Alberta game farms have been destroyed to date. In addition, a few workers involved in the program seroconverted to a positive skin test.

The source of the outbreak was traced to infected wapiti imported from the U.S. that were not detected during import inspection. Since January of 1989, diagnostic procedures for detecting Tb in wapiti have been improved but are still not failsafe.

Subsequent compensation for destroyed big game farm animals has been the source of aggravation within the cattle industry and among taxpayers because original settlements were substantially higher than that received for cattle destroyed for disease control. Up to $15 million compensation has been paid to game farmers in Alberta alone. Since 1988, bovine Tb has been confirmed in fallow deer in B.C. and Quebec, red deer, wapiti and hybrids in Ontario; and wapiti in Saskatchewan. All cases involved imported animals on game farms.

The devastating setback to the Alberta big game farm industry resulting from Tb eradication efforts has renewed the lobby to acquire breeding stock whether from the wild or via import.

Although the threat of Tb spreading to wildlife is real, the actual risk of this happening is unknown. There is at present no documentation that the disease agent has done so nor did it establish in cervids when bovine Tb was widespread in cattle in the 1920s and 30s. Bison in Wood Buffalo National Park is the only known case of bovine Tb established in free-ranging wildlife. The disease source apparently was cattle which shared the same range with bison at Buffalo National Park (now Camp Wainwright) in the 1920s.

Conclusion:

The examples of Tb and red deer hybrid entry into the province, in addition to several incidents involving individual operations attempting to circumvent game farm control regulations, is evidence that opponents of big game farming have very real and legitimate concerns.

It is very unlikely that disease/genetics testing procedures will improve sufficiently to prohibit additional entry of animals containing Tb or red deer genes and it is very possible that even more devastating disease agents (such as meningeal worm) would enter the province if import bans are lifted.

It is similarly unlikely that existing big game farmers will be required to upgrade their facilities to assure containment of their stock as well as prevent break-ins by wild ungulates. It is further anticipated that lobby pressure to capture wild stock will increase to the point where future political will may not be sufficient to refuse their requests.

Government regulatory agents which are not adequately equipped at present will not likely be provided with sufficient direction and resources to maintain adequate control of an expanding industry and prevent infractions which could result in the spread of serious diseases to our wildlife.

Philosophical Concerns

Concern:

The announcement that the Alberta government would encourage and facilitate the establishment of a big game farming industry resulted in strong vocal opposition from various public sectors based on a variety of arguments. There were however several arguing solely on a philosophic basis. Big game farming was seen by these groups and individuals as degrading to the aesthetic value of wild animals. The idea of private ownership of live wild animals for commercial purposes was considered distasteful and

unethical. In their opinion the fundamental North American idea of maintaining wildlife in public ownership (in general) was seen to be defiled.

In another vein, concern was expressed that big game farming may produce animals and products to such an extent that the values associated with viewing in the wild and acquisition of meat and products through hunting would significantly decline. It was feared that this in turn would see a decline in the will to protect and conserve the wild stock and its supporting habitat.

Conclusion:

Although there are several cases in Alberta where live wild animals are kept in captivity for commercial purposes (zoos, furfarms, birdgame farms, etc.) the philosophical points of view expressed have merit from cultural, historic and resource perspectives but because they are based on personal values and predictions they cannot be judged right or wrong.

Big game farming has however resulted in a real effect on conservation of wildlife in that a considerable amount of time and effort has been diverted away from regular wildlife management and enforcement efforts to accommodate the control necessary to establish the industry in the province over the past five years.

Summary

The foregoing describes the potential detrimental effects on our wildland and wildlife resources that a continuation of big game farming would have under a regulatory regime such as is currently in effect in Alberta. In summary these are:

- reduction in access to habitat on private lands by wild ungulates;
- reduction in public access to wildlife on private land;
- possible extension of the above issues to crown land;
- increase in options and incentive for illegal acquisition and disposal of wildlife;
- decrease in ungulates available in a wild setting;
- increase in possible genetic contamination of wild stock of some species;
- greatly enhanced chance of introducing untreatable, detrimental parasites and disease agents into our wildlife;
- degradation of traditional wildlife values;
- reduction in traditional wildlife resource management effort and incentive.

For these reasons the Alberta Chapter of the Wildlife Society believes that continuation of the big game farming industry is detrimental to the conservation and protection of wild species and their supporting habitats in Alberta. In addition, public access to these resources is diminished both in quantity and quality.

12

Morphology, Bioenergetics and Resource Use: Patterns and Processes

Lyle A. Renecker and
Robert J. Hudson

This chapter is a culmination, and more, of the varied information presented earlier in this book. In a comprehensible explanation, the authors synthesize a multitude of seemingly independent relationships into a set of rules as to how ungulates expend, acquire and allocate energy as they strive to locate and consume adequate levels of nutrients, complete their body growth, minimize heat loss during cold seasons, detect and avoid predators, achieve social dominance, and become reproductively successful. A central theme of this chapter is that body form, life history, behaviours, predator avoidance strategies and forage preferences of ungulates are all related in a meaningful way to each other and the preferred habitat of each species.

As this chapter explores such topics as form and function, nutrient requirements and supply, activity patterns and habitat preferences, it becomes clear that bioenergetics—the exchange of energy between the animal and its nutritional and thermal environments—offers the greatest insight into the fascinating adaptations and behaviours exhibited by Alberta's hoofed mammals.

INTRODUCTION

Daily patterns in use of time, habitat and food by wild ungulates are related in complex ways to their social, security, comfort and bioenergetic needs. Behaviours related to day-to-day living aim to maximize fitness by compromising these sometimes conflicting needs. Because some needs are more immediate than others, animals occasionally pre-empt food-searching and thermoregulatory concerns to deal with an immediate threat of predation or to enhance mating opportunities. However, the long-term concern is to maximize survival and reproductive contribution by acquiring energy with minimum effort and risk. This chapter explores the complex trade-offs involved and how this influences resource use.

FORM AND FUNCTION

How animals experience trade-offs and thus modify their behaviour is influenced by their specific anatomical, physiological and social characteristics. Body size is an important entry point for understanding adaptation since it influences almost every aspect of the animal's biology (Figure 12.1).

Physical Attributes

Organisms, like machines, seldom work the same if simply increased or decreased in size. For example, to support increasing weight, the cross-sectional area of the limbs and back must increase disproportionately. This principle extends beyond mechanical considerations to metabolic phenomena, ecological and social characteristics, and population dynamics. Mathematically, such

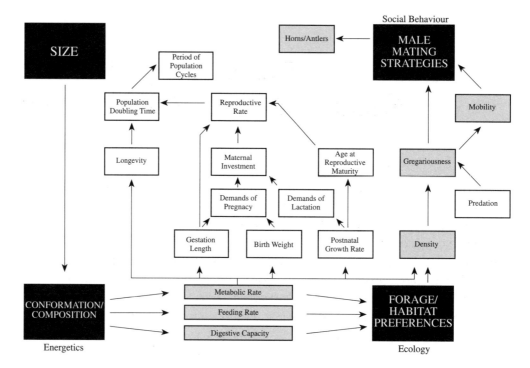

Figure 12.1
Interrelationships among size, energetics, ecology and social behavior of wild ungulates (Hudson, 1985).

relationships are described by the allometric equation $Y = aW^b$, where "Y" is the trait, "a" is the intercept, "W" is liveweight, and "b" is the slope. The value of "b", the curvature of the relationship, is most important: values of one describe isometric (linear) scaling, values of greater than one describe traits that increase more quickly than body size, and values of less than one (the most common pattern) describe traits that increase more slowly than size.

Weight

Alberta's ungulates range more than ten-fold in weight from 50 kg (pronghorn) to well over 500 kg (bison) (Table 12.1). Reported values are approximate, since season and range conditions profoundly affect body condition. Weights are usually taken during autumn hunting seasons (when weights are greatest) or in winter when animals can be easily captured (when weights have declined). Linear measurements such as skull dimensions, body length and shoulder height are relatively insensitive to short-term nutritional balance and give a good impression of frame size. The ratio of nutrition-sensitive (weight or chest girth) to insensitive (linear dimensions) measures can be used to score body condition (see Appendix 3).

Mature body size is highly heritable and seems to stay within relatively narrow limits. Suboptimal nutrition slows growth rates but only severe conditions early in life greatly reduce mature lean body mass. This suggests that mature size is highly adaptive, presumably shaped by such forces as thermal environment, locomotion, predation, and seasonal forage availability and quality. At least this holds for females, whose lives are not complicated by competition for breeding opportunities.

Most ungulates are sexually dimorphic because size improves competitive ability and confers greater opportunities to breed. In the most polygamous species, males may be 1.2 to 2 times heavier than females at maturity (Jarman, 1983; Georgiadis, 1985). Dimorphism tends to be a curvilinear function of the openness of habitat, increasing from forested to savanna habitats and diminishing in open grasslands (Geist and Bayer, 1988). The penalty for males living in the reproductive fast lane is heavier mortality. The sex ratio of dimorphic species is skewed in favour of females (Georgiadis, 1985), and the distortion increases under harsh environmental conditions (Flook, 1970).

Conformation

For mechanical reasons, the distribution of weight along the axial (spinal column) and appendicular skeleton (limb bones) is related to both size and locomotory patterns. Small, forest-dwelling ruminants tend to have more rounded backs, relatively short front legs, and saltatorial (bounding) gaits. Larger grassland ruminants have straight backs, relatively long front legs and cursorial (running) gaits.

Running speeds scale weakly with size among the world's ungulates. However, any pattern among Alberta's limited spectrum is masked by specific locomotory adaptations related to evasion of predators (Table 12.1). The fleetest of Alberta's wild ungulates is the pronghorn which uses this talent to advantage in open terrain. Bighorn sheep and mountain goat are relatively slow, but they make up for this with their agility in rough country.

Hard-ground species such as pronghorn, bison, and wapiti have tight hooves which splay little, even when running on soft ground. The dew claws, which serve no purpose on hard ground, have been lost in the pronghorn. On the other hand, deer, moose and caribou have loose ligaments which allow the cloven hoof to splay. Large dew claws and hooves and long legs are specific adaptations to snow (Telfer and Kelsall, 1984). Caribou occupy winter habitats with wind- or sun-crusted snow that supports their weight. However, snow in the winter habitats of moose is usually softer and seldom provides sufficient support so "wading" is a better strategy than "floating".

Incorporating both morphological and behavioural traits, Telfer and Kelsall (1984) ranked ungulates according to their ability to cope with snow (Table 12.2). In order of decreasing adaptation, Alberta's ungulates rank as follows: caribou, moose, wapiti, deer, bighorn sheep, bison and pronghorn. Mountain goats were not included in this comparison.

Feeding and Digestion

Diet, and consequently habitat selection, result from the differential scaling of metabolism and digestive capacity which forces smaller animals to feed more selectively (Demment and Van Soest, 1985). This is reflected in the remarkable adaptive radiation of ruminant digestion. On the basis of ecology, dentition, muzzle shape, salivary glands and alimentary tract, ruminants can be classified as grazers, browsers or mixed feeders (Hofmann, 1989). Within each category, species can be arranged according to selectivity which is generally inversely related to body size. Alberta's grazers are bison, bighorn sheep, and pronghorn. Mixed feeders include wapiti, caribou and mountain goat. Browsers are moose, mule deer and white-tailed deer.

Morphophysiological Specialization

The selenodont dentition of ruminants shows striking adaptation to diet. Because of the greater wear caused by their diet of coarse, dusty grasses, grazers have high crowned (hypsodont) molars and premolars to ensure they will last for the reproductive life of the animal. The incisor bar tends to be wider in grazers allowing more rapid forage intake at the expense of selectivity (Gordon and Illius, 1988). Grazers have larger masseter (chewing) muscles and smaller salivary glands than browsers.

Although fermentation volumes scale isometrically, grazers tend to fall above the interspecies relationship and browsers below (Van Soest, 1982). The overall size and proportions of the four-chambered stomach also reflect dietary adaptation (Figure 12.2). Grazers have relatively large rumens and omasa but small reticula and abomasa (Hofmann, 1989). Papillae are less evenly and densely distributed providing a lower effective absorptive surface. Browsers have relatively large reticula and abomasa, more open communication among stomach compartments, and heavy papillation.

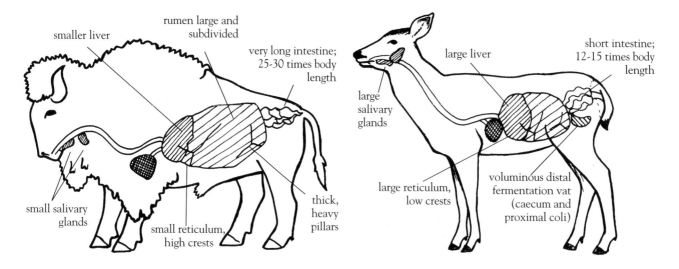

HIGH FIBER FOOD STRATEGIES
(plant cell wall)
slow passage and low
fermentation rate, cellulolysis

rumen large and subdivided

smaller liver

very long intestine; 25-30 times body length

small salivary glands

thick, heavy pillars

small reticulum, high crests

LOW FIBER FOOD STRATEGY
(plant cell content)
rapid passage, high fermentation rate,
amylolytic bacteria

large liver

short intestine; 12-15 times body length

large salivary glands

large reticulum, low crests

voluminous distal fermentation vat (caecum and proximal coli)

Figure 12.2

Anatomy of the ruminant digestive tract.

Digestion

The anatomical differences between grazing and browsing ruminants affect the digestive process (Renecker and Hudson, 1990). Because of the larger and more strongly subdivided foregut, the food of grazers is delayed, permitting relatively complete microbial fermentation before fine particles pass through the omasum to the lower tract for gastric digestion. The diet of browsers is passed rapidly and consequently is lightly fermented.

These two digestive strategies are appropriate given the fermentation patterns of their diets. Grasses ferment slowly but completely whereas the highly differentiated tissues of browse plants ferment quickly but plateau at a lower level. The optimal retention time where gut fill constrains intake is when about 50% of the fermentable portion has gone. Therefore, digestion coefficients, a standard agricultural measurement of the completeness of digestion, mean little to the success of animals in the wild. The optimal strategy is based on the trade-off between completeness of digestion and forage passage rate.

Intake

On low quality forages, gut capacity (volume of the ruminoreticulum, and fermentation/passage rates of digesta) limits forage intake. On very high quality forages, satiation may occur because nutrient requirements have been fully met. However, under free-ranging conditions, the ability of animals to meet their nutritional requirements is often constrained by the logistics of foraging, i.e., feeding rate (g/min) and foraging time (min/day).

One of the strongest determinants of feeding rate (g/min) is forage biomass (kg/ha) but different relationships hold for grass and shrub habitats and each herbivore species responds differently (Figure 12.3). Large indiscriminate grazers, small selective grazers and browsers each have their own relevant forage worlds.

Feeding rate is the product of bite rate (bites/min) and bite size (g/bite). Bite size is most strongly influenced by structural attributes of the plant such as leaf area, plant configuration, and for grasslands, tiller length and density. This relationship has a mechanical basis and is assumed to scale to the width of the incisor bar (Clutton-Brock and Harvey, 1985). Although this probably holds for grass swards, herbivores that strip forage (e.g., foliage) or use their tongues to prehend forage may achieve larger bite sizes than predicted from incisor width.

The main limit on bite rates is the time required to handle, wet, masticate, and swallow food items. Except in very sparse plant communities, bite rates are inversely related to bite size and perhaps dietary fiber. The extent to which bite size depresses bite rate varies among herbivores. In wapiti, handling efficiency is lower than in larger indiscriminate grazers such as bison. Of course, bite rates can also be related to the density and spatial arrangement of food items, and to barriers such as snow cover.

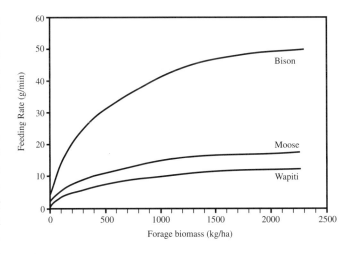

Figure 12.3
Foraging rates of bison, moose, and wapiti averaged from summer and autumn periods. Data from Hudson and Watkins (1986), Renecker and Hudson, (1986b), Hudson and Frank (1987).

Insufficient time available for grazing and low feeding rate may prevent wild ruminants from meeting their daily nutrient requirements. Normally, grazing time changes most adaptively in response to changing nutrient requirements and forage depletion, whereas foraging rate seems dictated largely by forage characteristics.

Social Behaviour

Species exploiting the higher productivity of open habitats attain higher densities and usually form groups to protect themselves against predators. For each individual (if similar to others in the group), the chance of being selected by a predator is inversely related to herd size. In the relative safety of the herd, individuals can spend more time grazing and thereby realize their potential for growth and reproduction. The cost is greater competition for forage and the consequent need to be more mobile. Optimal group sizes, therefore, vary with habitat and forage density. In forested habitats, trees rather than other animals provide security cover, and sparse forage resources do not permit aggregation.

Gregariousness changes the opportunities for males to maximize their reproductive fitness. Widely spaced individual females are best acquired by roving males (deer, moose). Small cohesive groups of females in patchy habitats can be held in harems (wapiti). Larger, less cohesive groups that are nevertheless predictable in their distributions are best served by territorial males, each attempting to exclude other males from areas where females are likely to be during the rut (pronghorn). Large, loose aggregations that are less predictable in their use of space are followed by males that breed according to rank dominance (bison). In all cases, males attempt to limit the choices available to females but scientists disagree on the degree to which females exercise mate choice.

These mating systems place different premiums on organs of combat and display. With the exception of two Asian species, musk deer (*Moschus*) and water deer (*Hydropotes*), all ruminants sport cranial appendages (ossicones in giraffids, horns in bovids, antlers in cervids). Among cervids, antlers are carried only by males, except for female caribou and rarely other species (Wishart, 1985).

Antler size increases faster than body size (hyperallometrically) and is generally related to the polygyny (ratio of breeding females to breeding males) of each species (Clutton-Brock *et al.*, 1980). However, the largest forms living in open country seem to become slightly less sexually dimorphic and carry slightly smaller horns or antlers than predicted from allometric relationships.

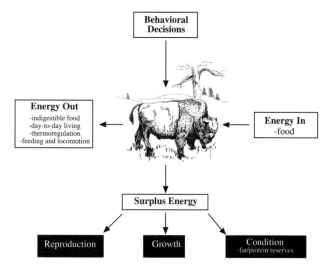

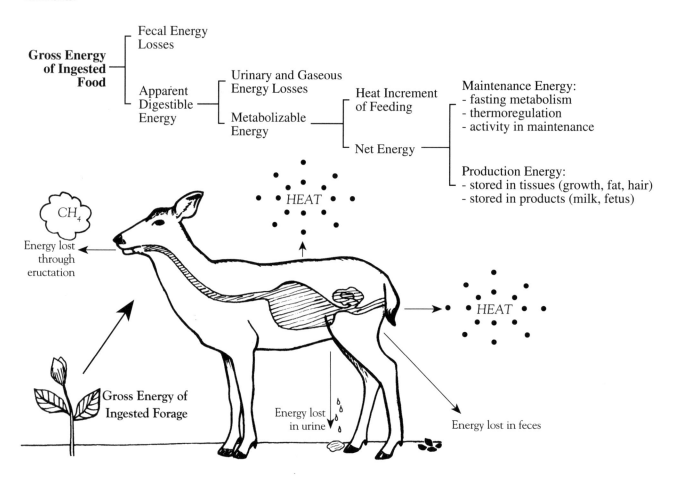

Figure 12.4
Ungulate energy budget.

Figure 12.5
Energy pathways of ruminants.

This may mean a number of things. Geist and Bayer (1988) feel that nutritional limitations in open habitats may reduce the adaptiveness of oversized weapons. There also may be an optimal mechanical size for any given fighting style which is exceeded in larger species. Perhaps, in large, loose aggregations, dominant males are not able to effectively restrict choices of females and "getting lucky" may be just that.

SEASONAL NUTRIENT REQUIREMENTS

The process of energy exchange with the environment and allocation within the animal body is called bioenergetics (Figure 12.4). To maintain homeostasis, ungulates require energy for basal physiological processes, thermoregulation and locomotion. Energy surplus to these needs is diverted to growth or reproduction. The pathways by which ruminants acquire, utilize, and lose energy are illustrated in Figure 12.5.

In addition to nutrient requirements for daily existence, ungulates must acquire a surplus of energy during the short period of plant growth for growth and reproduction. For young animals, growth rate is high during the first few months of life. Newborns must grow rapidly to avoid predation and to be adequately prepared for winter hardships. Beyond this need, ungulates exhibit rapid growth to attain an adequate body size to breed successfully at 16 months (white-tailed deer, mule deer, wapiti and moose) or 28 months (bison) of age. For mature animals, their goal is two-fold: a) to obtain adequate condition to breed, and b) to replenish fat stores to enhance winter survival.

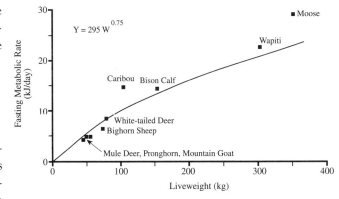

Maintenance

Basal Metabolism

Basal metabolism represents the minimal energy expenditure required for such essential physiological processes as cardio-pulmonary function, protein turnover and maintenance of ion gradients. In ruminants, this state is difficult to achieve experimentally so a standardized measurement at 72 hours after feeding is commonly used. This measurement is called fasting metabolic rate (FMR) and offers a suitable basis for calculating energy requirements. Since previous levels of feeding affect metabolic rate even after standardized fasts, the most reliable and interpretable measurements are from the winter period when animals are not growing.

Winter fasting metabolic rates of Alberta's hoofed mammals tend to be slightly above the interspecies mean of 295 $kJW^{0.75}$/d (Figure 12.6). Summer fasting metabolic rates of most temperate wild ruminants are considerably higher.

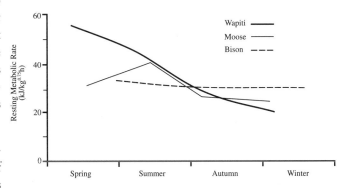

Energy expenditures of fed animals (resting metabolic rate, RMR) show even more marked seasonal fluctuations as a result of wide variations in forage intake and demands of growth, pregnancy, lactation, and thermoregulation (Figure 12.7). But there also is an underlying endogenous rhythm entrained by photoperiod (daylength).

Seasonal metabolic rhythms are obviously adaptive but it is not clear exactly how this is conferred. They may enable organisms to anticipate and prepare for predictable changes in environmental conditions, lowering requirements in winter and priming metabolic machinery for the brief pulse of plant growth in spring and early summer. Since winter energy expenditures of wild ruminants are similar to the interspecies mean, summer increases rather than winter declines appear most significant in seasonal adaptation.

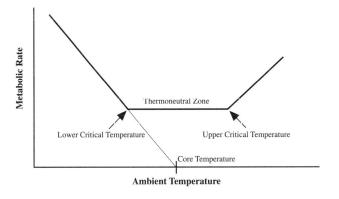

Thermoregulation

Animals must maintain body temperature within fairly narrow limits (Parker and Robbins, 1985). Over a wide range of thermal conditions, heat exchange with the environment can be sufficiently regulated by physical and behavioural means (Figure 12.8). Above the upper critical temperature, additional heat is released through such mechanisms as panting. Below the lower critical temperature, metabolic rate increases to produce heat to offset that lost to the environment.

Alberta's wild ruminants are quite resistant to cold perhaps because of the selective pressures of Pleistocene environments. Lower critical temperatures approximate –20°C for larger species (Table 12.3). Lower critical temperatures and thermal insulations of bison and moose are difficult to calculate because energy expenditures continue to fall with temperatures as low as are usually

Figure 12.6 (*top*) *Winter fasting metabolic rates of Alberta's hoofed mammals compared to the interspecies line for homeotherms.*

Figure 12.7 (*centre*) *Seasonal cycle of resting metabolism in several of Alberta's ungulates.*

Figure 12.8 (*bottom*) *Energetic response to thermal environments.*

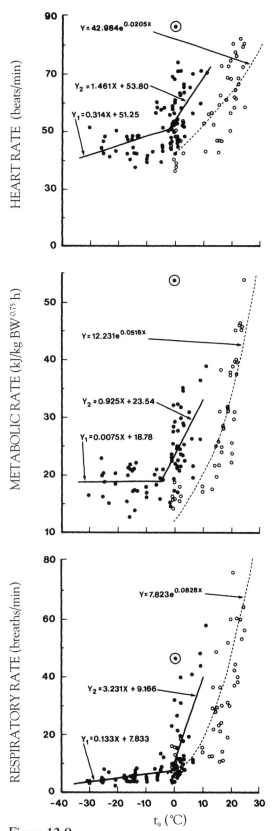

Figure 12.9
Effect of ambient temperature (t_a) on thermoregulation of moose (from Renecker and Hudson, 1986a).

encountered. Lower critical temperatures are determined by both insulation and thermoneutral metabolic rates. Insulation (reciprocal slope of relationship between metabolic rate and degrees below the lower critical temperature) is influenced by body size, condition, and pelage characteristics. Thermoneutral metabolic rate is influenced mainly by feeding level. Activity increases metabolic rate and makes animals feel warmer, but heat losses to the environment increase and thermal insulation is reduced (Gates and Hudson, 1979). Consequently, smaller wild ruminants remain bedded during periods of extreme cold.

Perhaps because humans are chilled by winters, disproportionate attention has been paid to cold stress in wild ruminants. However, for larger wild ruminants, there are many more days each year when animals are exposed to heat stress sufficient to depress feed intake and productivity. For much of the year, upper critical temperatures are on the order of 10°C for larger wild ruminants. A particularly difficult time for heat stress is spring when animals are still in winter coats. Moose have great difficulty dissipating surplus metabolic heat created by warm temperatures (Figure 12.9). In winter, heat stress occurs in moose between –5 and –2 °C, while in the summer extreme panting and heat stress occurs at 14 to 20 °C (Renecker and Hudson, 1986a).

Activity

Ungulates spend most of their day (>90%) foraging, resting/ruminating or walking between bedding and feeding sites. Thus, energy budgets can easily be calculated from activity budgets if the incremental costs of standing, travelling, and foraging are known.

Energy costs of standing in most domestic ruminants are on the order of 9% higher than energy expenditures while bedded. Experiments on moose, wapiti, and bighorn sheep suggest increments of 18–23%. This may be related to body conformation but must be at least partly due to the greater alertness of wild species. Metabolic rates are measured opportunistically and animals are more likely to bed when relaxed and stand when aroused. But whether expenditures of standing animals are higher for biomechanical or psychological reasons matters little to the construction of energy budgets.

Energy expenditures during locomotion scale linearly with velocity but vary little per unit distance (Fancy and White, 1985). Therefore, incremental costs can be conveniently expressed as energy expenditures associated with moving one kg of body mass over one kilometre (kJ/kg·km). For horizontal movement on hard substrates, this is close to 2.5 kJ/kg·km. Interspecies comparisons suggest that costs of locomotion scale close to the metabolic exponent. On inclines, the cost is 10 times this for each unit of elevation gained. Energy costs of locomotion in snow increase exponentially with sinking depths, approximately doubling by 60% of brisket height (Dailey and Hobbs, 1989).

Incremental costs of foraging include components of standing, eating, and travelling. The incremental cost of eating is less than 1 kJ/kg$^{0.75}$h. However, free-grazing animals expend 3–5 kJ·kg$^{0.75}$h because of the additional costs of searching for and selecting forage (Fancy and White, 1985). Since animals may spend 30–50% of their day foraging, daily energy requirements may increase by about 30% (Hudson and Christopherson, 1985).

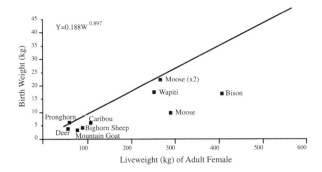

Reproduction

Gestation

Requirements for pregnancy (daily costs of fetal growth) depend on birth size and gestation length (Oftedal, 1985). Both parameters scale allometrically with maternal size (Robbins and Robbins, 1979; Western, 1979).

Newborn young dropped by small-bodied ungulates are a larger percentage of maternal weight than are those of larger species (Figure 12.10). Greater birthing difficulties might be expected for smaller species, except that this greater percentage of weight is often achieved by delivering twins. Moose have unusually small calves, but twins are common and total birth weights are accurately predicted by the interspecies relationship. Bison have small, single calves that, despite their small size, generally join the herd soon after birth.

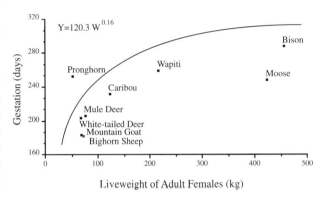

Gestation lengths of Alberta's ungulates (with the exception of the pronghorn) seem to scale differently than most of the world's artiodactyls, perhaps because most are tropical bovids (Figure 12.11). Since the optimal birth date in Alberta is late May to early June, rutting seasons peak a gestation-length earlier. Large ungulates such as bison rut first, followed sequentially by wapiti, pronghorn, moose, caribou, deer, mountain goats, and bighorn sheep.

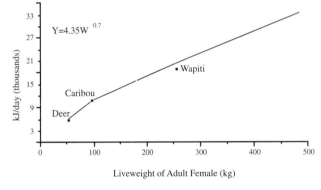

At least in theory, the dissimilar scaling of gestation length and birth weight should place proportionally heavier nutritional demands on pregnant females of smaller species. However, the precise value (0.897–0.16 = 0.737) is close to the metabolic exponent, which implies that demands are a constant proportion of the energy budget irrespective of maternal size.

Lactation

Although peak daily milk yields (kJ/d) can be modified greatly by artificial selection in dairy cattle and goats, energy yields in interspecies comparisons scale regularly with maternal size (Figure 12.12). This occurs despite wide differences in the chemical composition of milks (Table 12.4). Therefore, ungulates differ mainly in the amount of water they provide their nursing young. Among the world's ungulates, large ruminant species which nurse their young frequently ("followers" such as bison) produce dilute milks.

Milk production reaches a peak several weeks after parturition and gradually declines thereafter. Young ruminants wean gradually, so that nursing bouts become quite infrequent by early winter. Of course, the frequency and duration of nursing bouts are poor indicators of the amount of milk transferred since larger and older calves drink much more rapidly (Hudson and Adamczewski, 1990).

Figure 12.10 (*top*)
Birth weight of Alberta's wild ruminants compared with the interspecies mean.

Figure 12.11 (*middle*)
Gestation lengths of Alberta's wild ruminants compared with the interspecies mean.

Figure 12.12 (*bottom*)
Milk yield at peak lactation.

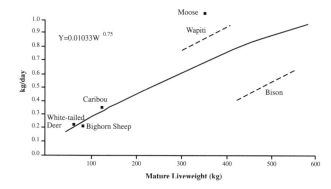

Growth

Growth Rates

Growth rates vary throughout the life of animals so selection of comparable points on the growth curve is important. The most common standard is growth rates of nursing young at peak milk production (growth rates tend to be constant from several days after birth to mid-lactation).

Compared with other mammals, ungulates have high growth rates (Figure 12.13). The adaptive significance of rapid growth can be traced to the importance of (1) quickly passing through the vulnerable early postnatal period when predation pressures are high; and (2) attaining sufficient size to cope with hardships imposed by seasonal environments. Among Alberta's ungulates, moose are exceptional for their rapid growth (over one kg/d) while bison grow rather slowly. It is of interest that cattle grow about as expected for animals of their mature size. Genetic selection for absolute growth rate in domestic animals has been achieved largely by selection for large mature weights.

Body mass seldom increases smoothly to a genetically-determined mature weight (Bandy *et al.*, 1970). Males show the most pronounced weight changes with precipitous drops in body weight during the rut. However, weights remain low throughout the winter months, even though rutting behaviour is suppressed. In animals that have been maintained on low planes of nutrition, weight loss and rutting activity are less marked and growth may ensue during the usual period of weight stasis (Renecker and Samuel, 1991).

Weight stasis or loss during winter is followed by exceptional compensatory growth following the flush of spring growth (Hudson *et al.*, 1985; Renecker and Samuel, 1991). Summer weight gain is strongly related to body weight and condition. Such compensatory growth may result from a combination of higher voluntary feed intake, improved efficiency of feed utilization, and increased body water. Of these, higher feed intake seems most important. Compensatory growth of permanent hard tissues (e.g., horns), however, is less responsive to the summer's superabundance of nutrients.

Composition of Gain

Energy requirements for growth are determined by the energy content of gain as well as the growth rate. Energy content reflects changing body composition, particularly fatness. Fat has an energy content of approximately 39 kJ/g whereas lean tissue contains only 5 kJ/g. As maturity is approached, the proportion of fat and hence energy content of gain increases. Since metabolizable energy is used with an efficiency of about 50%, energy requirements for live weight gain vary from 16–55 kJ/g.

SEASONAL NUTRIENT SUPPLY

Forage Biomass

Forage production can be divided into two basic categories: a) total biomass (includes all plant material accessible to the ungulate species within the foraging zone) and b) available biomass (includes only plant species and parts selected by a particular herbivore within the foraging zone). Available biomass is the preferred index because it represents a more realistic estimate of food supply, but it can be difficult to quantify.

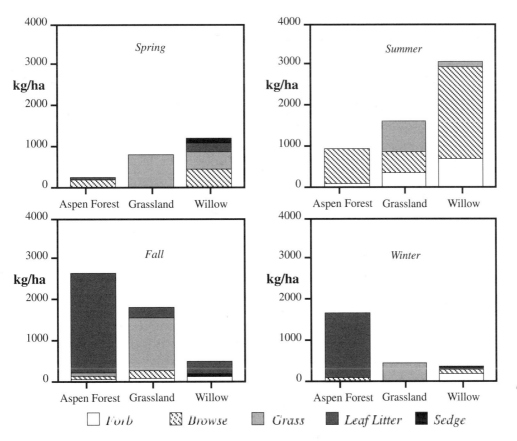

Eight main forage classes can be distinguished: a) forbs, b) grasses, c) sedges, d) browse (leaves and twigs from trees and shrubs), e) fallen leaves, f) bark, g) horsetails, and h) mosses and lichens. Although biomass is abundant in all forage classes during a brief period of active leaf growth in spring and summer, maturity of foliage causes a marked drop in available forage during autumn. This is particularly noticeable in forested areas, where available biomass is primarily browse. However, fallen leaves represent a potentially large usable resource during autumn, winter and spring. Winter snowfall and crusts also reduce available forage supply to wild ruminants. In aspen-dominated boreal forests of central Alberta, available herbage during winter is reduced 50–90% from summer productivity (Figure 12.14).

Figure 12.14
Seasonal supply of forage available to ungulates in the aspen-dominated boreal forest of Alberta.

Quality

Forage quality is influenced by plant development processes, herbivore effects and environmental factors (Figure 12.15). Nutritional quality of available woody forage declines as food becomes more fibrous during winter. Certain foods may have high concentrations of secondary compounds (alkaloids, terpenes, tannins) making them unsuitable for consumption. Similarly, heavy browsing may stimulate plant defenses and result in unpalatable food items. Thus, quality of winter food resources offered to a browser can be considerably less than that of grazing ungulates that utilize extensive grasslands and sedge meadows.

Seasonal changes in forage quality (Renecker and Hudson, 1988; Figures 12.16 and 12.17) are as dramatic as changes in biomass. However, staggered plant phenology offers an adaptive advantage to herbivores that track several different forage types. In boreal forests, plants respond to the disappearance of snow with a flush of green vegetation of high nutritive quality. During spring, forage crude protein (browse foliage = 20%, grasses = 25%, forbs = 30%) and dry matter digestibility (browse foliage = 55–77%, grasses = 73%, forbs = 70%) are high and provide the necessary surplus requirements for fattening and growth. However, as browse matures there is a reduction in readily

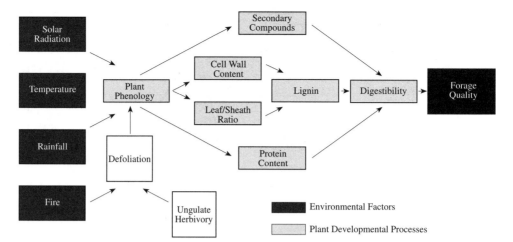

Figure 12.15
Forage quality model.

digestible cell solubles and leaf-to-stem ratios along with an increase in cell wall constituents. During winter, wild ungulates are hard-pressed to meet their maintenance energy and 7% protein requirement, since forage resources contain only 6–8% crude protein and have a digestibility of 27–45%. As days become warmer in early spring there is increased movement of highly digestible cell solubles and sugars through the bark cambium of shrubs and trees to the expanding leaves. This flow of nutrients and growth of meristematic tissue within bark lowers the concentration of secondary compounds and increases digestibility to about 65% for bark of trembling aspen, balsam poplar and willow; nevertheless, protein levels remain low at about 4 percent.

Estimation of seasonal change in the quality of forage is of paramount importance in assessment of range condition and, ultimately, ungulate condition. Diet quality can be determined through analysis of samples taken from ruminally or esophageally fistulated animals but the technique has limited use since these animals must be hand-reared and maintenance costs are high. Knowledge of chemical composition (in vitro or in situ digestibility; crude protein; or lignin, cellulose, hemicellulose, cell solubles, and ash content) aids in range assessment although it is difficult to interpret data unless diet composition is known. Recently, several authors have developed significant relationships between fecal protein and both dietary nitrogen and digestible dry matter intake (Renecker and Hudson, 1985). The advantage of this technique is that the animal makes the dietary choices in accordance with its perception of the environment, not man's.

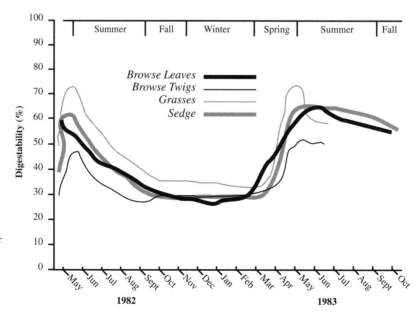

Figure 12.16

Seasonal change in quality of moose forage.

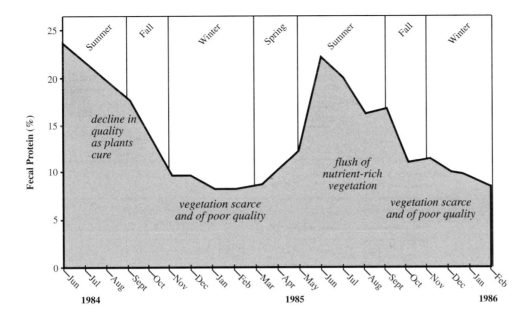

Figure 12.17
Seasonal change in forage quality in Elk Island National Park, as indicated by wapiti fecal protein.

The fecal protein index assumes that high fecal protein reflects high dietary quality. However, metabolic fecal nitrogen (nitrogen cost of digestion = enzymes, sloughed epithelial cells from intestine, etc.) also comprises a percentage of the fecal nitrogen. Interactions between diet composition, diet intake, and secondary plant compounds can affect this relationship and the proportion of nitrogen from these sources. For example, phenolics and tannins bind and precipitate both dietary and microbial protein thereby reducing nitrogen digestibility. Renecker and Hudson (1985) found that the regression between dietary and fecal nitrogen from free-ranging moose had a regression coefficient (slope) twice as large as from wapiti that fed primarily on grasses and alfalfa (Mould and Robbins, 1981). Because free-ranging moose consume browse containing large amounts of secondary compounds, their feces probably contain higher levels of metabolic fecal nitrogen and indigestible dietary nitrogen. Other studies have indicated that compounds present in phenolic and terpene resins of white birch and balsam poplar inhibit ruminal digestion even at relatively low concentrations. Concentrations of these secondary metabolites tend to increase with fiber content. Nevertheless, fecal protein serves as a valuable indicator of general fluctuations in range quality of a ruminant species. Since forage choice and chemical composition of the diet can vary among ungulates and geographical regions, relationships must be both species- and site-specific.

Seasonal change in crude protein content of wapiti feces has been monitored at Elk Island National Park (Figure 12.17). Fecal protein levels showed definite seasonal variations which coincided with shifts in plant phenology and range quality. This field technique reflected subtle shifts in dietary choice of wapiti during spring as a result of a late April snowfall. During this period, fecal protein (10.8%) reflected movement of wapiti from aspen forest habitat, where their diets comprised fallen leaves and new growth of grass and forbs prior to the snowfall, to sedge meadows (fecal protein = 7.7%) where sedge green-up and willow twigs were the principal foods until the heavy snow cover melted.

SEASONAL NUTRIENT BALANCE

The balance of nutrient demand and supply is reflected in seasonal changes in body weight and composition (Figure 12.18). During winter, it is not uncommon for ungulates to lose 15–20% of their peak autumn weight during winter. However, a weight loss of 30% can threaten survival, depending on the autumn condition of the animal.

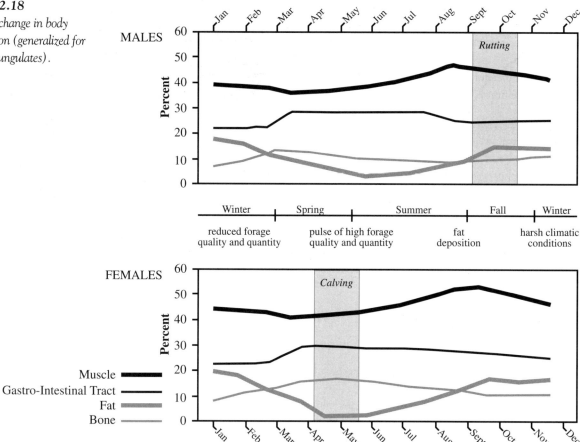

Figure 12.18
Seasonal change in body composition (generalized for northern ungulates).

Although both protein and fat are mobilized together, the greatest proportion initially, is fat. As winter progresses and fat depots are depleted, lean tissue provides most of the energy. However, its energy content is low and considerably more must be mobilized daily to fuel maintenance demands, so weight declines precipitously.

With the spring flush of plant growth, wild ungulates rapidly rebuild body reserves, replacing tissue depots in the reverse order they were mobilized. Considering only tissue energy content, efficiency of liveweight gain should decline as autumn approaches.

BEHAVIOURAL ADAPTATIONS

Although ungulates use body reserves as a buffer against environmental exigencies, they also deploy a number of physiological and behavioural mechanisms to smooth the seasonal disparity of energy supply and demand. Behavioural responses include habitat selection, diet selection, and activity budgeting.

Habitat Selection

Habitat selection is primarily a response to security, thermal comfort, and forage needs. The ungulate's goal is to balance these conflicting requirements. Habitat selection is species-specific, and choices will depend on physiological constraints and social needs of the species.

Requirements for security vary seasonally and are greatest when animals feel threatened. Ungulates are vulnerable at parturition and when accompanied by neonates, especially when the mother is in poor condition. To offset this disadvantage, ungulates select habitats consistent with their physical attributes and cryptic coloration. For example, escape cover is open grassland for a pronghorn, forest for a white-tailed deer or moose, distance for a wapiti, and rocky terrain for bighorn sheep and mountain goats.

The thermal environment is defined by ambient temperature, short-wave and long-wave radiation, wind and humidity. Habitat structure modifies these meteorological parameters in complex ways. Closed canopy forests reduce cold stress during winter, but shade provided by poplar and aspen forests during late spring is attractive during periods of high ambient temperatures. Moose exploit the thermal advantages of cool water in wetlands during hot summer days, which enables them to feed longer. Ungulates are often attracted to south-facing slopes to take advantage of daytime radiation during cold winters.

Although security and thermal cover are important, habitat selection is strongly influenced by relative foraging opportunities. Moose (Renecker and Hudson, 1992), wapiti (Watkins *et al.*, 1991), and presumably other species spend time in foraging habitats in direct proportion to foraging returns (measured as dry matter or protein intake rates). This is only one of several possible strategies. For example, they could use only the best habitats or only those better than the overall average, meanwhile sampling other habitats to adapt to changing conditions.

The pronghorn is the fastest mammal in North America, capable of attaining speeds of 100 kph. Large lungs, slender but well muscled legs and loss of dew claws all point to an animal adapted to speed.
Photo by J. Nolan.

Diet Selection

Herbivores are faced with deciding the optimal tradeoff between feeding rate and diet digestibility because the most nutritious forages also tend to be the most rare. Two main optimal foraging strategies have been identified (Pyke *et al.*, 1977). Time minimization describes patterns of foraging that allow animals to meet their basic requirements in the least possible time. This is expected to operate when animals are exposed to increased risk of predation or cold stress while foraging. The second strategy, energy maximization, describes behaviours that maximize nutrient capture (Westoby, 1974; Belovsky, 1978). In harsh environments, both strategies result in similar foraging patterns. As the disparity between forage availability and animal requirements widens, diet expansion is expected as the animal becomes less selective (Ellis *et al.*, 1976).

The way animals experience these trade-offs and therefore select diets reflects their morpho-physiological adaptations (Table 12.5). The diversity of ungulates found in Alberta is largely the result of the heterogeneous habitat types found within the province. The number of plants consumed by all hoofed mammals is extensive (Table 12.6).

Activity Budgets

Major activities for wild ruminants are feeding and lying/ruminating, while lesser amounts of time are spent grooming, walking, running and in social interaction (Figure 12.19). Activity patterns reflect the animal's behavioural adjustment to daily and seasonal variations in the environment. Although many factors determine activity patterns, the daily cycle of feeding and resting is dictated largely by the dynamics of rumen re-

Figure 12.19
Seasonal activity patterns of moose.

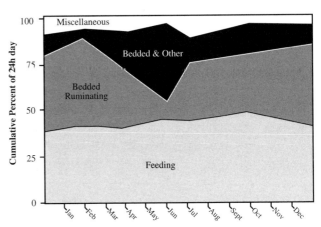

pletion and depletion. Therefore, much can be learned about regional and seasonal patterns by analyzing the factors influencing the length of feeding and ruminating bouts.

Feeding bout lengths are determined primarily by rumen capacity (rumen volume and time since last feeding) and foraging rate as influenced by forage biomass and structure. Large grazers have large rumens but also have potentially high feeding rates. Small browsers, on the other hand, have lower digestive capacities but generally low potential feeding rates. These factors tend to cancel one another, so generalizations about differences in feeding bout lengths are difficult to make.

Rumination bouts are proportional to the amount of cell-wall material (acid detergent fiber) in the rumen at the end of the preceding grazing bout. Rumination is required to reduce particle sizes so they pass the reticulo-omasal orifice. Grazers seem to pass smaller particle sizes so more rumination may be necessary. Also digestion and passage rates generally are lower among grazers so intervals between foraging bouts tend to be longer than among browsers.

Body size also is important. Small browsers such as deer have more feeding bouts (11/day) of shorter duration (56 minutes) than larger ruminants such as moose, which have 4–7 feeding bouts/day with an average length of 107 minutes (Renecker and Hudson, 1989). Similarly, small grazers such as bighorn sheep have shorter, more frequent feeding bouts than large grazers such as bison.

The same considerations allow interpretation of seasonal patterns. As diets become more fibrous from summer to winter, the duration of rumination bouts increases, as does total time spent ruminating.

SUMMARY

Bioenergetics, the study of energy exchanges of animals with their nutritional and thermal environments, offers insight into the basis of adaptation and behaviour of wild ruminants. Although the process is pre-empted by social and security imperatives, bioenergetic optimization remains a major long-term preoccupation of animals and determinant of their survival and reproductive success.

ACKNOWLEDGMENTS

We thank Wes Olson for data on fecal nitrogen levels of wapiti in Elk Island National Park. Special thanks to Donna Renecker for critical review of the manuscript.

TABLE 12.1

WEIGHTS AND MEASURES

	White-tailed Deer	Mule Deer	Caribou	Wapiti (Elk)	Moose	Prong-horn	Mountain Goat	Bighorn Sheep	Bison (Buffalo)
Average Liveweight (kg)									
Adult Male	95	95	180	320	450	56	85	117	681
Adult Female	70	70	115	230	418	45	62	65	450
Maximum Liveweight (kg)									
Adult Male	130	130	272	500	650	70	136	135	1090
Adult Female	90	90	150	320	450	56	95	80	613
Average Skull Length (cm)									
Adult Male	27.0	24.0	39.5	42.5	58.0	24.5	28.5	28.0	50.0
Adult Female	26.5	23.0	33.5	41.0	-	-	28.0	25.0	47.0
Average Skull Width (cm)									
Adult Male	11.5	11.5	17.5	18.5	22.0	8.5	8.5	13.0	35.5
Adult Female	10.0	10.0	15.0	15.0	-	-	8.0	12.0	30.5
Average Total Body Length (cm)									
Adult Male	187	177	259	231	274	142	154	183	340
Adult Female	170	163	223	228	185	141	91	161	267
Average Shoulder Height (cm)									
Adult Male	91	97	127	129	190	88	89	105	195
Adult Female	91	91	120	127	188	86	80	88	167
Average Chest Height (cm)									
	61	61	73	85	105	53	?	50	67
Average Tail Length (cm)									
Adult Male	28.5	19.0	17.5	16.0	14.5	10.5	12.0	12.5	34.0
Adult Female	25.0	17.0	17.5	15.0	15.0	9.7	10.5	10.0	35.0
Combined Antler Weight (kg)									
	1.5	2.0	12	16	35	-	-	-	-
Antler Cast	March/April	March/April	Nov./Dec.(Ad.M) May/June(Fem.) March(Sub.M)	January/May	January/March	November (sheath only)	-	-	-
Dental Formula (I C P M)[1]	$\frac{0\ 0\ 3\ 3}{3\ 1\ 3\ 3}$	$\frac{0\ 0\ 3\ 3}{3\ 1\ 3\ 3}$	$\frac{0\ 1\ 3\ 3}{3\ 1\ 3\ 3}$	$\frac{0\ 0\text{–}1\ 3\ 3}{3\ 1\ 3\ 3}$	$\frac{0\ 0\ 3\ 3}{3\ 1\ 3\ 3}$	$\frac{0\ 0\ 3\ 3}{3\ 1\ 3\ 3}$	$\frac{0\ 0\ 3\ 3}{3\ 1\ 3\ 3}$	$\frac{0\ 0\ 3\ 3}{3\ 1\ 3\ 3}$	$\frac{0\ 0\ 3\ 3}{3\ 1\ 3\ 3}$
Longevity (years)	10	15	18–20	15	25	12	16	15	>20
Maximum Speed (km/h)	60	40	75	50	56	100	-	50	58
References	Wishart, unpubl.; Halls, 1984; Hesselton and Hesselton, 1982	Wallmo, 1981 Mackie et al. 1982; Wishart, unpubl.	Edmonds and Bloomfield, 1984; Miller,1982	Peek,1982; Thomas and Toweill, 1982	Blood et al., 1967; Coady, 1982	Mitchell, 1971; Kitchen and O'Gara,1982	Wigal and Coggins, 1982	Lawson and Johnson, 1982; Blood et al., 1970	Reynolds, Glaholt, and Hawley, 1982

NOTE: Values presented in this table are approximated averages of several studies (recommended references are identified at the bottom of each column). Morphological dimensions and developmental events are highly variable, since they are affected by age, nutritional status, season, reproductive status, etc.

[1] I=incisors, C=canines, P=premolars, M=molars

TABLE 12.2

ADAPTATION OF UNGULATES TO SNOW

(from Telfer and Kelsall, 1984)[*]

	Deer	Caribou	Wapiti (Elk)	Moose	Pronghorn	Bighorn Sheep	Bison (Buffalo)
Morphological							
Chest Height (cm)	61	73	85	105	53	50	67
Foot Load Index (1-g/cm²)	51	81	33	35	28	64	28
Behavioural (1=poor, 5=excellent)							
Trail Marking	4	5	1	2	2	2	4
Selection of soft/ or shallow snow	5	4	4	3	3	5	3
Forage above snow	5	2	3	5	2	1	1
Digging for forage	1	5	3	1	2	2	4
Migration	3	5	5	3	3	4	3
Locomotion Technique	3	5	5	5	1	2	1
Morphological Index (MI)	112/200	154/200	118/200	140/200	81/200	114/200	95/200
Behavioural Index (BI)	21/30	26/30	21/30	19/30	13/30	16/30	16/30
Snow-Coping Index (MI+BI)/2	.63	.82	.65	.67	.42	.55	.49
Overall Rating (1=highest, 7=poorest)	4	1	3	2	7	5	6

[*] For both morphological and behavioural comparisons, higher values indicate better level of adaptation to snow. Morphological Index denominator (200) is an arbitrary reference.

TABLE 12.3

CRITICAL TEMPERATURES OF WILD RUMINANTS DURING WINTER

Species	Critical Temperatures (°C) Lower	Upper	References
White-tailed Deer	5	25	Parker and Robbins, 1985
Mule Deer	-20	5	Parker and Robbins, 1985
Caribou	<-40	20	Parker and Robbins, 1985
Wapiti (Elk)	-20	15	Parker and Robbins, 1985
Moose	<-30	-5	Renecker and Hudson, 1986a
Pronghorn	-16	-	Parker and Robbins, 1985
Mountain Goat	<-30	-	Krog and Monson, 1954
Bighorn Sheep	-10	-	Parker and Robbins, 1985
Bison (Buffalo)	<-30	-	Christopherson et al., 1978

TABLE 12.4

MILK PERCENTAGE COMPOSITION

(Oftedal, 1985)

Species	Solids	Fat	Protein	Lactose	Ash
White-tailed Deer	22.5	7.7	8.2	4.6	1.5
Mule Deer	24.4	10.9	7.6	5.4	1.4
Caribou	23.8	11.5	7.6	3.5	—
Wapiti (Elk)	19.0	6.7	5.7	4.2	1.4
Moose	21.5	10.0	8.4	3.0	1.5
Pronghorn	24.9	13.0	6.9	4.0	1.3
Mountain Goat	—	5.7	11.4	2.8	1.2
Bighorn Sheep	34.0	16.0	12.1	3.4	1.3
Bison (Buffalo)	14.6	3.5	4.5	5.1	0.8

TABLE 12.5

SEASONAL FORAGING PATTERNS

(values represent percent of diet)[*][†]

	Gram-inoids	Forbs	Shrubs/ Trees	Lichen/ Moss	Location	Reference
White-tailed Deer						
Spring	49	23	28	0	Camp Wainwright	Rhude and Hall, 1978 (3)
Fall	11	17	72	0	Camp Wainwright	Rhude and Hall, 1978 (3)
Winter	63	26	11	0	Camp Wainwright	Rhude and Hall, 1978 (3)
Mule Deer						
Spring	10	52	38	0	Camp Wainwright	Rhude and Hall, 1977 (3)
Fall	3	18	79	0	Camp Wainwright	Rhude and Hall, 1977 (3)
Fall	9	11	80	0	Camp Wainwright	Treichel and Dube, 1980 (3)
Winter	7	23	70	0	Camp Wainwright	Rhude and Hall, 1977 (3)
Winter	15	6	79	0	Jasper National Park	Cowan, 1947 (2)
Caribou						
Spring	5	5	5	85	Jasper National Park	Stelfox *et al.*, 1978 (4)
Summer	5	2	38	55	west-central Alberta	Edmonds *et al.*, 1984 (1)
Summer	26	6	23	45	Jasper National Park	Stelfox *et al.*, 1978 (4)
Fall	4	2	19	75	west-central Alberta	Edmonds *et al.*, 1984 (1)
Fall	5	3	2	90	Jasper National Park	Stelfox *et al.*, 1978 (4)
Winter	5	3	23	69	west-central Alberta	Edmonds *et al.*, 1984 (1)
Wapiti (Elk)						
Early Spring	73	1	25	2	Elk Island National Park	Renecker, 1989 (2)
Early Winter	37	4	59	0	Elk Island National Park	Renecker, 1989 (2)
Spring	43	20	37	0	Waterton Lakes N.P.	Stelfox and Tilson, 1985 (1)
Spring	84	16	0	0	Ministik Station	Nietfeld, 1983 (2)
Spring	90	2	8	0	Elk Island National Park	Cairns, 1976 (4)
Mid Spring	95	0	3	2	Elk Island National Park	Renecker, 1989 (2)
Late Spring	31	2	66	0	Elk Island National Park	Renecker, 1989 (2)
Summer	5	26	69	0	Waterton Lakes N.P.	Stelfox and Tilson, 1985 (1)
Summer	8	25	67	0	Elk Island National Park	Renecker, 1989 (2)
Summer	45	54	1	0	Ministik Station	Nietfeld, 1983 (2)
Fall	55	7	36	2	Elk Island National Park	Renecker, 1989 (2)
Fall	60	40	0	0	Ministik Station	Nietfeld, 1983 (2)
Fall	75	10	15	0	Cypress Hills Prov. Park	Treichel, 1979 (3)
Winter	25	0	75	0	Elk Island National Park	Cairns, 1976 (4)
Winter	40	4	26	16	Wolf Creek/Brazeau River	Morgantini and Olsen, 1983 (1)
Winter	55	3	42	0	upper Red Deer River	Salter and Hudson, 1980 (1)
Winter	70	1	19	10	upper Blackstone River	Morgantini and Russell, 1983 (1)
Winter	72	1	17	0	Ya-Ha-Tinda Ranch	Treichel and Hall, 1977 (3)
Winter	78	1	16	5	upper Red Deer River	Morgantini and Russell, 1983 (1)
Winter	82	1	16	1	upper Clearwater River	Morgantini and Russell, 1983 (1)
Winter	87	3	10	0	Ministik Station	Nietfeld, 1983 (2)
Winter	93	2	5	0	Ya-Ha-Tinda Ranch	Morgantini and Hudson, 1985 (1)
Winter	95	0	5	0	Oldman River	Berg, 1983 (1)
Winter	95	5	0	0	Waterton Lakes N.P.	Stelfox and Tilson, 1985 (1)
Winter	97	0	3	0	Jasper National Park	Cowan, 1947 (2)
Mid Winter	45	12	43	0	Elk Island National Park	Renecker, 1989 (2)
Late Winter	66	5	29	0	Elk Island National Park	Renecker, 1989 (2)

[*] These data are location- and time-specific. Populations in different locations, or at different times, may exhibit dissimilar foraging preferences.

[†] Diet determined according to the following techniques, indicated after the reference: (1) histological examination of plant cuticles in feces, (2) close observation of foraging bouts, (3) examination of stomach samples, (4) examination of forage plots or transects for utilization.

TABLE 12.5

SEASONAL FORAGING PATTERNS (continued)

(values represent percent of diet)*†

	Gram-inoids	Forbs	Shrubs/ Trees	Lichen/ Moss	Leaf Litter	Location	Reference
Moose							
Early Spring	0	2	98	0	0	Elk Island National Park	Renecker, 1989 (1)
Early Spring	1	0	58	0	41	Ministik Station	Renecker, 1987 (2)
Late Spring	1	0	99	0	0	Ministik Station	Renecker, 1987 (2)
Summer	1	25	74	0	0	Ministik Station	Renecker, 1987 (2)
Fall	0	0	100	0	0	Cypress Hills Prov. Park	Barrett, 1972 (3)
Fall	0	0	100	0	0	north-eastern Alberta	Nowlin, 1978 (4)
Fall	0	3	93	0	0	Cypress Hills Prov. Park	Treichel, 1979 (3)
Fall	6	10	55	0	29	Ministik Station	Renecker, 1987 (2)
Late Fall	3	17	80	0	0	Elk Island National Park	Renecker, 1989 (2)
Early Winter	0	5	95	0	0	Elk Island National Park	Renecker, 1989 (1)
Winter	0	0	100	0	0	north-eastern Alberta	Nowlin, 1978 (4)
Winter	0	0	100	0	0	Rock Lake	Millar, 1953 (2,3,4)
Winter	0	1	72	0	27	Ministik Station	Renecker, 1987 (2)
Mid Winter	1	13	96	0	0	Elk Island National Park	Renecker, 1989 (1)
Late Winter	0	0	100	0	0	Elk Island National Park	Renecker, 1989 (1)
Pronghorn							
Spring	25	57	18	0	0	south-east Alberta	Mitchell, 1980 (3)
Summer	13	62	25	0	0	south-east Alberta	Mitchell, 1980 (3)
Fall	13	37	50	0	0	south-east Alberta	Mitchell, 1980 (3)
Winter	10	47	43	0	0	south-east Alberta	Mitchell, 1980 (3)
Mountain Goat							
Spring	85	2	13	0	0	Smoky River	Kerr, 1965 (3,4)
Summer	78	9	13	0	0	Smoky River	Kerr, 1965 (3,4)
Summer	15	48	37	0	0	Smoky River	McFetridge, 1977 (1)
Winter	8	0	92	0	0	Smoky River	Kerr, 1965 (3,4)
Winter	29	36	35	0	0	Smoky River	McFetridge, 1977 (1)
Bighorn Sheep							
Spring	68	12	20	0	0	Waterton, Banff, Jasper NPs	Stelfox, 1976 (4)
Summer	60	26	14	0	0	Waterton, Banff, Jasper NPs	Stelfox, 1976 (4)
Summer	63	20	10	7	0	Ram Mountain	Johnson, 1975 (?)
Fall	40	35	25	0	0	Waterton, Banff, Jasper NPs	Stelfox, 1976 (4)
Winter	74	22	4	0	0	Waterton, Banff, Jasper NPs	Stelfox, 1976 (4)
Winter	96	3	1	0	0	Banff National Park	Shank, 1982 (1)
Winter	83	10	7	0	0	Jasper National Park	Cowan, 1947 (2)
Bison (Buffalo)							
Spring	92	8	0	0	0	Elk Island National Park	Cairns, 1976 (1)
Spring	97	1	2	0	0	Slave River, N.W.T	Reynolds, 1976 (1)
Summer	83	8	8	0	0	Slave River, N.W.T	Reynolds, 1976 (1)
Fall	92	4	2	0	0	Slave River, N.W.T	Reynolds, 1976 (1)
Winter	97	0	1	0	0	Slave River, N.W.T	Reynolds, 1976 (1)
Winter	93	0	7	0	0	Elk Island National Park	Cairns, 1976 (1)

* These data are location- and time-specific. Populations in different locations, or at different times, may exhibit dissimilar foraging preferences.

† Diet determined according to the following techniques, indicated after the reference: (1) histological examination of plant cuticles in feces, (2) close observation of foraging bouts, (3) examination of stomach samples, (4) examination of forage plots or transects for utilization.

TABLE 12.6

COMMON FORAGES

WD=white-tailed deer, MD=mule deer, CA=caribou, WA=wapiti, MO=moose, PR=pronghorn,
MG=mountain goat, BS=bighorn sheep, BI=bison.

Common Name	Scientific Name	Ungulate Species
Trees and Shrubs		
alder	*Alnus* spp.	MD, CA, MO, MG
alpine fir	*Abies lasiocarpa*	MD, CA, WA, MO, MG
aspen	*Populus tremuloides*	WD, MD, WA, MO, MG
balsam popular	*Populus balsamifera*	WD, MD, WA, MO
beaked hazel	*Corylus cornuta*	WA, MO
bearberry	*Arctostaphylos uva-ursi*	WD, MD, CA, WA, MG, BS, BI
black spruce	*Picea mariana*	CA
blueberry	*Vaccinium myrtilloides*	CA
bog cranberry	*Vaccinium vitis-idaea*	CA
buckbrush	*Symphoricarpos occidentalis*	WD, MD, WA, MO, PR
buffalo-berry	*Shepherdia canadensis*	MD, CA, WA, MO
choke cherry	*Prunus virginiana*	WD, MD, WA, MO
clematis	*Clematis* spp.	MO
crowberry	*Empetrum nigrum*	CA
Douglas fir	*Pseudotsuga menziesii*	MD, WA, MO, MG
dwarf birch	*Betula glandulosa*	WD, CA, WA, MO
high-bush cranberry	*Viburnum opulus*	MO
honeysuckle	*Lonicera* spp.	WA, MO, MG
jackpine	*Pinus banksiana*	WA
juniper	*Juniperus* spp.	WD, MD, MO, PR, BS
Labrador tea	*Ledum groenlandicum*	CA, MO
lodgepole pine	*Pinus contorta*	MD, WA, MG
low-bush cranberry	*Viburnum edule*	WA, MO, MG
paper birch	*Betula papyrifera*	WA, MO
pasture sage	*Artemisia frigida*	MD, PR, BS
pin cherry	*Prunus pensylvanica*	MO
pine	*Pinus* spp.	MD, CA, WA, MO
raspberry	*Rubus idaeus*	MD, WA, MO, MG
red-osier dogwood	*Cornus stolonifera*	WD, MD, WA, MO, BS
rose	*Rosa* spp.	WD, MD, CA, WA, MO, PR, MG, BS
sagebrush	*Artemisia cana*	MD, PR
Saskatoon (service-berry)	*Amelanchier alnifolia*	MD, WA, MO, MG, BS
shrubby cinquefoil	*Potentilla fruticosa*	CA, BS, BI
silver-berry	*Elaeagnus commutata*	WD, MD, WA, PR, MG
snowberry	*Symphoricarpos albus*	WD, MD, WA, PR, MG
spruce	*Picea* spp.	WA, MO
water birch	*Betula occidentalis*	WA, MO
wild gooseberry	*Ribes oxyacanthoides*	WA, MO, MG
willow	*Salix* spp.	WD, MD, CA, WA, MO, PR, MG, BS
Fallen Leaves		
aspen	*Populus tremuloides*	WA, MO
balsam poplar	*Populus balsamifera*	WA, MO
willow	*Salix* spp.	WA, MO
Bark		
aspen	*Populus tremuloides*	WA, MO
balsam poplar	*Populus balsamifera*	WA, MO
willow	*Salix* spp.	WA, MO
Forbs		
alfalfa	*Medicago sativa*	WD, MD, WA, PR
alpine milkvetch	*Astragalus alpinus*	WA, MG, BS
aster	*Aster* spp.	WD, MD, WA, BS
ball cactus	*Coryphantha vivipara*	PR
balsam-root	*Balsamorhiza sagittata*	MD
bluebells	*Mertensia paniculata*	WD, MD, MG,
bracted lousewort	*Pedicularis bracteosa*	CA
broomweed	*Gutierrezia sarothrae*	PR
bunchberry	*Cornus canadensis*	CA
butterfly-weed	*Gaura coccinea*	PR
Canada thistle	*Cirsium arvense*	MD, WA, MO, PR, BS

TABLE 12.6

COMMON FORAGES (continued)

WD=white-tailed deer, MD=mule deer, CA=caribou, WA=wapiti, MO=moose, PR=pronghorn, MG=mountain goat, BS=bighorn sheep, BI=bison.

Common Name	Scientific Name	Ungulate Species
clover	*Trifolium* spp.	WD, MD, WA, MO, BI
Colorado rubberplant	*Hymenoxys richardsonii*	PR
columbine	*Aquilegia* spp.	WD, MD
common knotweed	*Polygonum areastrum*	PR
common yarrow	*Achillea millefolium*	MO, PR, BS
cow parsnip	*Heracleum lanatum*	MD
dandelion	*Taraxacum officinale*	MD, WA, BI
everlasting	*Antennaria* spp.	WA, PR
fairy candelabra	*Androsace septentrionalis*	PR
false hellebore	*Veratrum eschscholtzii*	MD
fireweed	*Epilobium angustifolium*	MD, WA, MG, BS
fleabane	*Erigeron* spp.	MD, WA, MO
fringed gentian	*Gentianella crinita*	WD, MD, WA
goldenrod	*Solidago* spp.	MD, CA, WA, BS
goldon aster	*Heterotheca villosa*	PR
graceful cinquefoil	*Potentilla gracilis*	PR
groundsel	*Senecio* spp.	WD, MD, CA, WA, BS
harebell	*Campanula rotundifolia*	WD, MD, BS
hedysarum	*Hedysarum* spp.	WD, MD, WA, PR, BS
hemp nettle	*Galeopsis tetrahit*	WA
Indian paint-brush	*Castilleja* spp.	WD, MD, WA, MO
locoweed	*Oxytropis* spp.	BS
low bush cranberry	*Viburnum edule*	MO, MG
lupine	*Lupinus* spp.	WA
mertensia	*Mertensia* spp.	WD, MD, WA
moss phlox	*Phlox hoodii*	PR
mountain avens	*Dryas* spp.	CA
nettle	*Urtica dioica*	WA, MO
northern bedstraw	*Galium boreale*	BS
pasture sage	*Artemisia frigida*	MD, PR, BS
pea vine	*Lathyrus* spp.	WD, MD, WA, MO, BI
prairie crocus	*Anemone patens*	PR
prickly pear cactus	*Opuntia polyacantha*	PR
Sago pondweed	*Potamogeton pectinatus*	MO
sow thistle	*Sonchus* spp.	MD, WA,
twinflower	*Linnaea borealis*	CA, BS
water smartweed	*Polygonum amphibium*	WA
western wood lily	*Lilium philadelphicum*	WD, MD
wild heliotrope	*Valeriana sitchensis*	CA
wild raspberry	*Rubus idaeus*	MO, WA
wild strawberry	*Fragaria virginiana*	MD, WA, MG, BS, BI
wild tomato	*Solanum triflorum*	PR
wild vetch	*Vicia americana*	WD, MD, WA, BS, BI
yellow avens	*Geum aleppicum*	BI
yellow goat's beard	*Tragopogon dubius*	PR
yellow pond lily	*Nuphar variegatum*	MO
yellow sweet clover	*Melilotus officinalis*	PR, BS

Graminoids

barley	*Hordeum* spp.	WD, MD, WA
bent grass	*Agrostis* spp.	PR, BS
blue grama grass	*Bouteloua gracilis*	PR
bluegrass	*Poa* spp.	MD, WA, PR, MG, BS, BI
brome	*Bromus* spp.	MD, CA, WA, BS, BI
common cattail	*Typha latifolia*	WA, MO
common wheat	*Triticum aestivum*	WD, MD, PR
crested wheatgrass	*Agropyron pectiniforme*	WA
fescue	*Festuca* spp.	MD, CA, WA, MG, BS
hair grass	*Deschampsia caespitosa*	CA, WA
hairy wild rye	*Elymus innovatus*	WA, BS, BI
June grass	*Koeleria macrantha*	WA, PR, MG, BS, BI
manna grass	*Glyceria grandis*	BI
melic grass	*Melica* spp.	WA
needle grass	*Stipa* spp.	WA, PR

TABLE 12.6

COMMON FORAGES *(continued)*

WD=white-tailed deer, MD=mule deer, CA=caribou, WA=wapiti, MO=moose, PR=pronghorn,
MG=mountain goat, BS=bighorn sheep, BI=bison.

Common Name	Scientific Name	Ungulate Species
oat	*Avena* spp.	MD, WA, BI
oat grass	*Danthonia* spp.	WA, BS
reed grass	*Calamagrostis* spp.	WA, BS, BI
rye	*Secale cereale*	MD
sedge	*Carex* spp.	CA, WA, MO, PR, MG, BS, BI
timothy	*Phleum pratense*	MD, WA
wheat grass	*Agropyron* spp.	WD, WA, PR, MG, BS, BI
wire rush	*Juncus balticus*	BI

Horsetail

	Equisetum spp.	WD, CA, WA, MO, BI, BS

Mosses

	Pleurozium schreberi	CA
	Polytrichum piliferum	CA
	Racomitrium lanuginosum	CA

Lichens

reindeer lichen	*Cladonia* spp.	CA
reindeer moss	*Cladina* spp.	CA
	Alectoria glabra	CA
	Cetraria pinastri	CA
	Peltigera apthosa	CA
dog lichen	*Peltigera canina*	CA
	Stereocaulon spp.	CA
old man's beard	*Usnea* spp.	CA

Major References:

White-tailed Deer	*Kramer, 1972; Rhude and Hall, 1977*
Mule Deer	*Cowan, 1947; Sheppard, 1960; Flook, 1964; Kramer, 1972; Rhude and Hall, 1977*
Caribou	*Stelfox et al., 1978; Edmonds and Bloomfield, 1984*
Wapiti *(Elk)*	*Cairns, 1976; Salter and Hudson, 1980; Berg, 1983; Gates and Hudson, 1983; Morgantini and Olsen, 1983; Morgantini and Russell, 1983; Nietfeld, 1983; Morgantini and Hudson, 1985; Stelfox and Tilson, 1985; Renecker, 1989*
Moose	*Millar, 1953; Flook, 1964; Cairns, 1976; Nowlin, 1978; Telfer, 1978; Renecker, 1987; Renecker, 1989*
Pronghorn	*Mitchell and Smoliak, 1971; Barrett, 1974*
Mountain Goat	*Kerr, 1965; McFetridge, 1977*
Bighorn Sheep	*Wishart, 1958; Johnson, 1975; Stelfox, 1976; Shank, 1982*
Bison *(Buffalo)*	*Holsworth, 1960; Van Camp, 1975; Cairns, 1976; Reynolds, 1976*
General	*Nietfeld et. al., 1985; Green and Salter, 1987*

Glossary

(Term definitions often refer specifically to hoofed mammals.)

Abdominal cavity. The largest body cavity; contains digestive, reproductive and urinary organs. In mammals it is separated from the thoracic cavity by a muscular diaphragm.

Abomasum. The fourth chamber of the ruminant stomach. Site of enzymatic and acid hydrolysis of microbial cells and previously non-absorbed metabolites.

Age structure. Describes the contribution or number of various age classes (calves, yearling, adults) in a given population.

Alkaloids. Plant secondary compounds which may cause gastro-intestinal dysfunction when eaten by ungulates.

Altricial. Born in a relatively undeveloped state. In comparison to caribou, white-tailed deer fawns are altricial, and are hidden and less active during their first several days of life.

Anaerobic. An environment without oxygen, such as the rumen and reticulum of the ruminant.

Annulated. Possessing rings which indicate years. The horns of bighorn sheep and mountain goat or the cementum of teeth are examples.

Antilocapridae. An ancient group of ungulates which evolved in North America and is represented by today's pronghorn.

Antler cast. That period when antlers fall from the skull.

Antlers. Bony, deciduous (shed annually) appendages arising from the pedicels of the skull's frontal bones. Growing antlers are covered with a layer of skin, the velvet, which carries blood vessels and nerves supplying bone growth. The velvet is rubbed off leaving a bony structure. With the exception of caribou, they are confined to males of Cervidae (deer family). Their primary purpose is the establishment of social dominance.

Artiodactyla. Those hoofed mammals that have even numbers of digits. Include members of the family Tayassuidae, Cervidae, Bovidae and Antilocapridae in North America.

Beam. Major axis of antler from which tines arise.

Bez tine. The first tine above the brow tine of an antler.

Bolus. A unit of ingesta that passes along the esophagus.

Bovidae. The hollow-horned ungulates. Representatives of this family in Alberta are the mountain goat, bighorn sheep and the bison.

Brow tine. The first tine above the base of an antler.

Browser. An herbivore species that forages primarily on shrubs and trees.

Buccal cavity. Mouth cavity housing teeth and tongue in which food is procured, ground, mixed with saliva and rolled into a bolus (ball) prior to swallowing.

Caecum. Blind pouch located at junction of small and large intestines.

Calving interval. The average period of time between successive births from a single reproductive female.

Canine. The fourth tooth on either side of the lower jaw. In most ungulates, its appearance is incisor-like (incisiform). Upper canine teeth are absent from Alberta's ungulates, except for wapiti and caribou.

Carcass shrinkage. The amount of evaporative moisture lost from a carcass.

Carrying capacity. The number of individuals that the biological and physical resources of a habitat can support on a sustained basis.

Cell solubles. Contents within cell walls. Generally consists of highly digestible compounds including protein and simple sugars.

Cementum. A layer of cement-like material which attaches the root of teeth to the surrounding bone socket (alveolus).

Cervidae. Those ungulates with antlers. Representatives in Alberta are the white-tailed deer, mule deer, caribou, wapiti and moose.

Cheek teeth. Premolars and molars located in the rear of the mouth (buccal cavity) and used to masticate (break down) forage by grinding in a lateral and rotary direction.

Chest girth. The circumference of the chest immediately posterior to the front legs.

Chest height (cm). The distance between the ground and the sternum when the ungulate is standing upright on level ground.

Cloven hoof. Those hoofed mammals with two (split) hooves. All native Alberta ungulates are cloven-hoofed.

Colon. Also referred to as the large intestine. Major site of water absorption and formation of feces. Empties into rectum.

Compensatory growth. Accelerated body growth observed when animals receive additional food.

Compensatory mortality. Situations whereby animals killed by predators would otherwise have died from disease or poor body condition.

Conspecific. Of the same species.

Corpus luteum. Mass of yellowish, glandular tissue in the ovary formed from the Graafian follicle after ovulation.

Cow/calf ratio. Number of adult females in a population relative to the number of calves.

Crepuscular. Active at twilight, i.e., at dusk or at dawn.

Crown (of tooth). The part of the tooth farthest from the root, which comes into contact with an opposing tooth in the other jaw.

Cryptic. A condition of being difficult to detect; caused by coat spotting, posture, and obscuring an animal relative to its surrounding.

Cursorial. Adapted to or specialized for running.

Cusp. Projection or bump on occlusal surface of a tooth.

Deciduous dentition. The juvenile or milk dentition. Consists of incisors, canines, and premolars. Replaced by permanent or adult dentition.

Dental formula. A formula that describes the location and number of teeth. For most ruminants, the dental formula is I 0/3, C 0/1, P 3/3, M 3/3, indicating that there are 3 incisors (I) and 1 canine (C) on either side of the lower jaw, and 3 premolars (P) and 3 molars (M) on both sides of the upper and lower cheekteeth region.

Dentary bone. One of the pair of bones comprising the lower jaw (mandible).

Dentine. Hard material forming the major portion of a tooth; in most teeth surrounds the pulp cavity and contacts the enamel on the crown of tooth and the cementum at base of roots; sometimes exposed on surface of crown.

Dew claws. Hoofed remnants of side toes, located just above the main functional hoof (digit). They generally do not bear weight unless the animal is in deep snow or on a soft substrate. Found on all Alberta ruminants except pronghorn.

Diastema. Space on the dentary bone between the canines and the premolars.

Digesta. Food within the gastrointestinal tract that is in the process of being digested.

Digestibility. Refers to that proportion of the energy or nutrients within forage that is extracted within the digestive system and is available to the animal.

Digits. Toes. In ungulates digits are sheathed by hooves (unguis).

Dominance hierarchy. A social system in which several adult males remain together and establish a hierarchy based on physical and behaviour qualities. Those males occupying higher dominance positions generally monopolize breeding.

Dressed carcass. Includes the eviscerated carcass with head, lower legs, skin and organs removed.

Ear length. The length from the base of the ear notch to the ear tip.

Ectoparasite. A parasite on the external surface of an animal (e.g., a tick).

Egesta. Non-digested remains of forage that are excreted from the herbivore digestive system.

Enamel. Hard matrix of calcium salts which cover the crown of most teeth. The whitish, hard, outer layer of the tooth crown. Forms ridges on the occlusal surface (see infundibula).

Eructation. The process by which coarse forage in the rumen is returned to the mouth, where it is broken down through mastication.

Eruption. Refers to the emergence of a tooth through the gums.

Esophagus. Tube connecting the buccal cavity to the reticulo-rumen and through which digesta is transported during rumination.

Evisceration. The process of removing the gastro-intestinal tract and organs from an animal.

Fasting metabolic rate. The metabolic rate of a resting animal in a thermoneutral environment in a post-absorptive state. In this condition, the animal is not consuming energy for digestive processes or liberating heat from digestion.

Fecal nitrogen. The amount of nitrogen discharged by the animal in its feces. Since there is a positive relationship between fecal nitrogen content and forage nitrogen content and digestibility, fecal nitrogen can be used as a general index of forage quality and digestibility.

Feces. The remnants of forage after it has been processed by the gastrointestinal tract. Includes mucosal cells of the gut lining. Also referred to as egesta, scats, pellets, etc.

Feeding bouts. Those periods of the 24-hour day when animals most actively forage.

Fermentation. The anaerobic digestion of plant material in the rumen and reticulum of ruminants by microbes (protozoa, bacteria).

Fistula. An artificial opening in the esophagus or rumen that assists researchers examining forage intake and digestibility

Flehmen (lip-curl). A facial expression/behavior exhibited by males of certain species during the breeding season. Its function is not completely understood but seems to be involved in the analysis of pheromones that convey information about reproductive status of females. Flehmen is generally accompanied by lifting the upper lip and arching the head upwards.

Fluke. Trematode (flatworm) that exists as an endoparasite.

Foot-loading. Average weight (g/cm²) exerted on the bearing surfaces of the hooves. Foot load index calculated as 1 – g/cm².

Forbs. Non-woody broad-leaved dicotyledon plants growing in the herb layer.

Gastrointestinal tract. Those tissues involved in the digestion and absorption of nutrients.

Gestation. Time between conception (fertilization) and birth (parturition).

Graminoid. Grass-like; includes grasses and sedges.

Grasses. Plants that have hollow, jointed stems and leaves in two rows on the stem. The seeds are borne between two scales.

Grazer. An herbivore that forages primarily on grasses, sedges and forbs.

Gregarious. Those species that frequently assemble into herds. The most gregarious of North American ungulates are bison and caribou.

Guard hairs. Prominent, coarse hair in the pelage of mammals.

Habitat. That combination of biotic and physical variables in which a species occurs.

Harem. A grouping of animals during the breeding season containing numerous adult females and one sexually mature male. Dominant males in harems defend females from other reproductively active males.

Hectare. Square area defined by sides of 100 metres.

Herbivore. An animal that feeds primarily upon living vegetation.

Home range. Geographic area an animal or population of animals inhabits over an extended period of time.

Hoof. The horny, keratinized sheath (unguis) covering the toes of ungulates. The unguis curves almost completely around the end of the digit. Ungulate hooves come into direct contact with the ground and provide good traction and prevent wear.

Hoof length. See Figure 2.32.

Hoof width. See Figure 2.32.

Horn core. Bony, permanent structure extending from the frontal bone of the skull and enclosed by the horn sheath.

Horn sheath. Hard keratinized sheath which covers the horn core. Generally permanent, though shed annually from horn cores of pronghorn.

Horn. Unbranched and permanent structure projecting from the head and composed of an inner bony core formed from the frontal bone, and an outer layer of true horn formed from keratinized epidermis. Horns are present on many ungulates such as bison, cattle, goat, and sheep. They are used in the establishment of dominance and in defense. The horns of male pronghorn are atypical in that they branch.

Host. Animal that supports a parasite population.

Incisiform. Similar in appearance to the incisors. Refers specifically to the lower canines of ruminants.

Incisors. Teeth designed for cutting that are located in the foremost part of the jaw. In Alberta's native hoofed mammals, they are six in number and are restricted to the lower jaw.

Infundibula. Ridges of enamel on the occlusal surfaces of cheek teeth used to grind forage.

Ingesta. Forage that has been ingested and has not yet been digested. Found in mouth, esophagus and rumen.

Interdigital gland. Located between the hooves, this gland secretes a pheromone on the ground. Thought to be important in individual recognition and in retracing previous movements.

Keratinized. Impregnated with keratin, a tough fibrous protein.

Labial (buccal). Refers to the cheek side of the teeth.

Lactation. Production of milk from the mammary glands.

Licence. Purchased by a Wildlife Certificate holder for the purposes of hunting a specific species or group of species.

Lingual. Refers to the tongue side of the teeth.

Liveweight. Refers to the weight of a living ungulate. This weight may differ from fresh killed weight because of blood loss.

Lower critical temperature. The ambient (environmental) temperature at which animals begin to elevate their metabolic rate to create extra heat. This heat is used to compensate for extra heat loss to a cold environment.

Mandibular. Referring to the lower jaw.

Metatarsal gland. Epithelial gland located on the outside of the hind leg on the metatarsus.

Microbes. Generic term referring to anaerobic bacteria and protozoa inhabiting the rumen, reticulum, and caecum. These organisms perform a critical role in the degradation of refractory forage into a form usable to ruminants (i.e., volatile fatty acids).

Microhistological techniques. Refers to those analyses that examine the microscopic nature of the epidermis of plant material. The unique appearance of the cell wall of each plant species permits identification and quantification of diet composition.

Milk teeth. The first set of incisors, canines and premolars. This set will be replaced by permanent teeth.

Molars. Ridged cheek teeth that grind coarse forage by moving laterally across opposing teeth. Located posterior to premolars.

Molt. The yearly or seasonal shedding and replacement of hair.

Neonate. Newborn young.

Non-resident Wildlife Certificate holder. A resident of a province other than Alberta who has purchased a Wildlife Certificate.

Non-resident Alien Wildlife Certificate holder. A resident of a country other than Canada who has purchased a Wildlife Certificate.

Non-typical antlers. Antlers that do not have a structure that meets the criteria of "typical" of the Boone and Crockett Club. These antlers generally have either extra or misplaced antler tines.

Occlusal. The surface where two opposing teeth grind vegetation.

Omasum. Third chamber of the ruminant stomach which separates the rumen/reticulum from the acidic abomasum; finely partitioned by a leaf-like filter which prevents passage of coarse digesta and possibly absorbs water.

Palatability. The desirability of a plant for a herbivore. Characteristics of plants generally recognized to affect palatability include succulence, protein level and presence of secondary compounds.

Palmate. Palm-like (e.g., antlers of a moose).

Papillae. Small numerous projections located along the internal surface of the reticulo-rumen. Responsible for the absorption of nutrients, primarily volatile fatty acids.

Parasite. Organism that derives nutrients from another organism without generally inducing death.

Parturition. The process of birth.

Pelage. Hair or fur coat of an animal.

Penile button. The flap of skin and hair hanging below the abdomen.

Perissodactyla. Odd-toed herbivorous ungulates; includes horses, rhinoceroses, and tapirs.

Permanent teeth. Second set of incisors, canines and premolars which replace the milk (deciduous) teeth. Also include first and only set of molars.

Phenols. Plant secondary compounds that can reduce palatability of plants and may induce gastro-intestinal dysfunction in herbivores.

Phenotype. The physical expression of genotype, as affected by the environment.

Pheromone. Chemical substances which communicate information between individuals of the same species.

Polygamous. Males who breed more than one female during a reproductive season.

Population. Collection of interacting animals inhabiting the same area during the same general time period of the same species. Members of a population are not reproductively isolated.

Precocial. Newborn hoofed mammals that tend to follow their mothers and do not rely on crypsis and bedding to escape detection by predators.

Premolars. First three cheek teeth located in all four quadrants of the mouth of ungulates. Positioned anterior to the molars, they are used together to grind forage to increase surface area and improve digestion.

Preorbital gland. Located immediately anterior of the eye socket, this gland produces pheromones with a communication function. Also called antorbital gland.

Preorbital pit. Depression in skull anterior to eye orbit where preorbital gland is located. The depth of this pit is useful in distinguishing white-tailed deer and mule deer skulls (see Figures 12.14 and 12.15).

Resident Wildlife Certificate holder. A resident of Alberta who has purchased a Wildlife Certificate.

Resting metabolic rate. Term generally used to refer to metabolic rate (heat production) of an animal that is lying at rest. Does not necessarily mean that the animal is in a thermoneutral environment or in a post-absorptive state.

Reticulo-rumen. The first two sacs of the ruminant stomach; separated partially by the reticulo-rumen fold. Thin-walled papilla-lined structures that are the major site of anaerobic fermentation of forage and absorption of nutrients.

Roundworm. Unsegmented worms. Numerous species occur as parasites in the organs, muscles, and gastrointestinal tract of hoofed mammals.

Ruminant. A hoofed, even-toed mammal with a four-chambered stomach that chews its cud (i.e. brings food from the rumen back to the mouth for further chewing).

Rut. Mating season, characterized by reproductive receptiveness of females and sparring or displays among males.

Salivary glands. Several glands located near the mouth producing saliva. Saliva lubricates vegetation for easier swallowing and reintroduces nitrogen into the gastrointestinal tract.

Sampling intensity. The proportion of an area or population that is sampled. For example, if 250 km² of a total area of 1,000 km² are censused for ungulates, the sampling intensity would be 25 per cent.

Scent glands. Sweat or sebaceous glands modified for the production of an odoriferous secretion.

Secondary compounds. Plant chemical compounds such as alkaloids, phenols, and terpenoids that reduce palatability by creating gastrointestinal or neural disturbances within the herbivore.

Selenodont. Dentition characterized by premolars and molars with a crown pattern of longitudinally-oriented, crescent-shaped ridges formed by elongated cusps.

Shoulder height. The distance from the top of the shoulder above the scapula to the ventral mid-point of the digital pad.

Shrubs. Woody perennials with stems that live over the winter and branch from near the base.

Skull length. Distance from the most anterior part of the rostrum (excluding teeth) to the most posterior point of the skull.

Skull width. Greatest width of the skull, generally measured between the outer margins of the bones surrounding the orbits.

Small intestines. Portion of gastrointestinal tract located between the abomasum (true stomach) and the large intestine (colon). Function of the small intestine is the enzymatic digestion of forage and absorption of nutrients.

Straddle width. See Figure 2.32.

Stride length. See Figure 2.32.

Subunguis. Tissue on the inside of the keratinized hoof. It is generally softer in texture and offers traction on substrate.

Sustainable offtake. That percent of a population that can be harvested without inducing a downward trend in population numbers.

Tail gland. A gland found at the base of the tail of pronghorn. The function of this gland is unclear but may be to produce warning chemicals.

Tannins. A plant secondary compound that, when ingested, can bind protein in the gastro-intestinal tract of herbivores. The resulting precipitate is resistant to digestion.

Tapeworm. Cestode. Segmented flatworm that lives as an endoparasite. Adult stages generally live in the gastrointestinal tract of the host.

Tarsal gland. Scent gland located on the inner surface of the hind leg at the tarsus; thought to be involved in individual recognition. During the rut, bucks and does frequently urinate on their tarsal glands to deposit scent conveying identity and sexual status to the ground.

Terpenes. A group of aromatic plant secondary compounds that can reduce digestibility of forage.

Tick. Ectoparasite in the Order Acarina. Have an unsegmented abdomen and broad connection between abdomen and cephalothorax. Subadults have six legs and adults have eight legs. The "winter" or "moose" tick is a common ectoparasite of Alberta's moose and is responsible for major hair loss during some winters.

Tiller. A form of vegetative reproduction whereby a plant sends out a lower branch originating at the base of the plant. These branches may root and initiate a new plant.

Tine. An individual spike on an antler.

Trees. Woody, single-stemmed perennial plants that reach a mature height of at least 2.2 meters.

Typical antlers. An antler growth form that is considered normal and falls within the definition of typical antlers as outlined by such trophy organizations as the Boone and Crockett Club.

Underfur. Soft, often wooly, insulative hairs in the pelage of mammals.

Unguis. The hard, keratinized portion of a hoof.

Ungulate. Mammal that supports its weight on hooves, such as deer, cattle, sheep, antelope, goats, pigs, giraffe, horses and rhinoceroses.

Unguligrade. Hoofed; a foot structure in which only the hoof (unguis) contacts the ground.

Upper critical temperature. The ambient temperature above which metabolic rate is increased.

Velvet. The pilose skin covering a growing antler.

Volatile fatty acids. The major byproducts of anaerobic fermentation in the rumen. These acids (proprionate, acetate and butyrate) constitute a major energy source for the ruminant.

Weight load on track. The liveweight of an ungulate divided by the total surface area of its four hooves. Expressed as g/cm^2.

Wildlife Certificate holder. Any person 14 years of age or older who has purchased a Wildlife Certificate entitling him/her to purchase any number of species-specific hunting licences, or to apply for various special licenses issued through a lottery process or special draw.

Windpipe. Trachea. Cartilaginous tube that connects the mouth to the lungs.

Zoonosis. Any disease of wild animals that can be contracted by humans under natural conditions.

Capture and Restraint

Lyle A. Renecker and
Heather C.H. McIntyre

TABLE A2.1

PROJECTILES AND PROJECTOR MECHANISMS USED FOR CHEMICAL RESTRAINT OF UNGULATES

Method	Range	Description	Use	Manufacturer	Reference
Hand syringe	arms length 0–0.5 m	• hand operated	• with tractable animals in handling facility		
Pole syringe	arms length 0–2 m	• 0.9–4 m pole • can be telescopic springloaded • silent	• in handling facility • clover trap	Westergun Westerguard Ent. Kwik-way Kay Research Prod.	*Lynch, 1987* *Fowler, 1978*
Blow pipe	1–10 m	• 1–2 m plastic or metal tube (i.d. = 15–16 mm) • use air or liquid butane charged plastic darts; silent	• close range in corral or small capture pen	Dist-Inject, Peter Ott Telinject	*Lynch, 1987*
Bow	long range	• syringe attached to arrow	• remote immobilzation • not recommended • damage to animal high	custom: Donjoy Industries	*Hawkins* et al., *1967* *Lynch, 1987*
Pistols: CO$_2$	short range (depends on dart size)	• projects powder-charged aluminum darts; light weight • inconsistency in pressure	• in corral or trap	Palmer Chemical Equipment	*Lynch, 1987*
Pistols: Powder charged	short range	• projects powder charged aluminum darts	• in corral or trap	Dist-Inject, Peter Ott	*Lynch, 1987*
Rifle: N$_2$O	5–70 m	• equipped with pressure manometer to adjust pressure • silent • telescopic sight can improve accuracy	• in handling facility or field • 5–10 charges / gas cartridge, dependent on dart weight / pressure	Dist-Inject Model 50, Peter Ott	*Lynch, 1987*
Rifle: Powder charged	10–100 m	• 32 gauge shotgun stock that fires .22 caliber blanks • inexpensive but inconsistent • aluminum powder charged darts	• in field	Palmer Chemical Equipment	*Lynch, 1987*
Rifle: Powder charged	10–100 m	• uses aluminum darts which are constructed with O-ring seals • more consistent results, quieter	• in field or large corral	Dist-Inject Model 60, Peter Ott	*Lynch, 1987*
Rifle: Powder charged	10–75 m	• uses a pressure control metre to monitor gas through barrel	• in field or large corral	Zoolu Arms of Omaha	*Nielsen, 1982*
Rifle: Powder charged	10–100 m	• uses a pressure control metre to monitor gas through barrel	• in field or large corral	Paxarms Pneu-Dart	*Lynch, 1987*

VARIABLES TO CONSIDER BEFORE
CHEMICAL IMMOBILIZATION OF WILD UNGULATES

Variable	Comments
Individual/species differences	Be aware of the wide margin in variability among both individuals and species in how ungulates respond to chemical immobilization and the dose of drug required.
Behaviour/anatomy	Muscles of the upper hind leg, rump and shoulder are preferred as delivery sites for projectiles; avoid the neck and abdomen. Be aware of species behaviour and how an animal will respond after injection.
Animal condition	Avoid immobilizing animals stressed from pregnancy, rut, disease, or spring emaciation.
Stress-related factors	Minimize handling stress prior to and during immobilization; eliminate or reduce visual, auditory, olfactory and tactile stimuli. Avoid an underdose of etorphine as it can result in an excitatory phase from which the animal never exits. Plug the animal's ears with cloth; a loud noise could arouse it from anesthesia. Blindfold the animal with a towel or disposable diaper. This reduces water loss from eyes and protects them from injury. An injection of atropine (adult cow moose: 0.5 ml injection; 6 mg/ml solution) reduces excess salivation and stabilizes heart rate. Avoid topping up initial drug dosage with subsequent injections as it is impossible to determine the amount of active drug "on board" the animal. Therefore, it is difficult to determine the amount of time required for recovery, which eventually could jeopardize the animal's safety.
Topography/cover	Prevent access to cliffs and water where partially immobilized animals could injure themselves. Avoid immobilization in areas where dense cover will make it difficult to track the animal prior to the drug taking full effect. Lateral recumbency on a hard surface may result in radial nerve or muscle damage.
Weather/temperature	At air temperatures greater than 10°C, there is danger of hyperthermia. Cool the animal with water if rectal temperature exceeds 39.2–39.5°C. At air temperatures of less than -20°C there is danger of hypothermia. Use a blanket or solar sheet to cover the animal. At low temperatures, drug solutions may freeze, are often unstable at high concentrations, and may precipitate as temperatures approach 0°C or when subjected to rapid temperature change. High wind and rain influences the ballistics of the projectile and results in a poorly placed dart, incomplete injection if the needle strikes a bone, complete miss, or penetration of the abdominal wall.
Time of day	Avoid immobilization late in the day to prevent disorientation or loss of immobilized animal due to darkness.
Preparation	Have adequate help and all necessary supplies. An injection of antibiotic is recommended if surgical procedures are conducted on the animal. Position the animal upright, resting it on its sternum, with the neck up and head down. This allows for drainage of rumen fluid if the animal regurgitates and helps to prevent bloat. If bloat occurs the animal should be turned from side to side to help expel the gas and relieve the pressure. If aspiration occurs, additional immobilizing drug (50 mg of i.v. xylazine; was used by Renecker (1990) for adult cow moose immobilized with an initial combination of etorphine + xylazine) may be recommended to stop the reverse peristaltic reflex of the esophagus. Be prepared to give artificial respiration (alternately press and release the thorax) or use compressed oxygen and portable resuscitation equipment if respiratory depression occurs. If cardiovascular complications arise, administer the reversal drug.
Time of year	Know the innate changes that occur in metabolism of the animal species considered. Drug dosage will depend on this criterion (for example, metabolic rate is lower during winter than summer [see Renecker and Hudson, Chapter 12] and therefore less drug may be required).
Personnel requirements	Choose people that respond quickly and efficiently, make decisions as required, adhere to discipline, and are physically capable of laborious duties.
Human safety	Immobilization drugs are extremely dangerous to humans. Synthetic opiates such as etorphine and carfentanil are deadly and one drop could kill a human. Wear polypropylene gloves to avoid skin contact. Avoid spray from bottle when loading syringe. Always have human antagonist present and ready for injection when using etorphine. Everyone in the team should know CPR procedures.
Projectile delivery	Be familiar with delivery systems. Practice with an artificial target and assess the accuracy of the dart delivery system.

TABLE A2.3

CALCULATION OF DRUG DOSAGE AND PROCEDURE FOR INJECTION OF REVERSAL DRUGS FOR XYLAZINE-INDUCED SEDATION

There are a variety of drugs on the market for the immobilization of Alberta's ungulates (see Table A2.3). It is important to choose the proper drug and understand calculation of appropriate dosage

Dosage Calculation

1. Always weigh animals prior to immobilization for accurate body weights. Live weight can be estimated conservatively for wild animals.

2. For example, volume calculation of the reversal drug Yohimbine:

   Recommended dosage for yohimbine = 0.15 mg/kg

   Body weight of wapiti = 300 kg

   Concentration of drug solution (on drug label or recorded when drug is prepared) = 252 mg/50 ml

   Weight of drug required = 0.15 mg/kg x 300 kg BW of animal = 45 mg yohimbine

   Volume of drug required = $\frac{45 \text{ mg} \times 50 \text{ ml}}{252 \text{ mg}}$ = 8.9 mL yohimbine solution

3. The same calculation procedure can be applied to other drugs.

Injection procedures for yohimbine and 4-aminopyridine reversal drugs

1. Always load these drugs in separate syringes. If using the commercial product Antagonil, then only one syringe is required.

2. Drugs are always administered intravenously (i.v.) with consecutive injections in separate syringes. An intra-arterial injection will cause immediate convulsions and death. It is imperative that the person administering these drugs be certain that the needle has punctured a vein.

3. Always draw blood into the syringe before withdrawing the needle to insure that all the drug solution was injected into the vein.

4. Used syringes and needles should be disposed of via incineration.

5. Care should be taken to avoid accidental injection in humans, as it could cause death.

Potential problems with immobilized ungulates

1. Bloat.

2. Regurgitation and aspiration which can result in pneumonia.

3. Convulsions.

4. Excessive salivation.

5. Loss of sternal recumbency.

6. Radial nerve or muscle damage in large ungulates in a prone position for long periods of time.

7. Loss of thermoregulatory control.

8. Respiratory depression.

9. Kicking or arousal in response to loud noises because auditory senses are often extremely acute in immobilized animals.

TABLE A2.4

PHYSICAL CAPTURE TECHNIQUES USED FOR ALBERTA UNGULATES

Species	Alberta location	Technique	Reference
Caribou	Alpine tundra, west-central Alta.	hand-held net gun from helicopter	Barrett et. al., 1982
Wapiti	west central Alberta	enclosed plywood corral trap	Morgantini and Olsen, 1983
Wapiti	Waterton/Pincher Creek	enclosed plywood corral trap	Morgantini, 1990; pers. comm.
Wapiti	Ya-Ha-Tinda Ranch	corral trap	Morgantini, 1988
Wapiti	Elk Island National Park	clover trap	Renecker, 1991
Moose	Swan Hills - northwest Alberta	fence traps	LeResche and Lynch, 1973 Lynch, 1978 Lynch and Morgantini, 1984
Pronghorn	southern Alberta	oval throw net	Barrett, 1981
Bighorn Sheep	Prairie Bluff - southwest Alberta	box traps and drop net	Morgantini, 1988
Bighorn Sheep	southwest Alberta	corral trap	Festa-Bianchet, 1986
Bighorn Sheep	west central Alberta	corral trap	Wishart et al., 1980 Stemp, 1983

COMMONLY USED IMMOBILIZING DRUGS, THEIR PROPERTIES AND MODES OF ACTION

(some data from Hebert and McFetridge, 1978)

Properties/Actions	Succinyl-choline	Etorphine[1] & fentanyl	Carfent-anil	Ketamine	Xylazine	Ketamine & xylazine
Rapid Action	Yes	Yes	Yes	Partial	Partial	Yes
Wide safety margin	No	Yes	Yes	Yes	Yes	Yes
Reversible with antidote	No	Yes	Yes	No	Yes	Yes
Produces CNS depression	No	Unknown	Unknown	Yes/Partial	Yes	Yes
Produces predictable results	Partial	Yes/Partial	Yes/Partial	Yes/Partial	Yes/Partial	Yes
Allows control of immobilization with a second dose	No	Yes	Yes	Yes	Yes	Yes
Suitable for many species	Yes/Partial	Yes	Yes	Yes	Yes	Yes
Permits sternal recumbency	Yes/Partial	Yes	Yes	No	Yes	Yes
Low cost (CDN $)	Yes	No[2]	No	Yes	Yes/Partial	Yes/Partial
Easy to obtain	Yes	No	No	Yes	Yes/Partial	Yes/Partial
Human safety	Yes/Partial	No	No	Yes	Yes/Partial	Yes/Partial
Tissue residues	No	Unknown	Unknown	Unknown	Unknown	Unknown
Susceptible to freezing	Yes	Yes	Unknown	Yes	Yes	Yes
Sensitive to seasonal effects	Yes	No	No	No	Yes	Yes/Partial
Sensitive to sex and age	Yes	No	No	Yes/Partial	Yes	Yes/Partial
Sensitive to nutritional status	Yes	No	No	Yes/Partial	Yes	Yes
State of excitement	Yes	No	No	Yes	Yes	Yes
Harmful side effects	Yes	Yes/Partial	Yes/Partial	No	Yes/Partial	No

[1] no longer manufactured in North America

[2] immobilon is less expensive but not available in Canada

POSSIBLE SUPPLIES NECESSARY FOR EACH IMMOBILIZATION PROCEDURE OF AN UNGULATE

1. Polypropylene gloves.
2. Blindfold (towel or large baby diapers).
3. Cloth for ear plugs.
4. Paper towels.
5. Vaccutainers, vaccutainer needles and holder if blood is collected.
6. Atropine to reduce excessive salivation.
7. Rope to restrain legs of large ungulate, if necessary.
8. Immobilization and reversal drugs.
9. Syringes and needles.
10. Immobilization equipment, projectiles, and vaseline.
11. Long-acting injectable antibiotic, topical antibiotic, 95% ethanol, and distilled water.
12. Water to cool animal if immobilization occurs during a warm period or blanket for cool period.
13. Rectal thermometer and stethoscope.
14. Field data book and clock.
15. Resuscitation device.
16. Plastic bags for fecal samples.

CHARACTERISTICS OF COMMON IMMOBILIZATION DRUGS USED ON ALBERTA UNGULATES.

Drug	Maximum solubility in water (mg/ml)	Commercial concentration (mg/ml)	Susceptible to precipitation at maximum concentration or rapid temperature change
Xylazine	400	20 mg/ml or 100 mg/ml in 20 or 50 ml vials	yes
Ketamine	200	100 mg/ml in 10 or 100 ml vials	no
Yohimbine	9	—	yes[1]
4-aminopyridine	10	—	yes[1]
Etorphine	—	1 mg/ml in 20 ml vials	—
Diprenorphine	—	2 mg/ml in 20 ml vials	—

[1] Drugs will precipitate if mixed together at high concentrations.

DOSAGES OF IMMOBILIZATION AND REVERSAL DRUGS
AND THEIR EFFICACY FOR ALBERTA'S UNGULATES

Species	Immobilization Drug	Dosage (mg/kg)	Total Dose (mg)	Induction time (min)	Total Time Down (min)	Reversal Drug	Dosage (mg/kg)
Bighorn Sheep	xylazine	—	80-100	24	31	—	—
Bighorn Sheep	xylazine	—	100	—	—	—	—
Bighorn Sheep	xylazine & ketamine	—	—	—	—	yohimbine & 4-ap	—
Bighorn Sheep	xylazine & ketamine	—	—	—	—	Yohimbine & 4-ap	—
Bighorn Sheep	xylazine & Ketamine	—	—	—	—	yohimbine & 4-ap	—
Bighorn Sheep	xylazine & ketamine	—	—	—	—	yohimbine & 4-ap	—
Bighorn Sheep	xylazine & ketamine	—	81, 365	15	45[1]	—	—
Bighorn Sheep	xylazine & ketamine	—	160, 375	22	37[1]	—	—
Bighorn Sheep	xylazine & ketamine	—	52, 120	5.3	118[1]	—	—
Bighorn Sheep	xylazine & ketamine	—	73, 200	7.3	62.3[1]	—	—
Bighorn Sheep	xylazine & ketamine	—	262, 265	7.4	64.1[1]	—	—
Bighorn Sheep	xylazine & ketamine	—	243, 263	11.7	53.3[1]	—	—
Bighorn Sheep	xylazine & ketamine	—	170, 240	8.6	73.5[1]	—	—
Bighorn Sheep	xylazine & ketamine	—	225, 255	8.5	56[1]	—	—
Bighorn Sheep	xylazine & ketamine	—	80, 175	3.1	84[1]	—	—
Bighorn Sheep	xylazine & ketamine	—	92, 211	4.8	63[1]	—	—
Bighorn Sheep	sernalyn & anatran	0.9-2.5, 0.5-0.6	—	6-9	33-95	—	—
Bighorn Sheep	sernalyn & sparine	1.3, 0.6	—	6.8	62.5	—	—
Bighorn Sheep	sernalyn & anatran	1.4, 0.2	—	4.5	39.5	—	—
Caribou	etorphine	0.04		—	—	diprenorphine	0.098
Caribou	fentanyl, xylazine & azaperone	—	75, 50-100, 75-100	—	—	naloxone	20-40
Wapiti	succinyl choline	—	10-30	7	25	—	—
Wapiti	xylazine	0.8-3.9	—	5-38	1-several hrs	—	—
Wapiti	xylazine	—	300	—	—	—	—
Wapiti	xylazine	—	300	13	—	yohimbine	—
Wapiti	xylazine	—	350	26	—	yohimbine	—
Wapiti	xylazine	—	670	7	16	yohimbine & 4-ap	—
Wapiti	xylazine	1.19	—	5	—	yohimbine & 4-ap	0.15, 0.30
Wapiti	xylazine	0.68	—	10	—	yohimbine & 4-ap	0.15, 0.30
Wapiti	xylazine	1.1	—	—	—	yohimbine & 4-ap	0.15-0.18, 0.25-0.30
Moose	xylazine	1.02	—	17	—	yohimbine & 4-ap	0.15, 0.26
Moose	xylazine & etorphine	1.04, 0.02	300, 6.0	21.3	133.6	diprenorphine	0.56
Moose	xylazine & etorphine	1.3, 0.016	500, 6.0	21.0	144.6	diprenorphine	0.03
Moose	xylazine & etorphine	1.51, 0.02	475, 7.0	29	91	diprenorphine	0.04
Moose	xylazine & etorphine	0.92, 0.019	300, 6.0	13	89	diprenorphine	0.05
Moose	xylazine & etorphine	1.96, 0.025	550, 7.0	14	103	diprenorphine	0.05
Moose	xylazine	3.21	900	15	205	—	—
Moose	xylazine, etorphine	0.66, 0.04	164, 10	—	—	diprenorphine	0.07
Moose	xylazine, etorphine	0.66, 0.04	72, 10.4	—	—	diprenorphine	0.07
Moose	xylazine, etorphine	0.77, 0.031	200, 8	21.9	106.1	diprenorphine	0.06
Moose	xylazine, etorphine	0.53, 0.027	200, 10	17	88.3	diprenorphine	0.06
Moose	xylazine, etorphine	0.53, 0.027	175, 9	4.75	110.8	diprenorphine	0.055
Moose	etorphine	—	5-7	15	—	diprenorphine	—
Moose	etorphine	—	—	—	—	diprenorphine	—
Moose	succinyl choline	—	—	—	—	—	—
Moose	sernalyn	—	—	—	—	—	—
Moose	etorphine	—	5-7	3-44	—	diprenorphine	—
Moose	fentanyl & xylazine	0.14-0.53, 0.15-0.53	47-200, 50-200	3-24	—	naloxone	0.025-1
Moose	fentanyl & xylazine (hyaluronidase added)	0.13-0.3, 0.15-0.4	—	3-15; 3-10 for calves; 2-12 for adult	—	naloxone or levallorphan	0.025-0.1, 0.15-0.25
Mule Deer	xylazine	0.76	—	14	—	yohimbine & 4-ap	0.15, 0.29
White-tailed Deer	xylazine	0.65	—	10	—	yohimbine & 4-ap	0.15, 0.29

[1] Duration time = time from immobilization until animal stands

4-ap = 4-aminopyridine
etorphine = m-99
diprenorphine = M 50-50

Total Dose (mg)	Walking Time (min)	Sex	Weight (kg)	Age	Season	Reference
—	—	female	—	adult	Jan.-Mar.	Morgantini, 1990; pers. comm.
—	—	male	—	lamb	Jan.-Mar.	Morgantini, 1990; pers. comm.
—	—	female	—	adult	winter	Morgantini & Renecker, 1990; pers. comm.
—	—	male	—	lamb	winter	Morgantini & Renecker, 1990; pers. comm.
—	—	female	—	adult	spring/summer	Morgantini & Renecker, 1990; pers. comm.
—	—	male	—	adult	spring/summer	Morgantini & Renecker, 1990; pers. comm.
—	—	male	—	adult	March/April	Festa-Bianchet & Jorgenson, 1985
—	—	female	—	adult	March/April	Festa-Bianchet & Jorgensen, 1985
—	—	male	—	yearling	March/April	Festa-Bianchet & Jorgensen, 1985
—	—	female	—	yearling	March/April	Festa-Bianchet & Jorgensen, 1985
—	—	male	—	adult	May/Dec.	Festa-Bianchet & Jorgensen, 1985
—	—	female	—	adult	May/Dec.	Festa-Bianchet & Jorgensen, 1985
—	—	female	—	yearling	May/Dec.	Festa-Bianchet & Jorgensen, 1985
—	—	male	—	yearling	May/Dec.	Festa-Bianchet & Jorgensen, 1985
—	—	—	—	lamb	October	Festa-Bianchet & Jorgensen, 1985
—	—	—	—	lamb	Nov.-Jan.	Festa-Bianchet & Jorgensen, 1985
—	67-118	male	81-106	adult	autumn	Stelfox & Robertson, 1976
—	102.5	female	79.5	adult	autumn	Stelfox & Robertson, 1976
—	114.5	female	63.0	adult	spring	Stelfox & Robertson, 1976
7.8	—	—	—	adult	—	Fuller & Keith, 1981
—	—	—	—	adult	—	Haigh, 1978
	—		—	—	—	Anon. 1984
—	—	—	—	—	—	Anon. 1984
—	—	male	—	adult	winter	Morgantini, 1990; pers. comm.
25	4.7	male	—	adult	winter	Morgantini, 1990; pers. comm.
30	7	female	—	adult	winter	Morgantini, 1990; pers. comm.
37.5, 70	5	3 females & 1 male	—	adult	March	Renecker, 1991
—	15	male	—	adult	March	Renecker & Olsen, 1986a
—	12	female	—	adult	March	Renecker & Olsen, 1986a
—	8	male	—	adult	May	Renecker & Olsen, 1986b
—	19	3 females & 1 male	317-371	4.5	March	Renecker & Olsen, 1985
16	7.6	female	288	4.5	March	Renecker, 1990; pers. comm.
12	21.1	female	384	4.5	March	Renecker, 1990; pers. comm.
14	5	female	314	2.5	Nov.	Renecker, 1990; pers. comm.
16	4.0	female	325	2.5	Nov.	Renecker, 1990; pers. comm.
14	4	female	280	4.5	April	Renecker, 1990; pers. comm.
—	—	female	280	4.0	April	Renecker, 1990; pers. comm.
17.4	—	female	249	1.5	Sept.	Renecker, 1990; pers. comm.
18.2	—	female	260	1.5	Sept.	Renecker, 1990; pers. comm.
16	5.5	female	261	3.5	Dec.	Renecker, 1990; pers. comm.
20	2.6	female	376	3.5	Dec.	Renecker, 1990; pers. comm.
18	20.25	female	329	3.5	Oct.	Renecker, 1990; pers. comm.
10-14	2-12	—	—	adult	—	Lynch, 1981
—	—	—	—	adult	—	Lynch, 1978
—	—	—	—	adult	—	Lynch, 1978
—	—	—	—	adult	—	Lynch, 1978
10-14	4-25	males & females	—	adult	—	Lynch & Hanson, 1981
—	—	—	—	adult	—	Haigh et al., 1977
—	—	—	—	—	—	Haigh et al., 1977
—	3	—	68	adult	April	Renecker & Olsen, 1985
—	8	—	68	adult	April	Renecker & Olsen, 1985

TABLE A2.9

CHEMICAL AND TRADE NAMES OF IMMOBILIZING AND REVERSAL DRUGS USED FOR CHEMICAL RESTRAINT OF UNGULATES

Immobilizing Drugs		Reversal Drugs	
Drug Type/Generic Name	Trade Name	Generic Name	Trade Name
CENTRAL-ACTING DRUGS			
Narcotics			
carfentanil	Wildnil	naloxone hydrochloride	Narcan
etorphine hydrochloride	M-99	diprenorphine	M50-50
fentanyl citrate	Sublimaze, Innovar-Vet (includes droperidol), Fentanest	naloxone hydrochloride (also used as a human antagonist for etorphine)	Narcan
morphine			
Sedative analgesic			
xylazine hydrochloride	Rompun, BAY 1470	Yohimbine hydrochloride, 4-aminopyridine	Antagonil
Dissociatives			
ketamine hydrochloride	Ketaset, Vetalar, Rogarsetic, Kataject, Ketalar, Ketanest		
phenylcyclidine hydrochloride	Sernalyn, Sernyl		
PARALYZING/MUSCLE RELAXANT			
succinylcholine chloride	Anectin, Sucostrin, Quelicin, Scoline		
curare			
gallamine triethiodide	Flaxedil		
Tranquilizers			
promazine hydrochloride	Sparaine		
acetylpromazine maleate	Anatran		
benzodiazepines	Diazepam, Valium		
R51163	Wildtrans		

TABLE A2.10

SUPPLIERS OF CHEMICAL RESTRAINT EQUIPMENT, PROJECTORS, AND PROJECTILES

Company	Address
Donjoy Industries	Harare, Zimbabwe
Kay Research Products	1525 E. 53rd Street, Suite 503, Chicago, IL, 60615, USA (312) 643-9044
Kwik-way Manufacturing Co.	Sioux Falls, South Dakota, 57106, USA
Palmer Chemical Equipment	Palmer Village, P.O. Box 867, Douglasville, Georgia, 30134, USA (404) 942-4397
Paxarms Ltd.	P.O. Box 317, Timaru, New Zealand
Peter Ott	Basel, Switzerland (available in Canada from Biosonic Ltd., 5241 Calgary Trail Southbound, Edmonton, Alberta, T6H 5G8, Canada)
Pneu-Dart, Inc.	Williamsport, PA, 17701, USA, (717) 323–2710
Simmons Equipment	Zoolu Arms of Omaha, 10315 Wright St., Milwaukee, Wisconsin, 68124, USA
Telinject, L.C.	D67 Ludwigshafen, Germany
Westerguard Enterprises	Edmonton, Alberta, T5W 1N8

ACKNOWLEDGMENTS

We would like to thank all persons who provided personal data from their experiences in capture and restraint of wild ungulates in Alberta, with special thanks to Dr. Luigi Morgantini.

Indices of Body Condition and Nutritional Status

Jan Adamczewski

Information on the body condition of a hoofed mammal can reveal to a wildlife biologist much about the nutritional history of the animal. If enough animals are measured, the general health of the population, and its response to environmental quality, can be inferred. Identifying causes of body condition dynamics is not an easy task, however, as animals have endogenous (built-in) weight cycles cued by photoperiodism (daylight hours), are subjected to a seasonally variable forage supply, and allocate energy differently to bone, muscle and fat depending on the age and gender of the individual.

Some typical seasonal patterns in body condition of wild ungulates are described, and the criteria that a useful condition index must meet are presented. Indices of body condition and nutritional status are categorized into those useful for living and dead animals, and classified as to the period of time — recent, intermediate and long term — for which they assess an animal's nutritional history. The advantages and disadvantages of each measurement are listed in an extensive table. A thorough review of commonly used indices is offered and includes body mass measurements, body frame dimensions, weights of glands, organs, fat and muscle tissue and components of blood, urine and digesta. These measurements are best used broadly, together with indicators of population condition such as calf:cow ratio, recruitment rates of offspring, male:female ratio, and mortality rates of adults.

INTRODUCTION

Biologists and wildlife managers often want to know "how the animals are doing", as well as following population patterns. Severe winters in western Canada can result in widespread ungulate mortality, with dead animals typically showing depleted fat, emaciated muscles, and reduced pregnancy rates. Biologists have often used the animals directly as sensitive indicators of range condition and population quality, since animals integrate all positive and negative environmental influences: forage quality and quantity, population density, disease and various stresses. Various methods of measuring ungulate condition have been proposed, but "condition" can mean many things, and methods vary in sensitivity and ease of use. In this appendix, I would like to (1) briefly discuss seasonal changes in weight and condition of northern ungulates, (2) define the terms "body condition" and "nutritional status", (3) discuss some general sampling criteria, and (4) review methods currently used to assess body condition and nutritional status in ungulates.

Seasonal changes in weight and physiology of ungulates are complex and reflect both the environment and an endogenous (built-in) cycle guided by photoperiod (daylength). It was once thought that weight changes in ungulates simply reflected prevailing conditions: deer grew and fattened in summer and fall due to abundant good food, and they lost weight over winter due to severe weather and reduced access to forage. It was also thought that fat gained in summer allowed deer to "coast" through to spring. However, captive deer with free access to good food typically also eat less

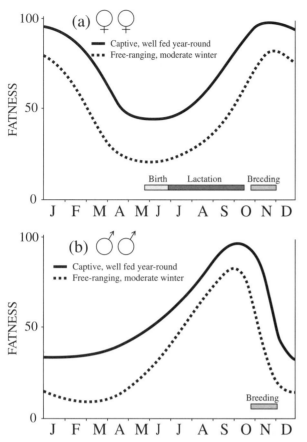

and lose weight and fat during winter; the seasonal cycle is similar to that in the wild, but less extreme. In free-ranging ungulates, environmental limits are superimposed on the underlying cycle (Figure A3.1). Seasonal weight changes are not limited to fat, as substantial changes in body protein, primarily in skeletal muscle, normally accompany changes in ungulate fat reserves. Photoperiod is likely the primary cue for seasonal changes in weight and metabolism, as it is for seasonal breeding and other physiological changes. Calculations of energy balance have shown that body reserves generally provide only a small supplement to food in winter, and are no guarantee of survival. Energy reserves may sometimes provide a crucial supplement to food, particularly with respect to reproductive costs, and they provide a sensitive index of past nutrition.

Seasonal cycles in ungulate weight and physiology can vary widely among sex and age classes, populations and years. Mature males typically reach peak fatness just before the rut and lose this reserve rapidly over a short period; they may be lean throughout winter (Figure A3.1). Breeding females tend to peak in condition later, and their most rapid fat loss is often at the end of winter. Weight loss and reduced food intake in winter are the norm in wild deer of various age classes, as is slowed growth of young animals. It is also typical of young deer, especially young of the year, to be leaner than adults; in early growth, lean tissue has priority over fat. Biologists must therefore measure "condition" of an animal in *relative* terms — relative to season, relative to the sex, age and reproductive status of the animal, and relative to previous values from that population or others.

Figure A3.1

Seasonal changes in fatness (arbitrary scale) of mature breeding does (upper) and mature bucks (lower); all animals on natural photoperiod and temperatures.
Based loosely on Riney (1955), Flook (1970), Larsen et al. (1985), and Suttie et al. (1992).

Condition measurements used to date can broadly be classified on three time scales:

1. Those measuring **recent** nutrition and health (days to weeks) — including measurements from blood, urine, feces and gut contents.

2. Those measuring the animal's body reserves, an **intermediate**, cumulative measure of nutrition (recent months and seasons), — including body weight and measures of fat and protein reserves.

3. Those measuring **long-term** population quality relative to habitat and other populations (years) — including linear body measurements and bone lengths.

All these measures and indices provide useful information, but none provides an adequate assessment on all three time scales. Bone lengths, for example, can be used to compare size and overall nutrition in different populations of deer, but they provide no information on recent winter conditions. Blood and urinary parameters can be used to make an assessment of health and recent nutrition, but typically respond within hours or days to altered nutrition, and generally provide little insight into fatness or body size achieved. In this review, measures of *body condition* are those which measure the state of the animal's body reserves of fat or protein, and measures of *nutritional status* are those which assess the animal's recent plane of nutrition.

An animal's health, nutritional status and body condition are related; many blood parameters are intimately affected by health as well as nutrition, and poor health or poor nutritional status will eventually reduce body reserves. However, an animal can be in poor condition and well fed at the beginning of spring; conversely, a deer may be in excellent condition but poorly fed after an early winter storm. The distinction is important, because condition and recent nutrition may separately affect productivity. For example, conception rates in fat sheep are relatively insensitive to recent diet quality but can be improved in lean sheep with a burst of good nutrition prior to breeding. Similarly, poor condition can impair early lactation, but this can be minimized with excellent nutrition.

Measures of nutritional status and body condition are most useful when used broadly, together with information on population characteristics, disease, and range quality. The choice of methods described here will depend on specific needs of the biologist or manager.

Timing of data collection is important in studies of condition and nutritional status. The onset and end of winter are key periods: measuring condition during early winter gives a cumulative measure of summer/fall nutrition, and nutritional stress is often most severe in late winter.

Wildlife managers generally are interested in *population* condition, but measurements are usually made on *individuals*, which are assumed to be representative of the population. Small sample numbers may be deceptive because condition can vary widely among individuals. Ten to 20 individuals of a particular age and sex class are generally minimal, although sample size will depend on the size of the population. Mature females, as the primary bearers of young, and calves, as the population recruits, are crucial to population productivity, and these are often the age/sex classes sampled.

Biologists commonly have access to ungulates in two ways: they can study live animals (free-ranging or immobilized) or dead animals. The following two sections briefly outline methods that have been used in dead and live ungulates. In each section some key methods are discussed; a more comprehensive listing is in Table A3.1.

METHODS FOR DEAD ANIMALS

Body condition

Body condition can be assessed readily in dead ungulates, particularly if the animals have just died (e.g., hunter kills). Measurement of total fat and protein requires that the animal be either dissected or ground and chemically analysed. Field conditions rarely permit such expensive, time-consuming procedures; in most studies the relative condition of animals is more important than their exact body composition. Simple indices of body fat and protein have been widely used, as have measures of body weight.

Fatness can be measured using indices such as depth of back fat, weight of fat around the kidneys, and fat content of the marrow in limb bones. Depth of fat over the longissimus dorsi muscle, between the 12th and 13th ribs, has been used for many years in grading beef carcasses, while wildlife biologists usually measure fat thickness as the maximum depth near the base of the tail. This measurement is of little value in very lean animals, but correlates well with total fat over a wide range in fatter animals. Weight of fat surrounding both kidneys, trimmed using Riney's (1955) technique (Figure A3.2), correlates reasonably well with total fat over a wide range although the separation of kidney fat from surrounding fat can be somewhat subjective in very fat animals. The use of the kidney fat index (dividing kidney fat weight by weight of the kidneys to account for animal size) is not recommended because kidney weight can vary widely with season and is not a good correlate of body size or weight. Fat content of the marrow of long bones provides a sensitive measure of fat depletion in its final stages but otherwise changes little. Although indices of fatness often correlate strongly with total fat, the relationships typically have considerable "scatter" due to individual variability. Comparisons are best made between groups of individuals, using a combination of indices.

Weights of individual muscles such as the gastrocnemius provide a simple, reliable index of skeletal muscle weight and body protein. This technique is less prone to subjectiveness than fat estimation, and the scatter of the relationships between individual muscle weight and total muscle/protein tends to be less than for fat indices.

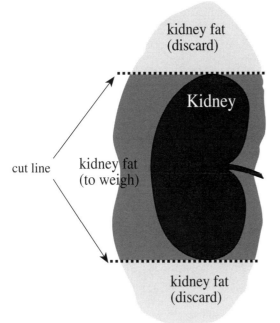

kidney fat
(discard)

Kidney

cut line   kidney fat
(to weigh)

kidney fat
(discard)

Figure A3.2
*Suggested method of
weighing kidney fat, based
on Riney (1955). Fat
within dotted lines is
stripped from both kidneys
and weighed. Best results
are obtained if kidneys are
allowed to cool in the
body cavity and gently
pulled and cut from
surrounding tissue.*

A method of scoring condition based on appearance of fat on the heart, omentum, kidneys, brisket and tailbase, and on fullness of musculature, was published by Kistner *et al.* (1980). This method permits a rapid, simple classification of condition in deer; its chief weakness, as with other condition scores, is the potential for variability among users.

Body weight has long been a key measure of growth and condition in animals. Its value is somewhat diminished in ruminants because gut contents, particularly in the rumen, can vary unpredictably and substantially. Many ruminants will attempt to compensate for low-quality forage by packing more of it into their rumens; their body weight may then be deceptively high. Ingesta-free body weight (IFBW) is the preferred measure of weight in ruminants but this requires tedious emptying of all gut chambers. Weight of the dressed carcass is more easily obtained and is strongly correlated with IFBW and body condition.

Nutritional status

A dead ungulate's nutritional status can be assessed from samples of ingesta (rumen contents, feces, etc.) and organ weights. If the animal has just died, then blood (serum) or urine can be collected and analysed for urea, creatinine and other parameters. Measurements from blood or urine are discussed later, with nutritional status in live ungulates.

Samples of rumen contents and feces have long been used to estimate diet composition and quality in ungulates. Composition of rumen contents and feces provides only a broad indication of diets, because some plants and plant parts (e.g., mushrooms) disappear rapidly and almost completely from the rumen while others (e.g., coarse grasses) remain for extended periods. Chemical analysis of dried rumen contents or feces for fiber and nitrogen can provide a good index of recent diet quality. Some caution is advised with the use of fecal or ruminal nitrogen because in some plants, a large proportion of nitrogen may be bound to phenolic compounds; in these cases the available nitrogen may be substantially less than the chemically analysed total. The analysis of fecal diaminopimelic acid (DAPA), produced only by bacteria, has been used as a measure of rumen microbial activity. Unlike many parameters measured in blood and urine, measurements from ingesta are more directly reflective of diets and less affected by complex physiological control.

Several organs and glands reflect altered nutrition by changes in weight and morphology; biologists have used some of these changes as indices of nutritional status. Liver and kidney weight may more than double from winter to summer; these weights provide a simple index of recent nutrition. The papillae (small finger-like projections) lining the rumen wall enlarge and increase their surface area rapidly in response to greater fermentation in the rumen. This surface enlargement can be measured using a technique of Hofmann (1982), and it is correlated with rate of nutrient absorption in the rumen. In deer, the thyroid gland shows a pronounced seasonal weight cycle, which is related to seasonal secretion of thyroid hormones (lowest in mid-winter, highest in mid-summer) and may provide an index of recent nutritional plane. The thymus gland also shows a seasonal weight cycle in deer but is not easily dissected for weighing.

Other data: linear measurements, population data and disease

Bone lengths and ratios are useful in comparing populations and in comparing year-to-year variation within a population. External linear measurements provide a useful size estimate but are often poorly repeatable and variable among observers. Estimation of body condition or weight from linear measures (e.g., girth-to-length) has not been very successful. Linear measurements provide little insight into body condition or nutritional status: a small deer can be quite fat and a large one can be emaciated.

Population characteristics can themselves be clear indirect measures of animal condition. High calf:cow ratios, a substantial proportion of young animals (particularly yearlings), high pregnancy rates in juvenile females, and a relatively balanced sex ratio are all characteristic of a healthy population in which individuals are well-fed and in good condition.

Diseases can have profound effects on ungulate populations. The significance of direct mortality has long been known but the importance of more subtle effects—reduced fertility, altered behaviour, increased vulnerability to predators—have only recently been widely recognized. Indications of disease are always worth noting, although they are not always related to condition. Many parasitic diseases (e.g., lungworms, abomasal nematodes) are most damaging at high ungulate densities. Some diseases strike despite good condition; others gradually weaken animals. To help in assessing a possible disease problem, the following information can be collected from dead animals: tissue abnormalities in colour, texture or size; feces to analyse for parasite eggs or larvae; numbers of animals affected; and geographical location.

METHODS FOR LIVE ANIMALS

Body condition

Measuring body condition in live ungulates has consistently proved difficult. There has been better success in measuring nutritional status of free-ranging ungulates, using blood, urine and feces (see following section). At present, condition of live ungulates can best be estimated from body weight, a measurement of subcutaneous fat or condition scoring.

Ungulates can be weighed in the field, although this is difficult for the larger species unless a helicopter or tripod is available. Body weight can be a deceptive measure of condition, as noted earlier.

Ultrasonography has been used extensively to measure subcutaneous fat thickness, and in some cases muscle area, in cattle, sheep and pigs. More recent ultrasound machines are portable and battery-powered, and fat depth can be measured accurately to within 1 mm. This technology has so far been little used in wild species. It is also possible to estimate fat thickness through a small incision in the skin. There are currently no methods for measuring other fat deposits in live ungulates.

In many mammals, the proportion of body fat can be estimated reliably by measuring total body water (inversely related to total fat for a given weight of animal). This method requires that an animal be restrained for at least half an hour. Total body conductivity can also be used to estimate body fat: lean tissues have a high water content and conduct current well, while fat has little water and conducts current poorly. A fatter animal of a given weight will have a lower conductivity. Unfortunately both techniques have limited value in ruminants because of variable and sometimes large proportions of gut contents and associated water, which must be assumed constant and known, in either approach to fat estimation. Body water markers have been used successfully in studies with captive deer fed a constant, known diet.

Condition scoring (a numerical score based on feeling the amount of subcutaneous fat on an animal) is a sensitive method of measuring fatness in the hands of a practised individual, but can be quite variable among observers. This method is widely used in domestic sheep, for example, and could be of value in wild ungulates if a single reproducible method of scoring was widely accepted.

Nutritional status

Nutritional status can be assessed in live ungulates using blood, urine and feces. Because urine and feces can be collected without capturing animals and can also be used to assess reproductive status, methods based on these have become increasingly attractive.

Although many blood parameters have been tested as indicators of condition or nutritional status, few have proved useful, either because they change rapidly in response to stress, or because they remain relatively constant despite large changes in diet or condition. Physiological regulation of nutrient supply in mammals is complex and its measurement does not yield readily to simple methods. Among the more useful measurements in blood are the hormones insulin-like growth factor 1 (IGF-1) and triiodothyronine (T3), and serum urea in relation to creatinine (U/C ratio). Baseline values from captive ungulates kept under known dietary conditions are essential background for this type of study.

IGF-1 is a growth factor produced primarily in the liver, and blood levels are strongly correlated with rate of lean body growth. IGF-1 levels are relatively stable in the blood and are highly sensitive to nutritional disturbance. This hormone has been little studied in wild ungulates but extensively in domestic ruminants, and is used as a sensitive measure of nutritional status in hospital patients. As with many hormones, its physiology is complex: IGF-1 levels are affected by lactation, disease, and apparently by season, independent of diet. With further study, IGF-1 may prove to be a sensitive measure of nutritional status in wild ungulates.

Triiodothyronine (T3) is a hormone produced by the thyroid gland, and its levels have been correlated with metabolic rate in many species. T3 levels are relatively stable in the blood and are reduced following poor nutrition. The physiology of T3 is complex and as with IGF-1, T3 levels may be sensitive to reproductive status and to seasonal effects, independent of diet.

Serum urea concentrations have been measured in relation to creatinine (a product of muscle breakdown) and this ratio has consistently shown a strong correlation with level of protein intake. Deer often show falling levels of this ratio through winter, as diet quality declines. Serum urea is also sharply elevated when animals have no fat remaining and are depleting body protein rapidly. However, nitrogen metabolism in ruminants is complex: season, independent of diet, may affect blood levels of nitrogenous compounds, creatinine output is not always constant, and both urea and creatinine may be elevated due to non-nutritional stress.

Measurement of urinary urea and creatinine (often from snow) provides data similar to those from serum, and does not require animal handling. Over winter, deer typically show declining urinary U/C ratios as diet quality declines, but a dramatic rise in this ratio indicates animals that have depleted their fat and are catabolizing body protein rapidly. This elevated urea can be distinguished from high serum urea associated with good food by the elevated urinary potassium which accompanies severe emaciation.

Feces can be collected either from immobilized animals or from the ground; fecal samples can be used as an index of diet quality, as noted earlier.

Other measures: assessment of reproductive status and stress levels

The reproductive status (e.g., pregnancy rates) of free-ranging ungulates is often of interest to biologists; in many species it is possible to determine pregnancy from feces and urine. These methods are based on the fact that metabolites of steroid hormones such as progesterone and estrogen are excreted both in the feces and in the urine. These metabolites are very stable and can be measured long after excretion. Pregnant caribou, like most mammals, have much higher serum levels of progesterone than non-pregnant caribou, and this elevated level is evident both in feces and in urine. A hormone found only in serum of pregnant females, pregnancy-specific protein B (PSPB) can also now be measured in urine. Reproductive status of males can be assessed by measuring testosterone metabolites in feces. Using these techniques, biologists can monitor both nutritional and reproductive status of ungulates without directly contacting the animals.

Although nutritional stress in winter can have major impacts on ungulate populations, stress can also result from crowding or disturbance by human factors. Such stress can be estimated physiologically, most commonly by measuring levels of cortisol in the blood. Cortisol is a hormone secreted by the adrenal glands and is elevated rapidly by stress. Metabolites of cortisol can also be found in urine and feces, providing a method for monitoring stress in free-ranging animals.

ACKNOWLEDGMENTS

My thanks to Brad Stelfox for his editorial help and to P.F. Flood and S. Tedesco for their thoughtful suggestions.

TABLE A3.1

A SUMMARY OF COMMON INDICES AND MEASURES OF CONDITION AND NUTRITIONAL STATUS

Index/Measurement	Definition	Advantages	Disadvantages	Suitable for: Dead	Live
Body Weights and Linear Measurements					
Total body weight	• weight of entire body (often excludes blood)	• usually correlated with condition, within a sex/age class	• gut contents often an unknown variable • hard to measure in field in large animals	✓	✓
Carcass weight	• weight of body minus head, hide, lower limbs, and internal organs	• well correlated with condition, within a sex/age class	• animals must be skinned and gutted • may be hard to measure in large animals	✓	—
Ingesta-free body weight	• weight of entire animal except for gut contents	• well correlated with condition • good measure of animal size	• requires entire gut to be emptied • may be hard to measure in large animals	✓	—
Body length	• animal length, from tip of nose to tip or base of tail	• easily measured • good measure of size	• little relation to condition or nutritional status • variably reproducible	✓	✓
Lengths of long bones—femur, mandible, metatarsus, metacarpus	• maximal length of bones	• easily measured • good reproducibility • useful in comparing populations or cohorts • preferred measures of animal size	• little relation to condition or nutritional status	✓	—
Shoulder height	• straight distance from tip of shoulder to hoof-tip or base of dew claw	• easily measured • measures animal size	• little relation to condition or nutritional status • variably reproducible	✓	✓
Chest girth	• circumference of animal, perpendicular to its long axis, taken just behind shoulder	• easily measured • sometimes a good correlate of body weight	• somewhat related to condition • variably reproducible	✓	✓
Hind foot length	• straight length of lower hind limb, from hoof tip to tip of tuber calcanei	• easily measured • good measure of animal size	• little relation to condition or nutritional status	✓	✓

A SUMMARY OF COMMON INDICES AND MEASURES
OF CONDITION AND NUTRITIONAL STATUS (continued)

Index/Measurement	Definition	Advantages	Disadvantages	Suitable for: Dead	Live
Measures of Body Fat and Protein					
Total body fat and protein	• all fat in ingesta-free body, extracted by suitable solvents, most commonly petroleum ether, and total protein measured by Kjeldahl method	• complete measure of fat and protein in body • standard for calibration of indices	• expensive • requires whole body to be ground and chemically analysed • time-consuming	✓	—
Anatomically dissected fat and muscle	• all tissue fat from carcass and viscera, and all muscle tissue	• includes most fat, especially in fat animals • muscle is major store of body protein	• expensive • requires whole body to be dissected • misses some fat, especially in lean animals, and protein in non-muscle tissues	✓	—
Depth of back fat	• maximum depth of subcutaneous fat, measured near base of tail	• easily measured • is quantitatively related to total fat in many species	• of little value in very lean animals • resolution not adequate to compare individuals similar in fatness	✓	✓
Ultrasound measurement of fat thickness	• ultrasound used to distinguish tissue layers; can be used to measure fat thickness	• allows repeated, non-invasive monitoring of fatness	• equipment expensive • can only measure subcutaneous fat, thus of limited use in lean animals • has been little tested in wild species	—	✓
Kidney fat weight (total or modified by Riney's (1955) technique)	• total weight of fat on both kidneys, often standardized by including only fat not extending beyond the long axes of the kidneys (see Fig. A3.2)	• easily measured • related quantitatively to total fat in many species, over a wide range in fatness	• kidney fat difficult to identify in some fat animals • resolution not adequate to compare individuals close in fatness	✓	—
Kidney fat index (not recommended)	• weight of fat on both kidneys X 100, divided by weight of both kidneys to account for body size	• easily measured	• kidney weight can vary widely with season and nutrition, thus weakly related to organism body size or weight	✓	—
Femur marrow fat (marrow from other long bones and from mandible has also been used)	• proportion of fat in marrow of central part of femur, extracted with solvents or approximated by assuming dried marrow is basically fat	• sensitive measure of fatness in lean and starving animals	• only useful in lean animals; stays at near-maximum over rest of range in fatness	✓	—
Fat content of individual muscles from carcass	• proportion of fat in dried muscle, extracted with suitable solvents	• has been suggested as proportional to total body fat	• reliability of technique has been questioned by other studies; apparently valid only in lean animals	✓	—
Fat and protein content of sawdust	• chemical composition of sawdust from serial sawing of carcass	• highly correlated with total fat and protein	• carcass destroyed • calibrated only in caribou	✓	—
Indicator muscles (such as the gastrocnemius)	• one or more muscles weighed as indices of total muscle weight and body protein	• highly correlated with total carcass muscle wt. and body protein • easily measured	• requires some dissection of carcass	✓	—
Fat content based on water estimation	• proportion of water in body can be measured with an injected marker and is inversely related to fatness	• potentially a valid method of estimating fatness in live animals	• requires animal to be tranquilized or quiet for at least half an hour • gut contents an unknown variable	—	✓

A SUMMARY OF COMMON INDICES AND MEASURES
OF CONDITION AND NUTRITIONAL STATUS *(continued)*

Index/Measurement	Definition	Advantages	Disadvantages	Suitable for: Dead	Live
Total body electrical conductivity	• electrical conductivity measured on a restrained animal; for a given weight a fatter animal will have lower conductivity	• rapid, simple method • non-invasive; works well in non-ruminants	• gut contents an unknown variable • animal must be weighed	—	✓
Fat cell volume or diameter	• diameter or volume of adipocytes from subcutaneous fat is in proportion to total fat	• potentially useful in live and dead animals • should be valid over a wide range of conditions	• untested in wild ruminants except caribou • requires histological equipment and samples must be from same site	✓	✓
Condition scoring	• method of rating condition by feel of subcutaneous fat deposits	• relatively easy to use • can be a sensitive measure when applied by an expert	• sometimes high variability among users	✓	✓
Kistner score	• condition score based on appearance of internal and subcutaneous fat and musculature	• rapid, simple method • distinguishes well among classes of body condition	• potential for variability among users	✓	—

Glands and Organs

Index/Measurement	Definition	Advantages	Disadvantages	Suitable for: Dead	Live
Liver weight	• weight of the liver depends strongly on the animal's recent nutrition; higher in well-fed animals	• easily measured • relatively responsive to recent nutrition	• could be affected by disease	✓	—
Kidney weight	• weight of the kidneys reflects level of recent nutrition	• easily measured • relatively responsive to recent nutrition	• could be affected by disease	✓	—
Index of rumen surface area	• measurement of surface enlargement of rumen papillae; enlarged surface indicates greater absorption of nutrients	• sensitive measure of recent diet quality	• requires specialized lab techniques	✓	—
Thyroid weight	• weight of the thyroid gland	• correlates with metabolic rate; thyroid secretion decreases after malnutrition	• few data available on weight change other than strong seasonal cycle	✓	—
Thymus weight	• weight of the thymus gland	• shows a strong seasonal cycle in deer • decreased by poor nutrition	• few data on factors affecting weight change • diffuse organ, hard to dissect	✓	—

Blood Constituents

Index/Measurement	Definition	Advantages	Disadvantages	Suitable for: Dead	Live
Urea/Creatinine ratio	• concentration of urea in blood, in relation to creatinine	• relatively sensitive to recent protein intake, so correlates with diet quality • stable blood levels	• levels may be affected by season and by non-nutritional stress • high levels may reflect good food or protein catabolism	✓	✓
Triiodothyronine (T3)	• level of triiodothyronine in serum	• correlated with metabolic rate and reduced following malnutrition • stable blood levels	• requires specialized lab assays • may be affected by season and reproductive status	✓	✓
Insulin-like growth factor I (IGF-1)	• serum levels of IGF-1	• highly correlated with rate of lean body growth • very sensitive to nutritional changes • stable blood levels	• requires specialized lab assays • affected by season, reprotive status, and disease	✓	✓
Other blood parameters	• readers are referred to reviews listed in references (e.g., Franzmann, 1985)	• may indicate disease • may show specific deficiencies	• rarely related to condition or nutritional status • results often rapidly altered by stress	✓	✓

Table A3.1

A SUMMARY OF COMMON INDICES AND MEASURES OF CONDITION AND NUTRITIONAL STATUS *(continued)*

Index/Measurement	Definition	Advantages	Disadvantages	Suitable for: Dead	Live
Ingesta, Feces, and Urine					
Diet composition assessed from rumen contents	• recent diet composition assumed in proportion to composition of rumen contents	• generally indicative of major food items eaten recently	• only a broad index of diet • expensive; specialized equipment required	✓	—
Diet composition assessed from feces	• recent diet composition assumed in proportion to fecal composition	• generally indicative of most major food items eaten recently	• only a very broad index of diet • expensive; specialized equipment required	✓	✓
Diet quality assessed from rumen contents and feces	• diet quality (fiber, lignin, nitrogen) in digesta assumed in proportion to same properties in diet	• results generally proportional to actual dietary values; a good index of diet quality	• few calibration studies • nitrogen levels may be deceptive due to unavailable or recycled nitrogen	✓	✓
Diaminopimelic acid (DAPA)	• product of microbial fermentation in rumen; produced only by bacteria	• correlated with level of microbial fermentation, thus a measure of recent diet quality	• requires specialized lab assays • few calibration studies	✓	✓
Fecal and urinary sex steroids	• sex steroids (progesterone, estrogen, testosterone) in feces and urine proportional to serum levels; can assess reproductive status	• non-invasive • can be used to assess pregnancy rates in free-ranging ungulates	• few calibration studies • specialized lab assays required	✓	✓
Fecal and urinary cortisol	• cortisol in feces or urine proportional to serum levels; cortisol elevated by stress	• non-invasive • may be used to monitor stress in free-ranging ungulates	• few calibration studies • requires specialized lab assays	✓	✓
Urinary urea/ creatine ratio	• ratio of urea to creatine in urine (may be collected from snow)	• noninvasive • sensitive to recent protein nutrition • can be used to identify severe malnutrition	• specialized lab assays required • may be affected by season and non-nutritional stress	✓	✓
Population Parameters and Disease					
Calf:cow ratio	• number of calves per 100 cows	• high ratio suggests good population condition	• can be affected by predation and other mortality	—	✓
Recruitment	• number of previous year's young as a percent of population	• high recruitment suggests a mild winter	• can be affected by predation and other mortality	—	✓
Male:female ratio	• ratio of males to females among adults in a population	• a highly unbalanced ratio (often few males) may suggest nutritional stress	• can be affected by hunting or other mortality	—	✓
Pregnancy rate	• number of breeding-age females pregnant in a population sample	• high rate generally indicates good population condition (esp. if high in juveniles)	• high pregnancy rate may persist despite wide variation in condition	✓	✓
Adult mortality	• mortality rates among adult sex and age classes	• high mortality of particular sex and age classes may suggest nutritional stress	• can be affected by hunting or other mortality	✓	✓
Evidence of viral, bacterial, or parasitic infections	• any indication of high incidence or prevalence of a disease (from dead or live animals)	• may indicate a pathogenic or stressful condition • may warn of future problems	• not necessarily related to condition or nutrition • some parasites are widespread but normal; some diseases kill despite good condition	✓	✓

Age Determination Techniques

J. Brad Stelfox

Accurate age information of ungulate populations is valuable to wildlife managers, as it tells biologists much about the numerical status of the population (stable, increasing, decreasing) and the environmental factors affecting it (predation, hunting, disease, forage quality). Using an assortment of tables and illustrations, this chapter reviews the most commonly used techniques including body and horn size, annuli (annual growth rings) of horns and teeth, tooth eruption sequence and tooth wear.

INTRODUCTION

Age determination techniques are useful both to the professional and the lay person. In addition to enabling curious recreationalists to estimate the age of "picked up" skulls found while hiking, and hunters of their bagged quarry, accurately-aged ungulates provide an invaluable tool to the wildlife manager. The primary management value of known-age individuals is the determination of the population's age-class composition. Monitoring of age-class composition over several years can reveal much about the dynamic structure of populations, such as mortality, maximum lifespan, whether the population is stable, expanding, or declining, and the susceptibility of specific age classes to hunting pressure and predation. Since an important goal of the wildlife manager is to maintain a "desirable" number of ungulates, as determined by biological, social and political forces, he can turn to age-class structure to gain insight into how the population is responding to such variables as predation, hunting, disease and forage. Different population age-class structures are depicted in Figure A4.1 to illustrate the impacts of hunting and environmental quality.

Numerous aging techniques have been used over the last several decades and the reader is directed to an excellent overview by Larson and Taber (1980). The purpose of this appendix is to present information, condensed into tables and figures, from which animals can be aged using dentition, horns, and antlers.

HORN DEVELOPMENT

When evaluating the usefulness of aging techniques, one must consider whether the measured attribute accurately reflects time (age), or if it is affected by such factors as nutritional status or physiological events. Such seasonal events as rutting, pregnancy, and forage quality can greatly affect body weight and composition (see Chapter 12 and Appendix 3), and therefore restrict the value of body conformation measurements for aging purposes. Unlike soft tissues, which often exhibit seasonal changes in weight, parameters such as frame size and bone length are less mercurial and therefore better indicators of age. The relationships between age, body height, and horn development for bighorn sheep (Geist, 1971) are illustrated in Figure A4.2. The figure also indicates the similar appearance of adult ewes and yearling rams. Shape and size of bison horns for different ages and gender are presented in Figure A4.3.

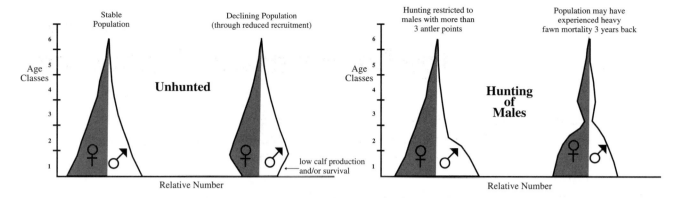

TOOTH ERUPTION SEQUENCE

During the early stages of life, the best indication of age is the sequence of tooth eruption. Since there is minimal geographic variation in the timing of eruption of particular teeth (as determined from known-aged individuals), examination of incisors, canines, premolars, and molars offers an accurate technique for young individuals (maximum age varying from 18 months in white-tailed deer to 3–4 years in bison). The position of each tooth is shown in Figure A4.4. The first premolar posterior to the canines or the diastema is technically referred to as premolar #2 (P2). This designation reflects the loss of premolar #1 (P1) during the evolutionary development of more advanced ruminants. The time at which each mandibular tooth erupts is detailed for each species in Table A4.1. Once the full complement of teeth have erupted and are in wear, other techniques are required to determine age.

CEMENTUM ANNULI

Since the 1960s, wildlife biologists have championed the merits of cementum annuli as an indicator of yearly intervals in the life of adult hoofed mammals. The alternating light and dark bands (annuli), which reflect the effects of seasonal environmental quality on body condition, can be counted on stained histological sections of incisor teeth. A common procedure for the counting of cementum annuli is the paraffin method, whereby the first incisor is removed, decalcified and cleared, then embedded in a paraffin matrix. A microtome is then used to remove a thin section (approx. 10 micron), which is stained, mounted, and examined under a microscope. Unfortunately, the cementum annuli for some species are more difficult to read than for others. Drawing on a wealth of experience in aging ungulate teeth, Matson (1981) has categorized ungulate species according to the degree of difficulty in interpreting cementum annuli. The least difficult are mule deer and mountain goat; white-tailed deer, wapiti and pronghorn are moderately difficult, and moose, bighorn sheep and caribou are most difficult. The general structure of the incisor root, and the location of annuli, are shown in Figure A4.4.

OTHER TECHNIQUES

Selected aging techniques of long standing are presented in Table A4.2. Most rely on the changing dimensions and shape of molariform teeth of adult ungulates. Although tooth-wear measurements have been shown to indicate the general age-class structure of a population, wear rate can be affected by such variables as the amount of soil on vegetation and abrasive minerals (e.g., silica) in forage.

Figure A4.5 illustrates the annulations found on the horns of mountain goat and bighorn sheep. When determining age with horns, particularly those of bighorn sheep, one must adjust estimates if the horn is broomed. Horn brooming occurs when males clash their horns together during the fall rut.

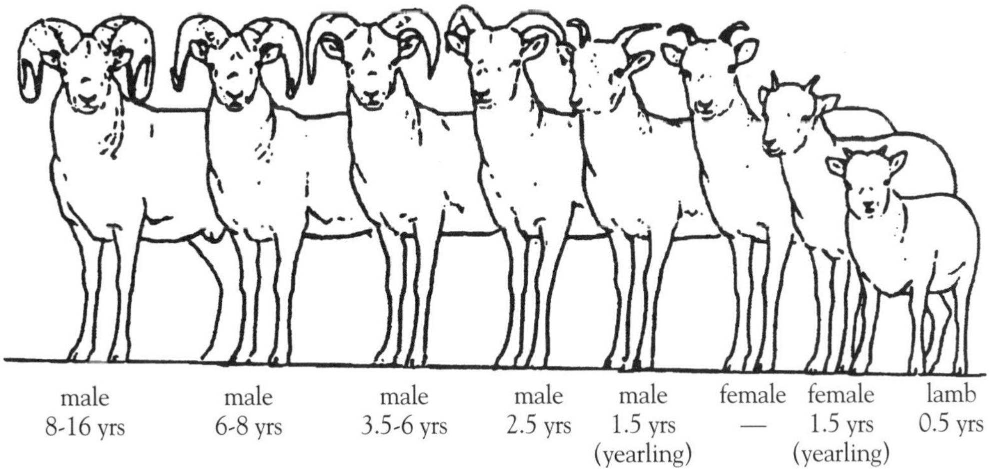

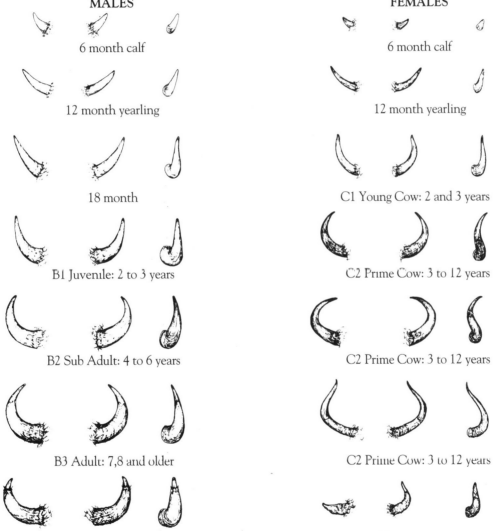

Figure A4.2
Body and horn size differences of bighorn sheep (Geist, 1971). Note similarities between adult females and yearling males. Illustration by Valerius Geist.

| male 8-16 yrs | male 6-8 yrs | male 3.5-6 yrs | male 2.5 yrs | male 1.5 yrs (yearling) | female — | female 1.5 yrs (yearling) | lamb 0.5 yrs |

MALES

6 month calf

12 month yearling

18 month

B1 Juvenile: 2 to 3 years

B2 Sub Adult: 4 to 6 years

B3 Adult: 7,8 and older

B4 Prime: older than B3

B5 Old: older than B4

FEMALES

6 month calf

12 month yearling

C1 Young Cow: 2 and 3 years

C2 Prime Cow: 3 to 12 years

C2 Prime Cow: 3 to 12 years

C2 Prime Cow: 3 to 12 years

C3 Old Cow: 12 to 20 years

C3 Old Cow: 15 to 25 years

Figure A4.3
Horn size and shape differences of bison (Anonymous, 1992). Illustration by Wes Olson.

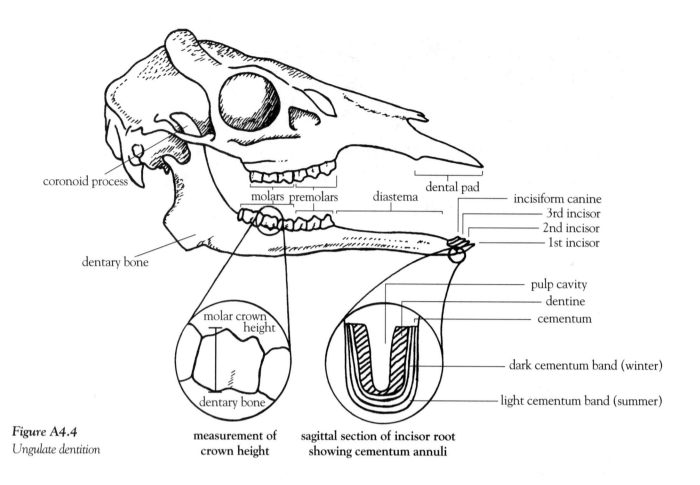

Figure A4.4
Ungulate dentition

measurement of
crown height

sagittal section of incisor root
showing cementum annuli

TABLE A4.1

TIMING OF MANDIBULAR TOOTH ERUPTION*

	White-tailed Deer	Mule Deer	Caribou	Wapiti (Elk)	Moose	Prong-horn	Mountain Goat	Bighorn Sheep	Bison (Buffalo)
Deciduous Teeth (in weeks)									
Incisor 1	Birth	< 2	Birth	Birth	Birth	1	1	Birth	Birth
Incisor 2	Birth	< 2	Birth	Birth	Birth	1	1	Birth	Birth
Incisor 3	Birth	< 2	Birth	Birth	Birth	1	1	Birth	Birth
Canine 1	Birth	< 2	Birth	Birth	Birth	1–5	1–4	Birth	Birth
Premolar 2†	1–3	10–12	Birth	< 4	1–2	1	1	Birth	Birth
Premolar 3	1–3	10–12	Birth	< 4	1–2	1	1	Birth	Birth
Premolar 4	10	10–12	Birth	< 4	1–2	1	1	Birth	Birth
Permanent Teeth (in months)									
Incisor 1	5–6	6–12	10–12	15	14–17	15–17	15–16	13–16	24–36
Incisor 2	6–12	12	10–12	18	14–17	26–29	26–29	24–36	24–36
Incisor 3	6–12	15	12–13	25	14–17	38–40	38–40	42–48	36–48
Canine 1	6–12	18–24	12–13	24	17	39–60	45–48	45–48	36–48
Premolar 2†	12–18	24	22–24	27	17	26–29	23–29	30–36	24
Premolar 3	18	24	22–24	27	17	26–29	23–29	30–36	36
Premolar 4	18	24	24–25	27	17	26–29	23–29	36–42	36
Molar 1	6–7	2–6	3–5	4	3–4	6–10	6–10	6	3–12
Molar 2	12–13	6–12	10–13	12	6–8	10–16	16–17	8–13	12–24
Molar 3	16–18	18–24	17–25	29	13–16	15–17	16–19	30–36	24–36

Important References

White-tailed Deer
Severinghaus, 1949

Mule Deer
Robinette et al., 1957;
Rees et al., 1966

Caribou
Miller, 1974

Wapiti (Elk)
Quimby and Gaab, 1957

Moose
Peterson, 1955

Pronghorn
Dow and Wright, 1962

Mountain Goat
Brandborg, 1955

Bighorn Sheep
Deming, 1952;
Hemming, 1969;
Stelfox and Poll, 1978

Bison (Buffalo)
Fuller, 1959

* *time of eruption refers to when the tooth is visible above the gum on the lower jaw.*

† *the first lower premolar has been lost during evolutionary development and is absent in North American ruminants.*

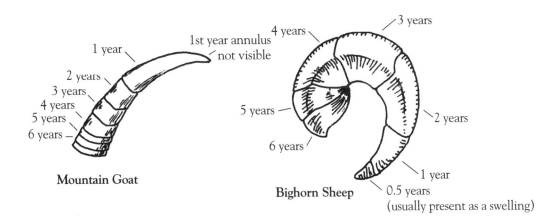

TABLE A4.2

COMMON AGING TECHNIQUES USING TEETH AND HORNS

(see explanations below)

Age	White-tailed[*] Deer	Mule[*] Deer	Caribou[*]	Moose[*]	Pronghorn[*]	Mountain Goat	Bighorn Sheep
	molar height	molar height/ width ratio	dentine/ enamel ratio	width/height molar age	# of infundibula	# horn annuli	#horn annuli
1.5 yrs							1
2.5 yrs	−1	0.33	1.0	32.1		2	2
3.5 yrs	−2	0.40	1.5	40.0		3	3
4.5 yrs	−3	0.45	2.5	49.5	18–20	4	4
5.5 yrs	−4	0.50	3.0	60.1	13–16	5	5
6.5 yrs	−5	0.54	4.0	60.1	10	6	6
7.5 yrs	−6	0.58	5.0	71.5		7	7
8.5 yrs	−7	0.62		71.5		8	8
9.5 yrs	−8	0.67		85.3		9	9
10.5 yrs	−9	0.73		85.3			
11.5 yrs		0.80		121.0			
12.5 yrs		0.88		121.0			
13.5 yrs		0.97		121.0			

[*] These indices of age must be used cautiously, as they are affected by the abrasiveness of forage. Populations inhabiting areas dissimilar in forage and soil characteristics would be expected to exhibit dissimilar tooth wear rates. Although tooth wear indices have largely been replaced by counts of cementum annuli, they still offer the biologist a "quick and dirty" field technique for estimating age.

White-tailed Deer Loss of molar crown height, in mm, from abrasive wear on forage. Values refer to accumulated loss of crown height from time when tooth is first in wear (Sauer, 1973). This technique requires knowledge of maximum unworn crown height in the studied population.

Mule Deer Molar tooth ratios, calculated by dividing the sum of the height of the 7 lingual crests into the sum of the 7 widths of the occlusal surface of the buccal side (Robinette et al., 1957).

Caribou D/E ratio where D = width of dentine and E = width of enamel. Both measurements refer to lingual crest of 1st mandibular molar (Banfield, 1954).

Moose Ratio of the width to the height of posterior buccal crest of mandibular M2 expressed as a percent of age (Peterson, 1955).

Pronghorn Number of infundibula counted on mandibular premolars and molars (Dow and Wright, 1962).

Mountain Goat Number of annuli counted on the horn sheath. Reduced horn growth in older animals restricts the usefulness of the technique to animals less than 10 years.

Bighorn Sheep Number of annuli counted on the horn sheath (most readily counted along inside curvature of horn). This technique requires 1 or 2 year adjustment for rams with badly broomed horns.

Field Dressing, Handling and Aging Big Game Meat

John G. Stelfox and
Shawn Wasel

This chapter is for those hunters who wish to learn (or review) the basic principles for handling their animal after it has been dispatched. If you follow these rules, you can be assured of minimal wastage of meat, and a more pleasant taste to your steaks and roasts. Topics which are discussed include bleeding of carcasses, evisceration, skinning, caping, cooling the carcass and appropriate aging of the meat. For those who bag an animal in a remote location, you may want to pay attention to the alternative field boning procedure. A few photographs have been added to illustrate some key points.

INTRODUCTION

It is the responsibility of the hunter to ensure that proper attention is given to the ungulate carcass once an animal has been killed. As described in Alberta's *Big Game Regulations* (1992), *"it is unlawful to allow the edible meat of any big game animal ..... to be wasted, destroyed, or spoiled"*.

Proper processing of the big game carcass can provide the hunter with significant quantities of meat. Wastage of meat is inherently poor wildlife stewardship and damages the perception of the hunting community by the general public.

PRELIMINARIES

After ensuring the animal is dead, affix the hunting tag to the animal as required in the hunting regulations.

If the cape or hide is to be saved for taxidermy purposes, then follow the directions for removing them as described later before proceeding with eviscerating (gutting) the animal.

There are four basic considerations in the preparation of a big game carcass:

1. All entrails and blood must be removed quickly to prevent tainting the meat and to speed the cooling process. This includes removing any blood-shot meat and wiping the carcass clean of blood after evisceration.

2. The meat should be thoroughly cooled, but not frozen, as quickly as possible. Large-bodied animals such as moose and wapiti will not cool properly if left unskinned if the temperature is much above freezing. Conversely, the hide can keep the meat from freezing in sub-zero weather.

3. If the air temperature is cold enough to cool the carcass, there are two advantages to leaving the hide on:
    a. If the animal has to be dragged before reaching a vehicle or camp, the hide will protect the meat and keep it clean;
    b. Aging the carcass in a cool place with the hide on keeps the meat from drying and darkening. However, similar results can be obtained by using a cheesecloth and/or porous-paper covering.

4. It is not necessary to remove the leg scent glands unless you can not avoid touching them frequently and then the meat. If you remove the glands, use a separate knife or wash the knife well before touching it to the meat.

EVISCERATION (GUTTING)

If possible, the head should be positioned downhill to allow gravity to carry blood from the animal and to reduce the risk of puncturing the stomach or intestines when making the long incision from the anus to the chest. Ideally, animals should be bled quickly. This will be accomplished by the bullet if it passes through organs or severs major blood vessels. Should this not happen, bleed the animal by severing the throat. If the hunter wishes to keep the hide intact for taxidermy or aesthetic reasons, the dorsal aorta (artery) can be severed from within the body cavity during the evisceration process.

With the animal on its side, or preferably on its back, make a long shallow cut through the skin along the lower midline from the anus (crotch) to the upper neck region. Starting at the lower end of this cut, near the lower belly, make a deeper cut through the thin abdominal muscles continuing forward up to the neck. Use the fingers of your non-knife hand to keep the entrails away from the knife. The rib cage needs to be split along the sternum using a meat saw, axe, or stiff knife. At this juncture, it should be possible to expose the abdominal and chest cavities. Be sure evidence of sex glands is retained as required by law.

As soon as the hunter is certain the animal is dead, the hunting tag should be attached to the animal as described in the hunting regulations. Photo by J.B. Stelfox.

Starting at the anus, make a circular cut around the rectum, being careful not to cut into the large intestine. Tie off the anus with a piece of cord to prevent faecal pellets from leaking into the body cavity. Now you are ready to remove the entrails. If possible, swing the head of the animal uphill.

Cut through the membrane (diaphragm) that separates the heart-lung area (chest cavity) from the stomach, liver, and intestines (abdominal cavity). Sever the windpipe (trachea) and esophagus in the neck region, then free them from surrounding tissue using a knife. Once free, pull windpipe and esophagus into the chest cavity then cut any connective tissue that holds the entrails to the interior body wall. Once the entrails have been pulled back to the stomach region, lay the animal on its side with the belly facing downhill. At this point, the entire gastro-intestinal tract (esophagus, guts, intestines) and abdominal and chest organs should slide out of the body cavity. Some remaining connective tissue may need to be cut to complete the process. The heart and liver can now be removed, cleaned, and cooled. If the heart is to be eaten, clotted blood in the ventricles should be removed.

If possible, hang the carcass by the head or lower legs from a tree or fence post. Place in shade if the temperature is warm. Hanging will encourage the remaining blood to drain away and for air to circulate and cool the meat. To improve air circulation, the rib cage can be propped open with a stick. It is advisable to remove any clotted blood, entrails, or blood-shot meat from the vicinity of the bullet/arrow wound(s). Wipe the inside of the carcass dry as wet meat can spoil quickly. If the weather is warm and the animal can not be hung up, prop the carcass up on logs to encourage air circulation and heat loss.

Sprinkling pepper on the exposed meat and covering the carcass with cheesecloth will reduce contamination from flies.

The metatarsal glands are used by deer to produce chemicals that convey information of dominance and threat to others. These chemicals can taint the taste of the meat, so hunters must be careful to avoid touching them when they skin their animal. Photo by H. Stelfox.

SKINNING

When removing the hide from the carcass, it is most convenient to suspend the carcass by the head or hocks. This also reduces contamination of the meat with dirt and hair. To remove the skin, make the following cuts through the skin:

- around the base of the head
- around the four legs at the knee joints
- along the inside of the four legs from the wrists/ankles to the ventral midline.

Remove the lower legs by cutting through the ligaments and then use the knife to carefully free the skin from the body. Once the hide begins to loosen, your fist or base of the knife can be used to knock the hide free while the other hand pulls the hide away from the carcass. The tail bone will have to be severed when removing the hide from the hind quarters. The bones of the tail (caudal vertebrae) will need to be removed from the hide to prevent spoilage. This can be done by making a cut down the middle of the underside of the tail and fleshing out the tail vertebrae.

Trim away excess meat and fat from the hide and salt it liberally with fine salt. Roll up the hide into a compact bundle with the hair out and place it in a cool location. The salt will draw the moisture from the hide so the next day the hide should be unrolled, drained and wet salt shaken loose. The hide should then be resalted with dry salt and laid flat to allow the hide to dry completely. The hide can then be stored, preferably loosely rolled, in a breathable container such as a burlap sac.

CAPING

If the trophy head is to be mounted, the hide from the head, neck and shoulders (the cape) must be removed from behind the shoulders to include the chest, upper front legs and down deep on the brisket. Never bleed a trophy animal that is to be caped by cutting the throat!

Begin removing the cape at a point on the back between the shoulder blades. Cut down each side of the shoulders to a point behind the front legs and extending to the mid-ventral cut at the brisket made during the gutting process. Next cut the skin around the upper front legs, extending the incision to the cut down each shoulder. Make a mid-dorsal cut along the back of the neck to a point between the ears. Cut from this point to the base of each antler or horn. After freeing the hide from around the antlers or horns, and the neck and shoulders, cut off the head. The head can be removed by cutting through the thick muscles at the base of the skull and disarticulating the first neck vertebrae from the rear of the skull. A sharp flexible knife makes this process much easier. Once most of the muscle and connective tissue has been cut, twist the head off.

You are now ready to skin out the head. Be especially careful around the ears, eyes, and lips. Using a sharp knife, remove the skin from the top of the skull until you reach the base of the ears (indicated by yellow cartilage). Cut down and forward through this cartilage to free the ears.

When you reach the eyes, place a finger under the top edge of the eyelid (from the outside) and pull the skin tight while cutting between the eyelid and the bone. Remember that the tear ducts are deep in some species (especially deer and wapiti) so you must cut deeply to avoid cutting through the skin. When you reach the corners of the mouth, insert fingers in the mouth and lift the lips. Cut the cheek muscles about 2 cm from the corner of the mouth. Skin close to the bone until the lower lip is free. Then skin out the muzzle up to the nostrils keeping close to the bone until the nose and upper lip are free. To free the nose you will need to insert your fingers into the nostrils to guide your knife as you cut down through the nose cartilage.

When the entire cape is free, excess fat and flesh can be removed at the skinning location or within a few hours at camp. The lips and nose should be split from the inside and excess tissue removed. To prevent the ear from rotting, it is necessary to separate the skin of the back of the ear from the cartilage. This can be done by cutting away excess meat at the base of the ear and, using a long blunt stick, invert the ear as you carefully separate it from underlying cartilage with a knife. Extreme care is required to avoid tearing the ear. If you feel uncertain about skinning the ears, eyes, and nose, it might be better to leave the cape intact on the head and have a taxidermist complete the task.

Blood should be removed from the cape quickly before it dries and stains the hair. Keep the cape clean and rolled up carefully (hide out). Salt the cape liberally with fine salt as soon as possible and roll up overnight. Let the water drain off and re-salt the next day. Then dry completely and store in a clean burlap sack so it can "breathe". Don't place capes or other hides in airtight bags as they will quickly rot.

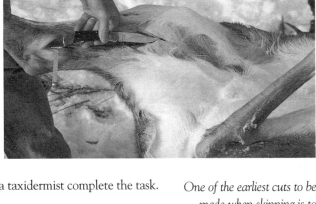

One of the earliest cuts to be made when skinning is to cut around the 4 legs at the ankle/wrist joints. Thereafter, a cut is made along the inside of each of the four legs to the ventral midline. Photo by H. Stelfox.

DEBONING

Under certain field conditions such as back-pack and horseback hunting, carrying out the entire eviscerated carcass is not possible. When faced with the prospect of packing out a mature bighorn ram or bull wapiti over many miles of rugged terrain, the hunter does not want to waste energy and effort carrying body parts that cannot be eaten. Deboning the carcass is an effective way to pack out all edible meat without wasting energy packing out bones and fat.

A word of caution if one chooses to debone a carcass in the field. The hunter must ensure that tagging, species identification, and evidence of sex requirements as defined in the hunting regulations are satisfied.

To make rolling of the carcass easier, the head and/or cape are typically removed first (this also will help limit the amount of blood spilled on the cape). The head is removed at the point where it articulates with the first vertebrae (atlas)—moving the head up and down will allow this hinge point to be more easily identified. A narrow-bladed knife is useful for inserting between the head and the atlas to sever the ligament thus making removal of the head easier. If the head is to

When making an incision along the belly, only the skin and thin abdominal muscles should be cut. It is important not to rupture the intestines or rumen, so use two fingers to depress the gastro-intestinal tract while running the knife above. Photo by H. Stelfox.

be packed out any distance the cape should be entirely removed. To further lighten the load, the lower jaw, tongue, nasal bones, brain, and flesh should be cut away.

The easiest way to debone an ungulate carcass is to first remove the hind legs by cutting from the inner thigh along the pelvis toward the base of the spine (moving the leg allows easier identification of the thigh joint). No sawing of bone is required as the leg is separated where the thigh bone articulates with the pelvis. The front legs can then be removed by grasping the leg, lifting away from the torso and cutting through the hide at the armpit toward the back. With all the limbs removed the next step is to cut away the backstraps. A cut is made straight down from each side of the spinal processes

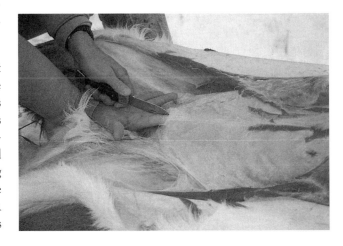

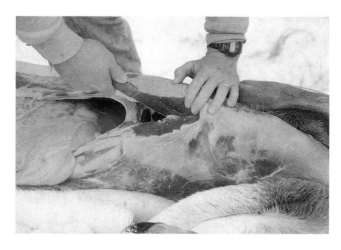

A strong knife, meat saw, or axe is needed to split the rib cage at the sternum. Once severed, the chest cavity is exposed and the heart and lungs can be removed. Photo by H. Stelfox.

to where the ribs attach to the vertebrae. This cut is continued from the point of the shoulder to the base of the spine. A lateral cut is then made lower down from the spine on each side where ribs are first apparent. The carcass can now be eviscerated by making a cut from the rectum to the base of the rib cage at the sternum. Above the abdominal cavity, along either side of the spine immediately behind the last rib, lie the tenderloins. These are easily removed by carefully cutting them away from the spine. The rib cage is then split in half longitudinally along the spine and the sternum with an axe or saw. The neck can be cut away from the carcass where it meets the anterior-most rib. All additional scraps of meat remaining on the pelvis can then be cut away. If the hide is to be retained intact, the animal should be skinned prior to deboning. If the animal is caped and the remaining hide is not to be packed out, the hide can be left on the carcass as deboning takes place to help keep the carcass clean. An effort should be made throughout the deboning process to prevent meat from being covered with debris and hair. With the animal deboned, the meat can easily be loaded and balanced in backpacks or pack boxes.

AGING THE MEAT

Big game carcasses should be "aged" for 5–15 days at a cool temperature (0–5 °C is optimal) as aged meat will be more tender. Keep the carcass dry, cool, clean, well-aerated, and protected from flies. If the carcass remains in the field during the aging process it should be hung where the wind will cool it at night and where it will remain dry. If daytime temperatures are warm hang the carcass in the shade or keep it wrapped in a heavy tarp or pannier in a cool place. Always have it hanging without a tarp covering at night so it will stay well aired and not get moldy.

In general, the aging period increases with larger carcasses and decreases with warmer air temperatures. Most carcasses are aged for one to two weeks. If aging is continued too long there is excessive carcass shrinkage and bacterial growth.

A Seasoned Hunter's Perspective

George Mitchell

Seasoned naturalist and hunter George Mitchell provides a fascinating perspective on ungulates and their management based on observing and hunting hoofed mammals in Alberta over six decades. He is one of the few active non-native hunters who can truly say he hunted during an era where it was done out of necessity to eat. Mr. Mitchell recounts some of his favourite hunting memories then touches on such topics as predator control, effects of fire on habitat, increased mechanization of sport hunting, and urbanization and loss of hunters.

It was 1931, in the dark days of the great depression, when I first started to hunt big game in Alberta. At thirteen years of age, I bagged my first hoofed mammal: a mule deer. On our homestead 10 miles southwest of Edson, I hunted not for sport or recreation, but out of necessity to put meat in the pot. At that time there was little work for adults, so we lived off the land. Vegetable stew was okay, but was better with some meat in it. It was not much trouble to grow a big garden and raise some cattle, but what little money we could get from our beef went to buy clothes and staples. If we needed meat to eat, there was no alternative but to hunt.

The only hoofed mammals near our homestead were mule deer and moose. The elk (wapiti) returned to the Edson area about 1936 and the white-tailed deer arrived in the 1950s. Mule deer were permanent residents and received the brunt of hunting pressure; the majority of moose did not migrate to where we lived until the deep snows of November.

The hunting season opened on the first of November and closed at the end of December. Legally, only males could be shot, but a hungry belly knows no law. It was everyone's ambition to shoot a two-year-old dry cow moose, which was usually fat—the same with doe deer. Although there was a regular season, it was rarely observed by the homesteaders. Between September and late December we simply hunted when we needed meat. Not a scrap was ever wasted, and my mother and sister canned venison for the summer months.

I cannot remember when I got my first licence, but it was many years after I started hunting. When I reflect back now, I cannot ever remember anyone considering that what we were doing was poaching, not even the one game officer or the police. They just said, "See that none is wasted." Two adults and six kids made sure of that at our house. One day a police officer dropped in for a visit and to have a look at our huge garden, as my dad was a great gardener. He said to my dad "Well, all you will need is some meat now. Send those boys out to get one of King George's cattle." When my father heard this, he replied "Oh, but the season is not open, and I think there are only two shells for the rifle." The policeman turned to my late brother Charles and asked, "What's the calibre of your rifle?", to which he replied, "A 32 special." The next day the policeman strode into the house and placed two boxes of shells on the table and said "Here, there is no need to go hungry. Policemen enjoy wild meat too."

A splendid old hunter by the name of Joe Millis took me under his wing and taught me how to hunt with horses. His mare, "Babe", and our black Arabian, "Rastus", were seasoned hunters, and generally saw the game first. When they stopped and their ears went forward, all you had to do was look in that direction. Apparently, big game were not alarmed by horses. If a deer was shot, it went home with us across the saddle. If it was a moose, we went back the next day with a team and wagon, or a sleigh if there was snow. While there were some old logging roads, there were no seismic lines criss-crossing the country. There were cutlines that were not wide enough for a team, but when the ground was snow-covered one of our Percherons, "Old Charlie", could skid moose out to where we left the sleigh.

When hunting on my own, I was on foot most of the time and walked hundreds of miles each season. If I had a two-dollar bill for every mile I walked while big game hunting, I would have been rich long ago. Although game was plentiful, dry leaves or crusted snow could make for hard hunting. Other times, while "still hunting", you were right on top of game when it jumped up and ran off through heavy timber without allowing you time to shoot.

I sincerely believe that we had abundant big game in the 1930s because of forest fires. While a lot of these were caused by lightning strikes, I am certain that many were set deliberately so that someone could get a job fire-fighting, even though the pay was only 15 cents an hour plus board. These fires burned over vast areas, and within two years there was a lush growth of new vegetation, the most prominent being fireweed, which was relished by mule deer. The new willow and poplar growth was four feet high and heavily utilized by moose. While deer did not use these areas when the snow deepened, the moose flocked to them and remained all winter.

From 1939 to 1940 I worked for the Alberta Forestry Service out of Mountain Park. What a variety of game I saw, including bighorn sheep, grizzly bear and unbelievable numbers of elk and moose. Their abundance, especially elk and moose, was a result of a huge fire that swept from Ruby Lake across to and east of Lovett, an area of approximately 35 by 20 miles.

A long-time friend and hunter, Harold McLaughlin, recalls when elk licences were first issued and how expensive they were. They were first available in 1933 and cost $50, which might as well have been $50,000 as far as resident hunters were concerned. In 1934, Harold and two friends chipped in to buy a $10 elk licence. Although they hunted hard in the Hargwen area along the McLeod River valley, they did not bag one. The next year, the license now reduced to $5, Harold hunted again and got his first elk. He said they were still scarce and in small bunches, but built up quickly in the late 1930s and 1940s after the big fires. This area was pristine wilderness, for only one horse trail and a single strand of telephone line connected the forestry cabins and fire lookouts. The burned-over area coupled with huge bunchgrass flats created ideal elk habitat, but more important was the fact that black bears were very scarce and there were no wolves.

The wolves moved in during 1943. The late forestry officer, Angus Crawford, wrote to me while I was overseas and informed me that he and his son Donny had seen their first wolves on Grave Flats. Incidentally, a forestry officer had reported seeing the first elk at Ruby Lake in 1929. In just ten years under ideal habitat and no predators, there had been an explosion of elk. The situation changed drastically, however, as the first oil road was pushed into Grave Flats from Mountain Park in 1954. In the post-war era, hunters flocked to Mountain Park along Highway 47 from Edson to Coalspur. This new road now took them into the heart of the best elk range at Grave Flats. Excessive losses of wildlife to hunters, wolves and native groups sounded the death knell for game in this area; loss of habitat due to regrowth of pine and spruce forests did not help either.

There are still a few elk and mule deer near the old townsite of Mountain Park, a few near Red Cap Mountain, but almost none on Grave Flats. Today, you seldom see a pile of droppings or "raked-up" trees, always good indicators that elk are around. One evening in September, 1940, I recall sitting on the north side of Grave Flats lookout watching over 250 elk scattered along Grave Flats and up Grave Creek which ran along the north side of the Red Cap Range. I also saw seven big bull moose in one bunch, their antlers flashing white in the late evening sun. Today you can drive through this area a week after a snowfall and rarely see a track. I believe that the only thing that will bring them back is to reduce predation by wolves and carry out some controlled burns.

While a few outfitters hunted this area, most hunted near Southesk or across the Brazeau River, as mountain goats could be found there also. Some that I knew were Tex Byers, Ray Mustard, and the Hagblads. When you met those outfitters on the trail, they were friendly and thanked you for helping with the maintenance of the trails. Today if you are hunting, friendly outfitters are the exception rather than the rule; most treat you as an interloper in your own country. This animosity has created a barrier between some resident hunters and outfitters, a situation that benefits neither party.

Thousands of homesteads were abandoned during the war or were incorporated into larger units for economic reasons. All this abandoned land went back to the government for back taxes. It is now public land, and a good thing, as a lot of it is grey-wooded soil and marginal farmland at best. This type of land will always be best-suited for wildlife, timber, mineral production or recreational pursuits such as hunting, fishing, camping and photography. There is no reason why multiple land-uses cannot coexist if managed in a proper way.

On the whole, there are relatively fewer hunters today in our population than there were in the 1930s. The population has become more urban and fewer parents are passing on the tradition of hunting to their children. The urban populations of today have no need to hunt for subsistence as we did in the 1930s. When I started we did not live to hunt, we hunted to live; it was as simple as that. Do not get me wrong: when I say there are not as many people hunting, this may be misleading. You seem to run into them everywhere you go during the hunting season.

ATVs and 4x4s have distributed hunters over a wider area by making use of old roads and seismic lines. While this decreases interactions between hunters, conflicts have lead to huge areas being closed to ATVs. These restrictions lead to concentration of ATVs in areas that were at saturation point already. I spoke to one hunter last fall who said, "I realize that everyone has the same right to hunt on public land as I do, but when I am here first and have my camp set up, I do not want some stranger coming along and tying his tent ropes to mine."

Where have we gone in the 58 years since I started to hunt? Well, I can remember when there was no female season, no tags, and you had to wear white while hunting. Clothing regulations went to red or blaze-orange, and now it is wear what you like. All game must now be tagged. A short time ago, the tag was put around the antlers on the deer family, now it has to be put on the tendon of the hind leg. Keeps you hopping just to keep up with the regulations.

Management of big game harvest has gone ahead by leaps and bounds. All the same, dedicated biologists are making important recommendations that are frequently not acted upon by elected officials, who are swayed far too often by the pleading of animal lovers, or others who are against hunting of any kind. I have often thought, and I have heard the same from many others, that we are managing the hunter, not the wildlife. A prime example is the policy of the government to try to increase the elk population to 15,000; an interesting proposal but unattainable the way they are going about it. They will never get them up to this number unless excessive predation by wolves is controlled. Incidentally, the states of Montana, Wyoming and Colorado each harvest approximately 15,000 elk every season. But while they have a bear problem, they have no wolves.

Extensive studies done in the Rocky Mountain House area indicated that wolves were the cause of low populations of elk, moose and deer. Another study done at about the same time on caribou in the Willmore Wilderness area reached the same conclusion. Wolves will have to be controlled, or there will be no caribou left. In 1987, a wolf reduction program was proposed. But it was never started because the anti-hunting group flew in a so called "wolf expert" from down east who knows as much about wolves and the wolf population in Alberta as I know about flying a space shuttle. So the ministers of Fish and Wildlife stopped the program. While wolves continue to increase, the game they prey upon is decreasing rapidly.

Big game animals that are hunted here each fall bring in millions of dollars to the economy. The governments of the Yukon, British Columbia and the state of Alaska at one time stopped their wolf-control programs. But due to a rapid increase in wolves, which made serious inroads into hoofed mammal populations, they had to start thinning out wolves. This caused a tremendous increase in the game there in just three years. It appears that a wolf control program in Alberta is unlikely. Many Alberta outfitters have stopped booking clients in some areas as there are no trophy elk left to hunt.

I often hunt on a farm east of Edmonton. The farmer, who was raised there, told me that when he was a boy there were no white-tailed deer, only a few mule deer, but you had to go miles south to find them. The majority of our best white-tailed deer hunting is now on private farms or ranch land. So do as I do: ask permission, and then help out when needed. Fix fences, cut wood, or help butcher a steer. My wife and I have hunted on the same farm for fifteen years. We know that when we are there, no one else will be. The farmer, when he has time, will spend a few hours hunting with us, as he enjoys it too.

The bighorn sheep are faring well and some outstanding rams are taken each fall. Many of them are well over the 180-point minimum for Boone and Crockett Club. I wonder how important wolf harassment of bighorn sheep is, as I have seen wolves chasing sheep right on top of Red Cap Mountain at 7,900 feet elevation. Moose, elk, and mule deer are in dire straits in the foothills and subalpine zones from one end of the province to the other. Some positive steps will have to be taken if we want them to be as abundant as they were in the 1950s and '60s.

The pronghorn were almost gone by the 1930s, but now there are many. So many in fact, that a couple of years ago, the Alberta Fish and Wildlife Division allowed those who were successful in drawing a non-trophy permit to take two pronghorn instead of one. They supposedly did this so that there would not be more hunters in the field, since all the antelope were on private land. This went over like a lead balloon with those hunters who did not get drawn, including quite a few ranchers who could not hunt on their own land. So much for management.

In conclusion, I feel that if we want to conserve our game animals, we must start paying attention to the dedicated field personnel who are closer to the situation than the elected officials. There is no use spending public funds to conduct studies unless they are acted upon. In my time I have seen the season left open on caribou, even to the taking of cows and calves, until they were almost gone. The same applied to mountain goats. Many hunters knew where they were going, as did the biologists, but no one would listen. They went down at the hunters' guns, by excessive predation, or through loss of habitat. We never seem to get alarmed until a crisis occurs.

My enthusiasm for hunting has not dimmed one bit. I just love to get out in the woods each fall to look for a grouse or a deer, and to set up camp with good companions. Shooting an animal is secondary. I am affluent enough to buy the best beef or fish, yet I find the challenge in going out and doing things my way. It is ingrained in me, as my old grandad, Charlie Wilson, was a famous game keeper in Yorkshire. He sent me his hand-tied flies to try on our trout and grayling. When I came home as a kid with enough fish to last us two days my mother would say, "We will never go hungry as long as you are around. You are just like your grandad." I am still proud today to be a skilled hunter and fisherman. It has given me much pleasure.

Boone and Crockett Club Scoring Forms

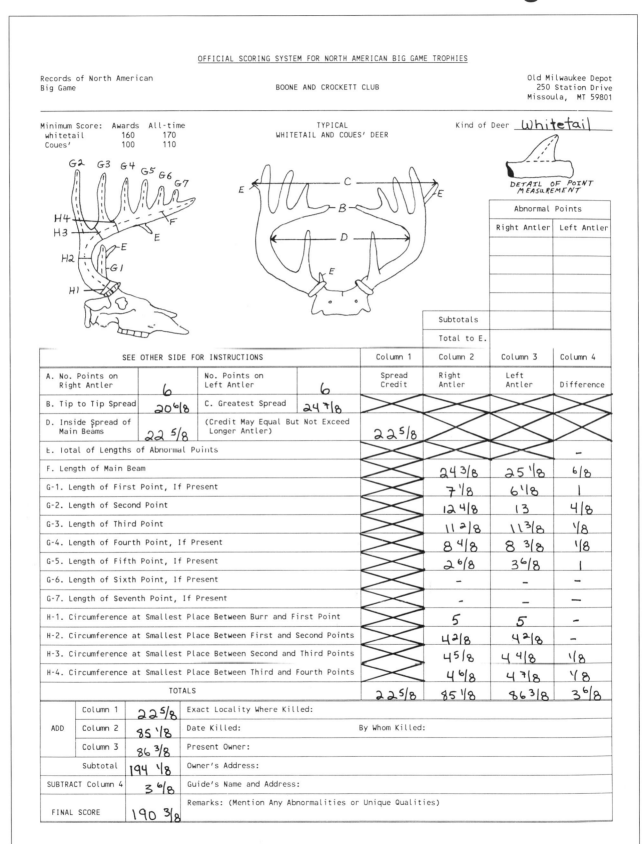

OFFICIAL SCORING SYSTEM FOR NORTH AMERICAN BIG GAME TROPHIES

Records of North American
Big Game

BOONE AND CROCKETT CLUB

Old Milwaukee Depot
250 Station Drive
Missoula, MT 59801

Minimum Score:	Awards	All-time
whitetail	160	170
Coues'	100	110

TYPICAL
WHITETAIL AND COUES' DEER

Kind of Deer **Whitetail**

DETAIL OF POINT MEASUREMENT

Abnormal Points	
Right Antler	Left Antler

| Subtotals | | |
| Total to E. | | |

SEE OTHER SIDE FOR INSTRUCTIONS				Column 1	Column 2	Column 3	Column 4
				Spread Credit	Right Antler	Left Antler	Difference
A. No. Points on Right Antler	6	No. Points on Left Antler	6				
B. Tip to Tip Spread	20 6/8	C. Greatest Spread	24 7/8				
D. Inside Spread of Main Beams	22 5/8	(Credit May Equal But Not Exceed Longer Antler)		22 5/8			
E. Total of Lengths of Abnormal Points							–
F. Length of Main Beam					24 3/8	25 1/8	6/8
G-1. Length of First Point, If Present					7 1/8	6 1/8	1
G-2. Length of Second Point					12 4/8	13	4/8
G-3. Length of Third Point					11 2/8	11 3/8	1/8
G-4. Length of Fourth Point, If Present					8 4/8	8 3/8	1/8
G-5. Length of Fifth Point, If Present					2 6/8	3 6/8	1
G-6. Length of Sixth Point, If Present					–	–	–
G-7. Length of Seventh Point, If Present					–	–	–
H-1. Circumference at Smallest Place Between Burr and First Point					5	5	–
H-2. Circumference at Smallest Place Between First and Second Points					4 2/8	4 2/8	–
H-3. Circumference at Smallest Place Between Second and Third Points					4 5/8	4 4/8	1/8
H-4. Circumference at Smallest Place Between Third and Fourth Points					4 6/8	4 7/8	1/8
TOTALS				22 5/8	85 1/8	86 3/8	3 6/8

ADD	Column 1	22 5/8	Exact Locality Where Killed:
	Column 2	85 1/8	Date Killed: By Whom Killed:
	Column 3	86 3/8	Present Owner:
	Subtotal	194 1/8	Owner's Address:
SUBTRACT Column 4		3 6/8	Guide's Name and Address:
FINAL SCORE		190 3/8	Remarks: (Mention Any Abnormalities or Unique Qualities)

I certify that I have measured this trophy on _____ 19 _____

at (address) _____ City _____ State _____
and that these measurements and data are, to the best of my knowledge and belief, made in accordance with the instructions given.

Witness: _____ Signature: _____

B&C OFFICIAL MEASURER | | | |

I.D. Number

INSTRUCTIONS FOR MEASURING TYPICAL WHITETAIL AND COUES' DEER

All measurements must be made with a 1/4-inch wide flexible steel tape to the nearest one-eighth of an inch. Wherever it is necessary to change direction of measurement, mark a control point and swing tape at this point. (Note: A flexible steel cable can be used to measure points and main beams only.) Enter fractional figures in eighths, without reduction. Official measurements cannot be taken until the antlers have air dried for at least 60 days after the animal was killed.

A. Number of Points on Each Antler: To be counted a point, the projection must be at least one inch long, with the length exceeding width at one inch or more of length. All points are measured from tip of point to nearest edge of beam as illustrated. Beam tip is counted as a point but not measured as a point.

B. Tip to Tip Spread is measured between tips of main beams.

C. Greatest Spread is measured between perpendiculars at a right angle to the center line of the skull at widest part, whether across main beams or points.

D. Inside Spread of Main Beams is measured at a right angle to the center line of the skull at widest point between main beams. Enter this measurement again as the Spread Credit if it is less than or equal to the length of the longer antler; if greater, enter longer antler length for Spread Credit.

E. Total of Lengths of all Abnormal Points: Abnormal Points are those non-typical in location (such as points originating from a point or from bottom or sides of main beam) or extra points beyond the normal pattern of points. Measure in usual manner and enter in appropriate blanks.

F. Length of Main Beam is measured from lowest outside edge of burr over outer curve to the most distant point of what is, or appears to be, the main beam. The point of beginning is that point on the burr where the center line along the outer curve of the beam intersects the burr, then following generally the line of the illustration.

G-1-2-3-4-5-6-7. Length of Normal Points: Normal points project from the top of the main beam. They are measured from nearest edge of main beam over outer curve to tip. Lay the tape along the outer curve of the beam so that the top edge of the tape coincides with the top edge of the beam on both sides of the point to determine the baseline for point measurements. Record point lengths in appropriate blanks.

H-1-2-3-4. Circumferences are taken as detailed for each measurement. If brow point is missing, take H-1 and H-2 at smallest place between burr and G-2. If G-4 is missing, take H-4 halfway between G-3 and tip of main beam.

FAIR CHASE STATEMENT FOR ALL HUNTER-TAKEN TROPHIES

FAIR CHASE, as defined by the Boone and Crockett Club, is the ethical, sportsmanlike and lawful pursuit and taking of any free-ranging wild game animal in a manner that does not give the hunter an improper or unfair advantage over such game animals.

Use of any of the following methods in the taking of game shall be deemed **UNFAIR CHASE** and unsportsmanlike:

I. Spotting or herding game from the air, followed by landing in its vicinity for the purpose of pursuit and shooting;

II. Herding, pursuing, or shooting game from any motorboat or motor vehicle;

III. Use of electronic devices for attracting, locating, or observing game, or for guiding the hunter to such game;

IV. Hunting game confined by artificial barriers, including escape-proof fenced enclosures, or hunting game transplanted solely for the purpose of commercial shooting;

V. Taking of game in a manner not in full compliance with the game laws or regulations of the federal government or of any state, province, territory, or tribal council on reservations or tribal lands;

VI. Or as may otherwise be deemed unfair or unsportsmanlike by the Executive Committee of the Boone and Crockett Club.

I certify that the trophy scored on this chart was taken in **FAIR CHASE** as defined above by the Boone and Crockett Club. In signing this statement, I understand that if this entry is found to be fraudulent, it will not be accepted into the Awards program and all of my prior entries are subject to deletion from future editions of *Records of North American Big Game* and future entries may not be accepted.

Date: _____ Signature of Hunter: _____

(Have signature notarized by a Notary Public.)

Copyright © 1993 by Boone and Crockett Club
(Reproduction strictly forbidden without express, written consent)

Records of North American
Big Game

BOONE AND CROCKETT CLUB

Old Milwaukee Depot
250 Station Drive
Missoula, MT 59801

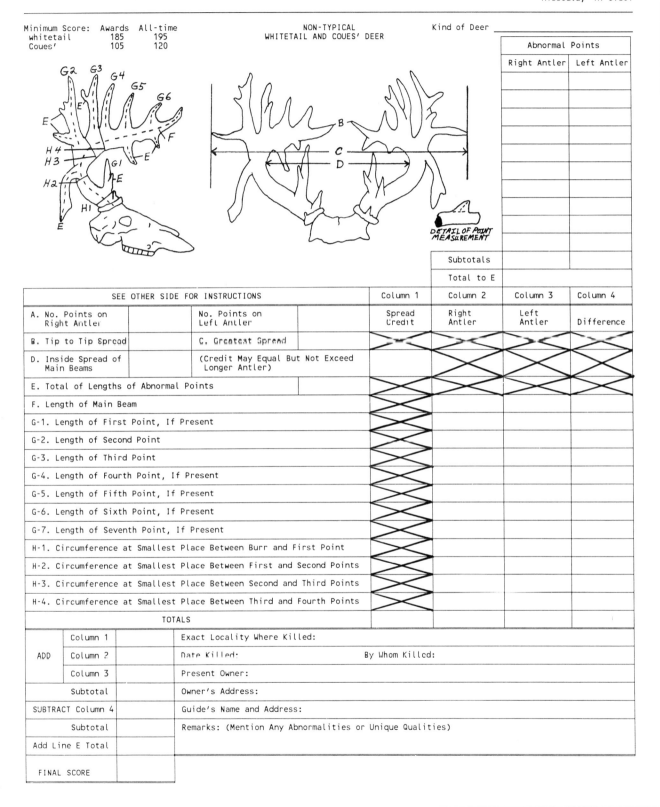

Minimum Score: Awards All-time
whitetail   185   195
Coues'   105   120

NON-TYPICAL
WHITETAIL AND COUES' DEER

Kind of Deer _____

Abnormal Points	
Right Antler	Left Antler
Subtotals	
Total to E	

SEE OTHER SIDE FOR INSTRUCTIONS				Column 1	Column 2	Column 3	Column 4
				Spread Credit	Right Antler	Left Antler	Difference
A. No. Points on Right Antler		No. Points on Left Antler					
B. Tip to Tip Spread		C. Greatest Spread					
D. Inside Spread of Main Beams		(Credit May Equal But Not Exceed Longer Antler)					
E. Total of Lengths of Abnormal Points							
F. Length of Main Beam							
G-1. Length of First Point, If Present							
G-2. Length of Second Point							
G-3. Length of Third Point							
G-4. Length of Fourth Point, If Present							
G-5. Length of Fifth Point, If Present							
G-6. Length of Sixth Point, If Present							
G-7. Length of Seventh Point, If Present							
H-1. Circumference at Smallest Place Between Burr and First Point							
H-2. Circumference at Smallest Place Between First and Second Points							
H-3. Circumference at Smallest Place Between Second and Third Points							
H-4. Circumference at Smallest Place Between Third and Fourth Points							
TOTALS							

ADD	Column 1		Exact Locality Where Killed:
	Column 2		Date Killed: By Whom Killed:
	Column 3		Present Owner:
	Subtotal		Owner's Address:
SUBTRACT Column 4			Guide's Name and Address:
	Subtotal		Remarks: (Mention Any Abnormalities or Unique Qualities)
Add Line E Total			
FINAL SCORE			

I certify that I have measured this trophy on _____ 19 _____

at (Address) _____ City _____ State _____
and that these measurements and data are, to the best of my knowledge and belief, made in
accordance with the instructions given.

Witness: _____ Signature: _____

B&C OFFICIAL MEASURER   [| | |]

I.D. Number

INSTRUCTIONS FOR MEASURING NON-TYPICAL WHITETAIL AND COUES' DEER

All measurements must be made with a 1/4-inch wide flexible steel tape to the nearest one-eighth of an inch. Wherever it is necessary to change direction of measurement, mark a control point and swing tape at this point. (Note: A flexible steel cable can be used to measure points and main beams only.) Enter fractional figures in eighths, without reduction. Official measurements cannot be taken until the antlers have air dried for at least 60 days after the animal was killed.

A. Number of Points on Each Antler: To be counted a point, the projection must be at least one inch long, with the length exceeding width at one inch or more of length. All points are measured from tip of point to nearest edge of beam as illustrated. Beam tip is counted as a point but not measured as a point.

B. Tip to Tip Spread is measured between tips of main beams.

C. Greatest Spread is measured between perpendiculars at a right angle to the center line of the skull at widest part, whether across main beams or points.

D. Inside Spread of Main Beams is measured at a right angle to the center line of the skull at widest point between main beams. Enter this measurement again as the Spread Credit _if_ it is less than or equal to the length of the longer antler; if greater, enter longer antler length for Spread Credit.

E. Total of Lengths of all Abnormal Points: Abnormal Points are those non-typical in location (such as points originating from a point or from bottom or sides of main beam) or extra points beyond the normal pattern of points. Measure in usual manner and enter in appropriate blanks.

F. Length of Main Beam is measured from lowest outside edge of burr over outer curve to the most distant point of what is, or appears to be, the main beam. The point of beginning is that point on the burr where the center line along the outer curve of the beam intersects the burr, then following generally the line of the illustration.

G-1-2-3-4-5-6-7. Length of Normal Points: Normal points project from the top of the main beam. They are measured from nearest edge of main beam over outer curve to tip. Lay the tape along the outer curve of the beam so that the top edge of the tape coincides with the top edge of the beam on both sides of the point to determine the baseline for point measurement. Record point lengths in appropriate blanks.

H-1-2-3-4. Circumferences are taken as detailed for each measurement. If brow point is missing, take H-1 and H-2 at smallest place between burr and G-2. If G-4 is missing, take H-4 halfway between G-3 and tip of main beam.

FAIR CHASE STATEMENT FOR ALL HUNTER-TAKEN TROPHIES

FAIR CHASE, as defined by the Boone and Crockett Club, is the ethical, sportsmanlike and lawful pursuit and taking of any free-ranging wild game animal in a manner that does not give the hunter an improper or unfair advantage over such game animals.

Use of any of the following methods in the taking of game shall be deemed **UNFAIR CHASE** and unsportsmanlike:

  I. Spotting or herding game from the air, followed by landing in its vicinity for the purpose of pursuit and shooting;

  II. Herding, pursuing, or shooting game from any motorboat or motor vehicle;

  III. Use of electronic devices for attracting, locating, or observing game, or for guiding the hunter to such game;

  IV. Hunting game confined by artificial barriers, including escape-proof fenced enclosures, or hunting game transplanted solely for the purpose of commercial shooting;

  V. Taking of game in a manner not in full compliance with the game laws or regulations of the federal government or of any state, province, territory, or tribal council on reservations or tribal lands;

  VI. Or as may otherwise be deemed unfair or unsportsmanlike by the Executive Committee of the Boone and Crockett Club.

I certify that the trophy scored on this chart was taken in **FAIR CHASE** as defined above by the Boone and Crockett Club. In signing this statement, I understand that if this entry is found to be fraudulent, it will not be accepted into the Awards program and all of my prior entries are subject to deletion from future editions of _Records of North American Big Game_ and future entries may not be accepted.

Date: _____ Signature of Hunter: _____

(Have signature notarized by a Notary Public.)

Copyright © 1993 by Boone and Crockett Club
(Reproduction strictly forbidden without express, written consent)

OFFICIAL SCORING SYSTEM FOR NORTH AMERICAN BIG GAME TROPHIES

Records of North American
Big Game

BOONE AND CROCKETT CLUB

Old Milwaukee Depot
250 Station Drive
Missoula, MT 59801

Minimum Score:	Awards	All-time
mule	185	195
Columbia	120	130
Sitka	100	108

TYPICAL
MULE AND BLACKTAIL DEER

Kind of Deer _____

DETAIL OF POINT
MEASUREMENT

Abnormal Points	
Right Antler	Left Antler
Subtotals	
Total to E.	

SEE OTHER SIDE FOR INSTRUCTIONS			Column 1	Column 2	Column 3	Column 4
A. No. Points on Right Antler		No. Points on Left Antler	Spread Credit	Right Antler	Left Antler	Difference
B. Tip to Tip Spread		C. Greatest Spread				
D. Inside Spread of Main Beams		(Credit May Equal But Not Exceed Longer Antler)				
E. Total of Lengths of Abnormal Points						
F. Length of Main Beam						
G-1. Length of First Point, If Present						
G-2. Length of Second Point						
G-3. Length of Third Point, If Present						
G-4. Length of Fourth Point, If Present						
H-1. Circumference at Smallest Place Between Burr and First Point						
H-2. Circumference at Smallest Place Between First and Second Points						
H-3. Circumference at Smallest Place Between Main Beam and Third Point						
H-4. Circumference at Smallest Place Between Second and Fourth Points						
TOTALS						

ADD	Column 1		Exact Locality Where Killed:
	Column 2		Date Killed: By Whom Killed:
	Column 3		Present Owner:
	Subtotal		Owner's Address:
SUBTRACT Column 4			Guide's Name and Address:
FINAL SCORE			Remarks: (Mention Any Abnormalities or Unique Qualities)

Boone and Crockett scoring form for mule deer (typical) • **205**

I certify that I have measured this trophy on _____ 19 _____

at (address) _____ City _____ State _____
and that these measurements and data are, to the best of my knowledge and belief, made in
accordance with the instructions given.

Witness: _____ Signature: _____

B&C OFFICIAL MEASURER [ ][ ][ ][ ]

I.D. Number

INSTRUCTIONS FOR MEASURING TYPICAL MULE AND BLACKTAIL DEER

All measurements must be made with a 1/4-inch wide flexible steel tape to the nearest
one-eighth of an inch. Wherever it is necessary to change direction of measurement, mark a
control point and swing tape at this point. (Note: A flexible steel cable can be used to
measure points and main beams only.) Enter fractional figures in eighths, without reduction.
Official measurements cannot be taken until the antlers have air dried for at least 60 days
after the animal was killed.

A. Number of Points on Each Antler: To be counted a point, the projection must be at
least one inch long, with length exceeding width at one inch or more of length. All points
are measured from tip of point to nearest edge of beam as illustrated. Beam tip is counted as
a point but not measured as a point.

B. Tip to Tip Spread is measured between tips of main beams.

C. Greatest Spread is measured between perpendiculars at a right angle to the center line
of the skull at widest part, whether across main beams or points.

D. Inside Spread of Main Beams is measured at a right angle to the center line of the
skull at widest point between main beams. Enter this measurement again as the Spread Credit
if it is less than or equal to the length of the longer antler; if greater, enter longer
antler length for Spread Credit.

E. Total of Lengths of all Abnormal Points: Abnormal Points are those non-typical in
location such as points originating from a point (exception: G-3 originates from G-2 in
perfectly normal fashion) or from bottom or sides of main beam, or any points beyond the
normal pattern of five (including beam tip) per antler. Measure each abnormal point in usual
manner and enter in appropriate blanks.

F. Length of Main Beam is measured from lowest outside edge of burr over outer curve to
the most distant point of what is, or appears to be, the Main Beam. The point of beginning is
that point on the burr where the center line along the outer curve of the beam intersects the
burr, then following generally the line of the illustration.

G-1-2-3-4. Length of Normal Points: Normal points are the brow and the upper and lower
forks as shown in the illustration. They are measured from nearest edge of beam over outer
curve to tip. Lay the tape along the outer curve of the beam so that the top edge of the tape
coincides with the top edge of the beam on both sides of point to determine the baseline for
point measurement. Record point lengths in appropriate blanks.

H-1-2-3-4. Circumferences are taken as detailed for each measurement. If brow point is
missing, take H-1 and H-2 at smallest place between burr and G-2. If G-3 is missing, take H-3
halfway between the base and tip of G-2. If G-4 is missing, take H-4 halfway between G-2 and
tip of main beam.

FAIR CHASE STATEMENT FOR ALL HUNTER-TAKEN TROPHIES

FAIR CHASE, as defined by the Boone and Crockett Club, is the ethical, sportsmanlike and
lawful pursuit and taking of any free-ranging wild game animal in a manner that does not give
the hunter an improper or unfair advantage over such game animals.

Use of any of the following methods in the taking of game shall be deemed UNFAIR CHASE
and unsportsmanlike:

I. Spotting or herding game from the air, followed by landing in its vicinity for the
purpose of pursuit and shooting;

II. Herding, pursuing, or shooting game from any motorboat or motor vehicle;

III. Use of electronic devices for attracting, locating, or observing game, or for
guiding the hunter to such game;

IV. Hunting game confined by artificial barriers, including escape-proof fenced
enclosures, or hunting game transplanted solely for the purpose of commercial
shooting;

V. Taking of game in a manner not in full compliance with the game laws or
regulations of the federal government or of any state, province, territory, or
tribal council on reservations or tribal lands;

VI. Or as may otherwise be deemed unfair or unsportsmanlike by the Executive Committee
of the Boone and Crockett Club.

I certify that the trophy scored on this chart was taken in FAIR CHASE as defined above by the
Boone and Crockett Club. In signing this statement, I understand that if this entry is found
to be fraudulent, it will not be accepted into the Awards program and all of my prior entries
are subject to deletion from future editions of *Records of North American Big Game* and future
entries may not be accepted.

Date: _____ Signature of Hunter: _____
(Have signature notarized by a Notary Public.)

OFFICIAL SCORING SYSTEM FOR NORTH AMERICAN BIG GAME TROPHIES

Records of North American
Big Game

BOONE AND CROCKETT CLUB

Old Milwaukee Depot
250 Station Drive
Missoula, MT 59801

Minimum Score: Awards All-time
225   240

NON-TYPICAL
MULE DEER

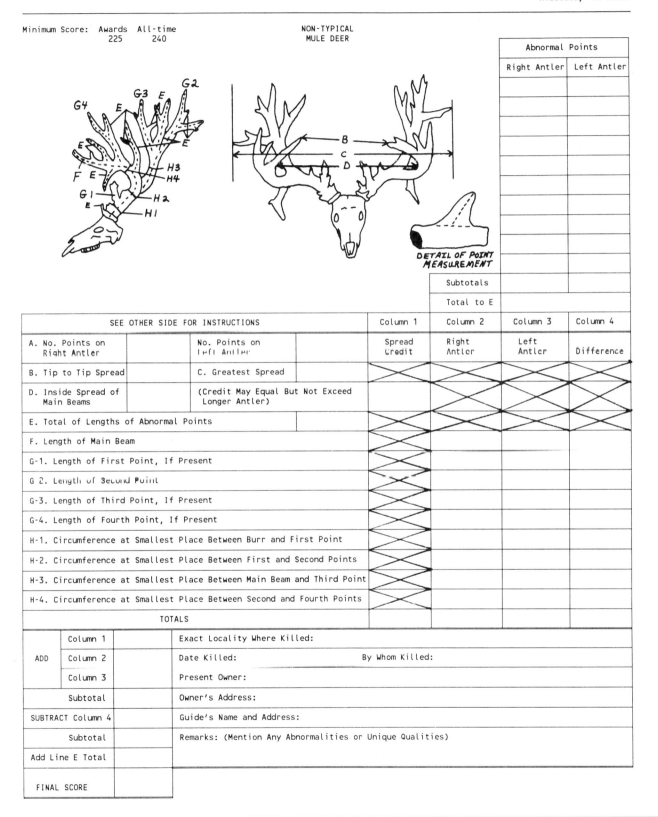

Abnormal Points	
Right Antler	Left Antler
Subtotals	
Total to E	

SEE OTHER SIDE FOR INSTRUCTIONS				Column 1	Column 2	Column 3	Column 4
A. No. Points on Right Antler		No. Points on Left Antler		Spread Credit	Right Antler	Left Antler	Difference
B. Tip to Tip Spread		C. Greatest Spread					
D. Inside Spread of Main Beams		(Credit May Equal But Not Exceed Longer Antler)					
E. Total of Lengths of Abnormal Points							
F. Length of Main Beam							
G-1. Length of First Point, If Present							
G-2. Length of Second Point							
G-3. Length of Third Point, If Present							
G-4. Length of Fourth Point, If Present							
H-1. Circumference at Smallest Place Between Burr and First Point							
H-2. Circumference at Smallest Place Between First and Second Points							
H-3. Circumference at Smallest Place Between Main Beam and Third Point							
H-4. Circumference at Smallest Place Between Second and Fourth Points							
TOTALS							

ADD	Column 1		Exact Locality Where Killed:
	Column 2		Date Killed: By Whom Killed:
	Column 3		Present Owner:
	Subtotal		Owner's Address:
SUBTRACT Column 4			Guide's Name and Address:
	Subtotal		Remarks: (Mention Any Abnormalities or Unique Qualities)
Add Line E Total			
FINAL SCORE			

I certify that I have measured this trophy on _____ 19 _____

at (address) _____ City _____ State _____
and that these measurements and data are, to the best of my knowledge and belief, made in
accordance with the instructions given.

Witness: _____ Signature: _____

B&C OFFICIAL MEASURER [ ][ ][ ][ ]

I.D. Number

INSTRUCTIONS FOR MEASURING NON-TYPICAL MULE DEER

All measurements must be made with a 1/4-inch wide flexible steel tape to the nearest
one-eighth of an inch. Wherever it is necessary to change direction of measurement, mark a
control point and swing tape at this point. (Note: A flexible steel cable can be used to
measure points and main beams only.) Enter fractional figures in eighths, without reduction.
Official measurements cannot be taken until the antlers have air dried for at least 60 days
after the animal was killed.

A. Number of Points on Each Antler: To be counted a point, the projection must be at
least one inch long, with length exceeding width at one inch or more of length. All points
are measured from tip of point to nearest edge of beam as illustrated. Beam tip is counted as
a point but not measured as a point.

B. Tip to Tip Spread is measured between tips of main beams.

C. Greatest Spread is measured between perpendiculars at a right angle to the center line
of the skull at widest part, whether across main beams or points.

D. Inside Spread of Main Beams is measured at a right angle to the center line of the
skull at widest point between main beams. Enter this measurement again as the Spread Credit
if it is less than or equal to the length of the longer antler; if greater, enter longer
antler length for Spread Credit.

E. Total of Lengths of all Abnormal Points: Abnormal Points are those non-typical in
location such as originating from a point (exception: G-3 originates from G-2 in
perfectly normal fashion) or from bottom or sides of main beam, or any points beyond the
normal pattern of five (including beam tip) per antler. Measure each abnormal point in usual
manner and enter in appropriate blanks.

F. Length of Main Beam is measured from lowest outside edge of burr over outer curve to
the most distant point of what is, or appears to be, the main beam. The point of beginning is
that point on the burr where the center line along the outer curve of the beam intersects the
burr, then following generally the line of the illustration.

G-1-2-3-4. Length of Normal Points: Normal points are the brow and the upper and lower
forks as shown in the illustration. They are measured from nearest edge of main beam over
outer curve to tip. Lay the tape along the outer curve of the beam so that the top edge of
the tape coincides with the top edge of the beam on both sides of point to determine the
baseline for point measurement. Record point lengths in appropriate blanks.

H-1-2-3-4. Circumferences are taken as detailed for each measurement. If brow point is
missing, take H-1 and H-2 at smallest place between burr and G-2. If G-3 is missing, take H-3
halfway between the base and tip of G-2. If G-4 is missing, take H-4 halfway between G-2 and
tip of main beam.

FAIR CHASE STATEMENT FOR ALL HUNTER-TAKEN TROPHIES

FAIR CHASE, as defined by the Boone and Crockett Club, is the ethical, sportsmanlike and
lawful pursuit and taking of any free-ranging wild game animal in a manner that does not give
the hunter an improper or unfair advantage over such game animals.
Use of any of the following methods in the taking of game shall be deemed **UNFAIR CHASE**
and unsportsmanlike:

I. Spotting or herding game from the air, followed by landing in its vicinity for the
purpose of pursuit and shooting;

II. Herding, pursuing, or shooting game from any motorboat or motor vehicle;

III. Use of electronic devices for attracting, locating, or observing game, or for
guiding the hunter to such game;

IV. Hunting game confined by artificial barriers, including escape-proof fenced
enclosures, or hunting game transplanted solely for the purpose of commercial
shooting;

V. Taking of game in a manner not in full compliance with the game laws or
regulations of the federal government or of any state, province, territory, or
tribal council on reservations or tribal lands;

VI. Or as may otherwise be deemed unfair or unsportsmanlike by the Executive Committee
of the Boone and Crockett Club.

I certify that the trophy scored on this chart was taken in **FAIR CHASE** as defined above by the
Boone and Crockett Club. In signing this statement, I understand that if this entry is found
to be fraudulent, it will not be accepted into the Awards program and all of my prior entries
are subject to deletion from future editions of *Records of North American Big Game* and future
entries may not be accepted.

Date: _____ Signature of Hunter: _____
(Have signature notarized by a Notary Public.)

Copyright © 1993 by Boone and Crockett Club
(Reproduction strictly forbidden without express, written consent)

Records of North American
Big Game

BOONE AND CROCKETT CLUB

Old Milwaukee Depot
250 Station Drive
Missoula, MT 59801

Minimum Score:	Awards	All-time
barren ground	375	400
mountain	360	390
Quebec-Labrador	365	375
woodland	265	295
Central Canada barren ground	330	345

CARIBOU

Kind of Caribou _____

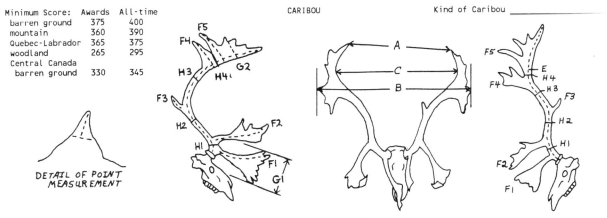

DETAIL OF POINT MEASUREMENT

SEE OTHER SIDE FOR INSTRUCTIONS		Column 1	Column 2	Column 3	Column 4
		Spread Credit	Right Antler	Left Antler	Difference
A. Tip to Tip Spread					
B. Greatest Spread					
C. Inside Spread of Main Beams	(Credit May Equal But Not Exceed Longer Antler)				
D. Number of Points on Each Antler Excluding Brows					
Number of Points on Each Brow					
E. Length of Main Beam					
F-1. Length of Brow Palm or First Point					
F-2. Length of Bez or Second Point					
F-3. Length of Rear Point, If Present					
F-4. Length of Second Longest Top Point					
F-5. Length of Longest Top Point					
G-1. Width of Brow Palm					
G-2. Width of Top Palm					
H-1. Circ. at Smallest Place Between Brow and Bez Points					
H-2. Circ. at Smallest Place Between Bez and Rear Point, If Present					
H-3. Circ. at Smallest Place Before First Top Point					
H-4. Circ. at Smallest Place Between Two Longest Top Palm Points					
TOTALS					

ADD	Column 1		Exact Locality Where Killed:
	Column 2		Date Killed: By Whom Killed:
	Column 3		Present Owner:
	Subtotal		Owner's Address:
SUBTRACT Column 4			Guide's Name and Address:
FINAL SCORE			Remarks: (Mention Any Abnormalities or Unique Qualities)

I certify that I have measured this trophy on _____ 19 _____

at (address) _____ City _____ State _____
and that these measurements and data are, to the best of my knowledge and belief, made in
accordance with the instructions given.

Witness: _____ Signature: _____

INSTRUCTIONS FOR MEASURING CARIBOU

All measurements must be made with a 1/4-inch wide flexible steel tape to the nearest
one-eighth of an inch. Wherever it is necessary to change direction of measurement, mark a
control point and swing tape at this point. (Note: A flexible steel cable can be used to
measure points and main beams only.) Enter fractional figures in eighths, without reduction.
Official measurements cannot be taken until the antlers have air dried for at least 60 days
after the animal was killed.

A. Tip to Tip Spread is measured between tips of main beams.

B. Greatest Spread is measured between perpendiculars at a right angle to the center line
of the skull at widest part, whether across main beams or points.

C. Inside Spread of Main Beams is measured at a right angle to the center line of the
skull at widest point between main beams. Enter this measurement again as the Spread Credit
if it is less than or equal to the length of the longer antler; if greater, enter longer
antler length for Spread Credit.

D. Number of Points on Each Antler: To be counted a point, a projection must be at least
one-half inch long, with length exceeding width at the point of measurement. Beam tip is
counted as a point but not measured as a point. There are no "abnormal" points in caribou.

E. Length of Main Beam is measured from lowest outside edge of burr over outer curve to
the most distant point of what is, or appears to be, the main beam. The point of beginning is
that point on the burr where the center line along the outer curve of the beam intersects the
burr.

F-1-2-3. Length of Points are measured from nearest edge of beam on the shortest line over
outer curve to tip. Lay the tape along the outer curve of the beam so that the top edge of
the tape coincides with the top edge of the beam on both sides of point to determine the
baseline for point measurement. Record point lengths in appropriate blanks.

F-4-5. Length of Points are measured from the tip of the point to the top of the beam,
then at a right angle to the lower edge of beam. The Second Longest Top Point cannot be a
point branch of the Longest Top Point.

G-1. Width of Brow is measured in a straight line from top edge to lower edge, as
illustrated, with measurement line at a right angle to main axis of brow.

G-2. Width of Top Palm is measured from midpoint of lower rear edge of main beam to
midpoint of a dip between points, at widest part of palm. The line of measurement begins and
ends at midpoints of palm edges, which gives credit for palm thickness.

H-1-2-3-4. Circumferences are taken as described for measurements. If brow point is
missing, take H-1 at smallest point between burr and bez point. If rear point is missing,
take H-2 and H-3 measurements at smallest place between bez and first top point. Do not
depress the tape into any dips of the palm or main beam.

FAIR CHASE STATEMENT FOR ALL HUNTER-TAKEN TROPHIES

FAIR CHASE, as defined by the Boone and Crockett Club, is the ethical, sportsmanlike and
lawful pursuit and taking of any free-ranging wild game animal in a manner that does not give
the hunter an improper or unfair advantage over such game animals.

Use of any of the following methods in the taking of game shall be deemed **UNFAIR CHASE**
and unsportsmanlike:

   I.   Spotting or herding game from the air, followed by landing in its vicinity for the
        purpose of pursuit and shooting;

   II. Herding, pursuing, or shooting game from any motorboat or motor vehicle;

   III. Use of electronic devices for attracting, locating, or observing game, or for
        guiding the hunter to such game;

   IV. Hunting game confined by artificial barriers, including escape-proof fenced
        enclosures, or hunting game transplanted solely for the purpose of commercial
        shooting;

   V.   Taking of game in a manner not in full compliance with the game laws or
        regulations of the federal government or of any state, province, territory, or
        tribal council on reservations or tribal lands;

   VI. Or as may otherwise be deemed unfair or unsportsmanlike by the Executive Committee
        of the Boone and Crockett Club.

I certify that the trophy scored on this chart was taken in **FAIR CHASE** as defined above by the
Boone and Crockett Club. In signing this statement, I understand that if this entry is found
to be fraudulent, it will not be accepted into the Awards program and all of my prior entries
are subject to deletion from future editions of *Records of North American Big Game* and future
entries may not be accepted.

Date: _____ Signature of Hunter: _____
(Have signature notarized by a Notary Public.)

Records of North American
Big Game

BOONE AND CROCKETT CLUB

Old Milwaukee Depot
250 Station Drive
Missoula, MT 59801

Minimum Score: Awards All-time
360 375

TYPICAL
AMERCIAN ELK (WAPITI)

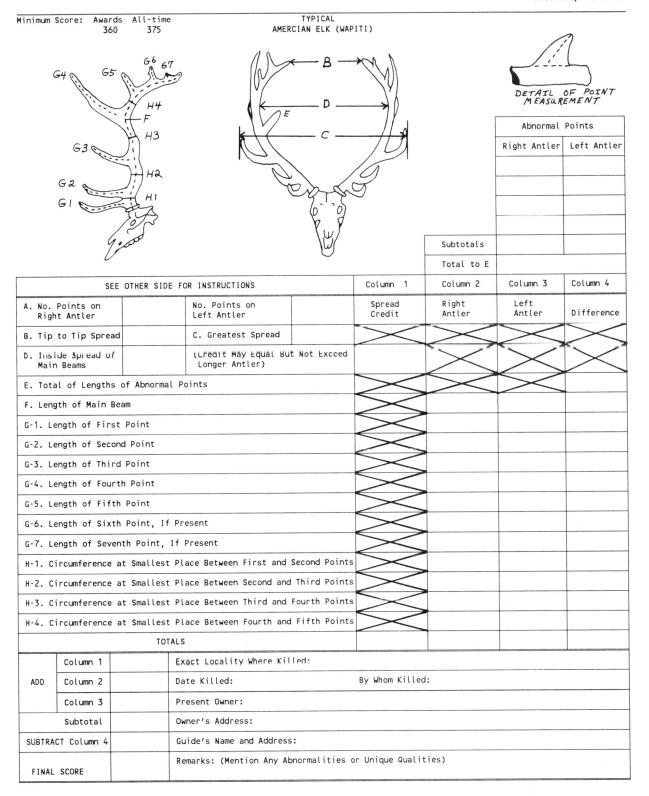

DETAIL OF POINT MEASUREMENT

	Abnormal Points	
	Right Antler	Left Antler
Subtotals		
Total to E		

SEE OTHER SIDE FOR INSTRUCTIONS				Column 1	Column 2	Column 3	Column 4
				Spread Credit	Right Antler	Left Antler	Difference
A. No. Points on Right Antler		No. Points on Left Antler					
B. Tip to Tip Spread		C. Greatest Spread					
D. Inside Spread of Main Beams		(Credit May Equal But Not Exceed Longer Antler)					
E. Total of Lengths of Abnormal Points							
F. Length of Main Beam							
G-1. Length of First Point							
G-2. Length of Second Point							
G-3. Length of Third Point							
G-4. Length of Fourth Point							
G-5. Length of Fifth Point							
G-6. Length of Sixth Point, If Present							
G-7. Length of Seventh Point, If Present							
H-1. Circumference at Smallest Place Between First and Second Points							
H-2. Circumference at Smallest Place Between Second and Third Points							
H-3. Circumference at Smallest Place Between Third and Fourth Points							
H-4. Circumference at Smallest Place Between Fourth and Fifth Points							
TOTALS							

ADD	Column 1		Exact Locality Where Killed:	
	Column 2		Date Killed:	By Whom Killed:
	Column 3		Present Owner:	
	Subtotal		Owner's Address:	
SUBTRACT Column 4			Guide's Name and Address:	
FINAL SCORE			Remarks: (Mention Any Abnormalities or Unique Qualities)	

I certify that I have measured this trophy on _____ 19 _____

at (address) _____ City _____ State _____
and that these measurements and data are, to the best of my knowledge and belief, made in
accordance with the instructions given.

Witness: _____ Signature: _____

                                                    B&C OFFICIAL MEASURER | | | | |

                                                    I.D. Number

INSTRUCTIONS FOR MEASURING TYPICAL AMERICAN ELK (WAPITI)

All measurements must be made with a 1/4-inch wide flexible steel tape to the nearest
one-eighth of an inch. Wherever it is necessary to change direction of measurement, mark a
control point and swing tape at this point. (Note: A flexible steel cable can be used to
measure points and main beams only.) Enter fractional figures in eighths, without reduction.
Official measurements cannot be taken until the antlers have air dried for at least 60 days
after the animal was killed.

A. Number of Points on Each Antler: To be counted a point, the projection must be at
least one inch long, with length exceeding width at one inch or more of length. All points
are measured from tip of point to nearest edge of beam as illustrated. Beam tip is counted as
a point but not measured as a point.

B. Tip to Tip Spread is measured between tips of main beams.

C. Greatest Spread is measured between perpendiculars at a right angle to the center line
of the skull at widest part, whether across main beams or points.

D. Inside Spread of Main Beams is measured at a right angle to the center line of the
skull at widest point between main beams. Enter this measurement again as the Spread Credit
if it is less than or equal to the length of the longer antler; if greater, enter longer
antler length for Spread Credit.

E. Total of Lengths of all Abnormal Points: Abnormal Points are those non-typical in
location (such as points originating from a point or from bottom or sides of main beam) or
pattern (extra points, not generally paired). Measure in usual manner and record in
appropriate blanks.

F. Length of Main Beam is measured from lowest outside edge of burr over outer curve to
the most distant point of what is, or appears to be, the main beam. The point of beginning is
that point on the burr where the center line along the outer curve of the beam intersects the
burr, then following generally the line of the illustration.

G-1-2-3-4-5-6-7. Length of Normal Points: Normal points project from the top or front of
the main beam in the general pattern illustrated. They are measured from nearest edge of main
beam over outer curve to tip. Lay the tape along the outer curve of the beam so that the top
edge of the tape coincides with the top edge of the beam on both sides of point to determine
the baseline for point measurement. Record point length in appropriate blanks.

H-1-2-3-4. Circumferences are taken as detailed for each measurement.

FAIR CHASE STATEMENT FOR ALL HUNTER-TAKEN TROPHIES

FAIR CHASE, as defined by the Boone and Crockett Club, is the ethical, sportsmanlike and
lawful pursuit and taking of any free-ranging wild game animal in a manner that does not give
the hunter an improper or unfair advantage over such game animals.

Use of any of the following methods in the taking of game shall be deemed **UNFAIR CHASE**
and unsportsmanlike:

  I.   Spotting or herding game from the air, followed by landing in its vicinity for the
       purpose of pursuit and shooting;

  II. Herding, pursuing, or shooting game from any motorboat or motor vehicle;

  III. Use of electronic devices for attracting, locating, or observing game, or for
       guiding the hunter to such game;

  IV. Hunting game confined by artificial barriers, including escape-proof fenced
       enclosures, or hunting game transplanted solely for the purpose of commercial
       shooting;

  V.   Taking of game in a manner not in full compliance with the game laws or
       regulations of the federal government or of any state, province, territory, or
       tribal council on reservations or tribal lands;

  VI. Or as may otherwise be deemed unfair or unsportsmanlike by the Executive Committee
       of the Boone and Crockett Club.

I certify that the trophy scored on this chart was taken in **FAIR CHASE** as defined above by the
Boone and Crockett Club. In signing this statement, I understand that if this entry is found
to be fraudulent, it will not be accepted into the Awards program and all of my prior entries
are subject to deletion from future editions of *Records of North American Big Game* and future
entries may not be accepted.

Date: _____ Signature of Hunter: _____
                                             (Have signature notarized by a Notary Public.)

Copyright © 1993 by Boone and Crockett Club
(Reproduction strictly forbidden without express, written consent)

OFFICIAL SCORING SYSTEM FOR NORTH AMERICAN BIG GAME TROPHIES

Records of North American
Big Game

BOONE AND CROCKETT CLUB

Old Milwaukee Depot
250 Station Drive
Missoula, MT 59801

Minimum Score: Awards All-time   MOOSE   Kind of Moose _Canada_
Alaska-Yukon   210   224
Canada   185   195
Wyoming   140   155

DETAIL OF POINT MEASUREMENT

SEE OTHER SIDE FOR INSTRUCTIONS	Column 1	Column 2	Column 3	Column 4
		Right Antler	Left Antler	Difference
A. Greatest Spread	61 3/8			
B. Number of Abnormal Points on Both Antlers				O
C. Number of Normal Points		12	10	2
D. Width of Palm		16 3/8	17 1/8	6/8
E. Length of Palm Including Brow Palm		42 2/8	40	2 2/8
F. Cirumference of Beam at Smallest Place		7	7 3/8	3/8
TOTALS	61 3/8	77 5/8	74 5/8	5 3/8

ADD	Column 1	61 3/8	Exact Locality Where Killed:
	Column 2	77 5/8	Date Killed: By Whom Killed:
	Column 3	74 4/8	Present Owner:
SUBTOTAL		213 4/8	Owner's Address:
SUBTRACT Column 4		5 3/8	Guide's Name and Address:
FINAL SCORE		208 1/8	Remarks: (Mention Any Abnormalities or Unique Qualities)

I certify that I have measured this trophy on _____ 19 _____

at (address) _____ City _____ State _____
and that these measurements and data are, to the best of my knowledge and belief, made in
accordance with the instructions given.

Witness: _____ Signature: _____

B&C OFFICIAL MEASURER

I.D. Number

Boone and Crockett scoring form for moose   •   213

INSTRUCTIONS FOR MEASURING MOOSE

Measurements must be made with a 1/4-inch wide flexible steel tape to the nearest one-eighth of an inch. Enter fractional figures in eighths, without reduction. Official measurements cannot be taken until antlers have air dried for at least 60 days after animal was killed.

A. Greatest Spread is measured between perpendiculars in a straight line at a right angle to the center line of the skull.

B. Number of Abnormal Points on Both Antlers: Abnormal points are those projections originating from normal points or from the upper or lower palm surface, or from the inner edge of palm (see illustration). Abnormal points must be at least one inch long, with length exceeding width at one inch or more of length.

C. Number of Normal Points: Normal points originate from the outer edge of palm. To be counted a point, a projection must be at least one inch long, with the length exceeding width at one inch or more of length.

D. Width of Palm is taken in contact with the under surface of palm, at a right angle to the length of palm measurement line. The line of measurement should begin and end at the midpoint of the palm edge, which gives credit for the desirable character of palm thickness.

E. Length of Palm including Brow Palm is taken in contact with the surface along the underside of the palm, parallel to the inner edge, from dips between points at the top to dips between points (if present) at the bottom. If a bay is present, measure across the open bay if the proper line of measurement, parrallel to inner edge, follows this path. The line of measurement should begin and end at the midpoint of the palm edge, which gives credit for the desirable character of palm thickness.

F. Circumference of Beam at Smallest Place is taken as illustrated.

FAIR CHASE STATEMENT FOR ALL HUNTER-TAKEN TROPHIES

FAIR CHASE, as defined by the Boone and Crockett Club, is the ethical, sportsmanlike and lawful pursuit and taking of any free-ranging wild game animal in a manner that does not give the hunter an improper or unfair advantage over such game animals.

Use of any of the following methods in the taking of game shall be deemed **UNFAIR CHASE** and unsportsmanlike:

I. Spotting or herding game from the air, followed by landing in its vicinity for the purpose of pursuit and shooting;

II. Herding, pursuing, or shooting game from any motorboat or motor vehicle;

III. Use of electronic devices for attracting, locating, or observing game, or for guiding the hunter to such game;

IV. Hunting game confined by artificial barriers, including escape-proof fenced enclosures, or hunting game transplanted solely for the purpose of commercial shooting;

V. Taking of game in a manner not in full compliance with the game laws or regulations of the federal government or of any state, province, territory, or tribal council on reservations or tribal lands;

VI. Or as may otherwise be deemed unfair or unsportsmanlike by the Executive Committee of the Boone and Crockett Club.

I certify that the trophy scored on this chart was taken in **FAIR CHASE** as defined above by the Boone and Crockett Club. In signing this statement, I understand that if this entry is found to be fraudulent, it will not be accepted into the Awards program and all of my prior entries are subject to deletion from future editions of *Records of North American Big Game* and future entries may not be accepted.

Date: _____ Signature of Hunter: _____
(Have signature notarized by a Notary Public.)

Records of North American
Big Game

BOONE AND CROCKETT CLUB

Old Milwaukee Depot
250 Station Drive
Missoula, MT 59801

Minimum Score: Awards All-time
80 82

PRONGHORN

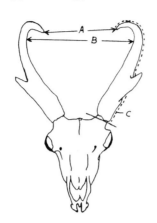
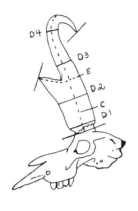

SEE OTHER SIDE FOR INSTRUCTIONS		Column 1	Column 2	Column 3
A. Tip to Tip Spread	2	Right Horn	Left Horn	
B. Inside Spread of Main Beams	8			Difference
IF Inside Spread Exceeds Longer Horn, Enter Difference		✕	✕	-
C. Length of Horn		17 5/8	17	5/8
D-1. Circumference of Base		5 7/8	5 7/8	-
D-2. Circumference at First Quarter		6 3/8	6 5/8	2/8
D-3. Circumference at Second Quarter		4 1/8	3 7/8	2/8
D-4. Circumference at Third Quarter		3 2/8	3 1/8	1/8
E. Length of Prong		6 1/8	6 3/8	2/8
TOTALS		43 3/8	42 7/8	1 4/8

ADD	Column 1	43 3/8	Exact Locality Where Killed:
	Column 2	42 7/8	Date Killed: By Whom Killed:
SUBTOTAL		86 2/8	Present Owner:
SUBTRACT Column 3		1 4/8	Owner's Address:
FINAL SCORE			Guide's Name and Address:
		84 6/8	Remarks: (Mention Any Abnormalities or Unique Qualities) HORN TIPS OVERLAP

I certify that I have measured this trophy on _____ 19 _____

at (address) _____ City _____ State _____
and that these measurements and data are, to the best of my knowledge and belief, made in
accordance with the instructions given.

Witness: _____ Signature: _____

B&C OFFICIAL MEASURER [ ][ ][ ]

I.D. Number

INSTRUCTIONS FOR MEASURING PRONGHORN

All measurements must be made with a 1/4-inch wide flexible steel tape to the nearest one-eighth of an inch. Wherever it is necessary to change direction of measurement, mark a control point and swing tape at this point. Enter fractional figures in <u>eighths</u>, without reduction. Official measurements cannot be taken until horns have air dried for at least 60 days after the animal was killed.

A. Tip to Tip Spread is measured between tips of horns.

B. Inside Spread of Main Beams is measured at a right angle to the center line of the skull, at widest point between main beams.

C. Length of Horn is measured on the outside curve on the general line illustrated. The line taken will very with different heads, depending on the direction of their curvature. Measure along the center of the outer curve from tip of horn to a point in line with the lowest edge of the base, using a straight edge to establish the line end.

D-1. Measure around base of horn at a right angle to long axis. Tape must be in contact with the lowest circumference of the horn in which there are no serrations.

D-2-3-4. Divide measurement C of longer horn by four. Starting at base, mark <u>both</u> horns at these quarters (even though the other horn is shorter) and measure circumferences at these marks. If the prong interferes with D-2, move the measurement down to just below the swelling of the prong. If the prong interferes with D-3, move the measurement up to just above the swelling of the prong.

E. Length of Prong: Measure from the tip of the prong along the upper edge of the outer curve to the horn; then continue around the horn to a point at the rear of the horn where a straight edge across the back of both horns touches the horn, with the latter part being at a right angle to the long axis of horn.

FAIR CHASE STATEMENT FOR ALL HUNTER-TAKEN TROPHIES

FAIR CHASE, as defined by the Boone and Crockett Club, is the ethical, sportsmanlike and lawful pursuit and taking of any free-ranging wild game animal in a manner that does not give the hunter an improper or unfair advantage over such game animals.

Use of any of the following methods in the taking of game shall be deemed **UNFAIR CHASE** and unsportsmanlike:

I. Spotting or herding game from the air, followed by landing in its vicinity for the purpose of pursuit and shooting;

II. Herding, pursuing, or shooting game from any motorboat or motor vehicle;

III. Use of electronic devices for attracting, locating, or observing game, or for guiding the hunter to such game;

IV. Hunting game confined by artificial barriers, including escape-proof fenced enclosures, or hunting game transplanted solely for the purpose of commercial shooting;

V. Taking of game in a manner not in full compliance with the game laws or regulations of the federal government or of any state, province, territory, or tribal council on reservations or tribal lands;

VI. Or as may otherwise be deemed unfair or unsportsmanlike by the Executive Committee of the Boone and Crockett Club.

I certify that the trophy scored on this chart was taken in **FAIR CHASE** as defined above by the Boone and Crockett Club. In signing this statement, I understand that if this entry is found to be fraudulent, it will not be accepted into the Awards program and all of my prior entries are subject to deletion from future editions of *Records of North American Big Game* and future entries may not be accepted.

Date: _____ Signature of Hunter: _____
(Have signature notarized by a Notary Public.)

Records of North American
Big Game

BOONE AND CROCKETT CLUB

Old Milwaukee Depot
250 Station Drive
Missoula, MT 59801

Minimum Score: Awards All-time   ROCKY MOUNTAIN GOAT   Sex _____
                  47   50

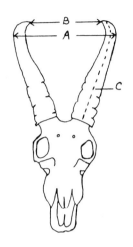
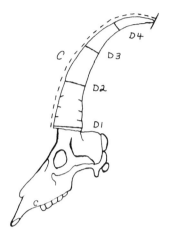

SEE OTHER SIDE FOR INSTRUCTIONS		Column 1	Column 2	Column 3
A. Greatest Spread		Right Horn	Left Horn	Difference
B. Tip to Tip Spread				
C. Length of Horn				
D-1. Circumference of Base				
D-2. Circumference at First Quarter				
D-3. Circumference at Second Quarter				
D-4. Circumference at Third Quarter				
TOTALS				

ADD	Column 1		Exact Locality Where Killed:
	Column 2		Date Killed: By Whom Killed:
SUBTOTAL			Present Owner:
SUBTRACT Column 3			Owner's Address:
FINAL SCORE			Guide's Name and Address:
			Remarks: (Mention Any Abnormalities or Unique Qualities)

I certify that I have measured this trophy on _____ 19 _____

at (address) _____ City _____ State _____
and that these measurements and data are, to the best of my knowledge and belief, made in
accordance with the instructions given.

Witness: _____   Signature: _____

                                                B&C OFFICIAL MEASURER   [ ][ ][ ]

                                                            I.D. Number

INSTRUCTIONS FOR MEASURING ROCKY MOUNTAIN GOAT

All measurements must be made with a 1/4-inch wide flexible steel tape to the nearest one-eighth of an inch. Wherever it is necessary to change direction of measurement, mark a control point and swing tape at this point. Enter fractional figures in eighths, without reduction. Official measurements cannot be taken until horns have air dried for at least 60 days after the animal was killed.

A. Greatest Spread is measured between perpendiculars at a right angle to the center line of the skull.

B. Tip to Tip spread is measured between tips of the horns.

C. Length of Horn is measured from the lowest point in front over outer curve to a point in line with tip.

D-1. Circumference of Base is measured at a right angle to axis of horn. Do not follow irregular edge of horn.

D-2-3-4. Divide measurement C of longer horn by four. Starting at base, mark both horns at these quarters (even though the other horn is shorter) and measure circumferences at these marks.

FAIR CHASE STATEMENT FOR ALL HUNTER-TAKEN TROPHIES

FAIR CHASE, as defined by the Boone and Crockett Club, is the ethical, sportsmanlike and lawful pursuit and taking of any free-ranging wild game animal in a manner that does not give the hunter an improper or unfair advantage over such game animals.

Use of any of the following methods in the taking of game shall be deemed **UNFAIR CHASE** and unsportsmanlike:

I. Spotting or herding game from the air, followed by landing in its vicinity for the purpose of pursuit and shooting;

II. Herding, pursuing, or shooting game from any motorboat or motor vehicle;

III. Use of electronic devices for attracting, locating, or observing game, or for guiding the hunter to such game;

IV. Hunting game confined by artificial barriers, including escape-proof fenced enclosures, or hunting game transplanted solely for the purpose of commercial shooting;

V. Taking of game in a manner not in full compliance with the game laws or regulations of the federal government or of any state, province, territory, or tribal council on reservations or tribal lands;

VI. Or as may otherwise be deemed unfair or unsportsmanlike by the Executive Committee of the Boone and Crockett Club.

I certify that the trophy scored on this chart was taken in **FAIR CHASE** as defined above by the Boone and Crockett Club. In signing this statement, I understand that if this entry is found to be fraudulent, it will not be accepted into the Awards program and all of my prior entries are subject to deletion from future editions of *Records of North American Big Game* and future entries may not be accepted.

Date: _____ Signature of Hunter: _____
                                       (Have signature notarized by a Notary Public.)

OFFICIAL SCORING SYSTEM FOR NORTH AMERICAN BIG GAME TROPHIES

Records of North American Big Game	BOONE AND CROCKETT CLUB	Old Milwaukee Depot 250 Station Drive Missoula, MT 59801

Minimum Score:	Awards	All-time	SHEEP	Kind of Sheep:_____
bighorn	175	180		
desert	165	168		
Dall's	160	170		
Stone's	165	170		

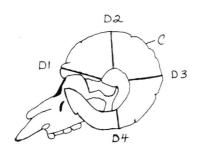 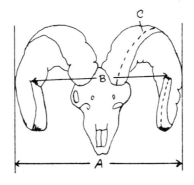 

MEASURE TO
A POINT IN
LINE WITH
HORN TIP

SEE OTHER SIDE FOR INSTRUCTIONS		Column 1	Column 2	Column 3
A. Greatest Spread (Is Often Tip to Tip Spread)		Right Horn	Left Horn	Difference
B. Tip to Tip Spread				
C. Length of Horn				✕
D-1. Circumference of Base				
D-2. Circumference at First Quarter				
D-3. Circumference at Second Quarter				
D-4. Circumference at Third Quarter				
TOTALS				

ADD	Column 1		Exact Locality Where Killed:
	Column 2		Date Killed: By Whom Killed:
SUBTOTAL			Present Owner:
SUBTRACT Column 3			Owner's Address:
FINAL SCORE			Guide's Name and Address:
			Remarks: (Mention Any Abnormalities or Unique Qualities)

I certify that I have measured this trophy on _____ 19 _____

at (address) _____ City _____ State _____
and that these measurements and data are, to the best of my knowledge and belief, made in
accordance with the instructions given.

Witness: _____   Signature: _____

B&C OFFICIAL MEASURER

I.D. Number

INSTRUCTIONS FOR MEASURING SHEEP

All measurements must be made with a 1/4-inch wide flexible steel tape to the nearest one-eighth of an inch. Wherever it is necessary to change direction of measurement, mark a control point and swing tape at this point. Enter fractional figures in eights, without reduction. Official measurements cannot be taken until horns have air dried for at least 60 days after the animal was killed.

A. Greatest Spread is measured between perpendiculars at a right angle to the center line of the skull.

B. Tip to Tip Spread is measured between tips of horns.

C. Length of Horn is measured from the lowest point in front on outer curve to a point in line with tip. Do not press tape into depressions. The low point of the outer curve of the horn is considered to be the low point of the frontal portion of the horn, situated above and slightly medial to the eye socket (not the outside edge). Use a straight edge, perpendicular to horn axis, to end measurement on "broomed" horns.

D-1. Circumference of Base is measured at a right angle to axis of horn. Do not follow irregular edge of horn; the line of measurement must be entirely on horn material, not the jagged edge often noted.

D-2-3-4. Divide measurement C of longer horn by four. Starting at base, mark both horns at these quarters (even though the other horn is shorter) and measure circumferences at these marks, with measurements taken at right angles to horn axis.

FAIR CHASE STATEMENT FOR ALL HUNTER-TAKEN TROPHIES

FAIR CHASE, as defined by the Boone and Crockett Club, is the ethical, sportsmanlike and lawful pursuit and taking of any free-ranging wild game animal in a manner that does not give the hunter an improper or unfair advantage over such game animals.

Use of any of the following methods in the taking of game shall be deemed UNFAIR CHASE and unsportsmanlike:

    I.   Spotting or herding game from the air, followed by landing in its vicinity for the purpose of pursuit and shooting;

   II.   Herding, pursuing, or shooting game from any motorboat or motor vehicle;

  III.   Use of electronic devices for attracting, locating, or observing game, or for guiding the hunter to such game;

   IV.   Hunting game confined by artificial barriers, including escape-proof fenced enclosures, or hunting game transplanted solely for the purpose of commercial shooting;

    V.   Taking of game in a manner not in full compliance with the game laws or regulations of the federal government or of any state, province, territory, or tribal council on reservations or tribal lands;

   VI.   Or as may otherwise be deemed unfair or unsportsmanlike by the Executive Committee of the Boone and Crockett Club.

I certify that the trophy scored on this chart was taken in FAIR CHASE as defined above by the Boone and Crockett Club. In signing this statement, I understand that if this entry is found to be fraudulent, it will not be accepted into the Awards program and all of my prior entries are subject to deletion from future editions of Records of North American Big Game and future entries may not be accepted.

Date: _____ Signature of Hunter: _____

(Have signature notarized by a Notary Public.)

Records of North American
Big Game

BOONE AND CROCKETT CLUB

Old Milwaukee Depot
250 Station Drive
Missoula, MT 59801

Minimum Score: Awards All-time
115 115

BISON

Sex _____

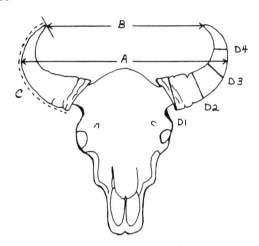

SEE OTHER SIDE FOR INSTRUCTIONS		Column 1	Column 2	Column 3
A. Greatest Spread		Right Horn	Left Horn	Difference
B. Tip to Tip Spread				
C. Length of Horn				
D-1. Circumference of Base				
D-2. Circumference at First Quarter				
D-3. Circumference at Second Quarter				
D-4. Circumference at Third Quarter				
TOTALS				

ADD	Column 1		Exact Locality Where Killed:
	Column 2		Date Killed: By Whom Killed:
SUBTOTAL			Present Owner:
SUBTRACT Column 3			Owner's Address:
FINAL SCORE			Guide's Name and Address:
			Remarks: (Mention Any Abnormalities or Unique Qualities)

I certify that I have measured this trophy on _____ 19 _____

at (address) _____ City _____ State _____
and that these measurements and data are, to the best of my knowledge and belief, made in
accordance with the instructions given.

Witness: _____   Signature: _____

B&C OFFICIAL MEASURER

I.D. Number

INSTRUCTIONS FOR MEASURING BISON

All measurements must be made with a 1/4-inch wide flexible steel tape to the nearest one-eighth of an inch. Wherever it is necessary to change direction of measurement, mark a control point and swing tape at this point. Enter fractional figures in eighths, without reduction. Official measurements cannot be taken until horns have air dried for at least 60 days after the animal was killed.

A.   Greatest Spread is measured between perpendiculars at a right angel to the center line of the skull.

B.   Tip to Tip Spread is measured between tips of horns.

C.   Length of Horn is measured from the lowest point on underside over outer curve to a point in line with the tip. Use a straight edge, perpendicular to horn axis, to end the measurement, if necessary.

D-1. Circumference of Base is measured at right angle to axis of horn. Do not follow the irregular edge of horn; the line of measurement must be entirely on horn material, not the jagged edge often noted.

D-2-3-4. Divide measurement C of longer horn by four. Starting at base, mark both horns at these quarters (even though the other horn is shorter) and measure the circumferences at these marks, with measurements taken at right angles to horn axis.

FAIR CHASE STATEMENT FOR ALL HUNTER-TAKEN TROPHIES

FAIR CHASE, as defined by the Boone and Crockett Club, is the ethical, sportsmanlike and lawful pursuit and taking of any free-ranging wild game animal in a manner that does not give the hunter an improper or unfair advantage over such game animals.
Use of any of the following methods in the taking of game shall be deemed **UNFAIR CHASE** and unsportsmanlike:

I.   Spotting or herding game from the air, followed by landing in its vicinity for the purpose of pursuit and shooting;

II.   Herding, pursuing, or shooting game from any motorboat or motor vehicle;

III.   Use of electronic devices for attracting, locating, or observing game, or for guiding the hunter to such game;

IV.   Hunting game confined by artificial barriers, including escape-proof fenced enclosures, or hunting game transplanted solely for the purpose of commercial shooting;

V.   Taking of game in a manner not in full compliance with the game laws or regulations of the federal government or of any state, province, territory, or tribal council on reservations or tribal lands;

VI.   Or as may otherwise be deemed unfair or unsportsmanlike by the Executive Committee of the Boone and Crockett Club.

I certify that the trophy scored on this chart was taken in **FAIR CHASE** as defined above by the Boone and Crockett Club. In signing this statement, I understand that if this entry is found to be fraudulent, it will not be accepted into the Awards program and all of my prior entries are subject to deletion from future editions of *Records of North American Big Game* and future entries may not be accepted.

Date: _____   Signature of Hunter: _____
(Have signature notarized by a Notary Public.)

Unit Definitions and Conversions

SYMBOL	UNIT	CONVERSION
Length		
μ	*micron*	10^{-6} meters
mm	*millimetre*	10^{-3} meters
cm	*centimetre*	10^{-2} meters
m	*metre*	39.4 inches (in) = 3.28 feet
km	*kilometre*	0.62 miles = 3281 feet
Weight		
mg	*milligram*	10^{-6} kg
g	*gram*	10^{-3} kg
kg	*kilogram*	1000 g = 2.205 pounds (lb)
t	*tonne*	1000 kg
Area		
m^2	*square metre*	10,776 square feet (ft^2)
ha	*hectare*	10,000 square metres = 0.01 km^2 = 2.47 acres
km^2	*square kilometre*	0.386 square miles = 100 ha
Energy		
J	*joule*	0.239 calories (cal)
kJ	*kilojoule*	1000 J
Volume		
ml	*millilitre*	1 cubic centimeter (cm^3) − 0.061 cubic inches (in^3)
l	*litre*	1000 ml = .220 Imperial gallon = .264 U.S. gallon
Temperature		
°C	*centigrade*	
Frequency		
kHz	*kilohertz*	

References

1. INTRODUCTION

Anonymous. 1992. *An illustrated guide to bison phenotypes*. Produced by the Taxonomy Subcommittee of the Wood Bison Recover yTeam, Edmonton.

Bork, A.M., Strobeck, C.M., Yet, F.C., Hudson, R.J., and Salmon, R.K. 1991. Genetic relationship of wood and plains bison based on restriction fragment length polymorphisms. *Canadian Journal of Zoology*, 69: 43–48.

Burns, J.A. 1992. (personal communication). Curator, Quaternary Paleontology, Provincial Museum of Alberta. Alberta Culture and Multiculturalism, Edmonton.

Jones, J.K., Hoffmann, R.S., Rice, D.W., Jones, C., Baker, R.J., and Engstrom, M.D. 1992. *Revised checklist of North American mammals north of Mexico, 1991*. Occasional Papers, The Museum, Texas Tech University No. 46. Lubbock, Texas.

Kurten, B., and Anderson, E. 1980. *Pleistocene mammals of North America*. Columbia University Press. New York, N.Y.

Neuman, P.W. 1971. *An examination of genetic variation in plains bison* (Bison bison bison) *and wood bison* (Bison bison athabascae) *and their hybrids*. Canadian Wildlife Service, Edmonton. Unpublished report.

Peden, D.G. and Kraay, G.J. 1979. Comparison of blood characteristics in plains bison, wood bison, and their hybrids. *Canadian Journal of Zoology*, 57: 778-784.

Stelfox, J.B., Peleshok, L., and Nietfeld, M.T. 1991. *A selected bibliography of research, management, and biology of Alberta's native ungulates*. Alberta Environmental Centre, Department of Environmental Protection, Vegreville.

van Zyll de Jong, C.G. 1986. *A systematic study of recent bison, with particular consideration of the wood bison* (Bison bison athabascae Rhoads 1898). Publication of Natural Sciences No. 6. National Museum of Canada, Ottawa, Ont.

2. IDENTIFICATION

Geist, V., and Karsten, P. 1977. The wood bison (*Bison bison athabascae* Rhoads) in relation to hypotheses on the origin of the American bison (*Bison bison* Linnaeus). *Z. Saugetierk.*, 42: 119–127.

Gilbert, B.M. 1990. *Mammalian osteology*. Missouri Archaeological Society. University of Missouri, Columbia, Mo.

Halfpenny, J. 1992. (personal communication). Freelance ecologist. Gardner, Montana.

Kennedy, A.J., and Carbyn, L.N. 1981. *Identification of wolf prey using hair and feather remains with special reference to western Canadian National Parks*. Canadian Wildlife Service, Edmonton. Unpublished report.

Wishart, W.D. 1984. Frequency of antlered white-tailed does in Camp Wainwright, Alberta. *Journal of Wildlife Management*, 49: 386–388.

Wishart, W.D. 1986. *The Wainwright deer herd (1966-1984): a comparative study of white-tails and mule deer*. Alberta Fish and Wildlife Division, Edmonton. Unpublished report.

Wishart, W.D. 1992. (personal communication). Adjunct professor, Department of Zoology, University of Alberta, Edmonton.

3. COMMUNICATION

Albone, E.S. 1984. *Mammalian semiochemistry — The investigation of chemical signals between mammals*. John Wiley & Sons, Chichester, U.K.

Altmann, M. 1956. Patterns of herd behavior in free-ranging elk of Wyoming *Cervus canadensis nelsoni*. *Zoologica* (N.Y.), 41: 65–71.

Bergerud, A.T. 1974. Rutting behaviour of Newfoundland caribou. pp. 395–435. In: *The behaviour of ungulates and its relation to management*. Volume 1. Geist V., and Walther F. (editors). IUCN Publication New Series 24. IUCN, Morges, Switzerland.

Bouckhout, L.W. 1972. *The behaviour of mule deer* (Odocoileus hemionus hemionus Rafinesque) *in winter in relation to the social and physical environment*. M.Sc. Thesis, University of Calgary, Calgary.

Bowyer, R.T. 1986. Antler characteristics as related to social status of male southern mule deer. *Southwestern Naturalist*, 31: 289–298.

Bowyer, R.T., and Kitchen, D.W. 1987a. Sex and age-class differences in vocalizations of Roosevelt elk during rut. *American Midland Naturalist*, 118: 225–235.

Bowyer, R.T., and Kitchen, D.W. 1987b. Significance of scent-marking by Roosevelt elk. *Journal of Mammalogy*, 68: 418–423.

Bromley, P.T. 1977. *Aspects of the behavioural ecology and sociobiology of the pronghorn* (Antilocapra americana). Ph.D. Thesis, University of Calgary, Calgary.

Bromley, P.T., and Kitchen, D.W. 1974. Courtship in the pronghorn (*Antilocapra americana*). pp. 356–364. In: *The behaviour of ungulates and its relation to management*. Volume 1. Geist, V., and Walther F. (editors). IUCN Publication New Series 24. IUCN, Morges, Switzerland.

Bubenik, A.B. 1982. Physiology. pp. 125–179. In: *Elk of North America — Ecology and management*. Thomas, J.W. and Toweill, D.E. (editors). Stackpole Books, Harrisburg, Pa.

Burghardt, G.M. 1977. Ontogeny of communication. pp. 71–97. In: *How animals communicate*. Sebeok T.A. (editor). Indiana University Press, Bloomington, In.

Cowan, I. McT., and Geist, V. 1961. Aggressive behavior in deer of the genus *Odocoileus*. *Journal of Mammalogy*, 42: 522–526.

Dawkins, R., and Krebs, J.R. 1978. Animal signals: Information or manipulation? pp. 282–309. In: *Behavioral ecology – An evolutionary approach*. Krebs, J.R. and Davies, N.B. (editors). Sinauer Associates, Inc., Sunderland, Mass.

de Vos, A. 1958. Summer observations on moose in Ontario. *Journal of Mammalogy*, 39: 128–139.

Espmark, Y. 1971. Individual recognition by voice in reindeer mother-young relationship. Field observations and playback experiments. *Behaviour*, 40: 295–301.

Geist, V. 1963. On the behaviour of the North American moose (*Alces alces andersoni* Peterson 1950) in British Columbia. *Behaviour*, 20: 377–416.

Geist, V. 1964. On the rutting behavior of the mountain goat. *Journal of Mammalogy*, 45: 551–568.

Geist, V. 1966. Ethological observations on some North American cervids. *Zoologische Beitraege*, 12 (N.S.): 219–250.

Geist, V. 1971. *Mountain sheep — A study in behavior and evolution*. University of Chicago Press, Chicago, Ill.

Geist, V. 1978. *Life strategies, human evolution, environmental design — Toward a biological theory of health*. Springer-Verlag, New York, N.Y.

Geist, V. 1981. Behavior: Adaptive strategies in mule deer. pp. 157–223. In: *Mule and black-tailed deer of North America*. Wallmo, O.C. (editor). University of Nebraska Press, Lincoln, Neb.

Geist, V. 1982. Adaptive behavioral strategies. pp. 219–277. In: *Elk of North America — Ecology and management*. Thomas, J.W. and Toweill, D.E. (editors). Stackpole Books, Harrisburg, Penn.

Geist, V. 1992. (personal communication). Professor, Department of Environmental Design, University of Calgary, Calgary.

Gunderson, H.L., and Mahan, B.R. 1980. Analysis of sonagrams of American bison (*Bison bison*). *Journal of Mammalogy*, 61: 379–381.

Hailman, J.P. 1977. *Optical signals*. Indiana University Press, Bloomington, In.

Halls, L.K. 1978. White-tailed deer. pp. 43–65. In: *Big game of North America — Ecology and management*. Schmidt, J.L. and Gilbert, D.L. (editors). Stackpole Books, Harrisburg, Penn.

Hirth, D.H. 1977. Social behavior of white-tailed deer in relation to habitat. *Wildlife Monograph*, 53: 1–55.

Kitchen, D.W., and Bromley, P.T. 1974. Agonistic behavior of territorial pronghorn bucks. pp. 365–381. In: *The behaviour of ungulates and its relation to management*. Volume 1. Geist, V. and Walther, F. (editors). IUCN Publication New Series 24. IUCN, Morges, Switzerland.

Krebs, J.R., and Dawkins, R. 1984. Animal signals: mind-reading and manipulation. pp. 380–402. In: *Behavioural ecology — An evolutionary approach*. Krebs, J.R. and Davies, N.B. (editors). Blackwell Scientific Publications, Oxford.

Lent, P.C. 1965. Rutting behavior in a barren-ground caribou population. *Animal Behavior*, 13: 259–264.

Lent, P.C. 1966. Calving and related social behavior in the barren-ground caribou. *Zeitschrift fuer Tierpsychologie*, 23: 702–756.

Lent, P.C. 1974a. Mother-infant relationships in ungulates. pp. 14–55. In: *The behaviour of ungulates and its relation to management*. Volume 1. Geist, V. and Walther, F. (editors). IUCN Publication new series 24. IUCN, Morges, Switzerland.

Lent, P.C. 1974b. A review of rutting behaviour in moose. *Naturaliste Canadienne (Que.)*, 101: 307–323.

Lott, D.F. 1974. Sexual and aggressive behaviour of adult male American bison (*Bison bison*). pp. 382–394. In: *The behaviour of ungulates and its relation to management*. Volume 1. Geist, V. and Walther, F. (editors). IUCN Publication New Series 24. IUCN, Morges, Switzerland.

Manning, A. 1979. *An introduction to animal behaviour*. Edward Arnold, London, U.K.

Moore, W.G., and Marchinton, R.L. 1974. Marking behaviour and its social function in white-tailed deer. pp. 447–456. In: *The behaviour of ungulates and its relation to management*. Volume 1. Geist, V. and Walther, F. (editors). IUCN Publication New Series 24. IUCN, Morges, Switzerland.

Moynihan, M. 1970. Control, suppression, decay, disappearance and replacement of displays. *Journal of Theoretical Biology*, 29: 85–112.

Müller-Schwarze, D. 1974. Social functions of various scent glands in certain ungulates and the problems encountered in experimental studies of scent communication. pp. 107–113. In: *The behaviour of ungulates and its relation to management*. Volume 1. Geist, V. and Walther, F. (editors). IUCN Publication New Series 24. IUCN, Morges, Switzerland.

Müller-Schwarze, D. 1987. Evolution of cervid olfactory communication. pp. 223–234. In: *Biology and management of the Cervidae*. Wemmer, C.M. (editor). Research Symposia of the National Zoological Park, Smithsonian Institution. Smithsonian Institution Press, Washington, D.C.

Murie, O.J. 1932. Elk calls. *Journal of Mammalogy*, 13: 331–336.

Park, E. 1969. *The world of the bison*. J.B. Lippincott, Philadelphia, Penn.

Pruitt, W.O. Jr. 1960. Behavior of the barren-ground caribou. *Biological papers of the University of Alaska*, No. 3. University of Alaska, Fairbanks, Alaska.

Richardson, L.W., Jacobson, H.A., Muncy, R.J., and Perkins, C.J. 1983. Acoustics of white-tailed deer (*Odocoileus virginianus*). *Journal of Mammalogy*, 64: 245–252.

Rideout, C.B. 1978. Mountain goat. pp. 149–159. In: *Big game of North America–Ecology and management*. Schmidt, J.L. and Gilbert, D.L. (editors). Stackpole Books, Harrisburg, Penn.

Smith, W.J. 1977. *The behavior of communicating*. Harvard University Press, Cambridge, Mass.

Smith, W.J. 1985. Consistency and change in communication. pp. 51–75. In: *The development of expressive behavior: Biology-environment interactions*. Zivin, G. (editor). Academic Press, New York, N.Y.

Spencer, C.C. 1943. The life history of Rocky Mountain bighorn sheep in the Tarryall Mountains of Colorado. *Journal of Mammalogy*, 24: 1–11.

Struhsaker, T.T. 1967. Behavior of elk (*Cervus canadensis*) during the rut. *Zeitschrift fuer Tierpsychologie*, 24: 80–114.

Tavolga, W.N. 1968. Fishes. pp. 271–288. In: *Animal communication — Techniques of study and results of research*. Sebeok, T.A. (editor). Indiana University Press, Bloomington, In.

Tavolga, W.N. 1983. Theoretical principles for the study of communication in cetaceans. *Mammalia*, 47: 3–26.

Walther, F.R. 1984. *Communication and expression in hoofed mammals*. Indiana University Press, Bloomington, In.

Wilson, E.O. 1975. *Sociobiology — The new synthesis*. Harvard University Press, Cambridge, Mass.

4. DISTRIBUTION

Alberta Fish and Wildlife Division (AFWD), 1974. *Management plan for moose in Alberta.* Alberta Fish and Wildlife Division, Edmonton.

Alberta Fish and Wildlife Division (AFWD), 1992. *Elk management plan for Alberta.* Alberta Fish and Wildlife Division, Edmonton.

Allen, J.R. 1985. *Aerial survey for ungulates in Priddis-Millarville and Bragg Creek areas, January 28, 1985 and March 22, 1985.* Alberta Fish and Wildlife Division, Edmonton. Unpublished report.

Barrett, M.W. 1980. Seasonal habitat associations of pronghorns in Alberta. pp. 174–195. In: *Proceedings: Ninth Biennial Pronghorn Antelope Workshop,* 1980: 174-195.

Blyth, C.B., and Hudson, R.J. 1987. *A plan for the management of vegetation and ungulates of Elk Island National Park.* Department of Animal Science, University of Alberta, Edmonton. Unpublished report.

Bradford, W. 1992. (personal communication). Warden, Jasper National Park.

Clarkson, P.L., Schmidt, K.P., and Gunson, J.R. 1984. *Evaluation of wolf-ungulate predation near Nordegg, Alberta: first year progress report, 1983–84.* Alberta Fish and Wildlife Division, Edmonton. Unpublished report.

Cowan, I., McT. 1950. Some vital statistics of big game on overstocked mountain range. *Transaction of 15th North American Wildlife Conference,* 15: 581–588.

Danielson, B.J. 1978. *History of elk hunting in Alberta.* Alberta Fish and Wildlife Division, Edmonton. Unpublished report.

Dwyer, M.V. 1968. *The ecological characteristics and historical distribution of the family Cervidae in Alberta.* M.Sc. Thesis. University of Alberta, Edmonton, Alberta.

Edmonds, J. 1992. (personal communication). Biologist, Alberta Fish and Wildlife Division, Edson.

Gunson, J. 1992. (personal communication). Biologist, Alberta Fish and Wildlife Division, Edmonton.

Johnston, A. 1973. *Nutritional value of range forages.* Agriculture Canada Research Station, Lethbridge, Alberta. Unpublished report.

Law, C.E. 1949. *Report on the introduction of elk (Cervus canadensis) from Elk Island National Park, June 1949.* Canadian Wildlife Service, Edmonton. Unpublished report.

Lloyd, H. 1927. Transfer of elk for restocking. *Canadian Field Naturalist,* 41: 126–127.

Lothian, W.F. 1981. *A history of Canada's national parks.* Volumes 1, 2, 3 and 4. Parks Canada. Ottawa, Ont.

Lynch, G. 1992 (personal communication). Biologist, Alberta Fish and Wildlife Division, Edmonton.

McCrory, W. 1967. *Absorption and excretion by mountain goats of minerals found in a natural lick.* Canadian Wildlife Service, Edmonton, Alberta. Unpublished report.

McFetridge, R.J. 1984. Wapiti in the Peace River region — limit of the species range. *Proceedings 1984 Western States and Provinces Elk Workshop.* April 17–19, 1984. Edmonton, Alberta.

Millar, J.B. 1953. *An ecological study of the moose in the Rock Lake area of Alberta.* M.Sc. Thesis, University of Alberta, Edmonton.

Nietfeld, M. 1983. *Foraging behaviour of wapiti in the boreal mixed-wood forest, central Alberta.* M.Sc. Thesis, University of Alberta. Edmonton, Alberta.

Nietfeld, M., Wilk, J., Woolnough, K., and Koskin, B. 1985. *Wildlife habitat requirement summaries for selected wildlife species in Alberta.* ENR Technical Report Number T/73, Alberta Fish and Wildlife Division, Edmonton.

Novakowski, N.S. 1963. *Total counts of bison in the higher density areas of Wood Buffalo Park.* Canadian Wildlife Service, Edmonton. Unpublished report.

Paulsen, A.C., and Bruns, E. 1977. *Elk Creek and Seven Mile Creek elk transplants, 1977.* Alberta Fish and Wildlife Division, Edmonton. Unpublished report.

Quaedvlieg, M., Gunderson, G., and Cook, A. 1972. *Goat transplant — 1972.* Alberta Fish and Wildlife Division, Edmonton. Unpublished report.

Ramey, R.R. 1992. (personal communication). Graduate Student, Cornell University, Ithaca, N.Y.

Redgate, R.M. 1978. *Behaviour and ecological considerations in the management of elk in the Camp 1, Athabasca Valley.* M. Ed. Thesis. University of Calgary, Calgary.

Renecker, L.A. 1992. (personal communication). Assistant Professor, University of Alaska, Fairbanks, AK.

Rippin, B. 1992 (personal communication). Biologist, Alberta Fish and Wildlife Division, St. Paul.

Smith, K. 1985. *Preliminary elk (Cervus elaphus) management plan for the Edson wildlife management area.* Alberta Fish and Wildlife Division, Edmonton. Unpublished report.

Smith, K. 1986. *Progress report: mountain goat capture and transplant activities in Alberta during 1986.* Alberta Fish and Wildlife Division, Edmonton. Unpublished report.

Smith, K. 1987. *1987 mountain goat transplant program.* Alberta Fish and Wildlife Division, Edmonton. Unpublished report.

Smith, K. 1992. (personal communication). Biologist, Alberta Fish and Wildlife Division, Edson.

Spalding, D. 1992. (personal communication). Pender Island, B.C.

Stelfox, J.G. 1964. Elk in northwest Alberta. *Land-Forest-Wildlife,* 6: 14–23.

Stelfox, J.G., Kuchar, P., and Bindernagel, J.A. 1978. *Range ecology of mountain caribou (Rangifer tarandus caribou) in Jasper National Park, 1971–1974.* Canadian Wildlife Service report for Parks Canada, Western Region, Calgary.

Watson, M., and Lynch, G. 1986. *Elk transplants to the Pelican Mountains and Amadou Lake area in 1982.* Alberta Fish and Wildlife Division, Edmonton. Unpublished report.

Watt, R. 1992. (personal communication). Warden, Waterton Lakes National Park.

Wishart, W. 1964. *Elk distribution in northeastern Alberta*. Alberta Fish and Wildlife Division, Edmonton. Unpublished report.

Wishart, W. 1992. (personal communication). Adjunct Professor, Department of Zoology, University of Alberta, Edmonton.

Woody, N. 1971, 1973. *General bighorn sheep files*. Warden Service, Canada Parks Service, Jasper. Unpublished report.

5. POPULATION DYNAMICS AND REPRODUCTION

Armstrong, G.G. 1967. *Antelope status, 1967.* Alberta Fish and Wildlife Division, Edmonton. Unpublished report.

Bloomfield, M. 1980. *Closure of the caribou hunting season in Alberta: management of a threatened species*. Alberta Fish and Wildlife Division, Edmonton. Unpublished report.

Bradford, W. 1992 (personal communication). Warden, Jasper National Park, Parks Canada.

Carr, H.D. 1976. *A summary of the development of Alberta's present elk population*. Alberta Fish and Wildlife Division, Edmonton. Unpublished report.

Coady, J.W. 1982. Moose *Alces alces*. pp. 902-922. In: *Wild mammals of North America*. Chapman, J.A., and Feldhamer, G.A. (editors). Johns Hopkins University Press, Baltimore, MD.

Edmonds, E.J. 1986. *Restoration plan for woodland caribou in Alberta*. Alberta Fish and Wildlife Division, Edmonton. Unpublished report.

Festa-Bianchet, M. 1988. Nursing behaviour of bighorn sheep: correlates of ewe age, parasitism, lamb age, birth date, and sex. *Animal Behavior*, 36: 1445-1454.

Flook, D.R. 1970. *A study of apparent unequal sex ratio of wapiti*. Ph.D. Thesis. Univ. Alberta, Edmonton.

Geist, V. 1971. *Mountain sheep. A study in behavior and evolution*. University of Chicago Press, Chicago, Ill.

Glasgow, W.M. 1987. *Status of white-tailed deer and mule deer in Alberta. 1987/86*. Alberta Fish and Wildlife Division, Edmonton. Unpublished report.

Gunson, J.R. 1988. *Management plan for elk in Alberta. Discussion Draft*. Alberta Fish and Wildlife Division, Edmonton. Unpublished report.

Gunson, J.R. and Edmonds, E.J. 1987. *Predator management for caribou restoration and elk enhancement in the Eastern Slopes of Alberta*. Alberta Fish and Wildlife Division report.

Hall, B. 1977. *Status and management of the Rocky Mountain goat (Oreamnos americanus) in the province of Alberta*. Alberta Fish and Wildlife Division, Edmonton. Unpublished report.

Halls, L.K. (editor) 1984 *White-tailed deer; ecology and management*. A Wildlife Management Institute book. Stackpole Books, Harrisburg, PA.

Hebert, D., Wishart, W., Jorgenson, J., and Festa-Bianchet, M. 1985. Bighorn status in Alberta and British Columbia. *Biennial Symposium of Northern Wild Sheep and Goat Council*, 1985: 48-55.

Hesselton, W.T., and Hesselton, R.M. 1982. White-tailed deer. pp. 878–901. In: *Wild mammals of North America*. Chapman, J.A., and Feldhamer, G.A. (editors). Johns Hopkins University Press, Baltimore, MD.

Kunelius, R. 1993. (personal communication). Warden, Banff National Park, Parks Canada.

Lynch, G.M. 1975. *Moose populations and seasons in Alberta*. Alberta Fish and Wildlife Division, Edmonton. Unpublished report.

Lynch, G.M. 1986. *Moose management strategy for Alberta. Draft report*. Alberta Fish and Wildlife Division, Edmonton. Unpublished report.

Lynch, G.M., and Pall, O.G. 1973. *Status of caribou management in Alberta*. Alberta Fish and Wildlife Division, Edmonton. Unpublished report.

Mackie, R.J., Hamlin, K.L., and Pac, D.F. 1982. Mule deer (*Odocoileus hemionus*). pp. 862–877. In: *Wild mammals of North America*. Chapman, J.A., and Feldhamer, G.A. (editors). Johns Hopkins University Press, Baltimore, Md.

Mercer, J. 1993. (personal communication). Assistant Chief Warden, Resource Management. Wood Bison National Park, Parks Canada.

Miller, F.L. 1982. Caribou (*Rangifer tarandus*). pp. 923–959. In: *Wild mammals of North America*. Chapman, J.A., and Feldhamer, G.A. (editors). John Hopkins Univ. Press, Baltimore, Md.

Mitchell, G.J. 1965. *Natality, mortality and related phenomena in two populations of pronghorn antelope in Alberta, Canada*. Ph.D. Thesis. Washington State University. Pullman, Wash.

Mitchell, G.J. 1980. *The pronghorn antelope in Alberta*. University of Regina Press, Regina, Sask.

Olson, W. 1993. (personal communication). Warden, Elk Island National Park, Parks Canada.

Peek, J.M. 1982. Elk (*Cervus elaphus*) pp. 851-861. In: *Wild mammals of North America*. Chapman, J.A., and Feldhamer, G.A. (editors). Johns Hopkins University Press, Baltimore, MD.

Quaedvlieg, M.T., Boyd, M., Gunderson, G. and Cook, A. 1973. *Status of the Rocky Mountain goat in the province of Alberta*. Alberta Fish and Wildlife Division, Edmonton. Unpublished report.

Redhead, B. 1992. (personal communication). Warden, Wood Buffalo National Park, Parks Canada.

Reynolds, H.W., Glaholt, R.D., and Hawley, A.W.L. 1982. Bison. Chapter 49. In: *Wild mammals of North America*. Chapman, J.A., and Feldhamer, G.A. (editors). Johns Hopkins University Press, Baltimore, Md.

Shackleton, D.M. 1985. *Ovis canadensis. Mammalian Species*, 230: 1–9.

Soper, J.D. 1941. History, range and home life of the northern bison. *Ecological Monographs*, 11: 348–412.

Stelfox, J.G. 1966. *Moose populations, harvests, range conditions and proposed 1966 seasons*. Alberta Fish and Wildlife Division, Edmonton. Unpublished report.

Stelfox, J.G. 1971. Bighorn sheep in the Canadian Rockies; a history: 1800–1970. *Canadian Field Naturalist*, 85: 101–122.

Stelfox, J.G. 1992. Population trends, and factors responsible in Rocky Mountain bighorn sheep of western Canada: 1800-1900. In *Ram of the Rockies*. D.R. Dean. Wayside Press Ltd. Vernon/Kelowna.

Watt, R. 1993 (personal communication). Warden, Waterton Lakes National Park, Parks Canada.

Watson, M. 1988. *Pronghorn antelope management plan for Alberta*. Alberta Fish and Wildlife Division, Edmonton. Unpublished report.

Webb, R. 1959. *Alberta's big game resources*. Alberta Fish and Wildlife Division, Edmonton. Unpublished report.

Wigal, R.A. and Coggins, V.L. 1982. Mountain goat (*Oreamnos americanus*). pp. 1008-1035. In: *Wild mammals of North America*. Chapman, J.A., and Feldhamer, G.A. (editors). Johns Hopkins University Press, Baltimore, MD.

Wishart, W. 1969. *Antelope historic review; estimated antelope population and harvest: 1903–69*. Alberta Fish and Wildlife Division, Edmonton. Unpublished report.

Wishart, W. 1972. History and management of the pronghorn antelope in Alberta. *Alberta Conservationist*, 1972: 20–22.

Wishart, W. 1980. Hybrids of white-tailed and mule deer in Alberta. *Journal of Mammalogy*, 61:716-720

6. PREDATION

Ackerman, B.B. 1982. *Cougar predation and ecological energetics in southern Utah*. M.Sc. Thesis, Utah State University, Logan, Utah.

Alberta Fish and Wildlife Division (AFWD). 1991. *Management plan for wolves in Alberta*. Wildlife Management Planning Series, 4: 87 pages.

Alberta Fish and Wildlife Division (AFWD). 1992. *Management plan for cougar in Alberta*. Wildlife Management Planning Series, 5: 91 pages.

Anderson, A.E. 1983. *A critical review of literature on puma* (Felis concolor). Colorado Division of Wildlife Special Report.

Ashcroft, G.E. 1986. Attempted defence of a lamb by a female bighorn sheep. *Journal of Mammalogy*, 67: 427-428.

Atkinson, K., and Janz, D.W. 1986. *Effect of wolf control on black-tailed deer in the Nimpkish Valley on Vancouver Island*. British Columbia Department of Environment. Unpublished report.

Ballard, W.B., and Larsen, D.G. 1987. Implications of predator-prey relationships to moose management. *Swedish Wildlife Research Supplement*, 1: 581–602.

Ballard, W.B., Spraker, T.H., and Taylor, K.P. 1981. Causes of neonatal moose calf mortality in south central Alaska. *Journal of Wildlife Management*, 45: 335–342.

Barrett, M.W. 1984. Movement, habitat use, and predation on pronghorn fawns in Alberta. *Journal of Wildlife Management*, 48: 542–550.

Bjorge, R.R., and Gunson, J.R. 1989. Wolf (*Canis lupus*) population characteristics and prey relationships near Simonette, Alberta. *Canadian Field Naturalist*, 103: 327–334.

Bruns, E.H. 1970. Winter predation of golden eagles and coyotes on pronghorn antelopes. *Canadian Field Naturalist*, 84: 301–304.

Carbyn, L.N. 1975. *Wolf predation and behavioural interactions with elk and other ungulates in an area of high prey diversity*. Canadian Wildlife Service, Edmonton. Unpublished report.

Carbyn, L.N. 1983. *Wolves in Canada and Alaska: their status, biology and management*. Canadian Wildlife Service, Edmonton. Report No. 45.

Carbyn, L.N. 1987. Gray wolf and red wolf. pp. 359–376. In: *Wild furbearer management and conservation in North America*. Novak, M., Baker, G.A., Osgard, M.E. and Malloch, B. (editors). Ontario Trappers Association, Toronto, Ont.

Carbyn, L.N., and Trottier, T. 1987. Responses of bison on calving predation by wolves in Wood Buffalo National Park. *Canadian Journal of Zoology*, 65: 2072–2078.

Carbyn, L.N., and Trottier, T. 1988. Observations on the defense of bison calves against wolf predation in Wood Buffalo National Park. *Arctic*, 41: 297–302.

Clarkson, P.L., Schmidt, K.P., and Gunson, J.R. 1984. *Evaluation of wolf-ungulate predation near Nordegg, Alberta: first year progress report, 1983–84*. Alberta Fish and Wildlife Division, Edmonton. Unpublished report.

Connolly, G.E. 1978. Predators and predator control. Chapter 24: In: *Big game of North America; ecology and management*. Schmidt, J.L. and Gilbert, D.L. (editors), Stackpole Books, Harrisburg, Penn.

Cowan, I. McT. 1947. The timber wolf in the Rocky Mountain National Parks of Canada. *Canadian Journal of Research.*, 25: 139–174.

Dekker, D. 1986. Population fluctuations and spatial relationships among wolves, *Canis lupus*, coyotes, *Canis latrans*, and red foxes, *Vulpes vulpes*, in Jasper National Park, Alberta. *Canadian Field Naturalist*, 103: 261-264.

Dekker, D. 1986. Wolf, *Canis lupus*, numbers and phases in Jasper National Park, Alberta: 1965–1984. *Canadian Field Naturalist*, 100: 550–553.

Dorrance, M.J. 1982. Predation losses of cattle in Alberta. *Journal of Range Management.*, 35: 690-692.

Edmonds, E.J. 1988. Population status, distribution, and movements of woodland caribou in west central Alberta. *Canadian Journal of Zoology*, 66: 817-826.

Edmonds, E.J., and Bloomfield, M. 1984. *A study of woodland caribou*. Alberta Fish and Wildlife Division, Edmonton. Unpublished report.

Errington, P.L. 1946. Predation and vertebrate populations. *Quarterly Review of Biology*, 21: 144-177.

Farnell, R., and McDonald, J. 1987. *The demography of Yukon's Finlayson caribou herd, 1982–1987*. Yukon Renewable Resources Program. Progress report.

Franzmann, A.W., Schwartz, C.C., and Peterson, R.O. 1980. Moose calf mortality in summer on the Kenai Peninsula, Alaska. *Journal of Wildlife Management*, 44: 764–768.

Fuller, T.K., and Keith, L.B. 1980. Wolf population dynamics and prey relationships in northeastern Alberta. *Journal of Wildlife Management*, 44: 583–602.

Gasaway, W.C., Stephenson, R.O., Davies, J.L., Shepherd, P.E., and Borris, O.E. 1983. Interrelationships of wolves, prey, and man in interior Alaska. *Wildlife Monographs*, 84.

Gunson, J.R. 1984. *Review of management and research of wolf–big game predation in Alberta.* Alberta Fish and Wildlife Division, Edmonton. Unpublished report.

Gunson, J.R. 1986. Wolves and elk in Alberta's Brazeau country. pp. 29–33. In: *Bugle: The Quarterly Journal of the Rocky Mountain Elk Foundation.*

Gunson, J.R. 1992. Historical and present management of wolves in Alberta. *Wildlife Society Bulletin*, 20: 330-339.

Hamlin, K.L., Riley, S.J., Pyrah, D., Dood, A.R., and Mackie, R.J. 1984 Relationships among mule deer fawn mortality, coyotes, and alternate prey species during summer. *Journal of Wildlife Management*, 48: 489-499.

Harrison, S., and Hebert, D. 1988. Selective predation by cougar within the Junction wildlife management area. *Biennial Symposium of Northern Wild Sheep and Goat Council*, 1988: 292-306.

Hornocker, M.G. 1970. An analysis of mountain lion predation on mule deer and elk in the Idaho Primitive area. *Wildlife Monographs*, 21.

Jalkotzy, M., and Ross, I. 1991. *The Sheep River cougar project. Phase III. Cougar prey relationships, progress report, 1990–91.* ARC Associates Resource Consultants, Calgary.

Keith, L.B. 1983. Population dynamics of wolves. In: *Wolves in Canada and Alaska; their status, biology and management.* Canadian Wildlife Service Report No. 45. Edmonton.

Larsen, D.G., and Gauthier, D.A. 1985. *Management program draft proposal — options for increasing moose members, southern Yukon.* Yukon Renewable Resources report.

Mech, L.D. 1973. *Wolf numbers in the Superior National Forests of Minnesota.* U.S. Agriculture and Forest Services, research paper NC 97.

Mech, L.D., and Delguidice, G.D. 1985. Limitations of the marrow-fat technique as an indicator of body condition. *Wildlife Society Bulletin*, 13: 204–206.

Messier, F., Barrette, C., and Huot, J. 1986. Coyote predation on a white-tailed deer population in Southern Quebec. *Canadian Journal of Zoology*, 64: 1134-1136.

Miller, F.L., Gunn, A., and Broughton, E. 1985. Surplus killing as exemplified by wolf predation on newborn caribou. *Canadian Journal of Zoology*, 63: 295–300.

Nolan, J.W., and Barrett, M.W. 1985. *A preliminary study of moose calf mortality in northeastern Alberta.* Alberta Environment Centre report. Vegreville.

Nowak, R.M. 1978. Evolution and taxonomy of coyotes and related *Canis.* pp. 3-16. In: *Coyote: biology, behavior, and management.* Bekoff M. (editor). Academic Press, New York, N.Y.

Oosenbrug, S., and Carbyn, L. 1985. *Wolf predation on bison in Wood Buffalo National Park.* Canadian Wildlife Service, Edmonton. Unpublished report.

Ozoga J.J., and Harger E.M. 1966. Winter activities and feeding habits of Northern Michigan coyotes. *Journal of Wildlife Management*, 30: 809-818.

Peterson, R.O. 1977. *Wolf ecology and prey relationships on Isle Royale.* U.S. National Park Service Science Monograph Series 11.

Pimlott, D.H., Shannon, J.A. and Kolenosky, G.B. 1969 *The ecology of the timber wolf in Algonquin Provincial Park.* Ontario Lands and Forest Research Paper 87.

Pimlott, D. 1970. Predation and productivity of game populations in North America. *International Congress of Game Biologists*, 9: 63–73.

Ream, R.R., Harris, R.B., Smith, J., and Boyd, D. 1985. Movement patterns of a lone wolf (*Canis lupus*), in unoccupied wolf range, southeastern British Columbia. *Canadian Field Naturalist*, 99: 234–239.

Robinette, W.L., Gashwiler, J.W., and Morris, O.W. 1959. Food habits of the cougar in Utah and Nevada. *Journal of Wildlife Management*, 23: 261–273.

Ross, P, and Jalkotzy, M. 1989. *The Sheep River cougar project. Phase III final report 1987–1989.* ARC Associated Resource Consultants, Calgary.

Ross, P, and Jalkotzy, M. 1990. *Winter food habits of cougars in southwestern Alberta: A progress report.* Abstract from Alberta Chapter of the Wildlife Society, 2nd annual meeting. March 23-24, 1991, Edmonton.

Ross, P., and Jalkotzy, M. 1989. *The Sheep River cougar project. Phase III cougar prey relationships, progress report 1989–1990.* ARC Associated Resource Consultants, Calgary.

Roy L.D., and Dorrance M.J. (in prep). Characteristics of lambs killed by coyotes in Alberta.

Schlegel, M. 1976. Factors affecting calf elk survival in north central Idaho; a progress report. pp. 342–351. In: *Proceedings: 56th Annual Conference Western Association Game and Fish Commission.* Sun Valley, Idaho. July 26–29, 1976.

Schmidt, K.P., and Gunson, J.R. 1985. *Evaluation of wolf-ungulate predation near Nordegg, Alberta: second year progress report, 1984–85.* Alberta Fish and Wildlife Division, Edmonton. Unpublished report.

Shank, C.C. 1977. Cooperative defence by bighorn sheep. *Journal of Mammalogy*, 58: 243-244.

Shaw, H.G. 1977. Impact of mountain lions on mule deer and cattle. Phillips, R.L., and Jonkel, C.J. (editors). pp. 17–32. In: *Proceedings: 1975 Predator Symposium*, Montana Forest Conservation Experimental Station, School of Forestry, University of Montana, Missoula, Mont.

Simons L.H. 1988. Apparent strangulation of an adult deer by a coyote. *The Murrelet*, 69: 48-50.

Stelfox, J.G. 1969. Wolves in Alberta: a history, 1800-1969. *Alberta Lands-Forests-Parks-Wildlife*, 12: 18-27.

Stelfox, J.G. 1973. *Predator-prey relationships in Canadian national parks.* Canadian Wildlife Service, Edmonton. Unpublished report.

Stewart, R.R., Kowal, E.H., Beaulieu, R., and Rock, T.W. 1985. The impact of black bear removal on moose calf survival in east-central Saskatchewan. *Alces*, 21: 403–418.

Teer, J.G., Drawe, D.L., Blakenship, T.L., Andelt, W.F., Cook, R.S., Kie, J.G., Knowlton, F.F., and White, M. 1991. Deer and coyotes: the Welder experiments. *Transaction of North American Wildlife and Natural Resources Conference*, 56: 550-560.

Theberge, G. 1985. Models of wolf-ungulate relationships: when is wolf control justified? *Wildlife Society Bulletin*, 13: 449-458.

Todd, A.W., Keith, L.B., and Fischer, C.A. 1981. Coyote demography during a snowshoe hare decline in Alberta. *Journal of Wildlife Management*, 45:629-640.

Wielgus, R.B. 1986. *Habitat ecology of the grizzly bear in the southern Rocky Mountains of Canada*. M.Sc. Thesis. University of Idaho, Moscow, Idaho.

7. PARASITES AND DISEASE

Blood, D.A. 1971. Contagious ecthyma in Rocky Mountain bighorn sheep. *Journal of Wildlife Management*, 35: 270–275.

Chalmers, G.A., Vance, H.N., and Mitchell, G.J. 1964. An outbreak of epizootic hemorrhagic disease in wild ungulates in Alberta. *Wildlife Diseases*, 42: 1–6.

Festa-Bianchet, M. 1988. A pneumonia epizootic in bighorn sheep, with comments on preventive management. *Biennial Symposium of Northern Wild Sheep and Goat Council*, 6: 66–76.

Foreyt, W.J. 1989. Fatal *Pasteurella haemolytica* pneumonia in bighorn sheep after direct contact with clinically normal domestic sheep. *American Journal of Veterinary Research*, 50: 341–344.

Foreyt, W.J., and Jessup, D.A. 1982. Fatal pneumonia of bighorn sheep following association with domestic sheep. *Journal of Wildlife Disease*, 18: 163–168.

Glines, M.V., and Samuel, W.M. 1989. Effect of *Dermacentor albipictus* (Acari: Ixodidae) on blood composition, weight gain and hair coat of moose, *Alces alces*. *Experimental and Applied Acarology*, 6: 197–213.

Lothian, W.F. 1981. *A history of Canada's national parks. Volume 4*. Parks Canada, Ottawa, Ont.

Onderka, D.K., and Wishart, W.D. 1984. A major bighorn die-off from pneumonia in southern Alberta; 1982–1983. *Biennial Symposium of Northern Wild Sheep and Goat Council*, 4: 356–363.

Onderka, D.K., and Wishart, W.D. 1988. Experimental contact transmission of *Pasteurella haemolytica* from clinically normal bighorn sheep causing pneumonia in Rocky Mountain bighorn sheep. *Journal of Wildlife Disease*, 24: 663–667.

Onderka, D.K., Rawluk, S.A., and Wishart, W.D. 1988. Susceptibility of Rocky Mountain bighorn sheep and domestic sheep to pneumonia induced by bighorn and domestic livestock strains of *Pasteurella haemolytica*. *Canadian Journal of Veterinary Research*, 52: 439–444.

Samson, J., Holmes, J.C., Jorgenson, J.T., and Wishart, W.D. 1987. Experimental infections of free-ranging Rocky Mountain bighorn sheep with lungworms (*Protostrongylus* spp.; Nematoda: Protostrongylidae). *Journal of Wildlife Disease*, 23: 396–403.

Samuel, W.M. 1987a. Internal parasites of Alberta's wild ruminants. *Proceedings: Alberta Game Growers' Association Conference*, 1: 71–78.

Samuel, W.M. 1987b. Moving the zoo or the potential introduction of a dangerous parasite into Alberta with its translocated host. *Proceedings: Alberta Game Growers' Association Conference*, 1: 85–92.

Samuel, W.M. 1987c. Parasitologist in a park: potential, problems, procedures and progress. *Park News* (Journal of the Canadian Parks and Wilderness Society), 23: 20–22.

Samuel, W.M. 1988a. What's bugging your deer. *Deer and Deer Hunting Magazine*, 12: 39–45.

Samuel, W.M. 1988b. The use of age classes of winter ticks on moose to determine time of death. *Canadian Society of Forensic Science Journal*, 21: 54–59.

Samuel, W.M., Barrett, M.W., and Lynch, G.M. 1976. Helminths in moose of Alberta. *Canadian Journal of Zoology*, 54: 307–312.

Samuel, W.M., Chalmers, G.A., Stelfox, J.G., Loewen, A., and Thomsen, J.J. 1975. Contagious ecthyma in bighorn sheep and mountain goats in western Canada. *Journal of Wildlife Disease*, 11: 26–31.

Samuel, W.M., Hall, W.K., Stelfox, J.G., and Wishart, W.D. 1978. Parasites of mountain goat, *Oreamnos americanus* (Blainville), of west central Alberta with a comparison of the helminths of mountain goat and Rocky Mountain bighorn sheep. *Proceedings: 1st International Symposium of Mountain Goat.*, 1978: 212–225.

Schwantje, H.M. 1983. *Bighorn sheep die-off workshop proceedings*. Unpublished report, Ministry of Environment, Victoria, B.C.

Schwantje, H.M. 1988a. *Evaluation of health status of Rocky Mountain sheep in southeastern British Columbia*. Wildlife Bulletin Number B–58, Ministry of Environment, Victoria, B.C.

Schwantje, H.M. 1988b. *Causes of bighorn sheep mortality and die off   literature review*. Wildlife Working Report Number WR 35. Ministry of Environment, Victoria, B.C.

Spraker, R.J., and Hibler, C.P. 1982. An overview of the clinical signs, gross and histological lesions of the pneumonia complex of bighorn sheep. *Biennial Symposium of Northern Wild Sheep and Goat Council*, 3: 163–172.

8. HUNTING AND HARVEST

Alberta Fish and Wildlife Division (AFWD), (in prep). Management plan for moose in Alberta. Alberta Fish and Wildlife Division, Edmonton. Unpublished report.

Alberta Fish and Wildlife Division (AFWD), 1989. Management plan for mule deer in Alberta. Alberta Fish and Wildlife Division, Edmonton. Unpublished report.

Alberta Fish and Wildlife Division (AFWD), 1990. Management plan for pronghorn in Alberta. Alberta Fish and Wildlife Division, Edmonton. Unpublished report.

Anonymous. 1986. *Alberta wildlife trophies. Official records of the Alberta Fish and Game Association. 1963–1985*. McIntosh Publ., North Battleford, Sask.

Armstrong, G.G. 1966. *Prairie deer harvests, 1966*. Alberta Fish and Wildlife Division, Edmonton. Unpublished report.

Barrett, M.W. 1970. *Antelope harvest statistics*. Alberta Fish and Wildlife Division, Edmonton. Unpublished report.

Barrett, M.W. 1971. *Antelope harvest statistics*. Alberta Fish and Wildlife Division, Edmonton. Unpublished report.

Barrett, M.W. 1972. *Antelope harvest statistics*. Alberta Fish and Wildlife Division, Edmonton. Unpublished report.

Barrett, M.W. 1973. *Antelope harvest statistics*. Alberta Fish and Wildlife Division, Edmonton. Unpublished report.

Boone and Crockett Club. 1988. *Records of North American big game*. Published by Boone and Crockett Club, Dumfries, Va.

Boxall, P.C., and Smith, L.C. 1986. *Characteristics of Alberta's hunters: 1974–1984*. Alberta Fish and Wildlife Division, Edmonton, Occasional Paper Number 1.

Burgess, T.E. 1973. *Alberta mule deer: present status and management considerations*. Alberta Fish and Wildlife Division, Edmonton. Unpublished report.

Dunn, F. 1993. (personal communication). Corporal, Royal Canadian Mounted Police, Sherwood Park.

Edmonds, J. 1986. *Restoration plan for woodland caribou in Alberta*. Alberta Fish and Wildlife Division, Edmonton. Unpublished report.

Gunson, J.R. 1987. *Management plan for wapiti in Alberta. Draft report*. Alberta Fish and Wildlife Division, Edmonton. Unpublished report.

Hofman, D. 1974. *Antelope harvest statistics*. Alberta Fish and Wildlife Division, Edmonton. Unpublished report.

Mitchell, G.J. 1965. *Natality, mortality and related phenomena in two populations of pronghorn antelope in Alberta, Canada*. Ph.D. Thesis. Washington State University, Pullman, Wash.

Ondrack, J. 1985. *Big game hunting in Alberta*. Wildlife Publishing, Edmonton.

Quaedvlieg, M., Gunderson, G., and Cook, A. 1973. *Tracking of transplanted goats on Shunda Mountain — 1973*. Alberta Fish and Wildlife Division, Edmonton. Unpublished report.

Schneider, M.E. 1983. *A summary of big game harvest statistics for species under authorization*. Alberta Fish and Wildlife Division, Edmonton. Unpublished report.

Schurman, S. 1976. *Antelope harvest statistics, 1975*. Alberta Fish and Wildlife Division, Edmonton. Unpublished report.

Schurman, S. 1977. *Antelope harvest statistics, 1976*. Alberta Fish and Wildlife Division, Edmonton. Unpublished report.

Schurman, S. 1977. *Antlerless mule deer harvest statistics, 1977*. Alberta Fish and Wildlife Division, Edmonton. Unpublished report.

Schurman, S. 1977. *Documentation of the 1977 non-trophy sheep season*. Alberta Fish and Wildlife Division, Edmonton. Unpublished report.

Schurman, S. 1978. *Antelope harvest statistics, 1977*. Alberta Fish and Wildlife Division, Edmonton. Unpublished report.

Schurman, S. 1978. *Antlerless mule deer harvest statistics, 1977*. Alberta Fish and Wildlife Division, Edmonton. Unpublished report.

Schurman, S. 1979. *Antelope harvest statistics, 1978*. Alberta Fish and Wildlife Division, Edmonton. Unpublished report.

Schurman, S. 1979. *Antlerless mule deer harvest statistics, 1978*. Alberta Fish and Wildlife Division, Edmonton. Unpublished report.

Schurman, S. 1979. *Antlerless white-tailed deer harvest statistics, 1978*. Alberta Fish and Wildlife Division, Edmonton. Unpublished report.

Schurman, S. 1979. *Results from the 1978 elk season*. Alberta Fish and Wildlife Division, Edmonton. Unpublished report.

Schurman, S., and Hall, B. 1977. *Antlerless white-tailed deer harvest statistics, 1976*. Alberta Fish and Wildlife Division, Edmonton. Unpublished report.

Sitton, G. and Reneau, J. (editors) 1992. *Boone and Crockett Club's 21st big game awards*. Published by the Boone and Crockett Club, Missoula, MT.

Stelfox, J.B., Peleshok, L., and Nietfeld, M.T. 1991. *A selected bibliography of research, management, and biology of Alberta's native ungulates*. Alberta Environmental Centre, Vegreville.

Todd, A.W. and Lynch, G.M. 1992. *Managing moose in the 1990s and beyond: results of a survey of opinions, attitudes and activities of Alberta's resident moose hunters*. Alberta Fish and Wildlife Division, Edmonton. Occasional Paper #8.

Wishart, W. 1968. *Non-trophy sheep kills — 1968*. Alberta Fish and Wildlife Division, Edmonton. Unpublished report.

Wishart, W. 1969. *Antelope historic review: estimated antelope population and harvest 1963–1969*. Alberta Fish and Wildlife Division, Edmonton. Unpublished report.

Wishart, W., and Hall, W.K. 1967. *Provincial antelope surveys and harvest, 1963–67*. Alberta Fish and Wildlife Division, Edmonton. Unpublished report.

9. MANAGEMENT

Boxall, P.C., and Smith, L.C. 1987. *Estimates of the illegal harvest of deer in Alberta: a violation simulation study*. Alberta Fish and Wildlife Division Occasional Paper 2. 51 pp.

Clark, J.D. 1988. The past in perspective: the northern mixedwood forest in Alberta. pp. 23–27. In: *Management of northern mixedwoods*. (Samoil (editor). Northern Forest Centre, Canadian Forest Service Information Report. NOR–X–296.

Connolly, G.E. 1981. Limiting factors and population regulation. Assessing populations. pp. 245-345. In: *Mule and black-tailed deer of North America*. Wallmo, E.C. (editor). Stackpole Books, Harrisburg, Pa.

Dorrance, M.J., Savage, P.J., and Huff, D.E. 1975. Effects of snowmobiles on white-tailed deer. *Journal of Wildlife Management*, 39: 563–569.

Edmonds, E.J., and Bloomfield, M. 1984. *A study of woodland caribou (Rangifer tarandus caribou) in west central Alberta, 1979–1983*. Alberta Fish and Wildlife Division, Edmonton. Unpublished report.

Ferguson, M.A.D. 1980. *Ungulates and cross-country skiing, Elk Island National Park, Alberta*. M.Sc. Thesis. University of Wisconsin, Madison, Wis.

Heinselman, M.L. 1981. Fire intensity and frequency as factors in the distribution and structure of northern ecosystems. pp. 7–57. In: *Fire regimes and ecosystem properties*. Mooney, H.A, Bonnickson, T.M., Christensen, N.L., Lotan, J.E. and Reiners, W.E. (editors). USDA Forest Service general technical report.

Hornaday, W.T. 1923. *Campfires in the Canadian Rockies*. Charles. Scribners Sons, New York, N.Y.

Lewis, H.T. 1982. *A time for burning*. University of Alberta Boreal Institute for Northern Studies. Edmonton, Alberta. Occasional Paper 17.

MacArthur, R.A., Geist, V., and Johnston, R.A. 1982. Cardiac and behavioural responses of mountain sheep to human disturbances. *Journal of Wildlife Management*, 46: 351–358.

Millar, W.N. 1915. The big game of the Canadian Rockies. pp. 100–124. In: *Conservation of fish, birds and game*. Commission of Conservation Canada. Methodist Book and Publishing House, Toronto, Ont.

Millson, R. 1985. *Emergency feeding program - 1984-85: completion report*. Alberta Fish and Wildlife Division. Unpublished report.

Murphy, P.J. 1985. *Methods for evaluating the effects of forest fire management in Alberta*. Ph.D. Thesis. University of British Columbia, Vancouver, B.C.

Rowe, J.S. 1972. *Forest regions of Canada*. Canadian Forest Service Publication No. 1300.

Smith, D.R., Anderson, D.R., and Smeltzer, J.R. 1989. Assessment of the violation-simulation method. *Wildlife Society Bulletin*, 17: 180–184.

Stace-Smith, R. 1975. The misuse of snowmobiles against wildlife in Canada. *Nature Canada*, 4: 3 8.

Stelfox, J.G. 1971. Bighorn sheep in the Canadian Rockies; a history 1800–1970. *Canadian Field Naturalist*, 85: 101–122.

Stelfox, J.G., Lynch, G.M., and McGillis, J.R. 1976. Effects of clearcut logging on wild ungulates in the central Albertan Foothills. *Forestry Chronicle*, 52: 65–70.

Stemp, R.E. 1983. *Heart rate responses of bighorn sheep to environmental factors and harassment*. M.Sc. Thesis. University of Calgary, Calgary.

Tande, G.F. 1979. Fire history and vegetation patterns of coniferous forests in Jasper National Park, Alberta. *Canadian Journal of Botany*, 57: 1912–1931.

Tomm, H.O. 1978. *Response of wild ungulates to logging practices in Alberta*. M.Sc. Thesis. University of Alberta, Edmonton.

Van Wagner, C.E. 1978. Age-class distribution and the forest fire cycle. *Canadian Journal of Forest Research*, 8: 220–227.

Yarmaloy, C.P.1984. *The impact of off-highway vehicles on big game: management implications for Alberta's east slopes*. Master of Environmental Design Project. University of Calgary.

Yarmaloy, C.P., Bayer, M., and Geist, V. 198?. On behaviour responses and reproduction following experimental harassment of mule deer does with all-terrain vehicles. *Canadian Field Naturalist*, 102:425-429.

10. ECONOMIC ASPECTS

Adamowicz, W.L. 1983. *Economic analysis of hunting of selected big game species in the eastern slopes of Alberta*. M.Sc. Thesis, University of Alberta, Edmonton.

Adamowicz, W.L., Asafu-Adjaye, J, Boxall, P.C. and Phillips, W.E. 1991. Components of the economic value of wildlife: An Alberta case study. *Canadian Field Naturalist*, 105: 423-429.

Asafu-Adjaye, J., Phillips, W.E., and Adamowicz, W.L. 1989. Towards the measurement of total economic value: the case of wildlife resources in Alberta. Department Rural Economy Staff Paper 89-16.

Boxall, P.C., and Smith, L.C. 1986. *Characteristics of Alberta hunters, 1974–1984*. Alberta Fish and Wildlife Division, Edmonton. Resource Economics and Assessment Occasional Paper No. 1.

Brookshire, D.S., Eubanks, L.S., and Randall, A. 1983. Estimating option prices and existence values for wildlife resources. *Land Economics*, 59: 1–15.

Brookshire, D.S., Eubanks, L.S., and Sorg, C.F. 1987. Existence values and normative economics. pp. 14–26. In: *Towards the measurement of total economic value*. Peterson, G.L., and Sorg, C.F. (editors). U.S. Department of Agriculture. General Technical Report RM–148.

Brookshire, D.S., and Smith, V.K. 1987. Measuring recreation benefits: conceptual and empirical issues. *Water Resource Research*, 23: 931–935.

Brusnyk, L., Westworth, D.A., and Adamowicz, W.L. 1990. *An evaluation of the landowner habitat program*. D.A. Westworth and Associates, Edmonton.

Coyne, A.G. 1990. *Economic effects of environmental quality change on recreation demand*. M.Sc. Thesis. University of Alberta, Edmonton.

Coyne, A.G., and Adamowicz, W.L. 1992. Modelling choice of site for bighorn sheep hunting. *Wildlife Society Bulletin*, 20: 26–33.

Cummings, R.G., Brookshire, D.S., and Schulze, W.D. 1986. *Valuing environmental goods; an assessment of the contingent valuation method*. Rowman and Allanheld, Totowa, N.J.

Filion, F.L., Duwors, E., Jacquemot, A., Bouchard, P., Boxall, P., Gray, P.A., and Reid, R. 1989. *The importance of wildlife to Canadians in 1987; highlights of a national survey*. Canadian Wildlife Service, Environment Canada, Publication Number CW66–103/1989E.

Filion, F.L., Jacquemot, A., Boxall, P., Reid, R., Bouchard, P., Duwors, E., and Gray, P.A. 1990. *The importance of wildlife to Canadians in 1987; the economic significance of wildlife-related recreational activities*. Canadian Wildlife Service, Environment Canada, Publication Number CW66–103/2–1990E.

McConnell, K.E. 1985. The economics of outdoor recreation. pp. 677–722. In: *Handbook of natural resource and energy economics*. Volume II. Kneese, A.V. and Sweeney, J.L. (editors). Elsevier Science Publishers, New York, N.Y.

Mendelsohn, R. 1987. Modeling the demand for outdoor recreation. *Water Resource Research*, 23: 961–967.

Sorg, C.F. 1982. *Valuing increments and decrements of wildlife resource: further evidence*. Ph.D. dissertation, University of Wyoming, Laramie, Wyo.

Sorg, C.F., and Nelson, L.J. 1986. *Net economic value of elk hunting in Idaho*. Rocky Mountain Forest and Range Experiment Station Resource Bulletin RM–12, Fort Collins, Colo.

11. COMMERCIALIZATION

Geist, V. 1983a. Game ranching. *Western Canada Outdoors*, 7: 10.

Geist, V. 1983b. Some problems associated with game ranching. *Western Canada Outdoors*, 7:1.

Geist, V. 1985a. A critique of game ranching in Alberta. In: *Proceedings: 1984 Western States and Provinces Elk Workshop*. Nelson, R.W. (editor), Edmonton, April 17–18, 1984.

Geist, V. 1985b. Game ranching: threat to wildlife conservation in North America. *Wildlife Society Bulletin*, 13: 594–598.

Griffin, J.F.T., Cross, J.P. and Buchan, C.S. 1991. Laboratory immunodiagnostic tests of tuberculosis in deer and exotic ruminants. In *Wildlife Production, Conservation and Sustainable Development*. Renecker, L.A. and Hudson, R.J. (editors). AFES Misc. Pub. 91-6, University of Alaska, Fairbanks.

Hudson, R.J. 1981. Agricultural potential of the wapiti. pp. 80–86. In: *60th Annual Feeders' Day Report*. Department of Animal Science, University of Alberta, Edmonton.

Hudson, R.J. 1983. Commercial wildlife production in western Canada. pp. 134–148. In: *Symposium on Fish and Wildlife Resources and Economic Development*. Sponsored by the Alberta Society of Professional Biologists and Alberta Fish and Wildlife Division, Edmonton, April 26–27, 1983.

Hudson, R.J. 1984. The potential of wild ruminants. *Agrologist*, 13: 14–15.

Hudson, R.J. 1985. Elk farming. pp. 10–12. In: *Proceedings: 1984 Western States and Provinces Elk Workshop*. Nelson, R.W. (editor). Edmonton, April 17–18, 1984.

Hudson, R.J. 1987. International venison industry. *Proceedings: Annual Alberta Game Growers' Association Conference*, 3: 1–4.

Hudson, R.J. 1990. Wildlife Ranching: Dancing with the devil? *Wildlife Running into the Future Conference*. University of Calgary, 2–5, May 1990.

Hudson, R.J., Drew, K.R., and Baskin, L.M. (editors) 1989. *Wildlife production systems: economic utilization of wild ungulates*. Cambridge University Press, Cambridge, UK.

Millar, J.B. 1986. *Perspectives on the status of Canadian Prairie Wetlands*. Canadian Wildlife Service. Unpublished report. Saskatoon.

Moore, N. 1992. (personal communication). Moore's Auctioneering, Alder Flats.

Renecker, L.A. 1988a. Game production developments in Canada and Alberta. *Proceedings: Annual Alberta Game Growers' Association Conference*, 3: 5–8.

Renecker, L.A. 1988b. Velvet production and the market goal. *Proceedings: Annual Alberta Game Growers' Association Conference*, 3: 59–61.

Renecker, L.A. 1989a. Overview of game farming in Canada. pp. 47–62. In: *Proceedings: 1st International Wildlife Ranching Symposium*, Valdez, R. (editor). Cooperative Extension Service — Wildlife, New Mexico State University, Las Cruces, NM.

Renecker, L.A. 1989b. Wapiti farming in Canada. pp. 118–140. In: *Proceedings 1st International Wildlife Ranching Symposium*; Valdez, R. (editor). Cooperative Extension Service — Wildlife, New Mexico State University, Las Cruces, NM.

Renecker, L.A., and Hudson, R.J. (editors). 1991. *Wildlife Production: Conservation and Sustainable Development*. AFES Misc. Pub. 91–6, University of Alaska — Fairbanks, Fairbanks, Alaska. 601 p.

Renecker, L.A., and Kozak, H.A. 1987. Game ranching in western Canada. *Rangelands*, 9: 215–218.

Samuel, W.M., Pybus, M.J., Welch, D.A., and Wilke, C.J. 1992. Elk as a potential host for meningeal worm: implications for translocation. *Journal of Wildlife Management*, 56: 629-639.

Telfer, E.S., and G.W. Scotter. 1975. Potential for game ranching in boreal aspen forests of western Canada. *Journal of Range Management*, 28: 172–180.

12. MORPHOLOGY, BIOENERGETICS AND RESOURCE USE

Bandy, P.J., Cowan, I. McT., and Wood, A.J. 1970. Comparative growth in four races of black-tailed deer. Part I. Growth in body weight. *Canadian Journal of Zoology*, 48: 1401–1410.

Barrett, M.W. 1972. *A review of the diet, condition, diseases and parasites of the Cypress Hills moose*. Alberta Fish and Wildlife Division, Edmonton. Unpublished report.

Barrett, M.W. 1974. Importance, utilization and quality of *Artemisia cana* on pronghorn winter ranges in Alberta. pp. 337–359. In: *Proceedings of 6th Biennial Antelope States Workshop*. Salt Lake City, Utah.

Belovsky, G.E. 1978. Diet optimization in a generalist herbivore: the moose. *Theoretical Population Biology*, 14: 105–134.

Berg, B.P. 1983. *Wild and domestic ungulate interactions in the Bob Creek area, southwestern Alberta*. M.Sc. Thesis. University of Alberta, Edmonton.

Blood, D.A., Flook, D.R. and Wishart, W.D. 1970. Weights and growth of Rocky Mountain bighorn sheep in western Alberta. *Journal of Wildlife Management*, 34, 451-455.

Blood, D.A., McGillis, J.R., and Lovaas, A.L. 1967. Weights and measurements of moose in Elk Island National Park, Alberta. *Canadian Field Naturalist*, 81: 263–269.

Cairns, A.L. 1976. *Distribution of food habits of moose, wapiti, deer, bison and snowshoe hare in Elk Island National Park*. M.Sc. Thesis. University of Calgary, Calgary .

Christopherson, R.J., Hudson, R.J., and Richmond, R.J. 1978. Comparative winter bioenergetics of American bison, yak, Scottish Highland and hereford calves. *Acta Theriologica*, 23: 49–54.

Clutton-Brock, T.H., Albon, S.D., and Harvey, P.H. 1980. Antlers, body size and breeding group size in the Cervidae. *Nature*, 285: 565–567.

Clutton-Brock, T.H., and Harvey, P.H. 1985. The functional significance of variation in body size among mammals. pp. 632–663. In: *Advances in the study of mammalian behavior*. Eisenberg, J.F. and Kleiman, D.G. (editors). American Society of Mammalogy Special Publication 7.

Coady, J.W. 1982. Moose (*Alces alces*). pp. 902–922. In: *Wild mammals of North America*. Chapman, J.A., and Feldhamer, G.A. (editors). John Hopkins University Press, Baltimore, MD.

Cowan, I. McT. 1947. Range competition between mule deer, bighorn sheep and elk in Jasper Park, Alberta. *Transactions of North American Wildlife Conference*, 12: 223–227.

Dailey, T.V., and Hobbs, N.T. 1989. Travel in alpine terrain: energy expenditures for locomotion by mountain goat and bighorn sheep. *Canadian Journal of Zoology*, 67: 2368–2375.

Demment, M., and Van Soest, P.J. 1985. A nutritional explanation for body-size patterns of ruminant and non-ruminant herbivores. *American Naturalist*, 125: 641–672.

Edmonds, E.J., and Bloomfield, M. 1984. *A study of woodland caribou* (Rangifer tarandus caribou) *in west central Alberta, 1979 to 1983*. Alberta Fish and Wildlife Division, Edmonton. Unpublished report.

Ellis, J.E., Weins, J.A., Rodell, C.F., and Anways, J.C. 1976. A conceptual model of diet selection as an ecosystem process. *Journal of Theoretical Biology*, 60: 93–108.

Fancy, S.G., and White, R., 1985. Incremental costs of activity. pp. 143–160. In: *Bioenergetics of wild herbivores*. Hudson, R.J., and White, R.G. (editors). CRC Press, Boca Raton, Fla.

Flook, D.R. 1964. Range relationships of some ungulates native to Banff and Jasper National Park, Alberta. pp. 119–128. In: *Grazing in terrestrial and marine environments*. Crisp, D.R. (editor). Symposium of British Ecological Society, No. 4. Blackwell, Oxford.

Flook, D.R. 1970. *A study in sex differential in the survival of wapiti*. Canadian Wildlife Service Report Series No. 11. Queen's Printers. Ottawa, Ont.

Gates, C.C., and Hudson, R.J. 1979. Effect of posture and activity on metabolic responses of wapiti to cold. *Journal of Wildlife Management*, 43: 564–567.

Geist, V., and Bayer, M. 1988. Sexual dimorphism in the Cervidae and its relation to habitat. *Journal of Zoology* (London), 214: 45–53.

Georgiadis, N.J. 1985. Growth patterns, sexual dimorphism and reproduction in the African ruminants. *African Journal of Ecology*, 23: 75–87.

Gordon, I.J., and Illius, A.W. 1988. Incisor arcade structure and diet selection in ruminants. *Functional Ecology*, 2: 15–22.

Green, J.E., and Salter, R.E. 1987. *Reclamation of wildlife habitat in the Canadian prairie provinces. Volume II. Habitat requirements for key species*. Prepared for Environment Canada and the Alberta Recreation, Parks and Wildlife Foundation by the Delta Environmental Management Group, Calgary.

Halls, L.K. 1984. *White-tailed deer: ecology and management*. Stackpole, Harrisburg, Penn.

Hesselton, W.T., and Hesselton, R. 1982. White-tailed deer (*Odocoileus virginianus*). pp. 878–901. In: *Wild mammals of North America*. Chapman, J.A., and Feldhamer, G.A. (editors). Johns Hopkins University Press, Baltimore, Md.

Hofmann, R. 1989. Evolutionary steps of ecophysiological adaptation and diversification of ruminants: a comparative view of their digestive system. *Oecologia*, 78: 443–457.

Holsworth, W.N. 1960. *Buffalo range and food habits of buffalo in Wood Buffalo Park*. Canadian Wildlife Service, Edmonton. Unpublished report.

Hudson, R.J. 1985. Body size, ecology and evolution. In: *Bioenergetics of wild herbivores*. CRC Press, Boca Raton, Fla.

Hudson, R.J., and Adamczewski, J.Z. 1990. Effect of supplementing summer ranges on lactation and growth of wapiti (*Cervus elaphus*). *Canadian Journal of Animal Science*, 70: 551–560.

Hudson, R.J., and Christopherson, R.J. 1985. Maintenance metabolism. In: *Bioenergetics of wild herbivores*. Hudson, R.J., and White, R.G. (editors). CRC Press, Boca Raton, Fla.

Hudson, R.J., and Frank, S. 1987. Foraging ecology of bison in aspen boreal habitats. *Journal of Range Management*, 40: 71–75.

Hudson, R.J., and Watkins, W.G. 1986. Foraging rates of wapiti on green and cured pastures. *Canadian Journal of Zoology*, 64: 1705–1708.

Hudson, R.J., Watkins, W., and Pauls, R. 1985. Bioenergetics of wapiti in the boreal forest. In: *Biology of deer production*. Fennessy, P.F., and Drew, K.R. (editors). Royal Society of New Zealand Bulletin.

Jarman, P. 1983. Mating systems and sexual dimorphism in large terrestrial mammalian herbivores. *Biological Reviews*, 58: 485–520.

Johnson, J.D. 1975. *An evaluation of the summer range of bighorn sheep* (Ovis canadensis Shaw) *on Ram Mountain, Alberta*. University of Calgary, Calgary.

Kerr, G.R. 1965. *The ecology of mountain goats in west-central Alberta*. M.Sc. Thesis. University of Alberta, Edmonton.

Kitchen, D.W., and O'Gara, B.W. 1982. Pronghorn (*Antilocapra americana*). pp. 960–971. In: *Wild mammals of North America*. Chapman, J.A., and Feldhamer, G.A. (editors). Johns Hopkins University Press, Baltimore, Md.

Kramer, A. 1972. *A review of the ecological relationships between mule and white-tailed deer*. Alberta Fish and Wildlife Division Occasional Paper No. 3. Edmonton.

Krog, H., and Monson, M. 1954. Notes on the metabolism of a mountain goat. *American Journal of Physiology*, 178: 515.

Lawson, B., and Johnson, R. 1982. Mountain sheep (*Ovis canadensis* and *O. dalli*). pp. 1036–1055. In: *Wild mammals of North America*. Chapman, J.A., and Feldhamer, G.A. (editors). Johns Hopkins University Press, Baltimore, Md.

Mackie, R.J., Hamlin, K.L., and Pac, D.F. 1982. Mule deer (*Odocoileus hemionus*). pp. 862–877. In: *Wild mammals of North America*. Chapman, J.A., and Feldhamer, G.A. (editors). Johns Hopkins University Press, Baltimore, Md.

McFetridge, R.J. 1977. *Strategy of resource use by mountain goats in Alberta*. M.Sc. Thesis. University of Alberta, Edmonton.

Millar, J.B. 1953. *An ecological study of the moose in the Rock Lake area of Alberta*. M.Sc. Thesis, University of Alberta, Edmonton.

Miller, F.L. 1982. Caribou (*Rangifer tarandus*). pp. 923–959. In: *Wild mammals of North America*. Chapman, J.A., and Feldhamer, G.A. (editors). John Hopkins University Press, Baltimore, Md.

Mitchell, G.J. 1971. Measurements, weights and carcass yields of pronghorns in Alberta. *Journal of Wildlife Management*, 35: 76–85.

Mitchell, G.J. 1980. *The pronghorn antelope in Alberta*. Alberta Fish and Wildlife Division, Edmonton.

Mitchell, G.J., and Smoliak, S. 1971. Pronghorn antelope range characteristics and food habits in Alberta. *Journal of Wildlife Management*, 35: 238–250.

Morgantini, L.E., and Hudson, R.J. 1985. Changes in diets of wapiti during a hunting season. *Journal of Range Management*, 38: 77–79.

Morgantini, L.E., and Olsen, C. 1983. *Pipeline construction and wild ungulates; results of a two year monitoring program along the Edson M/L*. Prep. for NOVA, An Alberta Corporation by Wildlands Resources Consultant, Calgary. Unpublished report.

Morgantini, L.E., and Russell, W.B. 1983. *An assessment of three selected elk winter ranges in the Rocky Mountain regions*. Prepared for Alberta Fish and Wildlife Division by Wildlands Resources Consultants, Edmonton. Unpublished report.

Mould, E.D., and Robbins, C.T. 1981. Nitrogen metabolism in elk. *Journal of Wildlife Management*, 45: 323–334.

Nietfeld, M. 1983. *Foraging behaviour of wapiti in the boreal mixed-wood forest, central Alberta*. M.Sc. Thesis. University of Alberta, Edmonton.

Nietfeld, M., Wilk, J., Woolnough, K., and Haskin, B. 1984. *Wildlife habitat requirement summaries for selected wildlife species in Alberta*. Alberta Fish and Wildlife Division Technical Report No. T/73. Edmonton.

Nowlin, R.N. 1978. Habitat selection and food habits of moose in northeastern Alberta. *Proceedings of North American Moose Conference Workshop*, 14: 178–193.

Oftedal, O. 1985. Pregnancy and lactation. pp. 215–238. In: *Bioenergetics of wild herbivores*. Hudson, R.J., and White, R.G. (editors). CRC Press, Boca Raton, Fla.

Parker, K., and Robbins, C. 1985. Thermoregulation in ungulates. pp. 161–182. In: *Bioenergetics of wild herbivores*. Hudson, R.J., and White, R.G., (editors). CRC Press, Boca Raton., Fla.

Peek, J.M. 1982. Elk (*Cervus elaphus*). pp. 851–861. In: *Wild mammals of North America*. Chapman, J.A., and Feldhamer, G.A. (editors). Johns Hopkins University Press, Baltimore, Md.

Pyke, G.H., Pulliam, H.R., and Charnov, E.L. 1977. Optimal foraging: a selective review of theory and tests. *Quarterly Review of Bioogy*, 52: 137–154.

Renecker, L.A. 1987. *Bioenergetics and behaviour of moose (*Alces alces*) in the aspen-dominated boreal forest*. Ph.D. Thesis. University of Alberta, Edmonton.

Renecker, L.A. 1989. *Seasonal nutritional cycles of ungulates in Elk Island National Park*. Report prepared for Elk Island National Park, Fort Saskatchewan.

Renecker, L.A., and Hudson, R.J. 1985. Estimation of dry matter intake of free-ranging moose. *Journal of Wildlife Management*, 49: 785–792.

Renecker, L.A., and Hudson, R.J. 1986a. Seasonal energy expenditures and thermoregulation responses of moose. *Canadian Journal of Zoology*, 64: 322–327.

Renecker, L.A., and Hudson, R.J. 1986b. Seasonal foraging rates of free-ranging moose. *Journal of Wildlife Management*, 50: 143–147.

Renecker, L.A., and Hudson, R.J. 1988. Seasonal quality of forages used by moose in the aspen boreal forest, central Alberta. *Holarctic Ecology*, 11: 111 118.

Renecker, L.A., and Hudson, R.J. 1989. Ecological metabolism of moose in aspen-dominated boreal forests, central Alberta. *Canadian Journal of Zoology*, 67: 1923–1928.

Renecker, L.A., and Hudson, R.J. 1991. Digestive kinetics of moose (*Alces alces*), wapiti (*Cervus elaphus*) and cattle. *Animal Production*, 50: 51–61.

Renecker, L.A., and Samuel, W.M. 1991. Growth and seasonal weight change as they relate to spring and autumn set points in mule deer. *Canadian Journal of Zoology*, 69: 744–747.

Reynolds, H.W. 1976. *Bison diets of Slave River Lowlands, Canada*. Canadian Wildlife Service, Edmonton. Unpublished report.

Reynolds, H.W., Glaholt, R.D., and Hawley, A.W.L. 1982. Bison. Chapter 49. In: *Wild mammals of North America*. Chapman, J.A., and Feldhamer, G.A. (editors). Johns Hopkins University Press, Baltimore, Md.

Rhude, P., and Hall, W.K. 1977. *Food habits of white-tailed deer and mule deer in Camp Wainwright, Alberta*. Alberta Fish and Wildlife Division, Edmonton. Unpublished report.

Rhude, P., and Hall, W.K. 1978. *Cattle observations in relation to deer food habits in Camp Wainwright, Alberta*. Alberta Fish and Wildlife Division, Edmonton. Unpublished report.

Robbins, C.T., and Robbins, B.L. 1979. Fetal and neonatal growth patterns and maternal reproductive effort in ungulates and subungulates. *American Naturalist*, 114: 101–116.

Salter, R.E., and Hudson, R.J. 1980. Range relationships of feral horses with wild ungulates and cattle in western Canada. *Journal of Range Management.*, 33: 266–271.

Shank, C.C. 1982. Age-sex differences in the diets of wintering Rocky Mountain sheep. *Ecology*, 63: 627–633.

Sheppard, D.H. 1960. *The ecology of the mule deer of the Sheep River region*. M.Sc. Thesis. University of Alberta, Edmonton.

Stelfox, J.G. 1976. *Range ecology of Rocky Mountain bighorn sheep in Canadian national parks*. Canadian Wildlife Service, Edmonton.

Stelfox, J.G., and Tilson, D. 1985. *Elk-livestock range interactions in the Waterton Biosphere Reserve, 1984–1985*. Canadian Wildlife Service, Edmonton. Unpublished report.

Stelfox, J.G., Kuchar, P., and Bindernagel, J.A. 1978. *Range ecology of mountain caribou* (Rangifer tarandus caribou*) in Jasper National Park, 1971–1974.* Canadian Wildlife Service report for Parks Canada, Western Region, Calgary.

Telfer, E. 1978. *Ungulate use in the Marmot Creek experimental watershed.* Canadian Wildlife Service, Edmonton. Unpublished report.

Telfer, E.S., and Kelsall, J.P. 1984. Adaptations of some large North American mammals for survival in snow. *Ecology*, 65: 1828–1834.

Thomas, J.W., and Toweill, D.E. 1982. *Elk of North America.* Stackpole, Harrisburg, Penn.

Treichel, B. 1979. *Cypress Hills elk and moose rumen analysis.* Alberta Fish and Wildlife Division, Edmonton. Unpublished report.

Treichel, B., and Dube, L. 1980. *Wainwright deer rumen analysis 1980.* Alberta Fish and Wildlife Division, Edmonton. Unpublished report.

Treichel, B., and Hall, B. 1977. *Ya-Ha-Tinda elk rumen analysis.* Alberta Fish and Wildlife Division, Edmonton. Unpublished report.

Van Camp, J. 1975. *Snow conditions and the winter feeding behavior of* Bison bison *in Elk Island National Park.* Canadian Wildlife Service, Edmonton. Unpublished report.

Van Soest, P.J. 1982. *Nutritional ecology of the ruminant.* O&B Books, Corvallis, Ore.

Wallmo, O.C. 1981. *Mule and black-tailed deer of North America.* Stackpole, Harrisburg, Penn.

Watkins, W.G., Hudson, R.J. and Fargey, P.L.J. 1991. Compensatory growth of wapiti (*Cervus elaphus*) on aspen parkland. *Canadian Journal of Zoology*, 69:1682-1688.

Western, D. 1979. Size, life history and ecology in mammals. *African Journal of Ecology*, 17: 185–204.

Westoby, M. 1974. An analysis of diet selection by large generalist herbivores. *American Naturalist*, 108: 290–304.

Wigal, R.A., and Coggins, V.L. 1982. Mountain goat (*Oreamnos americanus*). pp. 1008–1020. In: *Wild mammals of North America.* Chapman, J.A., and Feldhamer, G.A. (editors). Johns Hopkins University Press, Baltimore, Md.

Wishart, W.D. 1958. *The bighorn sheep of the Sheep River Valley.* M.A. Thesis. University of Alberta, Edmonton.

Wishart, W.D. 1985. Frequency of antlered white-tailed does in Camp Wainwright, Alberta. *Journal of Wildlife Management*, 49: 386–388.

A2. CAPTURE AND RESTRAINT

Anonymous. 1984. *Techniques for chemical restraint of Alberta wildlife.* Alberta Fish and Wildlife Division, Edmonton. Technical manual.

Barrett, M.W. 1981. Environmental characteristics and functional significance of pronghorn *Antilocapra americana* fawn bedding sites in Alberta Canada. *Journal of Wildlife Management*, 45: 120–131.

Barrett, M.W., Nolan, J.W., and Roy, L.E. 1982. Evaluation of hand-held net-guns to capture large mammals. *Wildlife Society Bulletin*, 10: 108–114.

Festa-Bianchet, M. 1986. Site fidelity and seasonal range use by bighorn rams. *Canadian Journal of Zoology*, 64: 2126–2132.

Festa-Bianchet, M., and Jorgenson, J.T. 1985. Use of xylazine and ketamine to immobilize bighorn sheep in Alberta. *Journal of Wildlife Management*, 49: 162–165.

Fowler, M.E. 1978. *Restraint and handling of wild and domestic animals.* Iowa State University Press, Ames, Iowa.

Fuller, T.K., and Keith, L.B. 1981. Immobilization of woodland caribou with etorphine. *Journal of Wildlife Management*, 45: 745–748.

Haigh, J.C. 1978. Capture of woodland caribou in Canada. pp. 110–115. In: *Proceedings of American Association of Zoo Veterinarians*, Knoxville, Tenn.

Haigh, J.C., Stewart, R.R., and Frokjer, R. 1977. Capture of moose with fentanyl and xylazine. *Proceedings: North American Moose Conference and Workshop*, 13: 107–118.

Hawkins, R.E., Autry, D.C., and Klimstra, W.D. 1967. Comparison of methods used to capture white-tailed deer. *Journal of Wildlife Management*, 31: 460–464.

Hebert, D.M., and McFetridge, R.J. 1978. *Chemical immobilization of North American game mammals.* Alberta Fish and Wildlife Division, Edmonton.

LeResche, R.E., and Lynch, G.M. 1973. A trap for free-ranging moose. *Journal of Wildlife Management*, 37: 87–89.

Lynch, G.M. 1978. Live trapping moose at mineral licks in Alberta. *Proceedings: North American Moose Conference and Workshop*, 14: 56–67.

Lynch, G.M. 1981. *Transplants of moose and elk from Elk Island National Park by Alberta Fish and Wildlife Division in 1980/81.* Alberta Fish and Wildlife Division, Edmonton. Unpublished report.

Lynch, G.M. 1987. Projectile mechanisms for chemical restraint of wildlife. *Proceedings Alberta Game Growers' Association Conference*, 1: 97–99.

Lynch, G.M., and Hanson, J.A. 1981. Use of etorphine to immobilize moose. *Journal of Wildlife Management*, 45: 981–985.

Lynch, G.M., and Morgantini L.E. 1984. Sex and age differential in seasonal home range size of moose in northwestern Alberta. *Alces*, 20: 61–78.

Morgantini, L.E. 1988. *Prairie Bluff bighorn sheep study 4–4 progress report January/September 1988.* Report prepared for Shell Canada by Wildland Resources Consultants, Edmonton.

Morgantini, L.E. 1990. (personal communication). Adjunct Professor, Department of Forest Science, University of Alberta.

Morgantini, L.E., and Olsen, C.D. 1983. *Pipeline construction and wild ungulates. Results of a two year monitoring program along the Edson mainline loop.* Report prepared for NOVA, an Alberta Corp. by Wildland Resources Consultants, Edmonton.

Nielsen, L. 1982. *Chemical immobilization in urban animal control work.* Wisconsin Humane Society, Inc. Milwaukee, Wis.

Renecker, L.A. 1990 (personal communication). Assistant Professor, University of Alaska, Fairbanks, AK.

Renecker, L.A. 1991. *Seasonal nutritional cycles of ungulates in Elk Island National Park.* Report prepared for Elk Island National Park, Ft. Saskatchewan.

Renecker, L.A., and Olsen, C.D. 1985. Use of yohimbine and 4–aminopyridine to antagonize xylazine-induced immobilization in North American Cervidae. *Journal of American Veterinary Medicine Association*, 187: 1199–1201.

Renecker, L.A., and Olsen, C.D. 1986a. Antagonism of xylazine hydrochloride with yohimbine hydrochloride and 4-aminopyridine in captive wapiti. *Journal of Wildlife Disease*, 22: 91–96.

Renecker, L.A., and Olsen, C.D. 1986b. Reversing rompun: the North American experience. *New Zealand Deer Farmer*, 28: 31.

Stelfox, J.G., and Robertson, J.R. 1976. Immobilizing bighorn sheep with succinylcholine chloride and phencyclidine hydrochloride. *Journal of Wildlife Management*, 40: 174–176.

Stemp, R.E. 1983. *Heart rate responses of bighorn sheep to environmental factors and harassment*. M.Sc. Thesis. University of Calgary, Calgary.

Wishart, W.D., Smith, K., Jorgenson, J., and Lynch, G. 1980. The evolution of capturing bighorns in Alberta. *Symposium of Northern Wild Sheep and Goat Council*, 1980: 590–600.

A3. BODY CONDITION

Flook, D.R. 1970. *A study of the sex differential in the survival of wapiti*. Canadian Wildlife Service Report Series No. 11.

Franzmann, A.W. 1985. Assessment of nutritonal status. pp. 239-259. In: *Bioenergetics of wild herbivores*. Hudson, R.J. and White, R.G. (editors). CRC Press, Boca Raton, Florida.

Hofmann, R.R. 1982. Adaptive changes of gastric and intestinal morphology in response to different fibre content in ruminant diets. *Royal Society of New Zealand Bulletin*, 20.

Kistner, T.P., Trainer, C.E., and Hartmann, N.A. 1980. A field technique for evaluating physical condition of deer. *Wildlife Society Bulletin*, 8: 11–17.

Larsen, T.S., Nilsson, N.O., and Blix, A.S. 1985. Seasonal changes in lipogenesis and lipolysis in isolated adipocytes from Svalbard and Norwegian reindeer. *Acta Physiologica Scandica*, 123: 97–104.

Riney, T.N. 1955. Evaluating condition of free ranging red deer (*Cervus elaphus*) with special reference to New Zealand. *New Zealand Journal Science and Technology*, 36: 429–463.

Suttie, J.M., White, R.G. and Littlejohn, R.G. Pulsatile growth hormone secretions during the breeding season in male reindeer and its association with hypophagia and weight loss. *General and Comparative Endocrinology*, 85:36-42.

A4. AGE DETERMINATION

Anonymous. 1992. *An illustrated guide to bison phenotypes*. Produced by the Taxonomy Subcommittee of the Wood Bison Recover Team, Edmonton.

Banfield, A.W.F. 1954. *Preliminary investigation of the barren ground caribou, Part II*. Canadian Wildlife Service, National Parks, Wildlife Management Bulletin Series, 1: No. 10B.

Brandborg, S.M. 1955. *Life history and management of the mountain goat in Idaho*. Idaho Department of Fish and Game, Wildlife Bulletin, No. 2, Idaho.

Deming, O.V. 1952. Tooth development of the Nelson bighorn sheep. *California Fish and Game*, 38: 523–529.

Dow, S.A., and Wright, P.L. 1962. Changes in mandibular dentition associated with age in pronghorn antelope. *Journal of Wildlife Management*, 26: 1–18.

Fuller, W.A. 1959. The horns and teeth as indicators of age in bison. *Journal of Wildlife Management*, 23: 342–344.

Geist, V. 1971. *Mountain sheep: A study in behavior and evolution*. University of Chicago Press, Chicago, Ill.

Hemming, J.E. 1969. Cemental deposition, tooth succession, and horn development as criteria of age in Dall Sheep. *Journal of Wildlife Management*, 33: 552–558.

Matson, G.M. 1981. *Workbook for cementum analysis*. Published by Matson. Milltown, MT.

Miller, F.L. 1974. Age determination of caribou by annulations in dental cementum. *Journal of Wildlife Management*, 38: 47–53.

Peterson, R.L. 1955. *North American moose*. University of Toronto Press, Toronto, Ont.

Quimby, D.C., and Gaab, J.E. 1957. Mandibular dentition as an age indicator in Rocky Mountain elk. *Journal of Wildlife Management*, 21: 435–451.

Rees, J.W., Kainer, R.A., and Davis, R.W. 1966. Chronology and eruption of mandibular teeth in mule deer. *Journal of Wildlife Management*, 30: 629–631.

Robinette, W.L., Jones, D.A., Rogers, G., and Gashwiler, J.S. 1957. Notes on tooth development and wear for Rocky Mountain mule deer. *Journal of Wildlife Management*, 21: 134–153.

Sauer, P.R. 1973. *Seasonal variation in the physiology of white-tailed deer in relation to cementum annulus formation*. Ph.D. Thesis, State University of New York, Albany, NY.

Severinghaus, C.W. 1949. Tooth development and wear as criteria of age in white-tailed deer. *Journal of Wildlife Management*, 13: 195–216.

Stelfox, J.G., and Poll, D.M. 1978. *Weights, measurements and tooth replacement of Rocky Mountain sheep in Canadian national parks, 1967–1971*. Prepared by Canadian Wildlife Service, Edmonton for Parks Canada, Calgary. Unpublished report.

Index

condition 155, 178
    scoring 181, 185
conductivity 185
conformation 143, 187
coniferous forests 49
contagious ecthyma 82, 88
copper 48
corpus luteum 166
corral trap 172
cortisol 183, 186
COSEWIC 110
cougar(s) 69, 76, 77, 78
cow:calf ratio 181
coyote(s) 69, 74, 86
creatinine 180, 182
critical temperatures 158
Crowsnest River 50
crude protein 151
crypsis 70
cursorial 73
cuticular scale pattern 8
Cypress Hills Provincial Park 51, 61, 85, 86,
    159, 160
cysts 87

D

daily gain 150
Dall's sheep 2
dental formula 166
dentine 166, 191
dentition 190
dew claw(s) 27, 143
diaminopimelic acid 180
diarrhea, bovine viral 88
diastema 166, 188
dietary nitrogen 152
digesta 166
digestibility 152, 155
digestible dry matter 152
digestion 143, 144
diprenorphine 173
disease 69, 138
displays 29
    courtship 30, 33
    dominance 32
    submissive 31, 32
    threat 31
    visual 31
distribution 45, 48
dominance 30, 35
dressed carcass 166, 180
drop net 172
droppings 7
drownings 72
drug dosage 172
dwarf shrubs 48

E

eagle, golden 69
ears 23
ecological
    regions 45
    separation 45, 46
economic
    aspects 119
    components 120
    importance 1
ecoregions 45

electrophoresis 64
elk. *See* wapiti
Elk Island National Park 24, 50, 51, 52, 61, 67,
    85, 86, 110, 153, 156, 159, 160
emaciation 171, 182
enamel 166, 191
encephalitis 88
energy
    budget 146
    expenditures 148
    metabolizable 150
    requirements 150
epithelial glands 33, 64
epizootic hemorrhagic disease 88
eructation 166
escape cover 46, 49, 155
esophagus 166
estrogen 186
etorphine 171, 173
Eurasia 2
European wisent 3
evolutionary history 4
ewe 5
expenditures 126

F

fallow deer 138
fasting metabolic rate (FMR) 147
fat 150, 154, 158, 179, 184
    content 184
    deposits 181
    stored 147
fawn 5, 70
fecal 7
    nitrogen 153, 156
    pellets 7
    protein 152, 153
feces 70, 86, 138, 166, 178, 181, 182, 183, 186
feed intake 150
feeding
    bouts 156
    rate 144
femur 183
fence traps 172
fermentation 143, 166
fiber 180
fibroma 88
fire 49
    return interval 115
    suppression 72, 74
fistula 166
flehmen 30, 40, 41, 166
fluke(s) 84
    large American liver 83, 84
    liver 85, 86
    rumen 84
followers 149
foot load index 158
foot rot 88
foot stamp 38
forage(s) 47, 69, 161, 162, 163
    biomass 144
    production 150
foraging
    patterns 159, 160
    preferences 47
    rate 145
    strategies 47

forbs 48, 151
foreleg kick 34, 35, 42, 43
forestry 1, 113
fossil records 3
frame size 187
front kick 34
frontal bone(s) 8, 9
functional response 70

G

gait measurements 21
Game Act 110
game farming 1, 110, 127, 139
game ranching 128, 133
gastro-intestinal tract 8
gastrocnemius 184
gene conservation 132
genetic contamination 137
genitalia 6
gestation 68, 149, 167
glacial 3
glacial refugia 3
Grande Cache 61
grasses 151
grazers 47, 143
grinding teeth 38, 39
grouse 76
growth 150
guard hairs 8
guide 98, 99
gut
    capacity 144
    fill 144

H

habitat
    management 112
    preferences 53
    selection 154
hair 8, 48
harems 145
harvest 117
heart 180
heat stress 148
herbicide 116
hider 25
hind foot length 183
homeostasis 146
hoof (hooves) 5, 21, 70, 143, 167
    click 38
horn(s) 3, 6, 8, 25, 97, 98, 167, 188, 189
    cores 9, 26
    development 187
horses 96
    feral 134
horsetail 151
human harassment 45
hunters 1, 8, 64, 117
hunting 1, 70, 72
    fee 131
    license fees 131
    regulations 192
    seasons 142
hybrid(s) 64, 67, 139
hyperthermia 171
hypothermia 171
hypsodont 143

resins 153
resting metabolism 147
retention time 144
reticula 143
reversal drug(s) 171, 172, 176
rhinotracheitis, infectious bovine 88
ringworm 88
roadkills 64, 72, 112
robe contour 74
rumen(s) 143, 156, 180, 185, 186
   capacity 156
rumination 148, 156
rump patch 23
running speeds 143
rut(ting) 6, 149, 150, 168, 178

S

sagebrush 49
salivary glands 143
salivation 171
saltatorial 143
satiation 144
scat(s) 5, 7
scent glands 193
scientific names 4
secondary compounds 152, 153, 168
security 155
sedges 151
selenodont 169
   dentition 143
sensory systems 31
serum urea 187
sexing 6
sexual
   dimorphism 142
   maturity 64
Sheep River 61, 76, 77, 78, 85
Sheep River Sanctuary 52
shoulder
   height 183
   hump 26
Siberian snow sheep 3
silica 188
Simpson, Jim 97
sinking depths 148
skull(s) 9, 10, 11, 12, 26
snow-coping 158
snowfall 151
snowshoe hare 76
sodium 48
soremouth 82
spectrograms 32, 33
stag and hind 5
sterile 64
stomach hair worm 84
straddle 21
Strathcona County 61
stride length 21
subcutaneous fat 181
submission 35
submissive displays 32
subunguis 169
sucking lice 89
suckling 25
Suffield 134

Suffield Military Base 61
sulfur 48
surplus killing 74

T

tactile communication 30, 34, 42, 43
tail 23
tannins 151, 153, 169
tapeworm(s) 84, 86, 87, 169
   common 86
   fringed 84
   hydatid 84
tapir(s) 2
tarsal glands 23
taxonomy 2
terpenes 151, 169
testosterone 8, 183
thermal
   cover 46, 155
   environment(s) 147, 155
thermoregulation 146, 147, 148
thread-necked worm 84
threat signals 34
thyroid 180, 182, 185
tick(s) 71, 87, 90, 169
tiller length 145
tine 169
tooth
   eruption 188, 190
   wear 188
track(s) 21, 22
   length 27
   width 27
trail marking 158
translocations 50, 51, 52, 130
trichostrongyle 84
triclabendazole 86
triiodothyronine 182
trophies 8, 104, 105, 106
tuberculosis viii, 86, 88, 110, 132–139

U

ultrasonography 181
ultrasound 184
unguis 1, 169
ungulate harvest 109
University of Calgary 64
upper critical temperature 147
urea 180, 182, 185, 186
urinary potassium 182
urination 6, 40
urine 70, 178, 180, 181, 182, 183, 186

V

values
   consumptive 121
   extra-market 122
   extramarket 126
   market 127
   non-consumptive 123
   non-use 123
   wildlife 121, 122
velvet 34, 129, 133

visual signals 30, 32, 36, 37
vocalizations 5, 25, 32, 33
vulva patch 6

W

Wainwright viii, 61
Wainwright Buffalo Park 50, 51, 52
walking gait 21
wallowing 6, 40
wapiti 1, 2, 4, 11, 15, 21, 26, 27, 31, 32, 33, 38,
   40, 42, 46, 47, 48, 57, 61, 63, 65, 66, 67,
   68, 86, 87, 92, 95, 102, 103, 105, 106,
   109, 115, 129, 130, 133, 135, 143, 145,
   147, 149, 153, 155, 156, 158, 159, 161,
   162, 163, 188, 190, 192
water deer 145
Waterton Lakes National Park 50, 51, 61, 67,
   159
weight loss 153
weights and measures 157
whipworm 84
white-tailed deer 1, 2, 4, 5, 10, 13, 21, 22, 23,
   25, 26, 33, 38, 40, 42, 46, 47, 48, 54, 61,
   63, 64, 65, 67, 68, 73, 76, 81, 82, 83, 85,
   86, 87, 88, 91, 92, 95, 96, 97, 100, 102,
   103, 104, 106, 109, 112, 115, 129, 130,
   131, 135, 137, 138, 143, 146, 155, 158,
   159, 161, 162, 163, 188, 190, 201
Wildlife
   Act 128
   Society 139
wildlife management units 108
windchill 48
winter tick(s) 72, 87, 88, 90
winterkill 64
wolf (wolves) 69, 70, 71, 72, 73, 74, 86, 118
   bison interactions 74
   control 74
wolverine 69
Wood Buffalo National Park viii, 4, 46, 50, 52,
   67, 72, 74, 107, 110, 133, 134, 139

X

xylazine 173

Y

Ya-Ha-Tinda Ranch 51, 61, 159
yak 86
yearling 5
Yellowstone National Park 51
yohimbine 172, 173

Z

zoonosis 169